Secret of the Spirit

سِرُّ الرُّوحِ

Sirr ar-Rūḥ

2007 teachings of

Sīdī Shaykh Muḥammad Saʿīd al-Jamal ar-Rifāʿī ash-Shādhulī

الله
نور السموات
والارض مثل نوره
كمشكاة فيها مصباح
المصباح في زجاجة الزجاجة
كأنها كوكب دري يوقد من شجرة
مباركة زيتونة لا شرقية ولا غربية يكاد
زيتها يضيء ولو لم تمسسه نار نور على نور
يهدي الله لنوره من يشاء ويضرب الله الأمثال
للناس والله بكل شيء عليم . صدق الله العظيم

Secret of the Spirit

سِرُّ الرُّوحِ

Sirr ar-Rūḥ

2007 teachings of
Sīdī S̲haykh̲ Muḥammad Saʿīd al-Jamal ar-Rifāʿī ash̲-S̲hādh̲ulī

God is the Light of the heavens and the earth.
His Light is like this:
there is a niche, and in it a lamp,
the lamp inside a glass, a glass like a glittering star,
fueled from a blessed olive tree from neither east nor west,
whose oil almost gives light even when no fire touches it
—Light upon Light—
God guides whoever He wills to His Light;
God draws such comparisons for people;
God has full knowledge of everything.
(Qurʾān 24:35)

Cover art: Huda al-Jamal
Cover design: Amīna Stader-Chan

ISBN 978-0-9762150-3-5

Printed in the United States of America

For information, address the Shādẖiliyya Ṣūfī Center
P.O. Box 100 Pope Valley, CA 94567
(877) 720-8143

Table of Contents
Chronological Order

Farm of Peace

10-Day Ramadan Retreat

University of Spiritual Healing and Ṣūfism, Years 2-3

University of Spiritual Healing and Ṣūfism, Year 1

Appendices and Indices

Table of Contents
By Topic

Healing Methods and Special Practices

The Secret of the Love of God

Jumʿah

Appendices and Indices

Acknowledgements

The editors would like to gratefully acknowledge the generous assistance given by many beloveds who stepped forward in every instance to contribute exactly what was needed.

We begin by thanking Amany Shalaby and Ibrāhīm Ali who translated simultaneously into English the teachings Sidi Muḥammad gave originally in Arabic. Their dedication to transmit not only the literal but also the transcendent meanings of the teachings will, we believe, give the reader greater access to the full richness of what Sidi offered.

In addition to translating 90% of the teachings reproduced in this book, Amany not only prepared Sidi's meals for him, but also provided translation for hundreds of students who met individually with Sidi seeking his guidance and help. She was in constant service to all of her spiritual brothers and sisters. Thank you, Amany, for all you give "for the Face of Allāh."

We want to acknowledge the directors and staffs of the following organizations for the support and resources they provided to both record Sidi's teachings and to make these recordings available to the editors. This includes Maṣṭūra and her excellent administrative team at the University of Spiritual Healing and Ṣufism; Ṣāliḥ Cotten, Lāṭif Sorensen and all those who staffed the programs held at the Shadhiliyya Ṣūfī Retreat Center in Pope Valley, California; Lailā Saratore, Ḥabīb Laman and their staff at the Midwest Ṣūfī School; Salīma Adelstein, Kāmila Dining and Waḥīda Kass who directed a large and capable crew that hosted the Ṣūfī School at the Farm of Peace; and Ḥakīma Graefer and her San Diego team.

We extend the biggest possible "Thank You!" to David Abdul Qādr Burdette who recorded 80% of the teachings reproduced in this book. His willingness to make these recordings available to our transcribers in "record" time, in spite of his already challenging work load, made a major contribution to the success of this project. Many thanks also to Ben Salīm Cranston and Vickie Jamīla Davies who also both worked generously "after hours" to provide recordings of the Midwest and Farm of Peace Ṣūfī School teachings respectively. In addition, we want to acknowledge the invaluable technical assistance given by Tom Noor Upshaw who definitely brings brilliance and humor to all things digital.

Our transcribing and editing team was dedicated, efficient, accurate and unfailingly willing to take on whatever needed to be completed: Salaam McLaughlin, Bilqīs Loeliger, Rabiā'ah Houle, Maryam Reimer, and Karīma Kelleher. You all were a blessing to work with.

Once again, with guidance from Sidi, Hūda al-Jamal created a stunning original painting that Amīna Stader has incorporated into a lyrical and beautiful cover design that so beautifully reflects her love of Allāh and His Way. Yūnus Wesley provided considerable expertise in Arabic, Islām and Ṣūfism whenever needed. We are sincerely grateful for the timely generosity of John Waḥīd McHugh which played a special role in launching the entire project. As always, we extend our gratitude to Ṣāliḥ Kent, our brother in the way, for his love, kind-heartedness and enthusiastic commitment to bring Sidi's teachings out to the widest possible audience.

Finally, we would like to acknowledge the deep inner sense of gratitude and blessings that all of us feel for the privilege of sitting in person with our guide around the "table of Allāh" as he serves all of us the "real food and the real medicine for all people without separation." Truly, Allāh is the One who sustains His creation.

Subḥāna rabbika rabbi-l-izzati 'ammā yaṣifūn
wa salāmun 'ala-l-mursalīn
wa-l-ḥamdu-li-llāhi rabbi-l-'ālamīn

Exalted is your Lord, the Lord of Might, far beyond their description.
And peace be upon the messengers.
And praise be to Allāh, Lord of [all] the worlds.

Editors

Wadūde Laird
Nūra Laird
Shams Deckter

December 2007

Introduction

بِسْمِ اللّهِ الرَّحْمـــَنِ الرَّحِيمِ
الْحَمْدُ للّهِ رَبِّ الْعَالَمِينَ
الرَّحْمـــنِ الرَّحِيمِ
مَـــالِكِ يَوْمِ الدِّينِ
إِيَّاكَ نَعْبُدُ وإِيَّاكَ نَسْتَعِينُ
اهدِنَــــــا الصِّرَاطَ المُستَقِيمَ
صِرَاطَ الَّذِينَ أَنعَمتَ عَلَيهِمْ غَيرِ المَغضُوبِ عَلَيهِمْ وَلاَ الضَّالِّينَ

In the name of God, the Universally Merciful, Singularly Compassionate
Praise belongs to Allāh, Sustaining-Lord of the worlds
the Universally Merciful, Singularly Compassionate
Sovereign of the Day of Judgment
You do we adore, and from You do we seek aid
Guide us to the straight path [the true Ṣūfism and the true Islām]
Not the path of those upon who is Your wrath, nor of those You have led astray.

We begin in the Name of Allāh. the Singularly Compassionate, the Universally Merciful. We witness that Allāh is the One, the Eternal, the All-Encompassing, the One who sustains all of His creation. We send our prayers and blessings to the Prophet Muḥammad, may the peace and blessings of Allāh be upon him, and to his family, his companions, and to all of the prophets who have brought one message of peace, love, mercy, justice and freedom. We pray to Allāh that this book will be pleasing in His sight and that it will bring healing, hope and wisdom to all people seeking to live in the unity of Allāh's Reality.

Over forty years ago when Sidi Muḥammad was a young man, his guide S̲hayk̲h̲ Muḥammad al-Hās̲h̲im at-Tilmisāni told him that Sidi Muḥammad would come to America one day to teach people the real Ṣūfism, which is the real Islām. Decades passed before Allāh gave the actual order for Sidi to come to this country.

Sidi has traveled from his home in Jerusalem to the United States many times since his first visit over ten years ago. As the guide of the peace, love and mercy, Sidi has traveled across America giving to thousands of people the gifts of Allāh's generosity: wisdom, healing, divine care and the way to proximity and union with the Beloved.

This year Sidi seems to have brought an extra urgency to his teachings. He believes it is of the utmost importance that the American people and their leaders learn the way of peace, love and unity. As the reader of this book will readily discover, Sidi repeatedly has "taken the cover off the secrets" of the Ṣūfī way so that the sincere student may receive fully the richness, wisdom and healing that lives inside these teachings.

This book gathers in one volume many of the teachings given to us from Allāh, glory be to Him, through the voice of Sidi Muḥammad al-Jamal during his visit to the United States in 2007. Teachings were given at the S̲had̲hiliyya Spiritual Retreat Center in Pope Valley, California, at the Farm of Peace in Warfordsburg, Pennsylvania, as well as additional "Ṣūfī School" programs in Chicago, Portland and San Diego. Additional teachings were given in the October 2007, sessions of the University of Spiritual Healing and Ṣūfism held in Santa Rosa and Napa, California. The University teaches principles of spiritual transformation, spiritual practice and healing under the direction of Sidi Muḥammad.

Most of the teachings were delivered in Arabic, simultaneously translated into English by Amany Shalaby and recorded on sight. Subsequently, they were transcribed by volunteers and sent to us for review, collation and final editing. Ibrāhīm Ali provided the translation services for the Sidi "Welcome Weekend" when he first arrived this year from Jerusalem in August 2007.

Every effort has been made to preserve the accuracy and the original flavor of what Sidi presented. However, as perhaps only other editors can truly understand, we have had to make countless decisions about what to include, omit, and interpret. We realize that we undoubtedly have made errors either of fact or judgment for which we alone are responsible and for which we seek Allāh's forgiveness.

Our prayer is that this book will provide the deepest possible spiritual support and healing for all people everywhere who seek to live the real religion of love, mercy, peace, justice and freedom, God willing.

Wadūde Laird
Nūra Laird
Shams Deckter

December 2007

Teachings on the Spirit (Ruh)

Ādam

Who in reality is the origin of all of the universe and, in summary,
his spirit is the seed of the tree of the universe,
and his presence is the fruit of the material tree of the world.

Just as the fruit expresses all the parts of the tree
and is expressed at the top of the tree,
Ādam is above all the parts of the existence,
whether they are above or below,
and he is a benefit and a harm to every part of the tree.

Each particle is given an appropriate name that fits the angels.
It is from the perfection of Ādam's state
that the names of Allāh were given
according to his benefit or harm,
his interest or his corruption.

Since he [Ādam] is created, Allāh is the Creator.
Since he is provided for, Allāh is the Provider.
Since he is a bondsman, Allāh is Lord.
Since he is a worshipper, Allāh is the Worshipped.

With respect to his being deficient, Allāh is his veil.
With respect to his being sinful, Allāh is the Forgiver.
With respect to his repenting, Allāh is the Acceptor of Repentance.
With respect to his being benefitted, Allāh is the Beneficent.
With respect to his being harmed, Allāh is the Protector.
With respect to his being poor, Allāh is the Rich.
With respect to his being weak, Allāh is the Strong.
With respect to his being unjust, Allāh is the Just.
With respect to his being oppressed, Allāh is the Avenger.
With respect to his being the lover, Allāh is the Beautiful.

From "The Station of Kẖalīfa Designated for the Human Being"
in *The Path to Allāh, Most High*

The Knowledge of the Spirit

Fi maʿrifat ar-rūḥ

Reprint from *The Path to Allāh, Most High*, available through Sidi Muḥammad Press[1]

Allāh says:

> And they ask you about the Spirit (ar-rūḥ).
> Say: "The Spirit [comes] by the order of my Lord,
> and you have been given but little knowledge." (Qurʾān 17:85)

The Messenger of Allāh, may the blessings and peace of Allāh be upon him, said:

> Allāh, glory be to Him, created spirits two thousand years before He created bodies. (Ḥadīth)
>
> The first thing created by Allāh was my spirit. (Ḥadīth)

Know that people are divided by the question of the spirit (rūḥ). The ancient, wise people, and scholars who followed them, spoke much about the spirit (rūḥ) and had many different ideas and opinions. They expended their thoughts on the question of the spirit. Most of them were lost. There is no greater arena for differences among people of intelligence, than there is over the question of the spirit. We will not take up much time in repeating what they said and what they imagined. Most of these sayings are the result of minds affected by illusion and imagination. Their eyes do not have the treatment of kohl nor are they affected by the light of guidance. The necessary treatment is the following of the prophets. Regarding what is said by imāms and scholars of true knowledge, some say, "It is a subtle body." Some say, "It is a contingency." Some say, "It is an essence established in itself, but it is created." The vast majority say, "Allāh has more knowledge." And this is a knowledge that Allāh has kept to Himself.[2]

---

[1] Sidi Muḥammad Press: www.sufimaster.org or (707) 765-0904

[2] "God named knowledge a spirit that the angels bring down upon the hearts of His servants." (see Qurʾān 40:15; Qurʾān 42:52; Qurʾān 16:2)

I say, surely the Messenger of Allāh knew Allāh, and Allāh granted or gifted him when He said, "He taught you what you did not know," and, "Surely the gift of Allāh upon you is very great." It is unlikely that he did not have the knowledge of the spirit. Did Allāh not say that He taught him what he did not know? And did Allāh not say, "Only the true knowers know it?"

These true knowers are the masters of traveling to Allāh. When they cross the nafs and its attributes and reach the fortress of the heart, they understand the nafs with the light of the heart, the heart that is enlightened by the light of adh-dhikr. When they cross the stations of the heart and reach the stations of the secrets, they understand the heart with the secrets. Then they cross the stations of the secrets and reach the world of the spirit, and know the secret with the light of the spirit (rūḥ). When they cross from the world of the spirit and reach the stations of the Hidden, they know the spirit (rūḥ) with the witnessing of the Truth (al-Ḥaqq). When they cross the stations of the Hidden and reach the gateway of the shore of the ocean of the ḥaqīqa, they know the Hidden Beauty with the light of witnessing. Then if they are annihilated by the tajallī of the attributes of the Majesty (al-Jalīl) from the "I"ness of existence, they reach the shore of the ocean of the reality (ḥaqīqa), and the "He"ness of the Truth (al-Ḥaqq) is revealed to them.

When they stand high in the ocean of "He"ness and are given the baqā'√ of divinity, then they know Allāh by Allāh, and they unify Him where they find Him. This is the "one of his moment" (al-waqt). This is the time of, "We will show them Our Signs on the horizons and in themselves until it becomes clear to them that this [message] is the Truth (annahu-l-ḥaqq)." When that day arises, he no longer needs a lamp or torch. This is the realization of the slave in the station of, "I am his hearing, his seeing, his tongue, and his support. Through Me he hears, he speaks, and by Me he strikes." In this state (ḥāl), how can there be any doubt about the knowledge of the spirit? And moreover, how can we even compare this with the state of the master of all Messengers and the beloved of the Lord of the World? He, the Messenger of Allāh, is the one who says:

> I know of what has been and what will be. (Ḥadīth)

Know that the spirit (rūḥ) is a subtle reality disclosed by the Lord. It is the first thing that the Divine Power ordered to "Be" in existence. I say it is lordly because it is an appendage to the Lordly Presence. Allāh says:

> I fashioned him and breathed into him from My spirit (ar-rūḥ) (Qur'ān 38:72)

It is a lordly jewel (al-jawhar) established in Himself.[3] And this is proven by the Messenger's saying:

> Allāh created spirits before bodies by 2000 years. (Ḥadīth̲)

The spirit (rūḥ) is not a body and not a contingency because it is the first thing in creation, the first created thing. It is simple, whereas ordinary bodies are complex, and contingencies require place. If ordinary bodies accept a form, they cannot accept a different form of the same genre, except by removing the first or disconnecting from the first form. The spirit is not described by this because it can take on a second form without disturbing the first and if it takes on another form it increases in strength. So it is not a body; it is a pure essential substance (al-jawhar). Its light is the most exalted and the closest to the presence. It is what is pre-disposed to the k̲halīfa of Allāh on the earth. It is the living, the seeing, the speaking, the knowing, the powerful, the willing, the subsisting (al-baqā'). It is vicegerency to Allāh. Allāh made this known by His saying:

> Say: "The spirit is from the command of my Lord." (Qur'ān 17:85)

That is, its nature is from the world of command, not from the world of creation.[4]

Allāh created many worlds, as has come to us in many Ḥadīth̲. The Messenger of Allāh said:

> Allāh created three hundred sixty worlds. (Ḥadīth̲)

In another narration he mentioned seventy thousand, and in another narration eighteen thousand. But all of these are circumscribed into two worlds, that is, the world of creation and the world of command or order. Allāh says:

---

[3] Al-jawhar is the primary matter sometimes called a jewel or a pearl. It is the spirit which is the lordly jewel (al-jawhar) from which life comes to be.

[4] The spirit, the lordly jewel has governance or command over the body and it never ceases its governing of a body or bodies in any world.

> His is the creation and the command. (Qur'ān 7:54)

The most blessed is Allāh, the Lord of the worlds. So the world of the dunyā, which is what is sensed with the five outward senses, is creation (kh̲alq), and He expresses the world of the Hereafter (al-ākh̲ira), which is perceived through the five inward senses, which are the intellect, the heart, the secret, the spirit (rūḥ), and the hidden, as order or command (amr).

The created (kh̲alq) worlds are the first great things that Allāh created for continuation (al-baqā') from the spirit (rūḥ), the intellect, and the pen. He called the worlds, "the world of command (amr)" because creation occured through His order, "Be," from nothing without the intermediary of any thing. As Allāh says:

> Does not the human being remember that
> We created him before when he was nothing? (Qur'ān 19:67)

Since His order is ancient, whatever He fashioned with the ancient order has continuation (al-baqā'), even though it may be contingent. He calls the world of creation, "creation" because He gives it existence through intermediaries of created things, and so He calls it created because Allāh created it to experience the fanā' (annihilation; death).[5]

So His words: "Say, the spirit is from the command of my Lord (Qur'ān 17:85)," are to let us know that the spirit is from the world of the command and the baqā', not from the world of creation and fanā', which is not as some people imagine.

So know that the spirit (rūḥ) that is attached to the power of the command "Be" is first of all, the spirit (rūḥ) of the Prophet, may the blessings and peace of Allāh be upon him, because he said:

> The first thing that He created was my spirit (rūḥ). (Ḥadīth̲)

and in another narration [he said]:

> The first thing that He created was my light. (Ḥadīth̲)

---

[5] Death here is defined as a station for the spirit which ends the configuration of its attachment to the body in this world.

If you say that the Messenger of Allāh has also said:

> The first thing that Allāh created was the intellect.

and he said:

> The first thing that Allāh created was the pen.

and he said:

> The first thing Allāh created was His lordly jewel.

[Then] know that the first being has to be one thing. Two different things cannot be the first in creation and in existence because if there are two, either they happened at the same time or in succession. If they happened simultaneously, then one cannot be called first in comparison to the other. If they happened in succession, then one had to be first and the other second. The first would have to have priority, but it is not possible to believe other than that the Prophet spoke the truth. Therefore he confirmed the beginnings of the first things.

The creation is one thing that has different names in accordance with their attributes. The attribute is what determines the name. There are many names, but the name the First One is the root and everything else is derivative. There is no doubt that the root of the creation of the existence or the cosmos was the Prophet of Allāh, may the blessings and peace of Allāh be upon him, because Allāh said, "Had it not been for you, I would not have created the universe."

The Prime Matter (al-jawhar al-hayūlā) is the Prophet, may the blessings and peace of Allāh be upon him, at the root of all manifestation and everything is a derivative of him. He was made the seed of the tree of all existence by the spirit, which is the presence of arrival (sidrat al-muntahā). Fruit comes from the branch of the tree, so his coming out was at a distance of two bow's length or closer.[6] For this reason he says, I

---

[6] Two bows length refers to His coming down to existence and the drawing closer to Him, completing a circle. Two arcs manifest from one circle so it is imagined that the line dividing the circle into two arcs is existence. Then one arc is identical to the other in respect to "He"ness and you are the dividing imagined line. "Or closer" is the removal of this imaginary thing so nothing remains but a circle.

am the last and the first," the last as in the coming out of the fruits and the first in creation, as the seed.[7]

From this we understand that the spirit of the Prophet of Allāh, may the blessings and peace of Allāh be upon him, was the first thing manifested by the power, and that he is the one denoted by the different names because he is the first matter in the shell of all existence.

He is called the Prime Matter. As it is related in the ḥadīth̲, Allāh created a Prime Matter, and in another narration a pearl (ad-durra). Allāh looked at it and it melted, and from it He created everything. With regard to his spirituality, he is called spirit. With regard to his light, he is called light. With regard to the excellence of his intellect, he is called intellect. And a distinction of his spirit, may the blessings and peace of Allāh be upon him, is his saying:

> The first thing Allāh created was the intellect.
> He said to it, "Draw nearer." And it drew near.
> He said to it, "Go away." And it went away. (Ḥadīth̲)

This is the state (ḥāl) of the spirit of the first that Allāh created, may the blessings and peace of Allāh be upon him. His spirit was knowledgeable (al-ʿārif) of all comprehension in the world of spirits, which is the unseen (g̲hayb). It was ignorant of its particularities, the knowledge of the generalities and particularities of the world of bodies in the world of witnessing through the five senses, and of the strengths of the humanity. It was knowedgeable of the generalities of the unseen (g̲hayb), and the witnessing (as̲h-s̲hahāda) of its particularities. So it is only through vicegerency that you may be knowledgeable of the unseen and of the seen.

Then He said to it, "Go." That is, go back to your Lord and turn away from the dunyā. He answered Him, "What concern do I have of the dunyā?"

And he returned to his Lord on the night of the ascension.[8] Such is the case with the Prophet, may the blessings and peace of Allāh be upon him.

---

[7] When a person has nearness to his Lord like this, then when he removes himself there is only the First and the Last. This is the disappearance of the cosmos in the wujūd of the Real.

[8] "Then he drew close, so He came down, and he was two bows length away, or closer." (Qur'ān 53:8-9). This is refering to the Prophet's mi'rāj or Night Journey.

Then He said to the intellect, "By My might and by My grandeur, I have not created a creation that is more beloved to Me than you." So this is the state (al-ḥāl) of him, may the blessings and peace of Allāh be upon him, that he was the beloved of Allāh and the most beloved in His creation. And Allāh said to the intellect, "Through you, I know; through you, I take; through you, I give; through you, I punish; and through you I reward." This is all describing the state (al-ḥāl) of the Prophet, ṣalla-llāhu ʿalayhi wa-sallam.

Whoever does not know the Prophet, may the blessings and peace of Allāh be upon him, as prophet and as messenger, does not know Allāh, even though he may have thousands of other evidences pointing to Allāh. Allāh says to the Prophet, "The means of knowing Me is through knowing you as a prophet. Anyone who knows you as a prophet, knows Me as Lord. Anyone who is obedient to you in the religion and in the sh̲arīʾa is obedient to Me. It is through you that I give; through your intercession I give the highest degree (daraja)."

As the Messenger of Allāh said:

> People need my intercession, even the Prophet Ibrāhīm. (Ḥadīth̲)

And Allāh says:

> It is through you that I punish, and through you that I reward.

And Allāh also says:

> And [remember] when Allāh took the covenant from the prophets.
>
> [He said], "Take from the Book and the Wisdom and then there will come to you a messenger confirming that which is with you [from My Revelations]. Believe in him and help him." He says, "Do you agree and will you take up My Covenant?" They said, "We agree."
>
> He said, "Then bear witness and I am with you from among the witnesses." (Qurʾān 3:81)

So Allāh took the covenant from every prophet He sent, to believe in Muḥammad, may the blessings and peace of Allāh be upon him; and every prophet taught his people to believe in him and to support his religion (ad-dīn). Those who believed in him from the previous nations before he was sent to this world are the people of the good reward. And those who did not believe in him from the previous people or the latter-day people are the people of "punishment." The words of Allāh are confirmed when He says, "It is through you that I reward and I punish."

Everything I have revealed through this knowledge of the spirit (rūḥ) is from the state (al-ḥāl) of the Messenger of Allāh, may the blessings and peace of Allāh be upon him. He has knowledge of the spirit (rūḥ) because the spirit (rūḥ) is his own self.

The Messenger of Allāh said, "Whoever knows himself knows his Lord." That is because when Allāh created Ādam and his progeny, He made them vicegerents (k͟hulafā') on the earth. Allāh says:

> And He made you vicegerents upon the earth.
> (Qur'ān 57:7, 6:165)

So it is a condition of vicegerency that the one who is made vicegerent should have gathered all the attributes of vicegerency.

Know that the spirit (rūḥ) is the k͟halīfa of Allāh. It is what gathers all His essential attributes – life, power, hearing, seeing, speech, knowledge, will, and baqā'. The body is the k͟halīfa of the spirit and it gathers all of its attributes, a gathering in the spirit which lets it know that it is the k͟halīfa of Allāh. Through this we know that the body is the k͟halīfa of the spirit because we find that the body before its connection to the spirit and after its disconnection from the spirit is devoid of any of these attributes. Had the spirit not been described by these attributes because of its vicegerency of the Ḥaqq, the body would not have been described by them. The spirit has baqā' forever, and the body has annihilation. I say that the baqā' is eternally a characteristic of the spirit. It is the root prior to the k͟halīfa. It is the spirit (rūḥ).

Also know that the spirits were all created from the spirit of the Prophet, may the blessings and peace of Allāh be upon him, as it is related in the ḥadit͟h of Jābir ibn 'Abdullah that his, may the blessings and peace of Allāh be upon him, spirit is the root of all the spirits of all the Friends of God ('āwliya') and this is why he is called the mother of all spirits (ummiyya).

Ādam, peace be upon him, was the father and mother of Eve. This is because when Allāh created the spirit of the Prophet, may the blessings and peace of Allāh be upon him, Allāh was—and there was nothing with Him except his spirit. There was nothing else that would be related to his spirit. Since his spirit is the first prior creation (bākūra) to which Allāh gave existence from the tree of existence, and the first thing pertaining to Him is His power, He gave him nobility by relating him to Himself, so He called him My spirit (rūḥ). Just as He called the first house that was made for the people, My house.

Then when He wished to create Ādam, He formed him and breathed into him of His spirit, that is, from the spirit which is related to Him - the spirit of the Prophet (an-nabī), may the blessings and peace of Allāh be upon him, as He says:

> I have fashioned him and I have breathed into him
> from My spirit." (Qur'ān 15:29, 38:72)

So the spirit of Ādam is from the spirit of the Prophet, may the blessings and peace of Allāh be upon him. The spirits of his sons also arrive through this proof. Allāh says:

> He made his progeny from a demeaned water. Then
> He formed him and blew his spirit into him. (Qur'ān 32:7-8)

Concerning Maryam, peace be upon her, He says:

> We blew into her from Our spirit. (Qur'ān 19:17)

The blowing was by Jibrīl, may the blessings and peace of Allāh be upon him, and the spirit is from the spirit of the Prophet, may the blessings and peace of Allāh be upon him, which is related to the divine presence. This is one of the secrets of his, may the blessings and peace of Allāh be upon him, saying:

> Ādam and whoever comes after him
> are under my banner until the Day of Judgment. (Ḥadīth)

The Prophet, may the blessings and peace of Allāh be upon him, made his ascension (miʿrāj) (Qur'ān 53:1-18) with his spirit through the picture of an angel, and so he knew Him with a true knowing. It came in the ḥadīth of the ascension that was narrated by ʿAbdullah ibn ʿAbbās and ʿAbdullah ibn Mas̲h̲rūd and other narrators. The Messenger said:

> Then we saw an angel. His feet were at the bottom of the lower earth and his head pierced the highest heaven. The width of every wing was the distance of 500 years, and between every two wings for the one traveling fast there was a distance of 500 years. There was light from the top of his head to the bottom of his feet. In every part of this light there were faces whose tongues were glorifying in every language that exists in this existence. No tongue was like another tongue and no eye was like any other eye. Eyes were like bolts of light and the lights could not be counted or conceived. At one side of the body was a red light, on another side, a yellow light, and on another side, a green light. Every part of this body glorified Allāh with a different form of glorification; and from these glorifications, Allāh created angels who glorify Him. Had he wished to swallow up the seven heavens in one scoop, he could have. (Ḥadīt̲h̲ Qudsī)

No angel is capable of looking at these lights, not even Jibrīl, or Mikāʾil or the Cherubs. This is the Great Spirit, which is mentioned in the Qurʾān. To him (the Prophet, may the blessings and peace of Allāh be upon him) arise the concerns of the seven heavens and the earth, and he takes them up to Allāh. He is the one upholding the veils, and he is the writer of ar-Raḥmān, ar-Raḥīm.

Know that he is the greatest spirit and the greatest light that was the first thing attached to the divine power by the power of, "Be." As was made manifest by the ḥadīt̲h̲ of the Prophet (may the blessings and peace of Allāh be upon him) – he said, "It is the spirit," which is mentioned in the Qurʾān when He said, "From the top of his head to the bottom of his feet is spirit." This is an indication that every face is from the faces in the origin of his spirit, in which the prophets, and friends of Allāh (ʾāwliyaʾ), and believers are rooted.

His saying, "Every tongue glorifies with a different language," is indicative of the different manifestations of creation and the different languages, and the differences between them. In this ḥadīt̲h̲ there is confirmation that the spirits of the angels are also derived from him in his saying that he, "takes the matters of the people of the heavens and the earth," meaning that he raises them to Allāh.

This is the state of the greatest spirit from whom all the spirits arise. He is the first spirit, the Beloved of Allāh, His Prophet, may the blessings and peace of Allāh be upon him. He informs us by his saying:

> All actions of my community are brought to me. I bless the good actions and I ask for fogiveness for the bad ones. (Ḥadīth)

He is the holder of all the veils. It is through him that the veils are lifted. He is the holder of the bridge which people cross, and he is the writer of ar-Raḥmān, since he is also called the pen. It is with his life that Allāh wrote the letters of all existence on the page of nonexistence. Allāh says, "If it had not been for you, I would not have created the universe."

So return to Allāh for help,
He is our support for success.
So understand.

The Realities of Lordship

al-ḥaqīqa-l-rabbaniyya

Reprint from *The Path to Allāh, Most High*,
available through Sidi Muḥammad Press[9]

Allāh says:

> We will show them Our signs in the universe,
> and in their own selves,
> until it becomes manifest to them that He is the Truth.
> (Qur'ān 41:53)

Know that when Allāh says:

> I was a Hidden Treasure and I loved to be known, so I created the creation to be known by them. (Ḥadīth Qudsī)

He created the creation, that is, the spirit of the creation in the darkness of the reality (al-ḥaqīqa). Then He sprinkled it with His light, that is the ancient light, and whoever was touched by that light will find guidance through that ancient light, to the essence of the ancient light, to arrival, and to knowledge of His essence and His attributes. These are al-majdhūb, the ones who are attracted, those who are accepted by the divine care. Whoever misses the light is misguided. He does not find his way to arrival or to the knowledge of Allāh. He is lost in the tree of creation; he suffers and does not bear fruit.

Know that the cosmos is a tree whose fruit is the human being and whose seed is the spirit of the Prophet, may the blessings and peace of Allāh be upon him. Allāh says:

> The first that He created was His spirit (Ḥadīth Qudsī)

This means that he, may the blessings and peace of Allāh be upon him, is the spirit who is ennobled by being connected to His spirit. Therefore, he said,
"I am from Allāh and the believers are from me," because they were created from the seed of his spirit in the same way that fruit grows on a tree. The tree was created from him and just as the seed carries the tree

[9] Sidi Muḥammad Press can be reached at www.sufimaster.org or (707) 765-0904.

within it, so also in the seed of the spirit of the Prophet is the capacity to make the world grow.

All parts of the seed are equal in kind and share the same nature, stillness, or motion. If its nature is stillness, we see it moving in development and growth, therefore there has to be a driver. If its nature is motion, its movement has to be either up or down. And when we see parts of the seed move up and parts move down we know that there has to be a mover or a doer with choice, power, and knowledge, who manages the affair of the seed in accordance with wisdom so that it becomes a complete tree with roots, branches, leaves, boughs, and fruit. He is the One Who establishes the different parts of the tree by His power and His will. This points directly to the authority of the One Who creates the tree and His power over it. Allāh says:

> Is it you who produced the tree, or are We the Producer?
> (Qur'ān 56:72)

Therefore it is by this kingship that He has authority over all the parts with the command, "Be," that is, be a branch or a leaf or a fruit. Through His will He makes what He wants. Allāh says:

> Allāh creates what He wills;
> surely Allāh has power over all things. (Qur'ān 24:45)

This is the proof that Allāh, glory be to Him, is the Doer, the Chooser, and the Wise.

So know Who makes the tree of the world from the seed of the Muḥammadan spirit in the beginning and Who makes it into the fruit of the world of the tree in the end. This is why Allāh says:

> He is the First and the Last. (Qur'ān 57:3)

That is, last in the form of the fruit and first in the form of the seed.

The prophets and friends (al-'āwliya') are the fruit on the branches of this tree, and higher (ad-daraja) than others, according to their ranks in nearness. As Allāh says:

> It is He Who has made you successors upon the earth

> and has raised some of you above others in degrees.
> (Qur'ān 6:165)

And:

> These are the messengers We endowed, one after the other.
> (Qur'ān 2:253)

And for that reason, the Prophet, may the blessings and peace of Allāh be upon him, said,

> Ādam and those after him
> are under my authority on the Day of Judgment. (Ḥadīth)

In nearness to the tree, he, may the blessings and peace of Allāh be upon him, arrives the distance of two bows lengths or less. Each prophet is a branch of this tree which is a reference to the time in heaven when He made the progeny of Ādam like offshoots coming out of the root of the tree.

This is why the human is referred to as the microcosm. Each person has the picture or form of the tree and the reality of the person's existence is hidden in it as the fruition of His power. So every spirit that has been touched by the light in the world of the spirit is the faith at the root of the tree and is moved by the light to the top, to the branches of the tree, which is the heart. This is accomplished through walking in the form of good actions commended by the sharīʿa. The actions of the faithful and their good deeds take them from the darkness of the material body to the light of the sharīʿa. The animal nafs that are attached to the dunyā and its appetites at the bottom of the tree are destined to move downward except for "those who have faith and good action." True faith (al-'īmān) is the acceptance of the word of Allāh which He spoke as a parable, in saying, "Lā 'ilāha 'illa-llāh." This is like a branch of the good tree, the tree of the unity which has its light from the heart whose root is firm.

The root of the tree, that is, the unity is fixed in the light and its place is the heart. Light is fixed in the heart and connected to it because the light and the heart are of the same nature. Their root is the unity and its branches, that is, the branches of what is rooted in the unity and the light of the unity. This is the tree of the humanity and the heavens of the spiritual world which gives fruit from the unity at all times, that is, in its time. It does this with the permission of its Lord. This means with no natural intercession, but by divine command just as Mūsā, may peace be upon him, was called. The one who walks through the tree reaches the tree of the unity from aspiration (al-himma).

> I am your Lord, so take off your shoes
> (the dunyā and the ākhira).
> You are in the holy deep valley. (Qur᾿ān 20:12)

That is, the holy presence which envelops the two abodes. Allāh says:

> And the heavens will be folded into His right hand.
> (Qur᾿ān 39:67)

From this tree comes what comes from the permission of your Lord, that is, the fruit of "I am al-Ḥaqq, glory be to Me." So understand.

Every rūḥ that was not touched by this light in the world of spirits turns to its dark material form. It dwells at the bottom of the roots of the tree of human appetites as Ādam dwelt with Eve. Allāh says that He created the rūḥ's pair from the rūḥ for the rūḥ to find rest with its pair.

> He has made mates for you from your selves. (Qur᾿ān 42:11)

So the nafs is created from the side of the rūḥ to find rest in it. Had it not found rest, it would not have been established in the world of bodies by exchange with it. This exchange should only happen within the bounds of a marriage. Then his resting in her is through the order. This is so that he may not be distracted from that which will give him salvation and redemption from the painful punishment of being distanced from the divine presence. He is established and connected in degrees (al-darajab) in the Garden of pleasure which is in the stations of nearness to the divine presence. Allāh says:

> Oh you who believe!
> Will I guide you to a trade that will save you
> from a painful torment. (Qur᾿ān 61:10)

And He says:

> The Messenger, and those who believe with him,
> struggle with their wealth and their selves. (Qur᾿ān 9:88)

You can see, with the light of faith, the bad ending of putting your reliance on the dunyā and its appetites. So you should leave this and turn toward the divine presence.

Mūsā, may peace be upon him, said to his people:

> Wait here. I see a fire in the distance.
> Maybe I can bring you a live brand from it,
> or maybe I can find directions at the fire. (Qur'ān 20:10)

He deprives himself of staying at the bottom of the roots of the tree of humanity. He struggles in the way of the humanity to release himself from himself in the world, and fulfils his pledge to Allāh. Allāh has bought from the believers their selves and their wealth, but in return they will have the Garden. He leaves the dunyā and its appetites and expends himself and his wealth. He rides the branch which connects to the branch of the heart until he reaches the heavens of the spiritual world and then produces fruit, which is never disconnected or forbidden to the end of time.

This is better for you, meaning that the profit from this place is better for you than resting at the bottom of the tree of the humanity and better than being satisfied with pleasures that come to an end if you but knew.

To rest at the bottom of the tree of humanity is to dwell in the pit of the Hellfire of the bottom of hell (al-jahannam) and to reside in it forever. If any part of the tree stays at the bottom of the roots of the tree of humanity and is not attracted by the force of the light that secures it to the branches of spirituality, referred to as the Garden, then it may never be released from al-jahannam. But what comes up from al-jahannam are the roots of the tree of humanity which are a part of the tree of the spirit and after a time, if it has even an atom's worth of light that was sprinkled in the world of the spirits, it will turn to the divine attraction.

The spiritual tree of the tree of the humanity has three classes. Allāh says:

> And you will be sorted out in three bands. (Qur'ān 56:7)

They are the Companions of the Left Side, the Companions of the Right Side and the Companions who have gone beyond.

1. The Companions of the Left Side

There is a class of people whom Allāh orders to be part of the tree who are known as the people of agony. These are the people of the Hellfire who are in it forever. As Allāh says:

> It is they who are the companions of the Hellfire.
> They dwell in it forever. (Qur'ān 2:81)

These are:

> The companions of the Left Side (al-'aṣḥābū-;-mash̲'amah). (Qur'ān 56:9)

2. The Companions of the Right Side

There is a class of people in the tree that Allāh describes as travelers with success from Allāh until they depart from the bottom sections of the tree and are released from the darkness of the nafs into the light of the spiritual world. These people are the righteous people and are called:

> The companions of the Right Side (al-'aṣḥābu-l-maymanah). (Qur'ān 56:8)

The righteous people or the people of ease are those who have gone through the Hellfire and have been saved from it by holding onto the light of faith. They enter the Garden of flowers and Allāh says,

> They are the companions of the Garden.
> They dwell in it forever. (Qur'ān 2:82)

These people are divided into two types:

1. A type whose nafs have been purified when they leave this world.

These are the ones who, if they enter the Garden on the Day of Judgment, the Hellfire will say to them, "Pass through, oh believer, for you are increased by the light of my flames." This is because when they entered al-jahannam with their nafs and appetites, and the Hellfire increased its flames, they quenched the flames with the light of their faith and kept themselves from following passion.

2. And a type whose nafs are purified in the Hellfire when they leave this world, as Allāh says:

> Truly he succeeds that purifies it; and he fails that corrupts it. (Qur'ān 91:9)

These people are a mixture of good and evil deeds because even though the light may have touched them and touched their spirits, the darkness of the attributes of the nafs has also taken them over. They mix good actions with bad actions. With good actions, which are the result of the light, the traveler walks toward Allāh, and with bad actions, which are the result of the darkness of the nafs, he turns away from Allāh. It is possible that Allāh may take these people by divine attraction. He may gift them. This means that He makes them turn toward Him by increasing their light, allowing their light to have authority over the darkness of their nafs. By relinguishing the flames of the passion and appetite of the nafs, they travel towards the Hellfire like the wind. Since part of the body of the spirit is predisposed to remaining in the humanity and part is predisposed to leaving it at death, the Messenger of Allāh said, "Allāh knows best what they are up to," meaning that if they are a people that were touched by the light, they do the work that leads them to the Garden, and if they are a people that were among those not touched by the light, they will do the work that leads them to the Hellfire.

3. The Companions Who Have Gone Beyond

The third class of people are the foremost ones (sāsābiqūna; those who have gone beyond (Qur'ān 56:10). They are the ones who are brought nearest to Allāh (al-muqarrabūn) from among the prophets and the 'āwliya. Allāh has predisposed them to be under the force of divine attraction. They are from the part of the seed of the tree of humanity in the stations of the nafs like the birds perched upon branches. In the stations of the heart, they are like the wind blowing toward the blossoms. In the stations of spirituality, they are like lightning, that is, like divine attraction enabling the skin of existence to have annihilation of the tree and to have baqā' in the fruits of the stations of arrival.

These are the ones whom Allāh loves to create so that He might be known by uncovering the hdden treasure. All other creatures are derivatives of their existence, just as all the parts of the tree are derivatives of the fruits.

Allāh says:

> I did not create the jinn and the humans except to worship Me. (Qur'ān 51:56)

In other words – to know Him. So why are they mentioned more than once as the foremost? This indicates that Allāh is foremost in leading them to His excellence. Allāh prepares them to be predisposed to receiving His beauty. He loves them and makes them ready to receive His protection. They love Him, so they are foremost by virtue of the preceding divine care toward them. They are also foremost in relation to other parts of the seed of the spirit because they were the first to come out of the tree of the humanity and to be established in the fruits of "āwliya, prophecy, and messengership according to their ranks in existence in the true humanity, and according to degrees of excellence, deficiency, smallness, and largeness in relation to their fruits.

They are also foremost in receiving divine love. Know that divine love is ancient and that the foremost are foremost in listening to the address of Allāh and in following His orders.

They are foremost in replying to Him when He asks,
"Do you come willingly or unwillingly?" They say, "We come willingly."
They are foremost in leaving nonexistence for the world of the spirits.
They are foremost in presenting themselves to the divine presence.
They are foremost in listening to Allāh's address to them,
"Am I not your Lord?" (Qur'ān 7:172)
They are foremost in replying. They say, "Yes!"
They will be foremost in being revived when the trumpet is blown.
They are foremost to cross the bridge;
foremost in traveling on the straight path.
They are foremost in speaking to Allāh and foremost in His looking at
them and entering the Garden and in seeing Allāh
when He makes tajallī with His slaves with His essence and His attributes.
Blessed and exalted and holy is Allāh.

Know that when spirits are addressed in the sacred fold near the Lord of the worlds, He says:

> Get down, each of you an enemy to the other. (Qur'ān 2:36)

That is, descend with bodies to the earth, and meaning that some of your rūḥ is an enemy because Allāh created the nafs through the combination of rūḥ and body. So the body is part of the rūḥ in the same way that Ādam and Eve are part of each other and the nafs is an enemy to the rūḥ which is its very self. As the Messenger of Allāh said:

> The greatest enemy to you
> is your nafs that is between your two sides. (Ḥadīth)

The rūḥ is also an enemy to the body because although its roots are in the presence, its reality is exalted and yearns for the meeting with its Lord. It was created out of nothing and ennobled by being given proximity to His presence so that it is only satisfied with that. So the spirit is the root or origin and everything else is a branch.

The rūḥ is seeking and the Ḥaqq is what it seeks. Because the spirit loves the Ḥaqq and the Ḥaqq is its Beloved it enjoins the nafs to come to the presence by force which is contrary to the nature of the nafs. The nafs is related to the earth and to its inhabitants; it is attached to the lowly material world (dunyā) because it originated from it. It was raised cultivating of its appetites and derives pleasure from them and wants to bring the rūḥ to the bottom of the material world (dunyā). Therefore it calls upon the rūḥ with force to help it in its satisfaction which is contrary to the nature of the spirit. So the rūḥ makes an enemy of the self and attaches itself to yearning (the exalted himma).

Both the rūḥ and the self have helpers in their mission. The advocates of the rūḥ are the intellect, the mind, and the heart, and they are aided by Allāh and His Messenger. The instruments of the rūḥ are the senses of the heart which have strength exemplified in action by following the commands of the sharī'ah and stopping with the prohibitions of the sharī'a so that the heart protects itself from the adversity of the "deaf, dumb, and blind; they are devoid of understanding." For this reason Allāh's Messenger said:

> In the body of Ādam's son there is a piece of flesh
> with which, if it is sound, the whole body becomes sound
> and if it is corrupt, the whole body becomes corrupt
> and this is the heart. (Ḥadīth)

The advocates of the nafs are passion and appetite and they are supported by the material world (dunyā) and the s̲hayṭān. Its instruments are the senses of the heart. These begin in childhood to the end of puberty and these help the nafs to take on the beauty of the world aided and abetted by the s̲hayṭān so that the nafs then commands to evil and superimposes its authority over the rūḥ. It jails the rūḥ in the prison of the natural animal world. As for the helpers of the spirit, the intellect, and the heart, at this point they are not able to help because of weakness and because their senses are incapable of receiving the support of Allāh and His messenger. So all the parts of the rūḥ remain at the bottom of the earth,

> [some that are] enemies to yourselves, (Qur'ān 64:14)

As Allāh says:

> And We said, "Get down, each of you [human and s̲hayṭān] an enemy to the other.
> And the earth will be your dwelling place
> and pleasure for a time,' " (Qur'ān 2:36)

That is, until the will of Allāh and His Ancient aided by His Wisdom will send the breezes of the Ḥaqqfrom the pure divine care.

> Then Ādam received from his Lord words [of guidance]
> and He turned to him [with mercy].
> Truly He is the Oft-turning, the Singularly Compassionate.
> (Qur'ān 2:37)

Oh our Lord we have been unjust to ourselves
by following the passions and appetites of the nafs.
And if You do not forgive us, that is,
if You do not cover us with Your grace and Your mercy
so that You may look upon us with the eye of mercy
and set Your gaze on the nafs that commands to evil
so that it no longer has ascendancy,
and if You make it willing to receive the order...
But this You give only to those upon whom You have mercy,
that You may release them from their prison terms
so that they may become sincere slaves.
If You do not do this,
then surely we are among those who have lost themselves

by following their passions and appetites
and who continue to be prisoners of the nafs in the lowest of the low,
jailed in the attributes of the body.

Oh Allāh, make us among those who receive Your guidance
and who follow Your desire.
Make us among those people whom fear does not overtake.
They do not fear that their nafs will have complete authority over them;
nor do they sorrow about what has past them by;
nor do they sorrow at the thought of giving up
the pleasures of the nafs and the animal appetites.

Oh Allāh, bring them to be Your k̲halīfa and forgive them.
Call upon their nafs with the order: "Return to your Lord."
Guide them with the tajallī of Your Beauty
to the presence of Your Majesty.

Know, my beloved, oh sincere seeker, oh intellegent seeker of the divine love, that I have explained to you what you need to start your journey from the lowest of the low of human nature to the highest of the high in the ranks of those who are nearest to their Lord. I have given you ample explanation and transparent clarification. I would like your end to be the musk that embellishes the holy spirits. When the holy spirits smells the fragrance of the gentle breezes of the Ḥaqq, it drives them to arrive at His presence, whereas these fragrances become a proof against the lowly ones because they are not capable of doing what the seeker needs to do. The seeker needs to act according to the realities of what is described in all the revealed Books.

Know that the ways to Allāh are as many as the breaths of creation. As for our way, that we wish to explain to you, it is one of the shortest of ways to reach Allāh. It is the clearest and the one with most guidance because although the ways are many, they can all be classified into three:

The Three Ways [available to the seeker]

1. The Way of Action

The first way is the way of the people of action. They are the ones who do a lot of fasting, praying, and recitation of the Qur'ān. They perform the pilgrimage, and so on. The ones who reach by this way are very few.

2. The Way of Spiritual Discipline

The second way is the way of the people of spiritual disipline. They change their character traits. They purify their nafs. They purify their hearts. They purify their spirit. They do what establishes their inward, which is the way of the pure ones. The people who arrive by this way are more than the first group, but those who have completion among them are very few. A beloved was asked, "In what station are you struggling with your nafs?" He answered, "I have been struggling with my nafs in the station of reliance on Allāh (at-taqwā) for thirty years." Then the first man asked, "If you are going to spend your whole life on building your inward, how long are you going to take to find annihilation in Allāh?"

3. The Way of Walking

The third way is the way of those who are walking the way of Allāh. This is the way of the intellgent ones from among the people of love, who are walking because of divine attraction. The people of arrival among them are more than in any other group. This is the select path. This is based on dying willfully. The Messenger, may the blessings and peace of Allāh be upon him, said, "Die before you die."

10 Principles Exemplifying the "Way of Walking"

1. Repentance

Repentance (at-tawba) is to turn to Allāh willingly, just as death is a turning to Allāh unwillingly. Allāh says,

> Return to your Lord, content and well-pleased. (Qur'ān 89:28)

This means letting go of all sins. Know that a sin is what veils you from Allāh. These are the ranks of the dunyā and the ākh̲ira. It is obligatory upon the seeker to let go of everything except Him; even to let go of existence – know that your existence is a sin greater than any other sin.

2. Asceticism

Asceticism (az-zuhd) in the material world (dunyā) means to let go of pleasures and appetites whether they are little or much; to let go of its wealth and high positions just as you are evidently going to do upon death. The reality of az-zuhd is that you are ascetic in the dunyā and the ākh̲ira. The Messenger of Allāh said:

> The dunyā is not permitted to the people of the ākhira,
> and the ākhira is not permitted to the people of the dunyā,
> and they are both not permitted to the people of Allāh. (Ḥadīth)

3. Reliance
Reliance on Allāh (at-tawakkul) is to let go of causality completely and to have complete trust in Allāh. This is the case with death. Whoever puts his reliance completely on Allāh, then Allāh is his help.

4. Satisfaction
Satisfaction (al-qanāʿa) is to let go of the appetites of the nafs and the pleasures of the animal body as is the case in death. You let go of everything, except what you absolutely need, so that you do not have excess in eating, clothing, or housing, and you take only what you absolutely need.

5. Seclusion
Isolation or seclusion (al-ʿuzla) is to let go of socializing with creation by being solitary, as is the case in death, except when you have to serve a gnostic shaykh who is a knower of Allāh and a complete ʾinsān al-kāmil. Then you are as the body of the dead with the washer. So with the shaykh, be as the body with the washer. Let him do as he wishes. Let him clean you with the water of ʾāwliyaʾ from other than Allāh. The shaykh is the one who gives strength to the spirit through khalwa and separation from the sensory, the dunyā, the shayṭān, the passions, and the appetites. This is how a doctor heals sick people. First he prevents them from taking what causes sickness. It is said that prevention is the best medicine.

6. Remembrance
Being in remembrance (adh-dhikr) at all times is to not do adh-dhikr of other than Allāh. You do not forget Allāh's saying, "Remember your Lord." This involves confirmation and negation: Lā ʾilāha ʾilla-llāh. By negation you remove all that corrupts, that leads to the sickness of the heart, chains the spirit, and gives strength to the nafs, producing ugly qualities, animal passions, and attachments to the two worlds. By confirming Allāh, you give strength to the health of the heart. This protects it from ugly qualities, gives increase to the light of Allāh, makes tajallī of the Ḥaqq, and for the rūḥ, the tajallī of His essence and His

attributes. The earth of the nafs is then full of the light of its Lord and free from the darkness of the attributes of the nafs.

> On [that] day the earth will be changed for another earth,
> and the heavens, and [all creatures] will come forth to Allāh,
> the One, the Irresistible Compeller! (Qur'ān 14:48)

Allāh says:

> So remember Me, I will remember you. (Qur'ān 2:152)

The one who remembers is replaced by the One Who is remembered and the remembered is replaced by the One Who remembers. So that the one doing adh-dhikr is annihilated in adh-dhikr and the continuation (al-baqā') is for the One remembered. He becomes the khalīfa for the one doing the remembrance. So if you seek the one doing the remembrance, you will find only the One Who is remembered, and if you were to seek the One remembered, you would find only the one doing the remembrance.

If you see Me, you see him,
and if you see him, you see Us.

7. The Return to Allāh

Returning to Allāh completely (at-tawajjuh) means not calling upon anyone except the Ḥaqq. And this is the case in death anyway. At that time there is no one to seek, no one to love, and no one to turn to except Allāh. If he was offered, at that time, all of the ranks of all of the prophets and messengers, he would not prefer them to Allāh for any moment. Know that if a truthful one turns to Allāh for one thousand years and then he turns his back for an instant, what he loses is more than what he gains.

8. Perseverance

Perseverance with patience (aṣ-ṣabr) is to let go of the appetites of the nafs through the struggle with it (and this is the case of death) and to be steadfast in weaning it from everything other than Allāh, to escape the appetites, to be straight in the perfect way, and to purify the heart and beautify the spirit.

Allāh, glory be to Him, says:

> And when they were patient,
> and when they were certain of Our signs,
> We appointed from among them leaders
> who guided by Our command. (Qur'ān 32:24)

9. Watchfulness

Watchfulness (al-murākabba) is to let go of one's own power as is the case in death. You are observant and watchful of the gifts of al-Ḥaqq. You expose yourself to the gentle breezes and turn away from "other." You are turned completely, engaged in the ocean of His love, yearning for the meeting. You rely upon your spirit, calling out for His help until Allāh opens the door of His mercy to you. You call out, with the light coming from the mercy of Allāh, that in a second the darkness of the nafs commanding to evil be removed. Otherwise it may take thirty years of struggle. Allāh says:

> Save the ones upon whom your Lord has mercy.
> (Qur'ān 11:119)

These are the elect. And more than that – Allāh changes the bad actions of the nafs into the good actions of the rūḥ. Allāh says:

> And who guards himself for Allāh,
> He will cover over his evil deeds
> and grant him a vast reward. (Qur'ān 65:5)

These are the purified ones (al-bar'ah).

Know that the good actions of the purified ones are the bad actions of those who draw near. So Allāh changes the bad actions of those who draw near through His gentle breezes. Allāh says:

> And whoever comes with a good deed will have better than it.
> (Qur'ān 27:89)

And:

> Whoever does a good deed,
> [Allāh] will increase the good of it for him. (Qur'ān 42:23)

This increase in goodness is from the gentle breezes of the Ḥaqq. This is the gift of Allāh that He gives to whomever He wills.

10. Contentment

Contentment (al-riḍā) is to leave the contentment of the self to enter into the contentment of Allāh through surrender to all His decrees from the azal, and to surrender to Allāh's management of his life without any objection.

Know that some have said, "I surrendered all my affairs to my Beloved. If He wishes, He gives me life and if He wishes, He takes it."

Whoever dies to his own will, meaning he lets go of the dark attributes, Allāh gives him a life with His light and this is out of divine care. Allāh says,

> Is one who was dead and We gave him life
> and made for him light by which to walk among the people
> like one who is in the darkness out of which he cannot emerge?
> (Qur'ān 6:122)

He gives them a light from the lights of beauty with which they walk, and with this light He says, "Through Me, he walks with people," that is, in the secrets of people he has the seeing of Allāh; he witnesses their ḥāl.

Know that whoever keeps his retreat (al-kh̲alwa) with these attributes, reaches happiness. The healing power of adh̲-dh̲ikr cuts him from ugly qualities and temptations and raises the veils, and raises the cloud from the sun of witnessing the Ḥaqq. He witnesses the truth and is given revelation and perfect manifestation.

Know that no one reaches the rank of guidance except by following:

> If you truly love Allāh, then follow me. (Qur'ān 3:31)

In this 'āyah I have found good tidings that are clearly for this nation. This is the station of love, that is, the love from Allāh, glory be to Him, for His Prophet, may the blessings and peace of Allāh be upon him, and this is by His saying:

> Allāh will bring a people whom He will love
> and they will love Him... (Qur'ān 5:54)

And it is for this that He says:

You are the best community that has been brought forth for [the good] of humanity. (Qur'ān 3:110).

I say, calling upon my Lord,
and calling upon His generosity,

Oh You Who created the tree of the world,
Who gave it the fruit of the sons of Ādam,
Who chose from among them, Muḥammad,
Oh our God, guide us to the straight path
and make us steadfast in Your right religion.

Oh our Lord, do not entrust our affairs to ourselves,
not even for the blink of an eye,
or less than that, or more than that.
Bestow upon us Your gifts and take us by You from us;
grant us the gift of Your existence in us.
Make us develop in the ocean of Your gifts
through the constancy of the tajallī
of Your jamāl and Your jalāl.

Oh God of all the worlds,
by Your mercy, Oh Most Merciful
and by Your generosity, Oh Most Generous.
I say all of this as a reminder
so whoever wishes may take a way toward his Lord.

The Human Body and the Connection of the Ruh

Reprint from *The Path to Allāh, Most High*,
available through Sidi Muḥammad Press[10]

Allāh says:

> And [remember] when your Lord said to the angels,
> "Surely I am creating a person out of dry clay
> transmuted from dark slimy mud.
> So when I have fashioned him and breathed into him
> from My Spirit, then fall down before him in prostration."
> (Qur'ān 15:28-29)

Allāh's Messenger said:

> Allāh fermented the clay of Ādam in His hands
> for forty mornings. (Ḥadīṯh)

The wisdom of creating the world is the creation of mankind because mankind is willing to accept the divine overflowing through which he has knowledge of his Creator. Mankind is the mirror of Allāh's attributes of al-jamāl and al-jalāl. He is the locus of the manifestation of the attribute of gentleness.

Allāh is the one who sees Himself in His mirror and witnesses the beauty of Himself and the jalāl of Himself through the light of divine overflowing. So He becomes a knower of Himself in His mirror and Lord of the jamāl and the jalāl and He is the Seer and the Seen.

As the Messenger of Allāh said:

> Beware of the insight of the believer
> because he sees with the light of Allāh. (Ḥadīṯh)

The human being is the beloved created for the purpose of gnosis. Allāh says:

> I love to be known, so I created the creation to be known.
> (Ḥadīṯh Qudsī)

---

[10] Sidi Muḥammad Press can be reached at www.sufimaster.org or (707) 765-0904.

Then know that the body began to be fashioned when Allāh looked at the gem He first created, and it froze and turned red. He looked again, and it melted and shook and turned into water. Then He looked at it again with a look of mercy and half of it froze, and from that He created the throne which shook. Allāh wrote on the throne:

Lā ʾilahā ʾilla-llāh

Then it became quiet and left the water as it was, shaking until the Day of Judgment.

In the throne is the prototype or mit͟hāl of all things created by Allāh. So it has come to us from the Reality that the gem was the first thing created, and it is the spirit of the Prophet, may the blessings and peace of Allāh be upon him, from which He created all existing things as is narrated in the ḥadīt͟h.

The throne went quiet (or stood still) when Allāh wrote:

Lā ʾilahā ʾilla-llāh Muḥammadur-rasūlu-llāh

because the throne was created from the light by the power of Allāh with the light of the name of Allāh and the name of the Messenger of Allāh, may the blessings and peace of Allāh be upon him. The throne and what is below it was created as a mirror for the attributes of the divinity and this is the container [Muḥammadur-rasūlu-llāh].

The heart is strong in the throne. This is why the Prophet said:

> Within the throne there is the likeness (al-timthāl)
> of everything Allāh created. (Ḥadīt͟h)

This means that the throne contains the likeness of everything and allows it to emanate from it in succession. The throne went quiet after the writing upon it, so that it would reach the perfection for which Allāh prepared it. So from the first glance toward the gem and through the change of its state into different modalities, Allāh, glory be to Him, was preparing for the preparation of the human body. As Allāh says:

> Every day He is upon a matter. (Qurʾān 55:29)

As I have mentioned before, when the time came for the leavening of the clay of the human body, Allāh sent Isrāfīl to the earth after Jibrīl and Mikā'il, peace be upon them, came back. It is said that, "Isrāfīl took a handful of dust (al-habā') from the face of the earth and threw it to the middle of the earth between Mecca and Ṭā'if." Isrāfīl did not care for the earth's complaint. He is also entrusted with seizing the spirit from the body (in death) as Allāh says,

> From her [the earth] We create you
> and into her We will return you. (Qur'ān 20:55)

The outer part of the earth is the skin (al-bush̲rā) and the inner part is called, "the adama" in Arabic. This is why the human is called Ādamic, because he was created from the adama of the earth, and he is called al-bush̲ra because his creation was also from the outside skin of the earth. Allāh says:

> Surely I am creating a mortal being from clay. (Qur'ān 38:71)
> ('innī k̲h̲āliqum-bas̲h̲aram-miñṭīn.)
> (I am creating a bushrā' from the earth.)

The Arabic word "bush̲rayya" refers to the outward picture and the Arabic word "adamayya" refers to the inward qualities.

Iblīs walked on the earth's face, and some parts of it touched his feet and some parts that were between his two feet were not touched by his feet or by his shadow. The inner body was created from the dust of his feet, and the outer body from the dust between his feet. The heart was created from dust not touched by the feet or by the shadow of Iblīs. This is the earth that was looked at by the gaze of ar-Raḥmān. Similiarly, when Ādam descended to the earth, he roamed all of the material world (dunyā). What he touched with his feet was given mercy and blessing and was enabled to became a city or a town. What was between his two feet became a village, and what was not touched became desert.

Know that the place of gnosis in the human being is a reality called the "dust" which ar-Raḥmān looked at on the day that the water became earth. What was not touched by Iblīs and his shadow is the core of the heart, the black dot, and it is around that dust that the body was formed. I mean by dust, that part which was taken out of the back of Ādam and was addressed, "Am I not your Lord?" And Allāh took the covenant with those who said, "Yes! Surely we bear witness [to that]." (Qur'ān 7:172)

Know that all of the matter which was taken from the bushrā of the earth was placed in the back of Ādam, peace be upon him. His body was the greatest in creation and he was of a very high stature. It is related that his head reached the clouds. After him, his sons became smaller and smaller. When the matter of his progeny was placed in the clay of Ādam, this is what was referred to as fermentation. Fermentation means the placing of character traits and meanings which were derived from the close angels, from the rebellious s̲hayāṭīn, from the different animals and plants, from the heavens and the two earths and what they contain of stars, planets, minerals, and gardens, and what they contain of pleasures and fires, and what they contain of pain. So the outward of Ādam was ennobled when he was leavened because of Allāh's two hands and these are the two attributes of gentleness and overpowering. So He placed in His clay what was expressing His gentleness and His overpowering. Therefore He made him the locus of manifestation of His attributes of gentleness and overpowering, which is specific only to his kind and is unlike all other creatures.

It is for this that He placed him there for forty days, so that the perfection of the ranks is four. One, ten, one hundred, and one thousand are perfect numbers based on one. He says, "That is a complete ten, and if you repeat it four times, you reach the utmost in perfection." So He is saying that "forty days" has a great secret in it. Allāh, Exalted is He, sprinkled some of His light on the clay of Ādam, peace be upon him, every morning of those forty days. The morning is indicative of the appearance of light. The dust of his progeny was already inside his clay.

Clay by its nature is dark, so whoever was touched by the light that morning was guided, and those who were not touched strayed in the darkness and never saw the light of day. These are the unfortunate ones, as indicated in the Prophet's saying:

> Allāh created creation in a darkness;
> then He sprinkled it with His light.
> Whoever was touched by the light was guided,

and whoever was not, lost his way. (Ḥadīt̲h)

In some narrations the forty days are forty thousand years, meaning that every day is a measure of one thousand years of what we count.

As we have said, the ranks of fashioning from the beginning started with the gaze on the gem in its different horizons. So first of all, the Maker fashioned the horizon of the mineral. Then it developed to the horizon of the plant, then to the horizon of the animal, then to the horizon of the angelic, and then to the horizon of the humanity. After the humanity was completely fashioned, so as to make it capable of receiving the divine overflowing without intermediary, the rūḥ became completely connected to the body. The connection of the rūḥ to the prime matter of Ādam is accomplished in stages according to the degree of the fashioning of the body. This starts with the dropping of the sperm in the womb, until it becomes a fetus, and until it reaches puberty.

The connection of the rūḥ of Ādam with his body happened in one gulp. Allāh says:

> And when I have formed him and breathed into him
> from My spirit. (Qur'ān 38:72)

At that point he was capable of receiving the divine overflowing and was ready for Allāh to make at-tajallī in him. The Messenger of Allāh, said:

> Allāh created Ādam and made at-tajallī in him. (Ḥadīth)

With this he reached the rank of receiving the station of the angels. He gained this rank with the secret of al-khalīfa which is the perfection of the station of the human being who was created for knowledge. Everything else that is in creation follows Ādam's creation; that of the tree is created as a follow-up of the fruit.

If you look closely, you will find that the whole tree is the fruit because the fruit is the power that turns to action. This is the same as the tree of all existence. It is full of the power and its fruit, which is the human spirit that comes out into action. If you look closely you find that the human being is called the "big man" or the "big world" or the "microcosm," and that the cosmos is a big human being. So it can be asked, "When anyone reaches his maturity, does he become worthy of Allāh's tajallī in him in the same way that He made at-tajallī in Ādam?"

The answer to this is in two parts. The first part is that it is in the way of Allāh that Ādam reaches the maturity of his full strength at forty years. This can be said to be the age of perfection of the body, and at this time the rūḥ is attached to the body in a complete way. If the mirror of the heart is not rusty with the rust of association and disobedience, and if it is not full of the darkness of the attributes of humanity, but if it is clean with lā ʾilāha ʾilla-llāh and it is pure of attachments to anything in the two worlds, then it deserves to become a place of the manifestation of the essence of Allāh and His mercy. And if anyone should reach this before the age of forty, this is a great honor, but it is an exception.

The second answer is that Ādam was created when He created the perfect creation. His fashioning was complete and his spirit was completely attached or connected to his body. The mirror of his heart was not rusted through acquiring animal desires, and when his rūḥ went up to his head, he sneezed. So the first action that ensued from him was a light action which was to say "al-ḥamdu-li-llāh" after sneezing. So the mirror of his heart was enlightened by the light of Allāh after thanking Allāh. This is the mind of the s̲harīʾah. So with the light of the s̲harīʾah, the darkness of nature was removed, and he became worthy of the tajallī of his Lord, al-Ḥaqq, according to Allāh's generosity, as He says in Qudsī:

> Whoever draws near to Me by a hand's span,
> I draw near to him an arm's length.

Ādam drew close to Allāh by praising Him, and Allāh drew nearer to him by saying, "May Allāh have mercy on you." So He has mercy on him with the tajallī of Lordship and He makes tajallī with all the ṣifāt and this is the meaning of when:

> And He taught Ādam the Names – all of them. (Qurʾān 2:31)

And by acquiring this rank, he goes beyond the horizons of the angels. Since they say:

> Glory be to You. We have no knowledge other than what You have taught us. (Qurʾān 2:32)

And from this Ādam gains the rank of the prostration of the angels. He was supported by the rūḥ of al-Quddūs, the holy spirit, and he was selected for vicegerency which was not given to any of the close angels.

As-salāmu ʿalaikum wa raḥmatu-llāh.

The Station of Khalifa Designated for the Human Being

Reprint from *The Path to Allāh, Most High*,
available through Sidi Muḥammad Press[11]

Allāh says:

> Oh Dāwūd,
> surely We have made you Our representative upon the earth,
> so judge between the people with justice,
> and do not follow [your own] desire,
> as it will cause you to stray from the Way of Allāh.
> Surely those who stray from the Way of Allāh [experience]
> a severe punishment for having forgotten
> the Day of Accounting. (Qur'ān 38:26)

The Messenger of Allāh, may the blessings and peace of Allāh be upon him, said:

> The k͟halīfa after me will last thirty-three years
> and after that there will be kingship and tyranny. (Ḥadīt͟h)

Know that the reality of the k͟halīfa is established upon three principles:

1. The first is annihilation, al-fanā'.
2. The second is the baqā'.
3. The third is steadfastness in surrender and satisfaction.

As for the fanā', it is the fanā' in relation to words and deeds. As for the baqā', it is the continuation of various actions in words and states. The one who is in the station of the k͟halīfa does not move without permission, and does not move from any state (al-ḥāl) except in accordance with the ḥāl established by Allāh for him. As for steadfastness in surrender and satisfaction, he is in opposition to his passions in everything so that he may seek the satisfaction of his Lord, the Lord of all the worlds.

Know that these principles are not established for the k͟halīfa, except that Allāh establishes them for him through His giving the fanā' in other

[11] Sidi Muḥammad Press can be reached at www.sufimaster.org or (707) 765-0904.

than Him, in other words, giving him the baqāʾ and establishing him in at-taslīm, the surrender and satisfaction with Allāh. This is confirmed by His saying:

> And well-pleased is Allāh with them
> and well-pleased are they with Him. (Qurʾān 5:119)

That is, when Allāh is pleased with him, Allāh makes him His vicegerent (k͟halīfa).

The Choice of the Human Being for K͟halīfa

Allāh, glory be to Him, says:

> Your Lord said to the angels,
> "I will place upon the earth a k͟halīfa" (Qurʾān 2:30)

Know that Allāh chose the human being for the role of k͟halīfa. And know also that the one chosen for k͟halīfa on earth is terrestrial and celestial. He is not just celestial like the angels or terrestrial like the animals. Allāh says, "I will place." He does not say, "I will create." There are two meanings in this. The first meaning comes from the verb "to make" which is more general than to create:

> [Is it not He] Who has made you stewards of the earth?
> (Qurʾān 27:62)

Making includes creation but with something more. He created him with the attribute of vicegerency, and not every created thing was chosen for k͟halīfa. Allāh said, "Oh Dāwūd, We have made you into a k͟halīfa upon the earth." In other words, He says, "We create you pre-disposed for k͟halīfa and then We give you its rank." The second meaning is that this "making" is specific to the knowledge of the order of the First (al-Awwal) in the malakūt, which is in opposition to the world of creation because creation consists of the world of bodies and sensory things. Allāh, glory be to Him, says:

> Without question His is the creation and the command
> (Qurʾān 7:54)

That is, the mulk and the malakūt. When Allāh refers to something that pertains to the world of the command, He is speaking about the "making" because the command is higher than creation or the act of creation. He says,

> Praise be to Allāh who has created the heavens and the earth
> and brought into being (made) the darkness and the light.
> (Qur'ān 6:1)

Since the heavens and the earth are sensory bodies, He refers to them as being "created," but since the darkness and the light are from the malakūt, He refers to them as being "made."

I say that darkness and light are in the realm of the malakūt because Allāh says:

> Allāh is the Protecting Friend of those who securely believe–
> He takes them from the shadows into the light. (Qur'ān 2:257)

These qualities are from the malakūt, not from sensory things because the light is the light of the rūḥ or the light of the guidance of faith. The "darkness" is a human attribute, like the darkness of unbelief and misguidance, as explained in many commentaries. Sensory darkness and light also fall under the creation of the heavens and the earth. So understand.

So when Allāh explains the body of Ādam, peace be upon him, He describes it in terms of creation. He says,

> Surely I am creating a mortal being from clay. (Qur'ān 38:71)
> ('innī kẖāliqum-basẖaram-miñṭīn.)
> (I am creating a bushra' from the earth.)

And when He gives us information regarding his spirituality, He mentions the "making." So He says that He is "making" a vicegerent upon the earth.

> [Is it not He] who made you stewards of the earth?
> (Qur'ān 27:62)

He selects the human being for the name "vicegerent" (kẖalīfa), and this is not given to any other existing thing.

So know that he is called kẖalīfa and know that the term kẖalīfa carries two meanings:

1. One meaning is that the kẖalīfa is a substitute for all existing things, but nothing is a substitute for the kẖalīfa because Allāh gathers in him what is in all the world of bodies and spirits.

2. In reality he is the kẖalīfa of everything and has been ennobled by this particularity. This nobility arises from Allāh's blowing of His spirit into him, as He says:

> [And I] breathed into him from My spirit. (Qur'ān 15:29)

No other creature in all the created worlds is given this nobility. This is what He means when He says:

> And undoubtedly We have honored the children of Ādam. (Qur'ān 17:70)

To be kẖalīfa for creation or for the Ḥaqq, blessed and exalted is He, is a specialty that is not afforded to any other existing thing.

Know that the human being is the kẖalīfa and the representative of Allāh in form and in meaning. As for his form, know that in reality his existence, in the outward, is different from the existence of the Ḥaqq because the existence of the human being is an "indicator" of the existence of his Creator, just as a building is a sign for the builder.

In reality the unity of the human being is different from the unity of the Ḥaqq;

the esssence and attributes of the human being
are different from the essence and attributes of Allāh;
the life of the human being is different from the life of Allāh;
the power of the human being is different from the Power of Allāh;
the will of the human being is different from the Will of Allāh;
the hearing of the human being is different from the Hearing of Allāh;
the seeing of the human being is different from the Seeing of Allāh;
the speech of the human being is different from the Speech of Allāh;
knowledge of the human being is different from the Knowledge of Allāh

And there is nothing in all of creation that can be the vicegerent as Ādam can be. Even though some creatures contain some of the attributes, they do not gather all the attributes of the Ḥaqq in the same way in which they are gathered in the human being and no attribute is reflected in any of these creatures as they are reflected in the mirror of the heart of the human being.

As for His "meaning" know that there is nothing in the world that takes on the light of Allāh and so reflects the lights of His attributes in the earth except the light of the insān al-kāmil because he is prepared to accept the overflowing light of Allāh. He has been given the light of the secret in the glass of the heart. This glass is in the niche of the body and in the glass of the heart is the oil of the spirit. Its oil gives out light from the purity of the intellect, even though it is not touched by fire. This light is the lamp of the hidden secrets, so that when Allāh wills to place a khalīfa upon the earth, the light of the beauty of Allāh manifests to the light of the human secret, and Allāh guides to His hidden light whomever He wills.

So the lamp of the human being is lit by the light of Allāh and he is upon a light from his Lord. So he becomes the khalīfa of Allāh on the earth of Allāh and manifests the lights of His attributes in the world with justice, goodness, and mercy to whomever deserves it, and with might and power, and wrath and punishment to those who deserve it. As Allāh, glory be to Him, says regarding His Prophet, may the blessings and peace of Allāh be upon him:

> Muḥammad is the Messenger of Allāh.
> And those with him are tough on al-kuffār
> (those who cover up the Truth)
> and merciful among themselves. (Qurʾān 48:29)

These attributes are not revealed to the animals, nor to coarse creatures in the world of al-mulk.

The two angels Hārūt and Mārūt objected to the progeny of Ādam – to those who followed passion, who were unjust, who killed and who caused corruption. They said, "Had we been placed as vicegerents (khulafāʾ), we would not have caused the corruption they do." So Allāh sent them down to the earth in human form and ordered them to judge between people with the truth. He warned them against associating anything with Allāh, and He warned them against performing acts of murder and drinking intoxicants. But after one month they had aready committed the first act of murder, drunk wine, and prostrated to idols. So know that the human being has been specifically chosen for khalīfa and for receptivity to the light of Allāh. If the angels had this particularity, they would not have committed these lowly acts. (see Qur'ān 2:102)

The prophets were protected from these vile qualities, even though they were human, because their hearts were lit by the light of the tajallī, and their bodies absorbed the light of their hearts inwardly and outwardly. When the earth of humanity is lit up with the light of the Lord, darkness is stripped away. So when the light of the "He"ness of the Ḥaqq blew away the darkness of the "I"ness of their contingent existence, and they received the baqā' in the existence of Allāh, they realized that they were the vicegerents (k̲hulafā') on the earth of Allāh and that they did not have true existence, nor did it belong to anyone else. Their existence was a pure receiving of the gift, which has existence only through the k̲halīfa of the existence of the Ḥaqq.

So whatever came from them in action or speech came from the station of the k̲halīfa of the Ḥaqq through Allāh's will and decree and power. In reality, they did not have existence or action. They realized that they were specified for k̲halīfa, and that this was not given to the angels who are veiled from seeing "other" and therefore veiled from witnessing the Ḥaqq. This was illustrated when Allāh tested them by saying that He was placing a k̲halīfa upon the earth. They said:

> Will You place upon it [one] who will corrupt it and shed blood
> [while] it is we who glorify Your praise and sanctify You?
> (Qur'ān 2:30)

If they had not been veiled, they would not have objected to Allāh's will. Furthermore, they would not have attributed acts to Ādam nor to themselves. If they had knowledge, they would have related acts to Allāh. As when Mūsā, peace be upon him, said:

> It is but Your trial of us,
> whereby You allow those to go astray whom You will
> and guide whom You will. (Qur'ān 7:155)

Mūsā attributes to Allāh what seems to appear from others. He saw others through the station of k̲halīfa. Even though he saw the actions of people, he turned them over to Allāh.

The Different Degrees of al-Kẖalīfa (or the functions of a deputy)

Allāh says:

> wa huwa-l-ladẖī ja'alakum kẖalāā'ifa-l-'arḍi.
> It is He Who has made you successors (kẖulafā') upon the earth and has raised some of you above others in degree.
> (Qur'ān 6:165)

Know that Allāh confirmed the vicegerency of the sons of Ādam by saying He is the One Who made them vicegerents on earth. He says that this is in degrees because in the rank of kẖalīfa He raises some above others. True vicegerency is to have authority in the mulk and in the malakūt as a representative of the Ḥaqq. Since Allāh is King of the outward cosmos in the material world (dunyā) and what is in it, and since He is the Disposer of Affairs in the malakūt, which is the inward of the universe in the ākẖira and what is in it, and since He is the Disposer of Affairs in the mulk and the malakūt in vicegerency, He disposes of things without the use of tools. He uses full power and a general will.

Allāh bestows upon the kẖalīfa "tools" with full capacity. As for the tools in the mulk, they are the limbs of the body and the five senses and everything pertaining to the body. As for the tools of the malakūt, they are the heart, the intellect, the secret, the spirit, the hidden, and all human powers, and everything that is connected to the rūḥ.

There are three ranks of the kẖalīfa:

1. The first rank belongs to those who use only the tools of the body. These people are divided into two categories:

    ★ Those whose toil is appreciated and who are rewarded for their actions. They use tools in accordance with the orders and prohibitions of the Maker for marriage, for provision such as in farming, and for the making of things such as the making of artifacts.

    ★ The second category are those who use the tools given to them according to the satisfaction of their nafs in opposition to the Orders of the One Who gave them the vicegerency and in opposition to His prohibitions. These are losers as a result of their vicegerency. They are like animals and are misguided.

2. The second rank belongs to the people who use the tools of the body and some spiritual tools. They are also divided into two categories:

   - Those who use these tools in accordance with the obligations and prohibitions of the One Who appointed them as vicegerents. These are the elect of the believers. They use their minds and intellects. They reflect upon the creation of the heavens and the earth. They see the signs of their Lord in the horizons and in themselves. They have certainty about the Ḥaqq. Their faith increases as their knowledge and their degree (daraja) and their nearness increases. Some of them use the heart after purifying their nafs. Their portion is the witnessing of the Ḥaqq and the unveiling of the realities in accordance with their usage of the hearts and other spiritual qualities.
   - The second category are those who use these tools for the satisfaction of their natural desires not in accordance with the s̲harīʿa and in opposition to the orders of the One Who gave them vicegerency and in opposition to His prohibitions. They use the intellect of a mind that is blemished by illusion and imagination; so they fall into the realm of His authority and are deprived of the happiness and dignity of succession.

3. The third rank belongs to those who use all the bodily and spiritual tools according to the orders and prohibitions of the One Who gave them vicegerency.

These are the prophets and the friends of Allāh (ʾāwliyaʾ). They have the highest rank in vicegerency and this is why Allāh chose Ādam for k̲halīfa. Others did not have these tools and were not pre-disposed for k̲halīfa. The excellence of Ādam above the angels is due to the many gifts he received from his Lord. Among these gifts is:

> He taught Ādam the Names – all of them. (Qurʾān 2:31)

He speaks about their names each beginning with the Arabic letters "alif" and "lām." "Alif lām" meaning everything. This means that there is nothing, except that Ādam knows its name and the meaning of the name. So He taught Ādam the names and the things named and their realities.

As an example: Allāh taught you the name "sheep," but this teaching goes beyond the abstract, so He taught you all the names. Therefore through your seeing you know whether it is black or white; through your hearing, He taught you the name of the sound it makes; through your smelling, He taught you the name of its smell; through your tasting, you know the name of its taste; and through your touch, He lets you know its quality.

This is true with all of the names. You know the attributes, the character traits, the particularities, the benefits, and the harms. He taught you with the force He gave you, with the intellect He gave you, and with the faith He gave you, all the names of His creation because every part of the name has a taste, a smell, a description, a particularity, a use, and a reality that only the human being knows because He created the human being in the best of forms. The human has the perception of the forms of everything, their meanings and their realities, and he has the tools to perceive these things.

Those in the highest rank of vicegerency have the perception to know the reality of things without any tools. The angels do not have these perceptions. All of them accept what pertains to the power of the angelic intellect. That is why when He placed Ādam before the angels and said to them:

> Tell Me the names of these if you are truthful. (Qur'ān 2:31)

That is, if you have the advantage over Ādam, by celebrating the praise and sanctity of Allāh, they said:

> Glory be to You, (Qur'ān 2:32)

They admitted their incapacity, and as an excuse for their objection, and confessing his qualification for succession. They said:

> We have no knowledge other than what You have taught us.
> (by what You grant us of sight in the mulk and the malakūt)
> (Qur'ān 2:32)

By this Allāh shows the excellence of Ādam over them in his knowledge of these things and in their incapacity to attain what he can. Just as the Qur'ān is a proof of the prophecy of Muḥammad, may the blessings and peace of Allāh be upon him, and of his excellence over the unbelievers when Allāh challenged them to bring something like what Muḥammad brought, the knowledge of the names was a proof of Ādam's vicegerency and superiority over the angels and their inability to produce the like of it. So when his perfection for the predisposition for kẖalīfa was proven, they prostrated to Ādam.

The excellence of Ādam is because Allāh taught him the names. Allāh taught him the attributes because He made his essence in His attributes a mirror that is capable of receiving the tajallī of the attributes of His jamāl and jalāl; Blessed is Allāh. As the Messenger of Allāh said:

> Allāh created Ādam and made tajallī in him. (Ḥadītẖ)

Through His tajallī he takes on His character traits and he is described by His attributes. This is the secret of the kẖalīfa and of the reality because the mirror becomes the kẖalīfa of the One Who manifests in it.[12]

Also among the proofs of the excellence of Ādam above the angels and of his deserving the rank of kẖalīfa is that the angels need Ādam to know about their names. Allāh says:

> Oh Ādam, tell them their names. (Qur'ān 2:33)

So Ādam is the first prophet and the first one to begin prophecy. He began by informing the angels about the order of the Ḥaqq and about his vicegerency. So the angels were his nation (ummah). The credit belongs to the Prophet over the nation.

Ādam in reality is the origin of all of the universe and, in summary, his spirit is the seed of the tree of the universe, and his presence is the fruit of the material tree of the world. Just as the fruit expresses all the parts of the tree and is expressed at the top of the tree, Ādam is above all the parts of the existence, whether they are above or below, and he is a benefit and a harm to every part of the tree.

Each particle is given an appropriate name that fits the angels. It is from the perfection of Ādam's state that the names of Allāh were given according to his benefit or harm, his interest or his corruption.

---

[12] According to Ibn al-ʿArabī it is through the Perfect One that Allāh looks at His creatures and dispenses His mercy.

Since he [Ādam] is created, Allāh is the Creator.
Since he is provided for, Allāh is the Provider.
Since he is a bondsman, Allāh is Lord.
Since he is a worshipper, Allāh is the Worshipped.

With respect to his being deficient, Allāh is his veil.
With respect to his being sinful, Allāh is the Forgiver.
With respect to his repenting, Allāh is the Acceptor of Repentance.
With respect to his being benefitted, Allāh is the Beneficent.
With respect to his being harmed, Allāh is the Protector.
With respect to his being poor, Allāh is the Rich.
With respect to his being weak, Allāh is the Strong.
With respect to his being unjust, Allāh is the Just.
With respect to his being oppressed, Allāh is the Avenger.
With respect to his being the lover, Allāh is the Beautiful, etc.

Know then that the human being in this respect is the recipient of every attribute, just like the mirror. He is the recipient of the attributes of Allāh, like gentleness and overpowering. This capacity for reflection of Allāh's attributes is increased by the nearness of the slave to Allāh. He achieves this nearness by purifying himself of ugly qualities, so that Allāh manifests Himself with the attribute of forgiveness. If he draws nearer to Allāh by purifying himself from the attribute of injustice, then Allāh manifests to him with His attribute of justice and then the slave carries this attribute of justice. He becomes the kẖalīfa of Allāh by the judgment of justice on the earth. This is the secret of His saying:

> When they draw near to me a hand's span,
> I draw near to them by an arm's length. (Ḥadīth̲ Qudsī)

You can proceed in this way with the rest of the attributes of Allāh. This is why Allāh says, "My slave, I am a living King, and I do not die. I am Eternal; if I say to a thing, 'Be,' it is. Obey Me, and I will make you a king, alive, eternally, and if you say to a thing, 'Be,' it will be."

Whoever obeys Allāh by using all the tools of the body and the spirit will attain to the kẖalīfa of this rank.

How the Spirit Enters the Body

Allāh says:

> Truly We created the human being in the best form.
> Then We reduced him to the lowest of the low –
> except for those who faithfully believe and do righteous deeds
> – theirs will be a reward unfailing. (Qur'ān 95:4-6)

Allāh's Messenger said:

> The creation of anyone of you is done by collecting him
> in the womb of his mother for forty days as sperm,
> then leech-like, then a morsel of flesh;
> then Allāh sends the angel with four words.
> Allāh says to the angel, "Write down his provision,
> action and life-span and whether he will be happy or wicked."
> Then He breathes from His spirit into him. (Ḥadīth)

Know that a person may do good things leading to the Garden all his life, and then he does one thing at the end of his life and enters the Hellfire, and vice versa.

Also know that the human spirit was created in the best of form, meaning with a predisposition to receive the divine overflowing without intermediary, and that the human is unique in this rank compared to other creations. This is because the human spirit is the first thing that pertained to the command, "Be," in existence without intermediary. As for other creatures, they receive this order through intermediaries. Because of this secret, Allāh says, in His teaching about the rūḥ:

> Say, the spirit comes by the order of my Lord. (Qur'ān 17:85)

Since the rūḥ is the first fact in relation to the power of Allāh, it is the closest thing in existence to the divine presence. It remained in the vicinity of the Lord of the worlds until Allāh [turned it back to the lowest of the low when He] placed the rūḥ in the human body. That is, He commands the spirit to be attached to the body. Do not think that the relationship of the spirit to the body is the same as the relationship of the body to the body. This attachment (the spirit to the body) is done through the blowing of the Ḥaqq without comparison to anything else. This is expressed in the Qur'ān and in the ḥadīth:

> [He] breathed into him (nafakhtu). (Qur'ān 15:29)

As for the truth of putting the rūḥ in the lowest of the low in the body, this means that its attention has been drawn away from the divine presence toward the sperm in the womb in order to care for it for forty days[13] until it becomes leech-like (al-'alaq) and then a morsel of flesh (al-mudgha). When He covers the bones with flesh the blowing of the rūḥ is then completed.

Please note, my beloveds, that it is in this way that the spirit is completely engaged in the care of the gross body. This is expressed by His saying:

> And then We reduced him to the lowest of the low.
> (Qur'ān 95:4)

In reality the rūḥ has not moved from its place in the vicinity of the Ḥaqq. For this reason Allāh says:

> We are nearer to him than the jugular vein. (Qur'ān 50:16)

If we look at the root of its formation, and see that it is the first thing that evolved out of the divine power, then we know that it is the closest thing to the presence. If we look at its place when it was driven to the lowest of the low, then it is the farthest away from the divine presence. When it turns and becomes a mortal (bashar), in reality it crosses the lights of the world of Spirits, then the world of the Throne, and the Footstool and the seven heavens, and what is in them of angels and the spirits who carry the Throne and the Footstool, and the heavenly souls, and the seven heavens, and the lowest of the low, since there is nothing under him or farther away from His presence. But because existent things in the world of bodies are the farthest away from the divine presence, if you look at the world of bodies, you find it the farthest away from the Throne. This is especially true of complex bodies, of which the human being is an example. If we look at the origin of his nature, we find that he is the nearest to the presence, and when we look at his abasement, we find that he is the lowest of the low and is farthest from the presence.

---

[13] Stage one of fetal development lasts for forty days and is known as "nuṭfa."

The farthest from the Throne is the nearest to the world of bodies (the ingredients from which the body is formed). The human body is nearer to real moderation and is therefore farther from material fundamentals. That is, the image of the human body is the farthest from the presence, and the spirit of the human body is the nearest. [14] And Allāh has combined the two:

> In order to test which of you is best in your [actions];
> and He is the Mighty, the Ever-forgiving. (Qur'ān 67:2)

Then know that the spirit,
by being attached to the highest place
and then abased to the lowest of the low in the body,
was pleased with the breath of Allāh.

But the spirit is veiled when it enters
the body of the human being and
becomes veiled and imprisoned
in the lowest of the low
until Allāh releases
whomever He wishes of His slaves with Divine Attraction
and His saying,

"Return to your Lord."

So understand, my beloved.

[14] According to Ibn al-'Arabī He makes Himself known to the form through the form, so the form comes to know Him through an affair to which it is naturally disposed.

The Return of the Ruh to the Presence

Reprint from *The Path to Allāh, Most High,*
available through Sidi Muḥammad Press[15]

Allāh says:

> Oh you soul whose self is at peace!
> (yāā-'ayyatuha-n-nafsu-l-muṭma'innah)
> Return to your Lord well pleased (al-rāḍiyah),
> well-pleasing (al-marḍiyyah).
> So enter [the ranks of] My worshippers and enter My Garden.
> (Qur'ān 89:27-30)

Know that when Allāh wanted to place a vicegerent upon His earth to represent His essence and His attributes, He created a spirit for it in the best of forms. Then He turned it to the lowest of the low, that is, the body, and veiled him with the veils of light and spiritual matters and the veils of the darkness of bodies. These are the two worlds of the seen and the unseen.

The number of veils is as the Messenger of Allāh, may the blessings and peace of Allāh be upon him, said:

> Allāh has seventy thousand veils of light and darkness. (Ḥadīth)

The veils of light are from the spiritual world, while the dark veils are from the visible world of bodies. With respect to those worlds, He gave the kẖalīfa spiritual and physical perception in order to know them. His kẖalīfa has knowledge of the hidden and the manifest when he is released from the prison of the body and when he returns to his Lord through divine attraction.

Allāh calls him "Spirit" when He blows into his body. He says:

> [I] breathed into him from My Spirit. (Qur'ān 38:72)

And He calls him nafs when the nafs returns to the presence. Allāh says:

> Oh nafs in complete rest and satisfaction (al-muṭma'innah),

[15] Sidi Muḥammad Press can be reached at www.sufimaster.org or (707) 765-0904.

> return to your Lord. (Qur'ān 89:27)

What He means by nafs here is His essence and the reality of His existence. So the nafs say, "You know what is in my self, but I do not know what is in Your self," that is, in Your essence.

For the human being, the nafs is a name that gathers his body (nafs al-marḍiyyah), his heart, and his spirit and this name defines and elaborates on all these different aspects. So in your return of the nafs to the presence is the return of the body, the spirit, and all of your existence. So when the Lord says, "Return to your Lord," and this is not perceived by hearing, Allāh helps the one who has at-tawbah, which is the return to the Ḥaqq, after He leaves you in error for awhile. Then He helps you to cross the seventy thousand veils of light and darkness. And you cannot cross these stations except by receiving that which was taken away when your spirit attached to your body. This allows you to take on light, purity, and subtlety. You need these qualities in order to fly back to your original home, where you came from. And this is possible with attraction to the order, "Return." You fly to the presence. The first station that the seeker transverses in the beginning of his walking is the station of the earth. So understand.

Earth, Water, Air and Fire

Know that the rūḥ is in the prison of the body. It is chained by four stations – earth, water, air, and fire. The rūḥ is not free of these except through faith and good action as decreed by the s̱harī'ah.

Allāh says:

> Then We reduce him to the lowest of the low,
> except for those who faithfully believe and do righteous deeds
> -
> theirs will be a reward unfailing. (Qur'ān 95:5-6)

Allāh says to him, "Move up!" (Qur'ān 58:11) righteous good word and deed. The crossing takes place with the dropping of every derived quality and with the holding onto every good quality in each of these stations. Whatever low qualities of the earth were taken, such as, lowliness, humiliation, meanness, and so on, these are let go of through the purification of the nafs. This is accomplished by dropping these attributes and taking on their opposites, which is the high yearning upon which the traveler rides.

The evils of "water" are lust and pleasure. The evils of "air" are pride, oppression, conceit, hypocrisy, hatred, and prejudice. The one walking should discard these bad qualities and replace them with their opposites. The evils of "fire" are anger, arrogance, haughtiness, greed, avarice, and envy. These are also to be replaced with their opposites. In crossing from one station to another – what is seen in the earth is ruins and pictures; what is seen in the air is walking on air, flying, and the ascension to heaven; what is seen in crossing the Hellfire are blazing flames, parched places, entering the Hellfire, and the like. It was for this reason that when the angels saw Ādam's body, consisting of the four elements, they said:

> Will You place upon it [one] who will corrupt it and shed blood? (Qur'ān 2:30)

They said this before they saw all these different components being brought together by the spirit, so they witnessed only animal traits.

He who sees with the sight of the malakūt, sees the hidden. It is seen and witnessed as Allāh says:

> We showed Ibrāhīm the dominion (malakūt) [of Allāh over]
> the heavens and the earth,
> that he might be of those who are certain. (Qur'ān 6:75)

And Allāh says:

> Do you not know that to Allāh belongs
> the sovereignity of the heavens and the earth? (Qur'ān 2:107)

The malakūt is witnessed by the angels, but the divine presence is hidden. They cannot "move up" to that presence, but man is a container for the sensory seeing world, a spirit in the unseen world of the malakūt that is not perceived, and a secret that is prepared to receive the divine light of overflowing. Man moves from the realm of the wayfarer, crossing the simple elements, progressing to the compound elements, then crossing the mineral world, the plant world, the animal world, the horizon of the human world, and ascending to the world of witnessing. He ascends to the world of the unseen, which is the malakūt, then to the jabarūt world, and to al-lahūt world, which is the unseen of the unseen. He witnesses the lights of the jamāl and the jalāl with the light of Allāh and becomes the kẖalīfa of the Ḥaqq, the knower of the unseen and the seen.

To Allāh belongs the world of the unseen and He does not reveal this except to those whom He chooses as a messenger from among the people. This is the hidden secret of the human being. It is the knowledge Allāh gave to Ādam that He did not give to the angels when they said:

> Will You place upon it [one] who will corrupt it and shed blood? (Qurʾān 2:30)

And He said, "I know what you do not know." The angels said what they said only because of their seeing into the earth (mulk) of the body of Ādam. Allāh made them say what they said so that we can know that these low qualities are present in our clay, so that we may strive in the purification of our nafs in order to be free of these qualities. In other words, the angel's knowledge of the nafs makes us realize that these bad traits are part of human nature.

Pope Valley Welcome Weekend

The story starts when Ādam left the Garden.
Allāh had brought him down to earth in a place now called Sri Lanka;
it used to be called Ceylon.
At that time, when Ādam descended, he was by himself.
Iblīs sent his followers to disturb Ādam.
So Ādam asked Allāh, "How can I rid myself of Iblīs' followers?"
Allāh gave him a divine order through the archangel, Jibrīl.
He told him that in this land there was a tree.
He described it to him, and Jibrīl, the archangel, showed him the tree.

The name of this tree in Syrianic is "Hiltīt."
This tree is very old.
When Jibrīl asked Ādam to cut a branch from this tree,
water came from it. He gathered that fluid,
and in two hours it had crystallized like a piece of mustard seed.
It is white and it has a very, very foul smell.
It would be very difficult for a human being to smell it.
Its taste is very, very bitter.
This [crystallized material] is whit.
It is used after reciting ʾāyat al-Kursī (Qurʾān 2:255)
for those who think they are afflicted by this Iblīs energy.

From "How to Heal All Diseases"

Travel from the Physical World to the World of Witnessing

"I am Traveling to My Lord"

from *He Who Knows Himself Knows His Lord*

Lā ʾilāha ʾilla-llāāāāāāh, Lā ʾilāha ʾilla-llāāāāāh, Lā ʾilāha ʾilla-llāāāāāh
Muḥammad rasūlu-llāh, Ibrāhīm rasūlu-llāh, Mūsā rasūlu-llāh,
ʿĪsā rasūlu-llāh ʿalayhim ṣalātu-llāh.[16]

Allāhumma anta-s-salām wa minka-s-salām
wa ilayka ya'ūdu-s-salām
tabārakta rabbanā
ya dha-l-jalāli wa-l-'ikrām[17]

As-salāmu ʿalaykum wa raḥmatu-llāh wa bārakatuhu.

Sidi in English: Greet us. Greet us with the love and the mercy, and the freedom and the justice and peace to us and to all humankind in every time and every place. Āmīn.

As-salāmu ʿalaykum wa raḥmatu-llāh wa bārakatuhu.

I thank Allāh and praise Him. May He make me remain strong, healthy in my body, healthy in my mind, healthy in my heart, healthy in my secret, healthy in my soul, and bring mercy through me from Him to you, so I can continue to bring the message of unity. I ask Him to bestow [strength, health, and mercy] upon me always, until I see the flag of freedom and justice fly on every home in this world without seeing any destruction, killing, or hunger.

---

[16] Sidi begins each gathering by affirming the unity of God and all of creation through the statement, "Lā ilāha ʾilla-llāh" which means, "There is no god but God." It can also be translated as, "There is no god worthy of worship except Allāh." Generally, Sidi will follow this by invoking the four prophets Ibrāhīm (Abraham), Mūsā (Moses), ʿĪsā (Jesus) and Muḥammad, may God's peace and blessings be upon them all.

[17] This translates as, "Oh Allāh, You are Peace, and from You comes Peace. Give us Peace. Blessed are You, oh our Lord, oh Lord of Majesty and Bounty."

I am certain that Allāh will fulfill His promise and bring this message to the whole world. He said:

> They [those who cover up the truth]
> want to extinguish Allāh's light with their mouths,
> but Allāh will not allow anything
> except that His light will be perfected
> even though the disbelievers hate [it]. (Qur'ān 9:32)

The time is very near. The time of the tyrants will be over on this earth. At that time you will hear the song of the freedom and peace everywhere in this world without discrimination and separation, because there is no difference in religion.

There is only one religion, the religion of unity, the religion of Allāh, in which there is no differentiation between black and white, female and male, rich and poor, because Allāh said:

> Oh people,
> We have created you from [a single pair] a male and a female,
> and made you into tribes and nations
> that you may know one other. (Qur'ān 49:13)

He also said:

> Truly! This, your religion (or nation) is one religion (or nation),
> and I am your Lord, therefore worship Me. (Qur'ān 21:92)

And this will be. The missiles and the planes and the weapons of destruction will vanish. You will see the dove of peace singing songs of peace. This is what we pray for and this is what we carry the message for. I hope deeply that you are one of those people who will sing the songs of love and peace.

You will start hearing from the deep book that I started six years ago. It is very deep. You have to open the ears of your heart and the inside of your heart. I would like you to be absent from this physical world. I would like you to open your heart and your ears and I would like you to listen to the word of Allāh and His Messenger. I grew up in this teaching. I was a young child, no more. I was raised under those people who carried this message. I hope that you will be raised with me the Day of Resurrection.

I love all people; it is my way to have friendship between men and women because we are all human beings. Allāh said, "Oh you people." He did not say, "Oh you man," or "Oh you woman." This is the truth. It is the human being who made this differentiation between a woman and a man. Does not everyone have a mother? Does not everybody have a father? It is the truth that you are created from dirt, dust. Do you know if the dirt is male or female? You do not know. You go back to what you were before. Be ashamed that you do not pronounce anything other than what Allāh said. Do not say that you are great; you are this or that, because you came from the earth and you will go back to the earth. You came as a sperm and you go back as a dead body. This is the truth, is it not? If anyone says this is not the truth, please tell me. But you are a holy person. How are you holy? Because Allāh has created you in His image. He ordered the angels to prostrate to this mirror.

This is why Allāh sent two books. Be careful. I will explain to you. The book that is seen, witnessed, is what you see in the earth and skies and heavens—everything in it - male, female. That is what you see with your eyes. This is witnessed, manifest. When Allāh manifested Himself, this is what manifested, what you see, what is witnessed.

Allāh has many worlds. Allāh created seven heavens and then made from the earth seven like them. This is in the book that was written, the witnessed book. In this book that is witnessed, there are some things you see and some things you do not see. The world of seven seas—the earth is a quarter [the size] of the oceans. How many human beings are on the surface of the earth? About five billion? How many animals are there? How many birds are there? How many trees are there? How many ants? How many worlds? They are all different worlds and they are all nations like you.

Listen to what Allāh says an ant said when Sulayman's army came along:

> Oh ants! Enter your dwellings, lest Sulayman [Solomon] and his hosts crush you while they do not see us. (Qur'ān 2:18)

The dogs are a nation. The fox and rabbits are all nations. Allāh said that there is nothing that does not supplicate and glorify Him. Everything knows what his supplication and his glorification is (Qur'ān 24:41). The water glorifies and the birds glorify. This is just a small portion of the seen. This is only on this small earth and the human being is destroying it, killing it with their planes. Meanwhile, the world under the seas so has many nations that no one can count them.

Allāh said there are seven heavens. Between the first heaven and the second heaven there are five hundred of Allāh's years. A day in Allāh's calculation is fifty thousand years. This also has worlds, a creation greater than us in so many ways. How many years between the first earth and the second earth? There are five hundred years and every one of them is filled with creation. All these creations know Allāh. There are believers and disbelievers among them. There are seven heavens. It is a great creation. There are jinn that are believers. There are angels that are believers; they sing only one song. The sun shines on the earth. There are seventy thousand suns and there is life in them. We are just a small planet of people. This whole earth is like the head of a needle compared to the creation of Allāh. We are destroying; we are killing, and we are doing what we are doing. We are just a small, tiny piece. All our life is very short—fifty or sixty years and we are gone. Why do we destroy? This is the world as seen and witnessed.

Everybody is holy, holier than any world. This world is where the names of Allāh (asma Allāh) have appeared. When He manifested Himself in His name, then the heart appeared. When He manifested Himself with a certain name, the trees came to be. When He manifested with His other names, the creation of the mountains and the hills came to be.

With His name also He created Ādam. He ordered the angels to prostrate to him, but one of them did not. The prostration was for the mirror of Allāh that was clear in Ādam. The prostration continues. If you read all of the holy books you will see that the angels are prostrating, and they never rise from this prostration. The one who prostrates to Allāh with honesty and sincerity will never raise his head. The prostration is to a mirror. That is why Allāh said:

> I created Ādam in My image. He is My mirror. (Ḥadīth Qudsī)

The angels prostrated to this mirror. He is Allāh, [there is] no one else but He. This is the book that is witnessed and seen.

What is the written book? Do you not know what it is? It is the Qur'ān with its letters and its meaning. Every letter has a meaning and it has a reckoning. Every reckoning carries seventy thousand meanings. That is why He said:

> Alif Lām Mīm (Qur'ān 2:1, 29:1, 30:1, 31:1, 32:1)

What does alif mean? This is the first letter of "bismi-llāh", the name of Allāh. Lām is "Lā 'ilāha 'illa-llāh." Mīm is for the one to whom the Qur'ān came—Muḥammad is His messenger. I need so much time if I am to translate and interpret all this reading. It takes so many days and so much time. The knowledge that the human being can reach in the Qur'ān is not even a drop in the ocean of knowledge. This Book is in the preserved tablet up there. This that we have is just notes. I cannot explain more. Bismi-llāh.

"I am Travelling to my Lord" on page 5 of *He Who Knows Himself Knows His Lord* is read from the beginning.

Travel with me. Do not stop; keep traveling to Allāh.

The reading continues until, "Then Allāh sent messengers in the same image, but at the same time they contained His hidden image."

That is why you are holy. That is why He said:

> If anyone kills a person,
> Or spreads mischief in the land –
> it is as if he has killed all humankind,
> and if anyone saves a life,
> it is as if he has saved the life of all humankind. (Qur'ān 5:32)

The reading continues to page 7, "You see some of them calling for Him, weeping, begging, invoking, moaning, standing or bowing or prostrating. This is a characteristic of walking the way to the Truth."

You cannot understand this language unless you follow the sharīʿa of the Prophet, ṣalla-llāhu ʿalayhi wa sallam. Everyone who claims he is a Ṣūfī and does not follow the sharīʿa is a disbeliever and he is ignorant. He has to abide by the sharīʿa of the prophets, so he can understand how they lived and how they walked with Allāh, and how they were happy with this religion in this life and the life after.

You can never reach excellence (iḥsān) if you do not pay the high price. The high price is to give your heart and your soul and your body to Allāh, to follow and abide by His rules and His prohibitions. That is what He told all His messengers, those who carried the message of unity from Ibrāhīm to Mūsā to ʿĪsā (Jesus) and to Muḥammad and all the prophets and all the rest. The Buddhists and the others do not know Allāh. We do not take anything from them because they are ignorant. They disobey what Allāh said. They do not have a book from Allāh.

Mūsā had the Torah come to him. ʿĪsā had the Evangel. Muḥammad had the Qurʾān. Ibrāhīm had the books. All the prophets carried the unity. They did not worship the cows. They did not worship the monkeys. They do not understand. That is why the knowledge of the Truth comes from following the s̲harīʿa and following what it contains. Anyone who follows the s̲harīʿa and does not follow the ḥaqīqa does not understand.

He must follow the s̲harīʿa like Ibrāhīm and emigrate like Ibrāhīm emigrated. Ibrāhīm said:

> I will emigrate for the sake of my Lord. (Qurʾān 29:26)

How can you emigrate to your Lord? Know Him, witness Him, and be in the place of witnessing. Witness Him with your eyes, with your heart and with your spirit. Do not stop with pictures and illusions. Allāh said, "I listen. I hear and I see." He hears and sees and knows and creates. Who else can create a hand? No one. Ever. He created everything in precise measure. Allāh does not like to play [games]. Allāh is the truth and He showed you the truth.

He manifested to you in His name. He said with His name He hears and He sees. If you have bad or diseased eyes, Allāh manifests with His name al-Baṣīr, and you are able to see. When He manifests with His name as-Samīʿ, the All-Hearing, you can hear. When He manifests with His name al-Ḥayy, the Living, you are alive. That is why Allāh created ninety-nine qualities, and He put all those qualities in you. Allāh said:

> [Allāh said] "Tell Me the names of these if you are truthful."
>
> [The angels answered] "We have no knowledge other than what You have taught us. Truly, You are the All-Knower, the All-Wise."

He said, "Oh Ādam! Tell them their names." (Qur'ān 2:31-2:33)

Then Ādam taught them. This is the kẖalīfa, because Allāh manifested in him. Do you see why you are holy? I do not say, "Oh man," or "Oh woman." I say, "Oh human, holy one." [Allāh says] "Why do you postpone following the commands? Why do you disobey Me? I came to you to know Me. My earth and My heaven did not contain Me, but the heart of My believing slave contained Me." I cannot say any more.

The reading repeats, "You see some of them calling for Him, weeping, begging, invoking, moaning, standing or bowing or prostrating. This is a characteristic of walking the way to the Truth."

Sidi in English: Yes, sure. It is very important to look deeper to know what I say. Do not wait. This is your time. God gives you a new creation now. Know Him now, not tomorrow.

The reading continues further down on the page, "At the end, the walking rests, but the epiphanies do not cease because the [divine] epiphany is endless. This is what the people of Allāh mean when they say, 'The ascending never stops, even after death.' "

There is no end. You get carried from station to station without end. There is no beginning. Allāh has no beginning and no end. You are His image; you have no beginning and you have no end. That is from the truth. I speak the truth. Not this body. The material is something different. I speak about your deep essence that Allāh manifested. He wanted to see Himself in what He created. You get carried from one world to another world—nothing but that.

When people say, "Allāh is no more," we need to know this will never happen. This is not true. No one thinks this except the ignorant. You have to stand up and investigate; what is speaking is not this tongue. This piece of meat is not the one that talks. Is it the eye filled with fluid that sees?

This is something you have to understand. You have to leave everything difficult and not stop with images, because they are illusion. This is just an image. When the human being dies if he is not ill, does he not he have two eyes? Does he not he have two ears? Does he not have a heart? Why does he not move? Why does he not speak? How far has the human being reached in knowledge? And this is just the tip of Allāh's knowledge. Allāh said to us that He created us from clay. The Messenger of Allāh said:

> In the body there is a heart.
> In the heart there is a spirit.
> In the spirit there is a secret.
> In the secret there is another secret.
> In the most secret there is another secret. (Ḥadīth)

There is divine emigration from

the world of mulk
to the world of malakūt,
to the world of jabarūt,
to the world of lahūt,
to the world of witnessing.

Travel from the physical world to the world of witnessing.

I have to stop here; forgive me. I hope that Allāh will give you understanding. This is just a small piece. I just wanted to tell you that the human being is holy and great. It is not for us to hate each other and discriminate between one another. The human is a holy picture. He has to have the love, the peace, the justice, the mercy, the infinite mercy, because Allāh is the Most Merciful.

This is a holy night. You do not stop. You have it all, but you do not see what kind of soul you have. This is a blessed night. I would like you to open your hearts. This is just a drop of the sweetness of Allāh. Allāh is the one who gives us His favor. We do not understand anything if we do not follow the sharī'a of His prophets, the sharī'a of beloved Muḥammad, Mūsā, 'Īsā, and Ibrāhīm, ṣalla-llāhu 'alayhim wa sallam. We have to be one of their children and not rebel against our fathers. We must not be disobedient children. Disobedience is something dreadful.

This is Friday, a blessed day. On this day Ādam was created. On this day the earth and the heaven were created. On this day the resurrection will take place. We pray to Allāh to bless you and to shower you with His favor and His mercy. Āmīn.

Who wants to renew his promise tonight? If you wish, I open the door for you.

The words you just listened to are divine words, Muḥammadan words. These are the words of Ibrāhīm and the words of Mūsā and the words of ʿĪsā, ṣalla-llāhu ʿalayhim wa sallam, because we do not discriminate between them. They are our beloveds and we are their children and they are pleased that we are their children. Inshā'a-llāh, you will be as such.

I am sure Allāh accepts everyone who loves Him. Allāh is love. For that reason it is impossible that He would not accept the one who loves Him. They love Him and He loves them. So come to Allāh with sincerity. Beware of not being honest, because Allāh says that He is with those who are honest. Allāh loves the sincere ones. This is known. This is the truth.

Be sure that you are truthful with Allāh. You have to keep your promise with Allāh. Be strong in your belief, be loving to Him. Give your self, your body, your spirit as a sacrifice to Him. Then Allāh will give you everything.

Allāh bought from the believers their selves and their wealth for the Garden. What is the price of this garden? The price is the love of Allāh. Without love, nothing happens. Show me one person who can live without love. Whether it is a human being, an animal, or a bird, it never happens. Can you live without love? You cannot. It is one of Allāh's secrets. Allāh has put it in our hearts.

We have to be straightforward with Allāh, follow the words of Allāh, and be honest and believing. Whatever you do, do it with honesty and love. If you love Allāh, listen to Him and obey Him. Then Allāh will hear from you. Do not betray. This is not from Allāh. Do not associate yourself with Allāh and then disobey. Do you accept it when somebody says he loves you, but does not love you? No. Humanity is built in love. When they left the love, they faced suffering, killing, destruction and hunger. Allāh blesses with love. Āmīn.

The True Meaning of Love

"I am Traveling to My Lord"

from *He Who Knows Himself Knows His Lord*

Lā ʾilāha ʾilla-llāāāāāāh, Lā ʾilāha ʾilla-llāāāāāh, Lā ʾilāha ʾilla-llāāāāāh
Muḥammad rasūlu-llāh, Ibrāhīm rasūlu-llāh, Mūsā rasūlu-llāh,
ʿĪsā rasūlu-llāh ʿalayhim ṣalātu-llāh.

Allāhumma anta-s-salām wa minka-s-salām
wa ilayka ya'ūdu-s-salām
tabārakta rabbanā
ya dha-l-jalāli wa-l-'ikrām

As-salāmu ʿalaykum wa raḥmatu-llāh wa bārakatuhu.

Good morning to you my beloveds. I thank Allāh for giving me His benevolence, for enabling me to return to you. I wish to bring to you new knowledge. I want to clarify how to be true children in the presence of your Great Beloved, Allāh, your Creator and Sustainer. He is the One Who Cares for all of His creation. He orders us to follow what He sent with His messengers, may Allāh's peace and blessings be upon them--from His sharīʿa, from His way, and from His truth.

This is the message of true unity. The world will never be happy except when following it—living it in their homes with their spouses and children. The world is full of suffering because the world has not followed this teaching. For that reason it has lost peace, love, mercy, freedom, justice and knowledge.

Ask Allāh in His greatness, "Who created all people to heal the corrupt and those who are sick in mind and heart?" Sickness of the heart and mind is stronger than sickness of the body. I am certain that Allāh is the one who created love and all that is good. He is the one who orders us to be one nation, loving each other, and to be patient, helpful and good to each other.

"I am Traveling to my Lord" is read from *He Who Knows Himself Knows His Lord*, beginning on page 7 continuing to the top of page 8. "The voyager also needs weapons that protect him from enemies – the shayṭān and the nafs."

These are not weapons as normal people understand them. Bombs and missiles are weapons that evil ones use in the wrong way. They kill each other, destroy homes and cut down trees. No, I am talking about divine weapons. These weapons are used to destroy evil, the s̲hayṭāns. They are used to kill those working to destroy humanity and knowledge of their Beloved, the one who created them and sustains them.

For this reason, Allāh gives us knowledge and understanding. These are divine weapons to be used without missiles or bombs—Allāh's missiles are greater than anything.

He gave us knowledge. He gave us love and taught us how to love. He gave us politeness and taught us how to be polite. He taught us how to follow the path of peace. He taught us how to be merciful so that we can give mercy to others.

He taught us also how to bring freedom to people. Allāh created us free. Did you not know that Allāh created you free inside your mother? He wants you to be free, but on His straight path. You cannot cut off your hand and say, "I am free to cut off my hand." You are not free to steal. This is not right. You are not free to do whatever you want and call it "freedom."

Allāh created you, oh human being, and perfected your creation so that you would use your hands for good, your eyes for good, your ears for good. Allāh created you to use your mind for goodness, not to kill humanity or create suffering. Freedom is a beautiful thing if you use it in the way Allāh wants. These are the greatest weapons when you are free in the divine way.

While walking on the street do not even step on an ant, because he was created by Allāh. Why would you kill it? Allāh created it. It has its own nation. It has its own tongue. It has its own ways. It has its own shape. It is not lawful for you to even kill a bee, because the bee gives you honey.

You want to be like the bee; have you ever seen a bee go through dirty trash? Allāh wants you to be like the bee. He does not want to see you rummaging through dirt. He wants you to have a beautiful fragrance and to be in flowers and roses [drinking the divine nectar]. This is true freedom.

Your freedom ends when you destroy another's freedom. Your freedom must originate from true knowledge, it must originate from Allāh. It cannot be filled with impoliteness, hatred and injustice toward others. It cannot be filled with indecency. This is the message Allāh wants us to carry and teach others. This is the strongest weapon.

True freedom is to care for people's hearts, their money and their lives. There is nothing in our hearts but love. We love whatever Allāh creates. We treat creation as Allāh has told us. It is not from love to break hearts. It is not merciful to be unmerciful to the poor, the hungry, and the orphans. It is not true freedom to steal other people's money. This cannot be.

Our teachings teach us to be aware of ourselves. They teach us to watch our hearts, our eyes, our ears. We cannot use our ears to listen to bad things [that might be said about other people]. We watch our tongues; we are not supposed to talk about people. We do not want to use our tongues except to speak the truth.

Allāh says that no one can say anything without two angels watching him (Qur'ān 50:17). Every word you utter is heard by an angel on your left and an angel on your right. Two angels are watching you whenever you utter anything. It is written, for example, "At this time, at this moment, on this day this man did this [action] and did this [other action] and wanted to do this [other action]." It is all written. "We did not leave anything out of this book."

From this place I say there must be a guide for the traveler. The airplane must have a pilot who knows the way. If not, what will happen to the passengers? They could lose their lives because the pilot is ignorant, without intelligence. For this reason the traveler must follow someone who knows both the s̲harīʿa and the ḥaqīqa. It is not lawful for the traveler to follow one who is not knowledgeable. It is not right for the traveler to follow someone who does not know. His guide must know all of the stations of the self, heart, and secrets.

This is not an easy matter, because the traveler wants to give everything to the guide. This is a dangerous thing. The traveler cannot give himself to the ignorant, to those who do not follow the s̲harīʿa of Allāh, to those who do not know the ḥaqīqa of Allāh. Those who pretend are not like those who follow the true teaching of Allāh and who are descendents of the Prophet, ṣalla-llāhu ʿalayhi wa sallam. This does not come from a teaching; it comes from Allāh. In the beginning it is a teaching; in the end it comes from Allāh and it is forever. When the knowledgeable person is born it is known that he will be a person of divine cognizance.

When Mūsā was born the Pharaoh decreed that every male child should be killed. Mūsā lived in spite of Pharaoh. Mūsā' mother put him in a basket and set the basket in the river. Then the wife of Pharaoh came, and this was from divine wisdom, and told her servant, "Bring that basket to me." At the time she did not have a son. Inside the basket was Mūsā. Pharaoh was afraid that a male would come and take his kingdom. Pharaoh's wife raised Mūsā. This was a divine order.

Another child was born around the same time who was called "the Samīrī." Who raised him and brought him up? The archangel Jibrīl. Who brought up the Prophet Mūsā? Pharaoh brought him up, because his wife wanted this young baby boy to be her child.

The Samīrī was the person who, when Mūsā went up the hill and came back, had gathered all of the gold and made a statue of a cow. When the statue came to life he told them, "This statue is your God. It is the God of Mūsā." This is the one who was taught by Jibrīl. If you can imagine, see divine wisdom in that the Samīrī was brought up by the archangel Jibrīl, while Mūsā was brought up by Pharaoh. This is the creation of Allāh. This is the will of Allāh. [18]

It is Allāh who guides you. The knowledge of Allāh has a sign; he sign is what he says, and his state or life.

His actions are truth.
His words are truth.
His state is with Allāh at all times.
His politeness and kindness are representative of Allāh.
His heart is filled with kindness.
He does not know hatred.
He always looks and sees with the eyes of Allāh.
He loves all of Allāh's creation.

---

[18] Regarding the Samīrī Sidi said in *The Sufi Realities*, "Look at this discrepancy: the one who was raised by archangel Jibrīl went off course, and the one raised by Pharaoh remained rightly guided. In reality, the Samīrī was the son of Pharaoh."

He carries no hatred.
His message is a divine message.
There is nothing in all of the knowledge that Allāh taught him
but to be a servant to all of Allāh's creation.

His states are divine states. Yes, he carries humanity, lives among creation and dwells with people. This relationship is a divine cover because Allāh did not will that he should be revealed in the physical world. Allāh's creation appears in two states: the subtle and the dense. Allāh appears in the human being in both the dense world and the subtle world.

How the True Human Being Lives in the Dense and Subtle Worlds of Creation

In the state of the human being he dwells with all of the people and he has two minds. One mind is the black mind of the physical world. He eats like he eats and he drinks like he drinks, but he follows the s̱harīʿa of his Lord. [He makes the distinctions] this is halāl, that is harām. This is right, that is wrong. He carries the message and s̱harīʿa of his Lord. If he says, "This is a male, this is a female. This is small, this is big," then this speech is from the world of the physical. He has to put the s̱harīʿa in its proper place.

But the truth, the ḥaqīqa, is something different. In the world of the subtle he does not see you as separate. He sees everything as one. He sees only the unity of Allāh. Everything he sees is a divine mirror of Allāh. Whenever he looks at something or someone he sees the divine image of Allāh. He loses the image of the human being. He follows the orders of his Lord. He is a divine mirror, so it is not in his knowledge whether or not you are a male or a female. Allāh said, "Oh human being." He did not say, "Oh women," or "Oh men." He said, "Oh people."

When Allāh created Ādam He ordered the angels to prostrate to him. Not to prostrate to the animal human being. The angels' names are from al-Laṭif (the subtle). He said to them:

> When I have fashioned him completely and breathed into him from My spirit, fall down prostrating yourselves unto him. (Qur'ān 15:29, 38:72)

What does the name "Ādam" mean? It is from the Arabic word "adim" meaning, "earth."[19]

> I have fashioned him completely
> and breathed into him from My spirit (Qur'ān 15:29, 38:72)

The body of Ādam is the one that carried this mirror of Allāh. For this reason Allāh wanted to see himself in Ādam. The body of Ādam is the one that carried this image of Allāh. Other than that, Ādam is just a piece of earth.

But the true prostration is for Allāh. After He asked the angels to prostrate to Ādam he asked Ādam to teach the angels [the divine names] He had taught Ādam. None of the angels knew the divine names. The first thing that manifested, that appeared, is the name of Allāh aḍẖ-Ḍẖāhir (the Manifest). There are ninety-nine qualities. It is important for you to understand all the meanings. God willing, you will understand.

The reading continues until, "There are seven of these stations. The first station is the station of dark inclinations where the soul (an-nafs) is called 'the self that commands,' an-nafs al-amarra. The second station is the station of the lights where the soul is called 'the self that blames,' an-nafs al-lawāmma."

There is a big difference here. As I said in the book *Music of the Soul*...this is a deeper meaning. In that book I wrote the stations of the nafs so that you could understand something of them. In this book, *He Who Knows Himself Knows His Lord*, I gave you a deeper meaning, because all of names of the different nafs stations are just one name—the one who is Allāh. I wanted to explain many other things and give you knowledge you did not have before so that you can follow it and reach. I was eager to keep seven stations.

When a child is born is the mother able to feed him meat right away? She cannot. She can give him only milk. In the beginning I gave you milk, just a little drop, and I insisted that you continue to read and write. So many people ask me, "Where am I? What station am I in?" I tell them, "Not yet. You have to walk because you are still a baby." How can I tell you to eat a piece of meat when you are just a baby?

---

[19] See page 39 for more information on this.

It became clear to me that my beloveds have grown up, and it is time for them to understand. I have been preparing this book for ten years. I have clarified everything in it. As your capacity to understand grows you will be able to understand more of it. For this reason I have described how to arrive at each station. I have described how to live with your nafs al-amarra which is a dark cover, a veil, a garment. You have to cross it and pass through it. The second station presents you with another garment you have to understand and pass through, little by little.

This does not mean that I was not watching you. I was never absent from you. If you were in Africa, I still would have seen you. For this reason I have made clear what you need to follow in each station. They are all names for one name—Allāh. For this reason the night before last I said:

> In the body there is a nafs,
> and in the nafs there is a heart,
> and in the heart there is a spirit (rūḥ),
> and in the rūḥ there is a secret (k͟hafī),
> and in the secret there is a secret,
> and in secret of the secret there is a secret,
> and in this secret there is yet another secret,
> and know that there is no god but Allāh.

At this time you begin to know yourself. You are a very holy one. You are not a human being. Yes, in the outside meaning you are a human being. You eat. You sleep. But really, you return to how God created you originally when He said to all His angels, "Prostrate to Ādam," (Qur'ān 38:71). Do you know who you are?

From this place, these are deep stations. I did not give these to you in the beginning. I am a farmer; I love the earth. When I went to plant, I had to clean the earth. I chose what to plant. Not everything is good to plant. I plowed the earth and I planted what I wanted to plant. You are my beloveds.

This book is very, very deep. I am certain that the person who reads it and writes it and understands it and does what is in it will be a true Ādam. He is the one who carries the divine mirror, not the human being that you see, not this human body. Did He not say, "There is no other god but Me?" Allāh does not need our prostration. He does not need anything. Everything is in His hand. He said to us:.

> I was a hidden treasure. I was a jewel.
> I was hidden treasure and I wanted to be known. (Ḥadīth Qudsī)

This was the love. He wanted to show His love to whomever He wants.

> For this reason I created the creation. (Ḥadīth Qudsī)

I took a piece of the earth from three places: from the holy mosque in Jerusalem, from the Ka'ba in Mecca, and from the place where the Prophet is buried. For this reason you are very special. Your body comes from these special places.

You are not an easy one. You are a great, holy creation. He says, "I perfected you with My hand." He created you and perfected you and put His spirit in you. This piece of clay does not amount to anything. Allāh wanted us to be a holy image so He could see it. So He breathed on it. He says:

> I created love in you so the love can spread to all creation.
> Be eager not to break this love.
> Use it with everything
> because you are My love and My beloved
> and there is nothing else.

For this reason you have to carry the unity. Know that there is no god but He. Allāh does not need the world. You are His image. If you follow His message and His path and His truth you will become Him, but in a human form that is holy, kind and beautiful because your beauty is from His beauty. You look for the deep love. The "ishq" is the deep love; you are the deep love and the beloved. You are the lover and the beloved. How beautiful! How great you would be if you followed the divine orders of Allāh! The lover of the Beloved is obedient.

What is the meaning of love if you do not obey the one whom you love? It does not have a meaning. Everyone has to die in his love. It is one love. This is why I say in a poem from my heart about the name of Laylā:

> Laylā, wherever you turn your face there is my face;
> wherever you turn your heart there is my heart
> because there is no difference for me at all.
> I can see you in every state.

There is no difference for me.
Wherever you are I do not see anything but myself in you.
I see you in my prostration and in my standing.

This is the truth. This is something of what I have written in this book. If I continued speaking for another year I could not finish. I just wanted to give you a little snippet. I know that you are holy and that you are the love, if you understand my meaning. At this point it becomes true for you in your hearts and spirits, for you and the ones around you. You will be like the rain when it falls to earth and the earth is dry. When the rain falls flowers spring forth: yellow, red, many different colors with many fragrances.

This is the way and the state of travelers. Each of them gives the truth with different fragrances and a beautiful image. This is the truth. We want to be like this from Allāh's mercy. We do not need killers. We do not need corrupters. This is the way Allāh wants it to be.

The reading continues until page 8, "The third station is the station of the secrets where the soul is called "the inspired self" (an-nafs al-mulhama).

Allāh opened the eye of your heart and the eyes in your head. When a child is born how soon does he open his eyes? After four days the newborn opens his eyes and is able to differentiate between his mother and father. You are the divine child. First you open your physical eyes, and then you open your divine eyes.

The reading continues, "The fourth station is the station of completion and perfection (al-kāmal) where the soul is called "the tranquil, secure self" (an-nafs al-muṭma'inna).

When you open your physical eyes and the eye of your heart sees things. fear leaves you. You are tranquil. You are in the safest place. You begin to move as a child does. You have trust.

The reading continues, "The fifth station is the station of connection, or reunion and communion, where the soul is called "the contented and the pleasing self" (an-nafs ar-rāḍiya).

It is known that children are born in the truth. I am not speaking about the human child. I am speaking about the divine child, the one carried by his mother who is the divine mother. When he sees from this place of truth he knows. He is tranquil. For this reason he was named "insan" or "ins." In Arabic "insan" ("human" in English) carries the meaning of being familiar with his surroundings. At this point he has no fear. If you give him a piece of dirt he will eat it. If you give him a flaming piece of charcoal he will take it. He does not have the ability to distinguish between these things yet, just as happened to Mūsā, ʿalayhi as-salām.

The reading continues, "The sixth station is the station of epiphanies (tajallī) of divine action where the soul is called "the pleased self" (an-nafs al-marḍiyya). The seventh station is the station of epiphanies of the names and the qualities where the soul is called "the perfect self" (an-nafs al-kāmila). When a person arrives in one of these stations, the station which is higher..."

I did not start with the explanation; I have only mentioned the names of the stations. God willing, we will begin the explanation.

The reading continues to page 9, "In the following chapters of this book, the epiphany of the actions, the names and the qualities will explained to you in detail, if Allāh so wills."

We are standing in front of the door. This is from Allāh's bounty. At this point you have to be polite. When you knock on the door you have to be qualified, preserved in His s̲harīʿa. You cannot come to Him without being pure. Your clothes have to be pure. You come with the ultimate politeness because Allāh has qualified you to become one of His beloveds. You have to carry the manners of Allāh. You have to carry the s̲harīʿa. What you say and what you do has to be divine. You cannot say you are a true Muslim and that you carry the s̲harīʿa unless you manifest this on earth through your actions.

Story of Ibrāhīm Being Thrown into Fire

If you say you are following the religion of Ibrāhīm, know that Ibrāhīm did not bow to statues and idols. Never! He was pure. For this reason he destroyed all idols. They [Nimrod and his enforcers] put him in the fire. He was not worried.

> When they propelled him toward the fire, but before he reached the fire, the angel Jibrīl came to him and asked him, "Ibrāhīm, do you want anything? Do you need any help?"
> At this point Ibrāhīm was in a divine state. He did not carry any humanity.
>
> He told Jibrīl, "I do not need anything from you. Allāh knows my state and He knows what I need."
>
> From the ultimate politeness Ibrāhīm said, "I do not need to ask because He knows what I need."
>
> Allāh then spoke to the fire. "We (Allāh) said: "Oh fire! Be cool and safe for Ibrāhīm (Qur'ān 21:69)

Ibrāhīm was able to walk out of the fire. The wood in the fire returned to its original state of trees bearing fruit for Ibrāhīm to eat. This is the traveler's destiny; this is His garden. Would you like to live in this Garden? Live there today, not tomorrow. Do not wait until after you die.

> The one who believes in Me is in the Garden today. (Ḥadīth)

Do not wait. You do not have to wait. When you give [everything] to Allāh now, He gives [everything] to you instantly.

For this reason you have to give yourself as a sacrifice. The man who wants to marry the most beautiful woman has to give himself; he has to provide her with everything. This is the unity of love: politeness, submission, patience, containment, knowledge and holiness. This is a divine creation. He cannot look at this creation without seeing divine love.

For this reason Allāh said, "Can you not see this in yourselves? If you have your Beloved within you, why are you looking outside yourselves for someone else? You have the love inside you. Why are you looking outside? We gave you a heart. We gave you eyes. The dwelling of the Beloved is in the heart."

Allāh said to us:

> My earth and My heavens do not contain Me.
> Only the heart of My beloved servant contains Me.
> (Ḥadīth Qudsī)

Allāh loves them and they love Him back. This is the true meaning of love. This is different than how animals love. Animals actually do know the meaning of love. Animals know the deep love. Can you not see the birds, how they dance and sing for each other? If you could just understand their language you would know how to love.

This is a subtle teaching. This is divine, subtle music. For this reason I say that this book (*He Who Knows Himself Knows His Lord*) is the essence of *The Music of the Soul*. This book is you.

I think this is enough. I thank Allāh. I thank you for listening. I hope that you understood what I wanted you to understand. I open my heart and give my heart to you to walk. I give to you with all my heart, with humbleness, with all politeness, without hesitation.

The Seventy-Thousand Veils between Humanity and Allāh

"I am Travelling to My Lord"

from *He Who Knows Himself Knows His Lord*

Lā 'ilāha 'illa-llāāāāāāh, Lā 'ilāha 'illa-llāāāāāh, Lā 'ilāha 'illa-llāāāāāh
Muḥammad rasūlu-llāh, Ibrāhīm rasūlu-llāh, Mūsā rasūlu-llāh,
'Īsā rasūlu-llāh 'alayhim ṣalātu-llāh.

Allāhumma anta-s-salām wa minka-s-salām
wa ilayka ya'ūdu-s-salām
tabārakta rabbanā
ya dha-l-jalāli wa-l-'ikrām

As-salāmu 'alaykum wa raḥmatu-llāh wa bārakatuhu.

Allāh has sent to me a glimpse from my Lord, and a secret from His secrets. My Lord has sent this to you in this moment while you were praying, seeking His pleasure, asking Him to open for you the great opening and true knowledge, asking Him for true healing for all those here and all those who are suffering in this world. I am certain that He accepted your prayers and your supplications. This is the first great news.

From this point on you should understand that if you are seeking help, ask for help from Allāh through our great beloved, the Prophet, ṣalla-llāhu 'alayhi wa sallam.

Know that, "He is closer to you than your jugular vein," (Qur'ān 50:16). He, glory be to Him, loves you more than you love Him. For that reason you should listen to what He says and obey Him. He says:

> And when My slaves ask you concerning Me,
> then [answer them], I am indeed near.
> I respond to prayers when they call upon Me. (Qur'ān 2:186)
>
> So they obey Me. They listen to and follow what I say.
> At that point I give them what they want.
> I give them my acceptance and my protection. (Sidi)

For this reason you must trust Him and surrender completely to Him because He has medicine for you. From Him comes medicine. He is the Protector, the Healer, and the Giver. He is jealous of whoever mentions Him. For this reason you should come forward for Allāh, trust Him, and stay up in the middle of the night and pray two rakāh. You must pray in complete submission when you want something, and He will give you want you want. He says, "My servant, be to me what I want and I will be to you what you want." This is Allāh.

I would like you to listen to this chapter and to understand it.

The reading begins on page 9 and goes to the top of page 10 of *He Who Knows Himself Knows His Lord*, "This is because Allāh is far beyond physical nearness and distance and He is beyond time and space and beyond all the characteristics of temporary existence."

This is a secret from Allāh's secrets. It is a mercy from Allāh to His creation and to His people. It would not be easy to know Allāh if Allāh were not helping you. If there were no help from Allāh then humans would suffer; this is what happened with Iblīs. Iblīs was one of the worshippers. Everywhere on this earth he prostrated to Allāh. What got him discharged from the Garden was his arrogance.

> When Allāh said to the angels, "Prostrate to Ādam"
> and all the angels prostrated except Iblīs,
> Allāh asked him, "Oh Iblīs, why did you not prostrate?"
> He said, "I am better than him.
> You created me from fire and you created him from clay."
> (Qur'ān 38:71-38:76)

Iblīs did not see the divine light; he stayed in darkness. He did not know that between him and Allāh there are seventy-thousand veils. There are seventy-thousand veils for those who are not surrendered to Allāh and who have not prostrated to Allāh. They have not obeyed Allāh. For this reason they are not able to see the light; they are able to see only the darkness. From the mercy of Allāh He created seventy-thousand veils between Him and His creation. There are seventy-thousand worlds like this one. There are seventy-thousand nations. Allāh said, "You are the best of nations that came to the people because you carry the flag of unity. For this reason when you declare unity and your acceptance of Allāh, those veils will dissolve in front of you. For this reason Allāh said:

> I am closer to you than your jugular vein. (Qur'ān 50:16)

When the human does not follow the order of Allāh he has big eyes, yet he is blind. He cannot see the eye of his heart. His eyesight does not become blind; it is his heart that becomes blind. How can the one who has no heart receive the light?

In this there is a reminder for the one who has a heart. If he listens with divine hearing and sees with divine sight he has to give up human pictures. At the moment he leaves the veils and his humanity behind he will see his Lord as Mūsā did. Have you heard Mūsā say to his Lord:

> And when Mūsā came at the time and place appointed by Us,
> and his Lord spoke to him,
> he said: "Oh my Lord! Show me [Yourself],
> that I may look upon You."
> Allāh said: "You cannot see Me, but look upon the mountain
> if it stands still in its place then you will see Me."
> So when his Lord appeared to the mountain,
> He made it collapse to dust, and Mūsā fell down unconscious.
> Then when he recovered his senses he said:
> "Glory be to You, I turn to You in repentance
> and I am the first of the believers." (Qur'ān 7:143)

When Allāh appeared to the mountain, Mūsā fell down unconscious. He was annihilated. He returned to his original life in divine light. He went to his origin. Allāh said:

> I am from Allāh
> and the believers are from me,
> and Allāh created all souls from me. (Ḥadīth)

At this point Mūsā realized. He went back to his humanity. He woke up. He was asleep because he was in his humanity. How can humanity stand in front of the divine light? When he saw Allāh he said, "My Lord, from what You have given me from Your goodness I am poor." This is divine politeness.

For this reason you have to be the Mūsā of your time, to be in the station of Mūsā. The people of gnosis realize that it is not possible for you to see Allāh if you are full of sins and evil, full of hatred and envy. Would you be able to sit next to a mule that has been dead for six days?

You would run away! You want to be near Allāh, but you smell like a decrepit thing. You have to cleanse yourself. You have to cleanse your body, your garment. The criminal wears an expensive garment, perhaps costing $100,000, but he is filled with hatred, envy and corruption. Between him and Allāh there are seventy-thousand veils. They are like insects. There is one kind of insect that if you spray it with a fresh fragrance it will die. It cannot accept a beautiful fragrance.

How can those who are veiled by their humanity (because their bodies are filled with bad things) perceive divine light? For this reason He said that we have to cleanse our bodies of all wrongdoings. "No person will reach Me except those who are pure. My love will come only to those who carry the message of unity, freedom and justice." Those are the ones who will never be veiled with the seventy-thousand veils. The seventy-thousand veils of darkness are not for the lovers of Allāh. It is for those who accept s̲hayṭān and stay away from Allāh. The light of Allāh will never be veiled from His lovers.

The reading continues, "The first veil is denser than the second veil...the nafs that command him to evil."

His nafs will tell him that he has reached, but he has not reached. For this reason he has to be careful in his walking. All of his actions must be pure for Allāh. He should have no hatred, envy or discrimination in his heart. He has to be a divine earth and a divine home. He should always give love to those who need it. He was created filled with love. He carries the olive branch that represents love. He accepts one faith: the essence of Allāh. It is all goodness. It is all giving. He is very generous in all of his actions. He smiles upon the weak, poor and needy. These are divine orders.

At this point the heavenly gardens will open for him
and he will see what the eye has never seen.
He will hear what the ear has never heard.
He will be carried from station to station.
He will penetrate through the seventy-thousand veils with one glance.

Allāh is the oil that lights the way for the one who follows Him. For this reason Allāh says that He is like:

> ...an olive tree that is not from the east or the west that can light by itself without any fire touching it. (Qur'ān 24:35)

Every creation of Allāh has this divine oil. For this reason [the divine human's] lights are always filled with divine oil. From this oil comes light that is stronger than any ordinary light.

The truth of the divine human is that he has two sides: the human animal and the divine human. The human animal wants to live as an animal with all of the attributes of an animal. As a human being he walks upon the earth and speaks, but his actions are just like those of the animal. His humanity is filled with filth. He has to remove this garment. How can he do this? He can do this by walking toward Allāh from station to station. He needs to wash with the water of divine knowledge. "From heaven We sent water to purify you."

When we listen to what Allāh says and follow it, our hearts fill with purity. At this point the creation becomes one ocean filled with love and divine knowledge. Through your obedience to Allāh you will be carried from one station to another. This is the truth. I ask Allāh to move you from the human animal to the divine human.

> The one who believes in Me is in the Garden today. (Ḥadīṯẖ)

The reading continues, "there are known characteristics for each level of the nafs."

The sālik (traveler) should know where he is in his walking. "Sidi, have I reached the fanā' station? Have I reached the baqā' station?" You should know where you are. You are the one who should know where you are. You do this by following the orders of Allāh. You have a scale which is like a thermometer used to measure temperature. The scale of Allāh is more refined than this scale of temperature.

For this reason you have to open your heart. If your heart has any envy or arrogance you know where you are. If your heart carries all of the names and attributes of Allāh and carries the qualities of Allāh such as "the Manifest" (aḏẖ-Ḏẖāhir) or "the Generous" (al-Karīm) or "the Subtle" (al-Laṭīf) then you know where you are.

As far as you are concerned, the guide does know where you are. If the guide is in Jerusalem and you are here in America he knows what you are doing. He has something better than a satellite. He has a divine satellite from Allāh.

He carries the name "as-Sattār," the One Who does not reveal secrets. What is this one doing? What is that one doing? He always prays for his children to make them firm in the path. He loves them more than they love him because Allāh will question him about the little and the big. For the one who has no sacrifice I am his sacrifice. This is the truth.

If the guide is someone who walks in the markets, then this is what Allāh made him to be. The Messenger received the revelation that, "Your Lord is One." (Qur'ān 112:1) The guide guides you to Allāh. He does not guide you to himself, because he is a servant and a slave.

From Allāh alone comes greatness. The guide is proud to wash the feet of his children with his hands until they know His real truth. He gives his heart and his blood and his body as a sacrifice for his children to reach the safe shore. That is his origin.

The reading continues, "Each nafs has its realm its state and its station and must walk in a particular way. The nafs of the commanding self is veiled by dark veils. But in other stations the nafs is veiled by luminous veils. Some of these veils are subtler than others."

Sidi in English: Open your ears and understand these words that Allāh sends for you! I would like for you to be awake, always.

The reading continues, "Therefore if the traveler in the first station is taught the first name ... publicly and secretly..."

I will clarify here how to be in the first station. I will give you a divine gift. Use it! From this point I tell you to read, write, understand and walk until you understand how to arrive at your essence and your Lord. This is the origin of your being. I do not want you to say, "I understand this book" and then put it on the shelf. The Messenger said:

> My Lord, my people took this book and then they abandoned it. (Ḥadīth)

How could they really understand it? If they understood it they would follow it to awaken their hearts and purify their bodies.

For these reasons I give you this advice which I repeat: you have to read and write and understand and follow what you read. I am very certain that you will reach the place of truthfulness of the divine King. This is the truth.

I think this is enough. This is a lot of food for you. I do not want to burden you. You have to be in divine marriage with Allāh. This is something that makes me very happy. This is divine music, divine remembrance.

How to Heal All Diseases, including Arrogance, Envy, Jealousy and Deception

Lā ʾilāha ʾilla-llāāāāāāh, Lā ʾilāha ʾilla-llāāāāāh, Lā ʾilāha ʾilla-llāāāāāh
Muḥammad rasūlu-llāh, Ibrāhīm rasūlu-llāh, Mūsā rasūlu-llāh,
ʿĪsā rasūlu-llāh ʿalayhim ṣalātu-llāh.

Allāhumma anta-s-salām wa minka-s-salām
wa ilayka ya'ūdu-s-salām
tabārakta rabbanā
ya d̲ha-l-jalāli wa-l-'ikrām

As-salāmu ʿalaykum wa raḥmatu-llāh wa bārakatuhu.

I praise Allāh. I ask Allāh to take your hands, to open your hearts, to lead you through this path, and for you to be knowledgeable and a carrier of this message of truth and unity; the message of peace and justice and freedom; the message that does not know any depreciation of or separation between human beings, whether or not they are black, white or any other color.

As Allāh said in His Book:

> Truly! This, your religion (or nation) is one religion (or nation), and I am your Lord, therefore worship Me. (Qurʾān 21:92)

There is only one God, and none of us [should] worship anything other than Allāh. No one [should] worship cows or any kind of animals or monkeys. So worship only Allāh.

Allāh has created everything. He created the heaven and the earth. And He created trees and what they carry. No one has been able to create even an ant. How can we worship other than Allāh? Allāh is the Creator. People call on Him in their languages. You speak in English; you ask Allāh. I speak with His name, Allāh. In the Hebrew they say, "Elohim." It means Allāh. This is the language of Ibrāhīm, ʿalayhi as-salām. People call upon Allāh in many languages, but the name is still the same. They all lead to the same [One].

His name is different in many languages, but it is still the same name, it is still Allāh. Is there any creator other than Allāh? No. He is the only creator. We can say that He is the only creator. We can agree on one thing, that He is the creator. Is that not so? Allāh is the creator.

He is the Creator. Is it not so? The meaning is One. Most importantly, you worship Him, because it is He Who created. And it is only lawful to worship and glorify the only One Who created.

There is nothing like Him.
There is nothing like Him.

It is not lawful for you to say, "Allāh is this; Allāh is that."

There is nothing like Him.
There is nothing like Him.

He was not created,
and He is not a father of anyone
and He is not a child of anyone, exalted is He.
He does not have a wife.
This is the nature of Allāh.

Allāh is not a human being, and He is not in any kind of picture you could ever come up with. He is distant from anything you could describe or make up. He knows Himself as His own essence. But His bounty is upon you, He manifests it to you in many, many manifestations, and He put its secret in everything.

In everything He has put a sign signifying that He is the One. For this reason we are His servants. We have to obey all of His orders. He wants us to be honest, believing, and knowledgeable—not ignorant. He wants us to determine our destiny as He prescribed it for us.

We follow what He says because what He sent with His Messenger is peace, love and justice. Happiness will happen for the one who follows this divine order. There will be no envy and no hatred. For this reason you can live in the Garden today, and not tomorrow.

You have to manifest the love Allāh brought down to earth. You must keep it pure and give life to whomever wishes for love and peace. This is the thing that unifies creation—unity—and nothing else. People are all one. Allāh is the Creator and He created them from one soul. He wants them to transcend all of the physical manifestations with which they identify themselves. They can do this only through knowledge of their Creator. Those who are ignorant of Allāh create all of the difficulties we have on earth, the atrocities that are committed in life.

I wish for and pray to Allāh to protect you and keep you, so that you may carry His message. So that you can carry what Allāh gives you to carry, and so that you can bring about peace, love and justice. Āmīn.

Before I start I want to tell you, as you know, Allāh created the jinn, humans and everything else. He created a thousand and thousand, a million thousand of creations in the seven heavens and seven earths. As it is, in the human creation there are also s̱hayāṭīn. They harm their fellow man, either with their hands, their eyes, or their ears. They work on not being straight, with full knowledge that Allāh has ordered them to be straight. They do not listen to what Allāh says. They spread corruption and kill others. These are the real evil human beings.

The ones who corrupt and harm others of the human race are the s̱hayāṭīn of the human race. And those human s̱hayāṭīn have friends among the jinn. They always work with them, and some of them have dear relationships with them. They set themselves apart to harm human beings. This is a problem the human race is suffering from. The human is in his house and he can hear voices and things that he cannot see; he gets disturbed by that in his sleep while he is in his home.

There are those of the jinn who are evil, who do not believe in Allāh. They follow Iblīs. Their father is Iblīs, the one who disobeyed Allāh at the beginning of creation. When Allāh asked the angels to bow to Ādam, only Iblīs refused. They have dedicated their lives to destroy human life.

So many people think they can stop the jinn's evil, but this [disease] can be treated only through certain knowledge. If you are not the inheritor of divine knowledge and if you are not knowledgeable, you will not be able to stop their evil. But for me, with the bounty of Allāh, I am able to do so. Allāh has given me what I need to help people who are unable to accomplish this.

The story starts when Ādam left the Garden. Allāh had brought him down to earth in a place now called Sri Lanka; it used to be called Ceylon. At that time, when Ādam descended, he was by himself. His grave is there. Iblīs sent his followers to disturb Ādam. So Ādam asked Allāh, "How can I rid myself of Iblīs' followers?" Allāh gave him a divine order through the archangel, Jibrīl. He told him that in this land there was a tree. He described it to him, and Jibrīl, the archangel, showed him the tree.

The name of this tree in Syrianic is "Hiltīt."[20] This tree is very old. When Jibrīl asked Ādam to cut a branch from this tree, water came from it. He gathered that fluid, and in two hours it had crystallized like a piece of mustard seed. It is white and it has a very, very foul smell. It would be very difficult for a human being to smell it. Its taste is very, very bitter. This [crystallized material] is used after reciting ʾāyat al-Kursī (Qurʾān 2:255), for those who think they are afflicted by this Iblīs energy.

In any house, if there are s̲hayāṭīn—human or jinn—and even if the s̲hayṭān has touched a person, put this [white crystallized material] on a piece of charcoal or wood and burn it. Use only about three grams. When you read ʾāyat al-Kursī and use this liquid any jinn inside a person or in the earth will run out of that place. If they do not run, they will choke to death. They will die right away. This is divine medicine from a divine order. I know it only through the bounty of Allāh to me. We have used it many times. We have forced many s̲hayāṭīn to leave many cities. I have a story.

Story of Sidi Using "Enemy of the S̲hayṭān" to Cure a City

One day fifteen years ago I was in Ammān, Jordan. There was a large building; it was rented for offices and other uses. In the evening, after mag̲hrib, there was a fight, a war. There were rocks flying about and commotion. More than a thousand people fled from it; nobody stayed there. Everybody left. Even King Ḥusayn of Jordan was there. He brought tanks and he brought the army, but he was not able to see anything. All they could see were rocks flying all over the place. This went on for seven weeks.

---

[20] "Hiltīt" is also the name Unāni medicine uses for the crystallized resin (also known as "asafoetida"). Traditinally, one use is to rub the crystallized resin on the bodies of epileptic patients; it is believed to drive the bad spirits (causing the convulsions) from the person.

At that time I was responsible for all of the courts in Jordan. It was my habit to go there once a month, just to follow up on the affairs of the courts. I had a friend there who was a judge. He said, "You came at the right time." He said, "See what happened. There is a war here, but we cannot see who is fighting us."

I told him jokingly, "You deserve more than this because you are making such corruption on the earth." Allāh says:

> And whatever of misfortune befalls you, it is because of what your hands have earned. And He pardons much. (Qur'ān 42:30)

This is it.

My friend put his hands on his hips and told me, "We have a real serious problem here and you are the only one who can solve it for us." I had my hands on my hips and I told him, "I cannot give you a word on this now, not until I see." Then, after the maghrib prayer I went to that place.

This complex contained over one hundred buildings. I looked at all the windows; there were so many windows broken. None of the windows were left, and no one had seen who broke all of these windows. I went inside the buildings and prayed two rakāh. I asked my Lord, and I looked. At a glance I saw that in the creation [those who caused this] had many different shapes, and I put the name of Allāh on them. I knew they were evil creatures and we had to fight them.

I went down to the market and I found a holy person. He carried the same medicine. I asked him if he had some of this medicine. I asked him to give me some of it. He gave me ten grams. I went back to the building, I lit some charcoal, and I read 'āyat al-Kursī three times. Then I put this medicine over the charcoal, I closed the door, and I left.

It was as if there was another war starting inside. They were all beating each other and the sound was so loud. The people from far away were looking at us as if to say, "What is going on?" But after one hour the rocks being thrown stopped, as if it had never happened. There was a foul smell, as if tear gas or something had been thrown into the buildings. After two hours, people came back to the buildings.

This is not imaginary. This is the truth. And the people knew about it, although I did not say anything about how it happened. When the word spread, the people possessed by jinn, and those that had jinn or thought they had s̲hayāṭīn in their houses, thought that I should put this thing to an end and get rid of the s̲hayṭān in every house that had a problem. Even in this valley [Pope Valley], in this place, if we light some of this medicine all of the jinn will go away.

This is not an easy medicine to get a hold of, because not everybody knows about it. If any of you wants, I have brought some to Ṣāliḥ to sell in the bookstore. You can find it there. But the only time you should use it is when you are sure, more than certain, that there are s̲hayāṭīn in that place. The most you can use is three grams or five grams. There is no way that the s̲hayṭān or devil in that place will not leave or choke to death. The s̲hayṭān or jinn leave the human being as if nothing happened.

If anybody thinks they have some problem like this, the medicine is here, at the store. We call it, "Enemy of the S̲hayṭān." That is its name, "Enemy of the S̲hayṭān." How do you fight the s̲hayṭān and its supporters among humans and jinn? It will have the same effect on the ones who makes magic, because the s̲hayāṭīn, whether human or jinn, will be inflicted with harm and disease from this until they repent and return to Allāh. This is the story of this medicine. Bismi-llāh, you can start.

"I am Traveling to My Lord" from *He Who Knows Himself Knows His Lord* is read from page 10 until, "As the traveler continues to remember and to strive, his nearness to his Lord strengthens until he reaches the lofty degrees of perfection."

This is the truth. At this point I want to clarify how to walk to Allāh. Where is the way to Allāh? How do you follow this road to Allāh? How do you follow the path of truth to save yourself from the life you are in? If the human being is filled with impurities, he has to look for a place to cleanse those areas of filth and dirt that cling to him from this life. He needs to find a place he can do this, he needs to find purifying water that will cleanse his body. By cleansing the "body," I do not mean cleansing the human body.

This human form is filled with disease. All of these diseases are connected to the nafs, because the nafs, the self, is filled with hatred, envy and discrimination, and it is totally connected to the lower life. All of these are diseases, and the sick self, the one that got these diseases, becomes diseased and it hates others. He becomes selfish, he wants everything to himself. His heart does not know any mercy and he becomes a human s̲hayṭān. How can we kill this human s̲hayṭān that wants to go to Allāh?

Allāh sent His messengers and brought down holy books through them. He put rules in these books, and orders. He said, "This is my straight path, so follow it." "If you follow My orders, you will be healed and you will reach Me." He forbade arrogance in us. He told us:

> If one has even a seed of arrogance, he will not go to Paradise. (Ḥadīt̲h̲)

Arrogance is a disease of the self, because the person sees himself as the highest and best of all people. He does not want to see good in others, and he wants to see all other people under his feet serving him. He wants to have them there, suck their blood, and take their wealth. This is a human s̲hayṭān. For this reason, we have to rid him of this s̲hayṭān. When that happens, his self becomes obedient and follows the orders of Allāh. Allāh says:

> Pride is My cloak and greatness is My robe,
> And he who competes with Me with respect to either of them
> I will cast into Hell. (Ḥadīt̲h̲ Qudsī)

Human beings are created. Their father is Ādam, their mother is Eve. They are all human. You were created from earth and every other person was created from the same earth. He is your brother. The arrogant one should not in any way look at his brother or sister as lower than himself. If you possess billions of dollars, if you are a president, you have to respect your other fellow humans because you were created from the same earth. You are a human being and he is a human being. So do not be arrogant; you have to be very humble. You have to be very polite. You have to remember that when you came, you were just a drop of semen. And at the end, you will be just a decrepit dead body. And between the time when you were semen and the time that your body ends, you are just a box of dirt.

This is your life. Is this not the truth? Just cover it up with clothes. Yeah, you look very elegant outside but your truth is completely different. This is the truth. Is there anyone who denies this? If you wear all silk and elegant clothing, does that change anything? No. Remember who you are. Do not say you are better than this and this, or her and him. You are a human being and he or she is a human being. Is it not so?

This human machine, this little small thing can stop you. If Allāh willed that He stop your heart for just a second, what would happen? One minute, what would happen? A doctor would not be able to cure himself; he would stand stunned. For this reason, the human being should know that he is weak. Allāh says:

> The human being was created in weakness (Qur'ān 4:28, 30:54)

If it was not for the mercy of Allāh, the human being could not stand. Allāh created everything with precision. This creation is a divine creation.

You find about three hundred and sixty veins in the human body, and there about three hundred and fifty other veins that spread out from them. If one vein is blocked, then you cannot do anything, just as if a wire gets destroyed in a car, it cannot do anything. Yes, just sit back in yourself with this condition, and they will put you in the hospital. They will put so much machinery and equipment on you that you will become a field experiment. They want to see what happens to you.

But does not Allāh, the One Who gave you things that work with precision, deserve worship? Is He not worthy of being respected and obeyed? So why does the human being become arrogant? Why is he not humble, knowing the essence of his body? Why does he look at people as incomplete? "I am white, I am better than all of the other people." "I am rich, I am better than all of the other people."

When you came to this earth you were crying, naked. You did not have anything. Then, Allāh gave you a mother and gave her breasts, and He put milk in those breasts, and put love in those breasts, with the knowledge that she carried you for nine months in her stomach. You were fed from inside, through her blood. And then what? You came to this earth. If Allāh did not put mercy and kindness in the heart of your mother who would have cared for you? Allāh is the One Who put all of these things in the mother to care for her child.

The human being has to remember this. He must know from whence he came, or how he comes into life. He is on a journey, a very short journey. Life is a very short journey. It is like a person who flies from one destination to another destination. Is it not so? The journey could be five hours, three hours, or one hour. Your life could go on for fifty, sixty, or seventy years. Most important is that it is going to end.

At that time, they put you in a place other than your house. They would not be able to bear your being there among them for even two nights, because your smell would disturb them. "Take him out now." "Where?" " Take him to his real mother, the earth." Mother Earth. "Bury him in the ground because he would harm us."

After two days, they just cannot handle it; they start looking, "Where is his money? Where did he put his money? What did he leave behind?" Many, many wait for the death of their parents; they want the money. Yes, they want the money; they are waiting for the money. "Yes, he is done. Take him away." Is that not the truth? This is the truth.

But the real, honest people, the people of love, the people of worship, the people of obedience to Allāh, are very eager to care for their parents. They are not able to leave them. As it was before, when the mother saw the child was ill, she was so disturbed she could not sleep. And if her child went away from her, she just worried, "Where is my child? What happened to my daughter?"

This is the truth of the human being. For this reason, you, human being, should know how to walk. For this reason it does not matter how much you own; it does not mean anything. If you are obedient to Allāh you can heal yourself from all diseases, from hatred, envy, all diseases, and put in their place love, peace, and mercy. You will be merciful toward yourself, because the mercy comes from you.

If you do not give mercy, you cannot receive mercy. How can you give love when you do not know what love is? The first step in walking is to heal yourself completely from the diseases of hatred and envy, and to replace them with love, mercy, freedom and giving. Through this you can return to Allāh. These orders are the s̲harī'a.

Allāh told you not to corrupt the earth. He told you not to steal. He told you to be straight. This is the s̲harī'a. This is from Allāh. This is the order of Allāh to us. How can I be a true believer while I kill? How can I be honest when I lie, I steal, I harm people and I steal their wealth? After that, I go and pray? You are just laughing at yourself. You have to be honest and sincere. This is one way of walking. If you put pictures and illusions in your mind that you are a great something, you are weaker than the fly that went into King Nimrod.

Story of how Nimrod Died: the Reward for Arrogance

Nimrod is the son of Canaan. He was the one who threw the Prophet Ibrāhīm into the fire. He is the example of arrogance. There was a little insect that went through his nose into his head. Allāh, through His wisdom, put this thing in his head to teach him a lesson about how he treated others and the suffering he caused them.

This is what the people of evil and arrogance need; this is their medicine. I am sure Allāh will send it to those who do not have mercy on the creation of Allāh, the killers, the people who steal people's money. I am sure He will send it to them one after another.

This little insect went into his head and Nimrod's servants said, "Look for somebody who can cure him."

Those they questioned said, "The only person who can heal him is one of Ibrāhīm's followers."

They asked, "Find us one who can cure King Nimrod."

Someone [Ibrāhīm] came and said, "I can cure him."

"How," they asked Ibrāhīm. They asked, "How can we heal him?"

Ibrāhīm said, "Take his shoes and beat his head."

Ibrāhīm went and told him, "This is the medicine for you. You are arrogant."

This is deep wisdom, the cure for arrogance. He took off his shoes and started hitting on his head with them. While he was hitting himself the little insect stopped buzzing in his head. When he stopped hitting his head, it started buzzing again. Yes. This cure came from a true believer and the king's shoes. If you are arrogant and you see yourself as great,

Allāh wants to show you. The best medicine is to be beaten with the lowest thing, the shoe. And he kept hitting himself until he died. This is the reward for the arrogant. Allāh said:

> The one who has a drop of arrogance in his heart will not enter the Garden. (Ḥadīth)

If you are following the order of Allāh, Allāh will tell you, "I will guide you to what will help you with this." Remember the first name from the names of Allāh. It is the great name, "Allāh." Say, "Ya Allāh, ya Allāh," always, when you are sitting, when you are walking, when you are standing, and in your sleep to seek help from Allāh. As long as you remember Allāh on your tongue and in your heart, your nafs, your ego will come into alignment with the divine.

At this time, your state will change from one condition to another. You see a world other than the one you were in, station after station, and so on. At this point, the nafs that has been ordered to do evil realizes, "I was terrible. I was stealing. I was killing." And the nafs begins holding itself accountable for all the things that it did, because the self starts hating these corrupt actions. The nafs does not want to go back to that lifestyle and it becomes ashamed of itself. How had it been envious? How had it hated? How had it been stealing and lying? At this time, the nafs begins to realize.

The name will help him clean this until his heart and tongue are in remembrance and Allāh will cause him to hate what he did before. He will become polite and kind to others, and will not say, "I am a boss," among his peers. He realizes that he is just a human being. He is polite with others, and he helps the needy. When he helps the weak and needy, he is helping himself. When he gives to the poor, he gives to himself. The One Who gave to him is Allāh. He gave him all that he is. Allāh gave him strength and he taught him how to earn.

For this reason while cleansing this nafs, the nafs is one nafs. This nafs used to order him to do evil, to perform misguided deeds. Allāh says:

> Truly, the self is inclined to evil... (12:53)

So you have to purify it. How can you steal and say, "I am going to pray?" How can you betray another and say, "I am going to pray?" Can you wear a garment that is filled with filth and dirt and come to pray? No. Allāh does not accept this. Allāh is Ṭayyib. Ṭayyib means, "good." Those nafs, pictures and illusions are diseases you need to get rid of. For this reason, Allāh said to His Messenger, "Say Allāh." Say Allāh. Say Allāh, and then leave them, and then you will leave those diseases behind.

This is the first station, and from there it continues. Watch yourself. Before you speak, you have to listen. What are you saying, what are you about to say? Are you going to say something about somebody? Is it from Allāh or from s̲hayṭān? If something you are about to say or have said is from the s̲hayṭān or nafs say, "astag̲hfiru-llāh." Do not go further. You have to be beneficent, very kind, a very good person. This is it. If you see someone putting harm in another's path, do you think that Allāh will accept this? Putting harm in people's way? Allāh says:

> Allāh is beautiful and He loves beauty. (Ḥadīt̲h)

He loves whatever is beautiful. Cleanliness is from faith. You cannot go to Allāh and carry all of this filth and pictures with you. All of those diseases are just filth. And no one can enter the house of Allāh unless he has been cleansed. This is just a little bit of what I have explained and detailed within this book.

The reading continues until page 13, "But before I begin I would like to explain some definitions and terms used by the people of realization. Ṣūfi: Becoming a Ṣūfi and following Ṣufism is to stand firm..."

Sidi in English: It is very important to open your ears for this meaning; I have explained very clearly to show you what the real meaning of "Ṣūfī" is. Who is a Ṣūfī? Not by talking. But He would like to see how you do, on the floor, on the ground, how you are. The Ṣūfī is very, very soft. But he does not leave anything from the order of Allāh because he sees that Allāh is watching him.

And Allāh judges him directly, not tomorrow. He sends something very strong for him. For that it is important to be very careful. If you do anything that is not right and say, "I am a Ṣūfī," like you steal, you do not pray—then He hits you. He hits you very hard. He is very patient, but when He sends something, it is more than you expected. Astag̲hfiru-llāh al-ʿaḏ̣hīm. Continue.

The reading continues until, "His state must be of its prohibitions in everything he says and does. His state must be observant of each breath and movement he makes and he must abide by Allāh's moral ethics..."

Allāh will hold you accountable for your own breath, the motions you make, and the steps you take. There is no space for cheating. If your beard came down to your stomach and you are turban-covered and your clothes are just so, Allāh would hear you and see you. There is no escape. There is no place to play and cheat, because Allāh sees you and hears you. He said, "My Lord." Allāh said:

> He will see the black ant, the steps and the path she takes,
> on the black rock in the middle of the night. (Ḥadīṯẖ Qudsī)

Allāh loves those who are honest and those who are sincere. Listen to what He says:

> People perish, except for those of knowledge.
> And those people of knowledge also will perish.
> And those people of action also perish,
> except for the sincere ones.
> And the sincere ones are in grave danger. (Ḥadīṯẖ)

Why? Because Allāh will hold everyone accountable for how sincere you are. What have you done to have people say about you, "You are generous." Why did you give? Why did you give charity? Do you want people to think of you and your beneficence? Do you want to just pretend and give, just so people can praise you? Or that people will think about you in a certain way? This is what they call "riyāʾ," hypocrisy. You have to do what you do for the sake of Allāh, not to get feedback from people that you are a kind man or a good person.

You obey your Lord because you love your Lord. You just do what you do for the sake of Allāh, because He ordered you to. And He loves the one who listens to Him. At this point, you find goodness. There is no space for s̲ẖayṭān in this work. If you do it because people will say something good about you, s̲ẖayṭān will be happy. But if you do it for the sake of Allāh, s̲ẖayṭān does not have space for that.

Everything you do should be for the pleasure of Allāh. Listen and obey. From this place, you can find help from Allāh, protection from Allāh. Be among those who are honest and sincere. Do not give any of your actions and deeds to the s̲hayṭān. The s̲hayṭān will lead you to be arrogant and hypocritical. Whatever you do, do it for the sake of Allāh. Whatever you do in giving to the needy or poor, do it for the sake of Allāh. Allāh who created them knows everything you do, and He will reward you on that scale.

The reading continues to page 14, "So one can see Allāh in his worship by being actualized in the station of excellence as is expressed in the saying of the Messenger of Allāh, ṣalla-llāhu 'alayhi wa sallam, "Excellence is to worship Allāh as if you are seeing Him."

Āmīn. Okay, enough. This is enough. Ins̲hā'a-llāh, in a few days I will send this book to be published—in not more than two weeks, and it will be ready for everyone. I hope Allāh helps us to understand every word that He sent from my heart and to explain more. And my words are always: read, write, and understand. It is not right to buy the book and put it on the shelf. I want you to put it in your heart, and to follow what you understand. I am sure if you read it, you will see. Allāh will help you and He will open the door for you to understand what I wrote.

This book is like a drop from the ocean of the knowledge of Allāh. I am nothing. But what He gave, I put down. If I were to explain this book really, maybe I would need one year. These are the words of Allāh, some of the words of Allāh. I am nothing. Without Him, I cannot make anything. He makes me; I am thankful. I thank Allāh because He makes me a slave for Him. It is a very holy gift, if He accepts me to be His slave, and to carry His message and to give it for all the beloveds who heard this voice. I pray now that . . .

I pray to Allāh that you are sincere in your actions, and kind among one another. We should all be one umma as Allāh wants us to be, so that we can carry His message of peace, justice and freedom. Āmīn.

Chicago Teachings

The angels have light.
How can you see this angelic light?
If you are truthful, sincere and honest with Allāh,
especially toward the last third of the night,
and when you are devoted to Allāh
(with nothing in your heart but Allāh),
and your heart is devoid of hate, envy and jealousy
and all of these qualities,
and you are full of love and mercy,
the angels will come.
They will descend upon you and surround you.

From "Make Your Inner Ḥajj Today"

Bad Character Traits to Avoid

"Veils and Repentance"

from *He Who Knows Himself Knows His Lord*

Lā 'ilāha 'illa-llāāāāāāh, Lā 'ilāha 'illa-llāāāāāh, Lā 'ilāha 'illa-llāāāāāh
Muḥammad rasūlu-llāh, Ibrāhīm rasūlu-llāh, Mūsā rasūlu-llāh,
'Īsā rasūlu-llāh 'alayhim ṣalātu-llāh.

Allāhumma anta-s-salām wa minka-s-salām
wa ilayka ya'ūdu-s-salām
tabārakta rabbanā
ya dha-l-jalāli wa-l-'ikrām

As-salāmu 'alaykum wa raḥmatu-llāh wa bārakatuhu.

I ask Allāh, glory be to Him, to protect you, your children, and your loved ones. May He push away all disasters, afflictions and diseases from you and from all of your loved ones. Because you are, as I know, the beloveds of Allāh who are carrying the message of the truth, which is the message of unity—the true message of Allāh. It is the message of all the prophets, and it is the message of peace, love, mercy, justice and freedom for the whole world. It is the message that was brought by our master guide and beloved, Muḥammad, may the peace of Allāh be upon him. Allāh said:

> We have not sent you but as a mercy for all the worlds.
> (Qur'ān 21:107)

He was an example of divine politeness, courteous manners. Allāh said that he had the greatest ethics. He was the example who demonstrated divine courtesy and good manners. He, the Prophet, 'alayhi as-salātu as-salām, said:

> The one who disciplined me, trained me and taught me this courtesy is my Lord, Allāh. (Ḥadīth)

He also said:

> The best of all the good is the best ethics. (Ḥadīth)

I hope that all of you now are ready to receive the words that emerged from the Prophet's tongue as he received them from his Lord. They were sent to him as a Qur'ān, a divine recitation. The Qur'ān teaches us how to be polite with Allāh and with the creatures of Allāh. It shows us how the Prophet used polite and courteous manners with all of the people who came to him.

It is not as those who claim things...It makes me so sad because some people say that they are on the Ṣūfī path, the path of purification, but they do not abide by divine law; they do not follow divine law. They do not pray; they abandon prayer and they do not follow the guidance and instruction sent down upon the Prophet, ʿalayhi as-salātu as-salām.

Some claim that they are advanced, that they are muqqadams. Some claim that they are master teachers or this or that, but these names do not mean anything to Allāh. What Allāh really loves and what His Messenger loves is for us to adorn ourselves with the ethics of Allāh and His Messenger. Our Messenger, may the peace of Allāh be upon him, taught us how to be polite and courteous with others. Allāh sent upon his heart a divine recitation, the Qur'ān, saying:

> And had you been severe and harsh hearted,
> they would have broken away from about you. (Qur'ān 3:159)

It was narrated that a large group of Christians came to the Messenger, may the peace of Allāh be upon him. They came to meet and visit with him in the beginning of his mission for Allāh. The Prophet's companions did not have a full understanding of the message and were not perfectly using good manners and politeness. They tried to push these people away—they refused to allow them to meet the Prophet. But the Prophet saw what was happening and stopped them. He went out to the Christians and was very polite with them. He embraced them and told his companions:

> The way you behaved is not the way of Allāh.
> It is not the ethics of the Messenger and Allāh
> because all people are the creatures of Allāh
> and these people are the followers
> of the Messiah, ʿĪsā (Jesus), ʿalayhi as-salām,

[the sound is lost for a few minutes]

...sheets and welcome them to sit. He and ordered them to cook for them and he said, "You must be very generous with them." For he, may the peace of Allāh be upon him said:

> All people are the children of Allāh.
> The one who is most beloved of Allāh
> is the one who is most beneficial to others. (Ḥadīth)

In our way there is no difference between black and white, rich or poor. There is no difference between men and women. We all are equal. We are brothers and sisters because Allāh says:

> Oh people,
> We have created you from [a single pair] a male and a female,
> and made you into nations and tribes,
> so that you may know one another.
> Truly, the most honorable of you with Allāh
> is he who is most pious. (Qur'ān 49:13)

And this is what we love, and this is what we carry: the message of justice.

Whoever claims to be a muqaddam or naqīb by saying he has this rank in the path must behave accordingly. He must never backbite others, speak badly about them, or claim to be advanced in the Ṣūfī way with a high rank on the path. Allāh said the following in the Qur'ān about backbiting:

> And do not spy on or backbite one another.
> Would one of you like to eat the flesh of his dead brother
> or sister? You would hate it. (Qur'ān 49:12)

Backbiting is like eating flesh. He said, "You should not backbite your brother or sister." You should come directly to your brother or sister and try to tell them what you think in a polite way. You should go to him and say, "Oh brother, I think that is wrong." But you should not go and publicize it on the computer and talk about him in a bad way. These are not the ethics of Allāh or His Messenger.

The Prophet, may the peace of Allāh be upon him said:

> Religion is giving good advice to people.

People asked him, "To whom should we give advice?"

He said, "The advice should be for the sake of Allāh,
for the sake of His book,
for the sake of His Messenger,
and everyone should advise another. (Ḥadīth)

You can advise one another, but you do not have the right to tell a person something in a way that is not approved of by Allāh. You may notice that a person is not doing his divine duty, or he is doing it in a wrong way. You may see that a person is not praying, that sometimes he misses the prayer. Go to him directly and advise him. Talk to him and tell him that this is not permissible because it is like repelling Allāh. But you should not go around to other people saying, "Do you believe that so and so is not praying?" No, this is not the way of Allāh. It is not the way of Ṣūfism or purification.

We should advise each other, but in a good way. We have to command what is good and prevent what is it evil, but not in a cruel way, in an impolite way. No, we have to be polite. We have to be very polite.

This is why I say, "Whoever has come to Allāh and accepted the way of Allāh must repent for all he has done, all mistakes like this that he has made with others. You must seek forgiveness from Allāh for what you have done. If you do not seek forgiveness from Allāh then your actions will not be accepted. Allāh will not accept your actions unless you repent from the mistakes you are making—even if you keep reciting Qur'ān or doing this ritual or that ritual. You must repent."

But there are conditions for repentance. One of the conditions is to go to the one you have wronged, the one you backbit. Apologize to him and ask him to forgive and to pardon you. If the person forgives and pardons you, then Allāh will accept you, your actions and your repentance. Do not act as if you are bigger than that person, or that you are too big to apologize. Do not allow conceit or arrogance to overtake you. Go and tell the person you are sorry. The greatest person and the closest to Allāh is the one who respects others and does not feel shame from apologizing and admitting a mistake. This is the truth.

I came here, asking Allāh, glory be to Him, to surround you with His special care. I hope that anyone who has committed wrongs among you will repent to Allāh and not continue making the same mistakes. Allāh, glory be to Him, says:

> The one who comes with repentance and a full heart,
> I will transform their bad deeds into good deeds
> and rectify their deeds and his affairs. (Qur'ān 5:39)

He also said in His direct conversation with the Prophet, the Ḥadīth Qudsī, which is the divine conversation:

> Oh My worshippers, if you had not committed sins,
> I would have created people who committed sins
> so that they would come to Me and ask for forgiveness
> and I would bestow forgiveness upon them.

The nature of the human being is to commit mistakes, to fall into error. But the best of those who commit mistakes are the ones who come and admit those mistakes and ask for pardon. This is something so great to Allāh. I pray to Allāh that you are ready, that you become ready to declare your repentance, especially because we are very close to the holy month of Ramaḍan.

In only a few days the month of Ramaḍan will start. Ramaḍan is the holy month of repentance. It is also the month of forgiveness and mercy. This is why I invite you to rush to repentance, and to be steadfast with your repentance because it is a good chance and repentance is a great thing. Ṣāliḥ will start to read for us from the new book, *He Who Knows Himself, Knows His Lord.*

It took me six years to write this book. It is a very deep book and I hope that you will benefit from it, because it is based in the holy book of Allāh and His secrets. It is also written from the Ḥadīth, the narration of the words of the prophets and our Master Messenger, ṣalla-llāhu ʿalayhim wa sallim, and all of the holy, truthful, authentic Books. I would like you to hear something in this station we are in.

I wanted to come to you even before I rested from my trip to say, "Peace be upon you," and to offer a gift to you, a divine gift. Open your hearts and your spirits. Not your physical bodies, because this does not benefit you. These physical bodies actually bring bad things to their possessors. The Messenger of Allāh said:

> Allāh does not look to your physical bodies
> and how you look and what your color is.
> He looks to your deeds and your intentions. (Ḥadīth)

This is the true scale with which Allāh measures things. There are many people who spread corruption on earth, but their words are so sweet. Look at their actions—do not look at their words. You will find them to be thieves and murderers, spreading corruption across the earth.

Story of the Two Birds and the Fisherman

Do not be like the bird that saw a fisherman one cold winter day. The fisherman had a gun with him and he found two birds. He wanted to shoot one of them. The one bird said to the other bird, "Look at that fisherman, tears are streaming down his face." But the other bird said to him, "Do not be stupid! Look at his hand. Look at what he is doing!"

Do not be deceived by the sweet words of some people. Look at their actions. This is why Allāh said:

> The most hateful thing to Allāh is when you say that which you do not do. (Qur'ān 61:3)

"Veils and Repentance" on page 57 of *He Who Knows Himself Knows His Lord* is read from the beginning until page 60, "So witnessing is a necessity that happens as a result of tiresome struggle and practice, and from poverty and surrender to Allāh, ṣalla-llāhu 'alayhi wa sallim."

There is a great difference between what you say and what you do. It is a must to be sincere in directing yourself fully toward Allāh. It was narrated that our most beloved Messenger said:

> People are destroyed
> except for the knowledgeable ones among them.
>
> But the knowledgeable ones are also destroyed
> except for the ones who perform good actions.
>
> But the doers of the good actions are all destroyed
> except for the ones who are sincere in their actions.
>
> But the sincere are also destroyed,
> because Allāh actually brings them to account
> according to the secret of the sincerity of their actions.
> (Ḥadīth)

This means that your matter is not judged by what you say, because you might be saying something, or even doing something, because you want to be praised by others. People can be deceived by a person because he or she is doing good, he is saying all of the right words, but behind others' backs he is backbiting them. He is just doing good deeds in front of people so that he can be praised for being the leader; he is this or that; he is great.

But the One Who is really great is the One Who created you and provided for you without saying, "I created you; I did this so you have to do that in return." He just wants you to acknowledge that you are His servant and slave, and that He is the Creator and Provider. He continues to provide for you, and He does not ask you to give Him food, money or anything in return. Allāh is not in need. He created jinn and humans just to worship Him (Qur'ān 51:56). He wants to be known, acknowledged.

It is not that I have to work to be a great s̲hayk̲h̲ to have people praise me, or that I have to tell others that I am advanced in the path so that that people say how great I am. This is not permissible. I must actually become a servant – polite, with good manners, and be courteous to others. I have to love all people without discriminating between them about who is great and who is not, who is big and who is not. The Messenger said:

> All people are the children of Allāh.
> The one who is most beloved of Allāh
> is the one who is most beneficial to others. (Ḥadīt̲h̲)

I must carry love for all. I must carry peace, justice and mercy for all people without discrimination. I must rush to help anyone I see in need – the poor, the needy and the sick.

Allāh created you this way, equal, from a pair, from a mother and father. Is this not so? Did He create you from a father different than my father? No. Did He create your mother from a different mother than someone else's? No. All people are equal because they all go back to Ādam and Eve, the great father and mother. This is the Reality and the creation of Allāh. From dust our bodies were created and to dust they will return. Is this not so? Have you ever seen a corpse, someone who passed away, and found it made of gold? It is from dust, and it will be analyzed and end up as dust whether he was rich, poor, white or black. This is why we must know and realize that we are from one father and mother, and we should be merciful and helpful to each other.

We should never envy or become jealous of each other. Never. We should never be envious. Why do you envy your brother? Why are you making separation between you and him? Were you made out of pearl and he is made out of wood? The things that people go through are crazy. This is how people act—it is crazy. But if someone passes away his family cannot allow him to be in the house for more than two days. Why? Because he stinks. Is this not the reality?

Then why do humans become arrogant? Why does someone think he is bigger and better than someone else? Why does he want to harm another? Why does he backbite another? Why does he not help his brother? This is what humanity needs. It is our message: the message of unity, the message of peace, love, justice and mercy that creates equality between all people without discrimination.

This can be done by following the commands of Allāh, the divine law that was sent and explained through the messengers of Allāh, ṣalla-llāhu ʿalayhim wa sallam. We must act according to these teachings. If we deviate from these teaching, may Allāh forbid, we are rebellious ones.

I ask Allāh, glory be to Him, for you to be ready to declare your repentance from all of your past deeds. Repent from all that you have done in the past, because Ramaḍan is imminent, and Ramaḍan demands that we be repentant. We must repent from all of our past sins—the sins we committed against our selves, against our brothers and sisters, against other people deviating from Allāh's commands. You must declare it with complete sincerity.

Whoever is ready to declare a sincere repentance let him do it, because this is Friday and Friday is the best day on which the sun rises. On a Friday Ādam was created. Also, the heavens and the earth were created on Friday, so it is a blessed day. If you want to repent I am opening the door of repentance for you. Whoever is ready to repent, come to me. Come to me, repent, declare your repentance in front of me and in front of your Lord.

Your repentance is for Allāh. This repentance is the repentance of the physical body, the repentance of the soul for what that human did with his body. What did he do? He must look. What did his physical body do? He might have lied with his tongue or backbitten someone. He might have slept with someone other than his wife or husband. He might have committed betrayal, theft, or anything with his body that is not in accordance with divine law. This repentance is a repentance of the body, of the soul; it is a repentance of the tongue. Allāh says in the Qur'ān:

> That the recording angels receive [record all of your actions], one sitting on the right and one on the left. (Qur'ān 50:17)

For this reason you must repent from whatever your tongue has uttered that it should not have uttered.

Why did you harm someone with your hand? Your hand must repent. You might have been envious of someone and sent that envy through your eyes, so your eyes should repent. You might have looked at someone and said, "Oh, I am better than so and so." Why did you use your mind, your intellect, to invent things that hurt humanity? You might have been involved in that. You might have sold poisons to people or done this or that. You must repent for that and be sincere with Allāh.

If you are a physician, you must repent if you did something wrong during your practice. Also, if you are a teacher or a lawyer, or any other profession, you must repent from what you did wrong during your practice. This is the repentance of the physical body, but it is the repentance of the soul, as well. It is the repentance of the body and what it contains.

What does it contain? What does the belly contain? If a person earned money in ways that are impermissible, then the money is not rightfully his. But he used it to buy food that he ate, and in doing so, he ate the rights of others through his belly.

How did you use your eyes? Did you use them in the right way? Because you will be brought to accountability for what your eyes did. Allāh created the human body in the best of forms, pure and clean, and you must never throw it away. You must keep and preserve it; you must keep it pure and clean as you were given it. You must never use your body except in the ways that were commanded by Allāh. This is the repentance of the physical body and the second level comes, the repentance of the soul.

The repentance of the soul is that you will not listen to your selfish ego, envy others, or listen to the whisper of the s̲hayṭān when it whispers,

"You should not be fasting, praying, or doing this or that." Everything has its own way, and so this is the repentance of the soul. If Allāh wills, we will explain these things with accuracy later. But for now, we should understand that one should not be praying and lying at the same time, or praying and stealing, or praying and murdering others. We must never be praying and cheating another or deceiving people. This is a deviation from divine law. We must be accurate, sincere, honest and alert in what we do.

I spread my hand to you now. Everyone can put his hand on the back of his brother or sister...

Sidi gives the promise.

Make Your Inner Hajj Today

"I am Traveling to My Lord "
from *He Who Knows Himself Knows His Lord*

Lā ʾilāha ʾilla-llāāāāāāh, Lā ʾilāha ʾilla-llāāāāāh, Lā ʾilāha ʾilla-llāāāāāh
Muḥammad rasūlu-llāh, Ibrāhīm rasūlu-llāh, Mūsā rasūlu-llāh,
ʿĪsā rasūlu-llāh ʿalayhim ṣalātu-llāh.

Allāhumma anta-s-salām wa minka-s-salām
wa ilayka ya'ūdu-s-salām
tabārakta rabbanā
ya dha-l-jalāli wa-l-'ikrām

As-salāmu ʿalaykum wa raḥmatu-llāh wa bārakatuhu.

This is the last day in which I will be with you in my physical being, but my spirit, my heart and my inmost secret will always stay with you, forever. This is because the spirit is a divine spirit; it never vanishes. Because Allāh says in the Qurʾān:

> I have fashioned him completely and breathed into him from My spirit. (Qurʾān 15:29, 38:72)

This means the human spirit is eternal, and I mean the human spirit that cares enough to preserve its essence and adorn itself with the lofty ethics of Allāh, following His natural law and commands, and following His most beloved Messenger, ṣalla-llāhu ʿalayhi wa sallam.

These are the spirits that will continue forever. Spirits are like groups. Those who knew one other in heaven will know one other on earth, and those who did not know each other there will know not each other here, or will be repulsed by the other.

All spirits come from the spirit of the Great Creator.
He is the Beautiful and he is the Majestic.
He is the Source of Peace.
He is the Merciful and He is the Wise; wisdom comes from Him.
He is Just and He created everyone free.
In His world there is no hate; there is no envy.

His whole existence is within you as well. Allāh will never forsake the people who promised Him to be His servants. He will always provide for them from His spirit, the spirit of divine beauty and divine love. He will always provide them with that. These spirits will never cease chanting praise for their Lord. They will always continue to be kind, polite, full of love, peace and mercy, singing the song of love for all those who are suffering across the earth, and praying for them. How can we arrive at this state? By surrendering to the Most Beloved and following His laws and commands.

I pray that Allāh, glory be to Him, will keep you in the circle of divine love and divine life. May He push all low desires away from you, because these low desires are full of harm, envy, jealousy and hate between people. May He protect you from these selfish and low desires.

I hope you will keep your promise, the promise you gave. It was the promise of the physical body, of the soul and heart. I would like you to use your physical body only in the way that Allāh wants you to use it, so that your heart will be full only with love and peace.

Do not listen to your ego and its lower desires. Do not listen to most people. If you listen to people then you will get confused, and the s̲h̲ayṭān will keep whispering in your ear and confuse you. But if you preserve Allāh's qualities then you will listen to Him. Otherwise, you will listen to the s̲h̲ayṭān and you will be confused, looking at his illusions and pictures.

Iblīs keeps whispering to the lower self, the animal self, for it to follow its desires. So people are confused because of the ego and its desires, and Iblīṣ' whispers, but those upon whom Allāh has mercy will be protected from that. When you offer good deeds, know that you are offering them for the sake of your own self. The Messenger of Allāh said:

> Your own worst enemy is the self between your two sides. (Ḥadīt̲h̲)

He said this because it can allow Iblīs to possess and control you.

How can you be possessed and controlled by Iblīs and serve him? This will happen if you do not follow the commands of Allāh. He will get you from the door of envy and jealousy; he will tell you, "Look at that person.

He has a high position and wealth and he does not deserve it. I deserve it. I wish I had it." And you wish bad things upon your brothers and you envy them. But the pious person does not listen to his ego. He does not listen to the ego that pushes him to envy, to hate and to conspire against his brother.

Be like our master guide Ibrāhīm who always said:

> ...the Lord of the Worlds Who has created me, and it is He Who guides me. (Qur'ān 26:77-26:78)

What does it mean that he has his Lord with him? It means he will always follow the commands of Allāh, the law of Allāh, and will not listen to his lower desires or to his ego. He said:

> I will emigrate for the sake of my Lord. (Qur'ān 29:26)

> It is He Who guides me (Qur'ān 26:78)

> And when I am ill, it is He Who cures me. (Qur'ān 26:79-80)

The pilgrimage here is an inner pilgrimage, a spiritual pilgrimage. The Messenger of Allāh said that deeds are judged by the intentions behind them, so whoever emigrates for the sake of marrying a beautiful woman or acquiring wealth will have what he wishes for. But the one who does his pilgrimage and travels towards Allāh will arrive at Allāh. The one who travels on the way to the s̲hayṭān will arrive at the s̲hayṭān, and will start to listen to the s̲hayṭān whisper and will get lost.

People come to me asking, "Sidi, I wish I had this spouse or this job or that job. Do you think I will have it?" People ask me and I marvel at these questions. The one who comes to Allāh with a whole heart, a full heart, and has direct connection with Him, will know and will be given to. Because Allāh says:

> And when My slaves ask you concerning Me,
> then [answer them], I am indeed near.
> I respond to prayers when they call upon Me. (Qur'ān 2:186)

Allāh sees and hears.

Make your relationship directly with Him. It does not mean you do not consult me. You can consult me, but I will tell you to go, ask Allāh and be polite, to have good manners with Allāh. Ask Allāh because He is close to you. He is never far away from you. He is closer to you than your jugular vein (Qur'ān 50:16). So do not say, "Allāh is not listening to me. I prayed and He is not listening." Because Allāh says, "I hear and I see." He told His Prophet Mūsā, 'ālayhi as-salām:

> Fear not, truly! I am with you both, hearing and seeing.
> (Qur'ān 20:46)

Allāh sees and hears so beware; do not lie to Allāh.

The s̲hayṭān will come to you in different pictures. He will appear to you in different forms. So beware. Do not ever say or claim, "Oh, Allāh told me so. I heard Allāh saying that to me," believing illusions and pictures. You cannot see Allāh unless you become the complete devotee to Allāh; you must have complete manners, be pious, follow His commands and avoid His prohibitions, in full surrender to His Majesty. In that station the Beloved is never absent.

You are His beloved when you feel love, when you actualize love on earth, and when you surrender and obey Him without looking right or left. Do not stop with illusions, imaginings and pictures.

Be one who remembers Allāh,
Be one who is obedient to Him
like those who love one another for the sake of Allāh,
who gather to remember Allāh,
who are polite to one another,
who do not envy one another,
who do not feel jealous of one another,
but rather, who cooperate.

They eat from one container and they drink from one drink.

By container, I mean the divine container, which can contain everything in creation. Allāh warns us against eating something impure, unclean. This means: do not use your ears to listen to gossip. Do not use your tongue to curse people, to backbite people, or to hurt people's feelings.

This divine container must be full of humility, love, peace and mercy—completely.

You must be as active as the honeybee. Have you ever seen a honeybee going eating garbage? No, it picks all of the beautiful flowers and fruits and sucks their nectar. These are the beautiful flowers that have a sweet fragrance and a sweet taste. Here Allāh gives us an example for those of us who believe, who have faith. This living, tiny creature goes and chants while flying. Have you not listened to its sound? It is not singing; it is not like any ordinary sound; it is chanting praises for Allāh. It is in prayer. Allāh said everything prays for Him and glorifies Him and praises Him (see Qur'ān 24:41), but you do not understand the language.

Every creature has its own prayer. Listen to the whistling of the tree branches and leaves; they pray. Listen to the waves of the ocean and the rivers; they pray, too. Do you not hear the waves? Sometimes they come in a strong, powerful way, with loud sound saying, "I am a creature of Allāh. Allāh sent me to challenge the oppressors and the tyrants." Some people think of themselves as powerful and very big, but no, Allāh is the Most Powerful. There is no one who is big or powerful without Him. This is a reminder, a reminder to anyone who has a heart, listens or witnesses. Anyone who has a heart full of the knowledge of Allāh and full of divine ethics can understand that.

The heart is the divine Throne. The heart knows only pure goodness, peace, justice, love and mercy. I am talking about the human heart that Allāh gave you as a gift. I am not talking about the piece of flesh, the organ, I am talking about the invisible heart, your innermost being. They open you in surgery and say, "This is your heart." No, you have another heart. The heart is that through which Allāh can give you inspiration. Know that Allāh also operates the heart organ, because through it He allows you to walk and to work in this life.

He is giving you a great gift of tajallī. He gave you the gift of living; you are alive. Life comes from Him; everything is from Him. You must be conscious and alert. Allāh gave you hearing so that you could listen to Him. He gave you a tongue so that you could talk with Him. How do you talk with Him? You speak with Him through your prayer (ṣalāh) and through remembrance (dẖikr). You speak with Him through all of the pure, good words that you use to communicate with people. It is not permissible for you to violate anyone because Allāh says in the Qur'ān:

> That the recording angels receive [record all of your actions], one sitting on the right and one on the left. (Qur'ān 50:17)

Allāh created this earth for you and gave you what you needed. Did you create it? You cannot create even the wing of a mosquito—or anything. You cannot; you cannot create these things. The only creator is Allāh. He is the One Who gave you all of these organs. So you must use your limbs and senses in the way that Allāh wanted you to use them.

You must always be in worship. But we do not mean that you continuously pray and do remembrance. That is part of what you do, but you can still be in worship when you talk with people. When you use your tongue not to deceive, but to speak kindly and justly, you are in worship.

Allāh gave you a hand. When you use your hand to do good and partake of permissible things, that is worship. If you are at your job and you are honest, sincere and fair, then you are in worship. If you do not like something and you speak the truth, you are in worship. But if you fight, feel jealous, attack people and backbite, and you claim to have knowledge that you do not have, then that is not using your limbs in the right way.

For example, a man comes with his wife to a physician, and he brings with him a child. The father loves the child very much because he resembles him. He cannot refuse anything the child requests, and so he cannot reject his requests.

The female child is the same. She requests things from the mother and the mother responds. The father and the mother feel happy if the child is happy; they feel sad if the child is sad; they feel sick if the child is sick.

I say to those who claim they know, and in reality do not know, that they should never deceive people. If they were truly guides or spiritual physicians, they would feel for people's pain and would not deceive it. I am talking about spiritual healing. Spiritual healing is known only to those who follow the way of Allāh.

The child goes to the physician and the physician looks in his eyes. The physician looks into the eyes and thinks he can see the unseen through the eyes. Then he says to the parents, "Your son is possessed by a jinn."

The parents bring the child, and the physician sees that he is not feeling well, so he tries to say, "Your child is possessed by jinn," but how can he know this? He cannot just know by looking at the child like that. He must be, himself, a child of God.

He must listen to the child, and ask him what his complaint is. He must give him hope, be gentle with him, and give him love and understanding and not scare or terrify the child. He does not let the parents be terrified either. Give them love; give them divine love. Give them the sweetness of Allāh. Listen to their complaints; listen to their pain.

But then he starts to say, "Your child is possessed by pain; I see this and I see that." He is listening to his own illusions and pictures, terrifying the child and the parents. This is wrong. It is like he is sitting in front of a television, seeing all the pictures the s̱hayṭān is presenting to him; then he says, "I see this and I see that." He goes to sleep at night and sees the same type of s̱hayṭānic pictures and dreams; he wakes up and h tells people, "I see this. I see that."

But in reality the little child has nightmares when he watches television too much and sees terrifying movies. He is not possessed, he just has nightmares from scary television.

My children, everyone has two intellects:

1. The mind, the apparent intellect
2. The inner intellect

The mind, the outer intellect, is that which interacts with daily life and sees pictures and all outer things. The brain starts to record all of these pictures, interactions and experiences. No matter who you are and how great you are, this happens. Your brain will record everything you experience, and you will see the outer pictures.

Everything is recorded with the outer intellect, with the mind. Even the words you hear are recorded. This is how Allāh created it. Compared to this, the computer is nothing. It cannot record all of this. The divine computer is very, very accurate and does not miss an iota, but records all.

Many things happen today because of the machines humans have invented. Those who stay in front of the computer and television a long time will become affected by it, especially children. If children stay in front of the television and the computer too long, playing wild games, they will have nightmares and scream at night, and the mother will say, "Why is my child screaming and having nightmares? He saw a monster in a dream. He saw an animal attacking him." Then she will take the child to someone who claims to understand and have knowledge, and claims he is a spiritual physician.

If you are truly a spiritual physician, your heart must be vast. You must understand that you are talking to a pure human, an innocent one like an angel, a little child. You must bow down to this innocent spirit who has seen only Allāh so far. He does not comprehend all of what people are doing. He does not know lying and deception and all of that yet, because he is an innocent spirit.

Listen to him. Do not tell him what you think you see, because he is actually the spiritual physician, the true one, not you. Do not give him something beyond his comprehension and tell him there is a jinn possessing him. That will terrify him. Actually, if you say such a thing, the jinn are in your own head.

The jinn do not actually have a way to enter his pure spirit. He is only a child. He did not commit any sin. He is very pure; he did not do anything wrong. He is not rebellious against Allāh. Why would a jinn dare to or be able to possess him? Allāh says in the Qur'ān:

> Certainly, you will have no authority over My slaves,
> except those who follow you of the astray ones. (Qur'ān 15:42)

He says that to Iblīs and the jinn. This child is an innocent spirit. He did not commit any sin. He did not do anything wrong. He is innocent and faithful to Allāh, very truthful and sincere. So you must talk with him gently and not tell him he is possessed by a jinn. You must listen to him and understand—analyze and understand.

The Ṣūfī physician, the spiritual physician, must understand through Allāh. How does this happen? Through the children of Allāh, actually, he can gain understanding. They are innocent, pure and gentle spirits, so you should listen to them, not tell them. And if you have to tell them something, tell them only good things.

The Messenger of Allāh said:

> Your smile in the face of your brother or sister is charity. (Ḥadīth)

A smile is a healing method for another soul. So you smile in the child's face and you make him feel secure and at peace. Children cannot be possessed by jinn ever, because they are still pure and innocent. But parents, sisters, and healers in our ṭarīqa must understand that nightmares come from computer games and from movies and what they see on television. Nightmares happens because this outer intellect, the mind, records everything in the brain and then projects it back.

But the inner intellect only knows Truth, the Reality, because it is a divine intellect. The metaphoric, outer intellect that interacts with the outer world is limited. But the inner spirit has no limit, and cannot be contained within something with dimensions. It is limitless. That is why in the Qur'ān Allāh says:

> Say: "The spirit is from the command of my Lord."
> (Qur'ān 17:85)

It is the secret and it belongs to Allāh alone.
It is the divine secret that Allāh put in everything alive.

The divine spirit has no limit. It is limitless, because it is a lordly spirit. The physical being is limited, but Allāh has no boundaries and He is not limited by time, space or anything. We cannot resemble Him. We cannot say that Allāh is a man or a woman. No, Allāh is beyond all of that, He transcends all of that, and the human spirit is a secret that Allāh gave to us. This is why we must surrender to divine commands. Divine commands lead us to pure goodness, to what is good for us.

There are holy spirits and pure, innocent spirits. Who are these spirits? They are the ones who have truly submitted to Allāh and followed His commands. They achieve this through their walking the way to Allāh continuously, unceasingly; it is through their remembrance of Allāh, their service to people, and their goodness to everyone.

Whenever a group of people comes together to remember Allāh,
angels surround them and
Allāh mentions them in His high assembly of angels (Ḥadīth Qudsī).

The angels have light.
How can you see this angelic light?
If you are truthful, sincere and honest with Allāh,
especially toward the last third of the night,
and when you are devoted to Allāh
(with nothing in your heart but Allāh),
and your heart is devoid of hate, envy and jealousy
and all of these qualities,
and you are full of love and mercy,
the angels will come.
They will descend upon you and surround you.

In the beginning you might not be able to see them, and you may be unconscious of their presence. But if you continue to be truthful you will actually see their light. You will see that you are surrounded by light. A noble angel will come to you to remember Allāh with you. When you see this light, know that he is an angel. But know he will not come to you unless you are truly pure, devoted to Allāh, and devoid of all bad qualities.

If you are otherwise, for example, not praying, not devoted to Allāh, lying and deceiving people, then Iblīs will come to you with illusions, so that you think you saw this and that. If you obey Iblīs, he will keep obeying you, too, and keep providing you with illusions and pictures. But if you obey your Lord, our Lord, then Iblīs, his troops, and his followers will never be able to approach you because Allāh promised:

> Certainly, you will have no authority over My slaves,
> except those who follow you of the astray ones. (Qur'ān 15:42)

Allāh said so in the Qur'ān because, "They are My beloveds, they remember Me, they are conscious of Me, they serve Me."

The ones who can see the light of the angels are the ones who are sincere and honest in whatever they do, in their jobs in their relationships with people. When you love good for people, you are continuously in prayer. Even in your job when you are kind to people and just, then you are in prayer. Why? Because you are following Allāh's commands to be honest, sincere, faithful, working hard and serving others. Then you are worshiping even when you are doing your job. When you have mercy on poor people, on sick people, then you are in prayer.

Prayer is not only in the mosque, synagogue or church. True prayer is in everything you do. If you are a pious person and you are in complete surrender to Allāh, everything you do becomes worship. So even when you sleep you are in worship, because Allāh commanded you to rest. When you do that you are obeying Him.

But people do not do that, instead they go play on the computer all night or watch television, and they do not rest, and so they lose the connection to Allāh. "I was just doing something because I cannot sleep." "I want to do this or that on the computer, or watch this or that on television," This violates the rights of your body. The Prophet, ʿalayhi as-salātu as-salām, said:

> Your body has a right upon you.
> Your soul has a right upon you.
> Your wife has right upon you.
> Your house has a right upon you.
> Your children have a right upon you.
> And your Lord has a right upon you. (Ḥadīth̲)

Everyone has a right over you, so you must give everyone their due, including your own self and body. If you do this you will come to be in continuous worship. This is the walking of the seeker on this path. He must achieve this station.

This is the true essence of true Ṣūfism, which is the way of purity. In the Ṣūfī way we do not allow anyone who should be lazy and claim to be a Ṣūfī. Laziness does not belong to Ṣūfism. Allāh wants us to be active, to be strong, to give love, and to help and serve the poor, the needy and the sick. This is something I wanted to explain in the beginning, but now I will have Ṣāliḥ read.

"I am Travelling to My Lord" on page 1 of *He Who Knows Himself Knows His Lord* is read from the beginning to page 16, "If the meaning becomes strong within you, it will clarify your action and the essence, and when the mastery of watching increases you will see that He is the Eternal for

His slave without action! This is the meaning of witnessing everything, but this is a tasting matter..."

He wants to transform you from the sensual world
and the world of illusions, phantoms and pictures
to the world of the Creator –
from the world of creation to the world of the Creator.

He wants to transform you from the sensual into the witness.
With your own eyes you see,
and when you transform to the realm of the Creator
you see with your inside.

He wants to transform you from the realm of illusion and imagination
to the realm of Reality that does not disappear and annihilate.
It is always there.

He does not want you to become like a donkey going in a circle.
He wants to transform you from the world of the formation
to the world of divinity, to His presence.

If He had not created a tongue for you, you would not be able to talk. If He had not given you hands, you would not be able to work. He wants you to preserve the gifts He gave you and use them in the right way. He gave all of these instruments to you: eyes, lips, tongue, hands, legs, and intellect as a gift, a deposit. He asks you to preserve it, to protect it and to use it in a certain way.

When you always refer everything to Allāh, then you will receive guidance from Him on what you should do. Then your actions become strong and good, and your life becomes the way Allāh wants it to be for you. You live in the Garden now. That is what Allāh wants. So Allāh says:

> The one who believes in Me, lives in the Garden now. (Ḥadīt͟h)

He does not live in the Garden later after he dies. It starts now. He wants you to use these gifts in a way that makes you happy, that takes you into the Garden now. Suppose you are working for a boss and at the end of the month he says, "This is your salary," after you have worked the whole month. Allāh is not like that. If you are working on something now, He gives to you now. He strengthens you now. He provides you with love and pure goodness right away. You always receive goodness from Him; you receive a reward from Him, right away. Our master guide Ibrāhīm said:

> I will emigrate for the sake of my Lord. (Qur'ān 29:26)
>
> It is He Who guides me (Qur'ān 26:78)
>
> And when I am ill, it is He Who cures me. (Qur'ān 26:79-80)

Some stupid people misunderstand this. They claim, "Oh Allāh gave me an illness. He is the one who gave me this accident. He is the one who does these horrible things to me." No, Allāh never ordered you to speed in your car. He did not tell you to drink alcohol and drive. He did not order you to do such things. He said you must understand the natural law, the balance. You must care for your own life and the life of others. So do not accuse Allāh of doing evil. You are the one who is doing evil. You say, "Allāh gave me this illness. Allāh gave me this accident. Allāh is the one who is ordering me to divorce my husband." No, Allāh does not order us like this.

Allāh ordered you to be polite, to be loving, to care for yourself, to care for what is between your hands, and to care for others. But the reality is that you listen to your lower desires, your stupidity and to Iblīs. Did Allāh give you two eyes to see the road? Did He give you two ears with which to listen? Then how is it you claim, "Oh, Allāh brought me this accident, this illness." No, it is what your hands earned. And Allāh pardons a lot (Qur'ān 42:30).

This is the truth. This is the reality. Someone comes complaining to me, "My mother violated me or my father abused me." You must ask why he abused you, why she abused you. You must understand that it is not from Allāh. Allāh never told your mother or your father to abuse you.

What happens is that the human becomes sick with a heart that is full of dirt, illusions, pictures, and imaginations. He leaves his human form and enters his animal form, and becomes devoid of love and mercy. In this state a person violates the rights of another. It is not Allāh; it is not Allāh Who orders anyone to do this. The one who abuses a child will receive his punishment. The consequences will come to him. Allāh will judge him.

If you were abused and you are truly innocent then forget the past.
Do not get stuck in the past. Look at the present.
You cannot change the past, so do not keep looking at it.

Be the child of your moment, the present moment.
Make your reconciliation with Allāh.
Rely upon Him, depend upon Him, and surrender your future to Him.
Seek refuge in Him; He will never forsake you.
He will heal your pain.
He is the First Healer.

And Allāh will surely heal the one
who truly comes to Him with a full heart.
This is the Truth; this is Reality.

Do not incline to those who oppress themselves and others – the ignorant ones, the stupid ones – do not listen to them. Do not listen to monsters, oppressors, and tyrants who abuse others, and misuse control and power of them. They want to have control and power over others because they listen to their own s̲hayṭān. Do not listen to them.

Believe that Allāh is Love. Allāh is the Source of Peace. Allāh is Merciful. His Mercy contains everything. Seek refuge in His Mercy, then. Do not swim in dirty water. This dirty water is polluted by ignorant ones, sinners, oppressors, by those who love power. Seek pure water. Seek pure water that is devoid of poisons and dirt.

What is pure water? It is divine knowledge that Allāh sent to us through His messengers, lovers and beloveds. It is the message of unity, which is the message of Reality, which does not know anything but love.

I ask Allāh to take your hands and help you to arrive at Him.
I say this and I seek forgiveness for myself and for you,
and glory be to Him,
He is far transcendent over what they attribute to Him.

Today is a day of witnessing.
I ask Allāh to make you witness Him
and supply you from His own existence.
May He protect you, your children and your brothers and sisters,
and families and even your parents who have passed away.

May He make you one of those who carries the message of unity,
the message of love, peace, justice, freedom and mercy.
May He preserve love in your hearts forever.

Now it is the time to give the promise, the promise of the inmost secret of being. Whoever is ready to give this promise, the deep promise, come to me because it will transform you and help you to travel quickly on your way to Allāh.

Keep your limbs and senses always pure, they are meant to be used in pure ways. Be polite with Allāh and always obey Him. This pilgrimage journey means you annihilate and get consumed in Allāh, and you fill your heart with Allāh and only Allāh. I ask that you open your hearts.

Sidi gives the promise.

What Will Remain For You After You Die?

"I am Traveling to My Lord "

from *He Who Knows Himself Knows His Lord*

Lā 'ilāha 'illa-llāāāāāāh, Lā 'ilāha 'illa-llāāāāāh, Lā 'ilāha 'illa-llāāāāāh
Muḥammad rasūlu-llāh, Ibrāhīm rasūlu-llāh, Mūsā rasūlu-llāh,
'Īsā rasūlu-llāh 'alayhim ṣalātu-llāh.

Allāhumma anta-s-salām wa minka-s-salām
wa ilayka ya'ūdu-s-salām
tabārakta rabbanā
ya ḏha-l-jalāli wa-l-'ikrām

As-salāmu 'alaykum wa raḥmatu-llāh wa bārakatuhu.

Welcome to you. I greet you from the bottom of my heart—a heart that is full of love, full of beauty, full of mercy, full of freedom, justice, peace and love for all of the children of humanity, regardless of their color, ethnic group or gender. I greet you in the name of the belief of the unity, the unity that knows no discrimination and no separation, no difference between white, black, or yellow, no difference between rich and poor, between man and woman, because Allāh is One. He is the One, the Unique, the Eternal One Who knows no discrimination between people, because He says in the Qur'ān:

> Oh people, We have created you from [a single pair] a male and a female. (Qur'ān 49:13)
>
> It is He Who has created you from a single soul. (Qur'ān 7:189)

We are not talking about a single woman and a single man. We were created from a single soul, which is the human soul. It is not as some people claim that that is black or white, that this is a man, and this is a woman. It is not like that in reality. Allāh says to us:

> We have certainly created man in the best mold. (Qur'ān 95:4)

He fashioned you in the picture He wanted. But He created you from a single soul (Qur'ān 7:189) and from that soul He created its mate. Allāh says in the Qur'ān:

> I have fashioned him completely
> and breathed into him from My spirit (Qur'ān 15:29, 38:72)

He is speaking about the human, any human. Any human is from the Light of Allāh. So that human being is holy. Allāh created humans from one soul (Qur'ān 7:189). Their Lord is one Lord. They are from one spirit. So the one who discriminates or makes separation between people based on their color, ethnic group, gender, wealth or poverty is deviating from the natural laws of Allāh. Allāh is beautiful, He is the Beautiful, and He created human beings in His reflection, after His own image, resembling Him (Ḥadīth). So every human being is created in that image, that reflection.

Is there anyone who can create an ear, an eye or a foot? No human can do this. The Creator is one and only, He is the one Lord. So in Allāh's creed there is no discrimination. There is no separation. His name is Love. His name is Justice. His name is the Wise. Whoever does not believe in this is deviating from Allāh's teachings and His natural law. He is actually covering up the truth and ridding himself of his own humanity. Let him then search for his real humanity and gain it back. If he does not believe in the humanity of his own brother or sister, then let him find his own humanity because he has lost it.

Is the other human a descendant of Iblīs? No, Iblīs is the one who confuses people, creates this kind of separation, and starts fights between people. He makes the human being lose his human nature and start to attack his brothers and sisters. He makes them make separation and discrimination, saying, "This is black; this is white; this is rich; this is poor, and this and that." He is making separation. Or he says, "This person is a boss and those people are followers." No, there is only the Great One. It is Allāh. There is only the Beautiful. It is Allāh. There is only the One, Allāh. And everything that Allāh created belongs to Allāh; it is related directly to Allāh.

That is why Allāh says to us in the Ḥadīth Qudsī:

> I created Ādam in My image. He is My mirror. (Ḥadīth Qudsī)

That means that the human being is the luminous mirror, the divine mirror, the mirror with which the human will adorn himself and in which he will see his beauty. So any human who belittles others, no matter how big or how powerful he is, is deviating from Allāh's natural law. And there is a doubt that he is still a human, and acting as a human.

Our own creed is the creed of unity. We believe in unity. We are like one heart, one hand and one spirit. In our way there is no discrimination; there is no separation between people. I love all people, no matter where they are and how they are.

My children total more than five million people across the world. In Africa they are my beloveds; they are my children. I love their children. I care for their women, in Indonesia and also in other countries (Europe and America). They are all my beloveds, and it is my great honor to wash the feet of all of these beloveds because they are the creatures of Allāh. They are carrying the reflection of the Real. How can I be the lover of Allāh and not love His creation. How could I not love all people? How can I?

Allāh and His Prophet, ṣalla-llāhu ʾālayhi wa sallam, said:

> All people are the children of Allāh.
> The one who is most beloved of Allāh
> is the one who is most beneficial to others. (Ḥadīth̲)

In our creed we are the people of unity, the people who carrying the message of Ṣūfism, the message of taṣawwuf, purity. It is the message that carries the natural law, the divine law of Allāh. It knows no discrimination. So all houses are the houses of Allāh in our way. You, human being, are also a house of Allāh. This is why destroying a house is like destroying all of the other houses, because you are the house of Allāh, you are His mirror.

Have you not seen the earth when it brings forth its plants? Have you seen the flowers; red, yellow, and white, and they all are watered by what? The water is the same. It is one, and the One Who waters it is One. He is the One Who originated it, created it in all of its beauty, perfection and excellence, because Allāh is the Beautiful. He does not know other than beauty.

Why did He create you beautiful? He created you beautiful, but you want to make yourself dirty. Why do you lie? Why do you become arrogant? Why do you envy? Why do you steal? Why do you kill? Why do you hate others? Who are you to hate others? Have you not been a tiny, insignificant drop? You came from that. Is that not how you started out? What is your end? Your end is to be a corpse that returns to dust. This is true about the human physical form. So how is it that you become arrogant?

But understand that you are also a precious essence. If you look at your reality, you find that you are carrying the divine image, the divine reflection, in fullness. The angels prostrated to that divine reflection in you. Isn't that so? Allāh says in the Qur'ān:

> So, when I have fashioned him completely and
> breathed into him from My spirit,
> then fall down prostrating yourselves unto him.
> (Qur'ān 15:29, 38:72)

Who is Ādam? You are Ādam. She is Ādam. He is Ādam. You came in a different appearance on the outside, but you are Ādam; you are the human being. Allāh said:

> I have fashioned him completely
> and breathed into him from My spirit (Qur'ān 15:29, 38:72)

How is it that you belittle others? How dare you? How can you keep from kissing and hugging them and washing their feet? How can you keep from doing that, because they are no different from you! Whether you like it or not, they are no different from you.

Your mother carried you in her womb and carried him as well. So every mother carried her own child in her own womb, there is no difference between anyone in this regard. We all came into the world the same way. Every human carries the divine qualities and is the reflection of Allāh.

But those who rebel and refuse to wear the garments of Truth: divine Love, divine Wisdom, divine Justice, divine Mercy, become the children of Iblīs. They are ejected from the Mercy of Allāh. They do not experience the Mercy of Allāh, even if they appear pious, cover their hair with scarves, wear ḥijāb and claim to be praying.

Allāh says:

> Truly, prayer prevents indecent and evil deeds. (Qur'ān 29:45)

True prayer is surrendering to Allāh and humbling oneself to Allāh. True prayer prevents one from doing what common sense denies, and prevents the one who is praying from performing ugly actions. He does not steal, murder, hurt others, make use of others, go and put ugly words on the internet and distribute it to people to read, attacking others. This is not the way of Allāh. Allāh said to us in His Holy Book:

> And do not spy on or backbite one another.
> Would one of you like to eat the flesh of his dead brother
> or sister? You would hate it. (Qur'ān 49:12)

No one likes to do that, but what is your opinion? Can you do that? Can you eat the raw flesh of your brother or sister?

When you speak in an ugly way about someone or backbite your brother or sister, you are eating his flesh. You are not only eating his flesh, but it is like eating dead flesh that is been there for six days. Can you imagine what that might be like? Would you be able to eat it? What you are doing is the same.

The one who backbites and says ugly things about others, and describes them in ugly ways and attacks them, is attacking Allāh Himself. This is more severe than denying Allāh and covering up His Reality. It is deviating from the natural law of Allāh. Allāh says, in the Qur'ān:

> And undoubtedly We have honored the children of Ādam.
> (Qur'ān 17:70)

That is why we must respect the human being and not let our conceit and arrogance take us over and say, "That person..." Do not think of yourself as becoming rich or becoming a leader, a boss or a muqaddam, advanced in spiritual rank. Do not think of yourself as that, because in the end you will die and you will stink. Your body will stink and you will be equal to the corpse of a donkey. How can you feel arrogant about that?

Why do you treat people with arrogance, as if you are better than they are? Be polite. Be courteous and have good manners. Whoever is acting like that that with others must stop. The true walker on this path of purification, of Ṣūfism, must be polite, must have courteous manners with others. He is carrying and representing divine law, which knows only love. It does not know rebellion; it does not know hate. So he must adorn himself with godly, lofty ethics.

Know that all the messengers since Ādam, Ibrāhīm, Mūsā, Nūh (Noah) and ʿĪsā (Jesus), ʿalayhim as-salām, had good manners. Who is ʿĪsā? He was the king of mercy, beauty and peace. Are his followers really embodying these qualities today? Look. Look at them. Very rarely will you find someone like that. Look at Muḥammad, the Prophet, may the peace and blessing of Allāh be upon him. Allāh says about him that he was sent as a mercy for all the worlds (Qurʾān 21:107). He told him in the Qurʾān:

> And had you been severe and harsh hearted,
> they would have broken away from about you. (Qurʾān 3:159)

They would not have followed him and surrounded him. So the one who claims to be a Muslim, a Jew or a Christian, a follower of Muḥammad, Mūsā or ʿĪsā, but backbites people, is cruel to them or harms them with his tongue, eyes or hand, is deviating from the laws of Allāh. The prophets are innocent of his actions because they have been polite. They have had the best manners. The true believers in God and His Messenger must always be full of love, and must never break the heart of anyone.

Our most beloved Prophet Muḥammad said:

> Have mercy on the people on earth
> so that the One in heaven will grant you mercy. (Ḥadīth)

He also said:

> The one who does not give mercy will not receive mercy. (Ḥadīth)

Those who harm humanity and hurt people will suffer the consequences of doing so in this life and in the next. He said, “Do not belittle anything because even the mountain is made up of tiny specks of dust.” (see Qurʾān 20:105, 56:5) So you were created from a tiny drop, an insignificant drop, or did your mother create you from something different—from a gem or a precious pearl or something? No, you were created the same way as all the other creatures – they are created in different ways, but from the same tiny insignificant drop.

Allāh gave us the teaching of how to behave through the messengers and the Prophet, ṣalla-llāhu ʿalayhim wa sallam. He taught us how to live in a good way, and so he ordered us to marry and to build families within divine boundaries, not like the human created it—boundaryless.

Look at families today. Most of them are destroyed. Who did that? Those who deceive people, violate them and make use of them. Our way of unity orders us to preserve the human being from the time he is still in the uterus of his mother to when he becomes strong and is able to function in life. We respect his life all the way. We respect his feelings. We protect his existence and we never break someone's heart. It is not permissible to backbite and talk badly about others.

Allāh said to us in the Qurʾān:

> Truly, the prayer prevents from indecent and evil deeds. (Qurʾān 29:45)

True prayer is that which prevents people from doing what common sense denies and from performing ugly actions.

The one who deceives Allāh will end up being apart from Allāh. The message of unity is with us, which is the message of true taṣawwuf, the message of becoming pure. He gives great care to following the teaching that Allāh sent down through His messengers according to His natural law. People claim that, "Oh, we will become Ṣūfīs but we will not pray the same way they are praying; we will not do these practices." Our master guide Mūsā said, "Oh Allāh, with all the riches that you brought to me, I am still Your poor slave." Allāh says to people in the Qurʾān:

> But Allāh is rich, and you are poor. (Qurʾān 47:38)

Are there any rich people who will stay here for eternity? Can a rich person stay in his palace, luxurious car, yacht or airplane forever? He will not remain there. He cannot, just as much as the ant cannot remain in this world. When they go to the grave, they take nothing with them. If you do not believe me, go look at them in their graves and see what they took with them. Did they take any of their materialistic wealth with them? They stole, but they left what they stole to others. Their children were waiting for them to die so they could take all of it for themselves. So, they stole what their father stole. The Prophet said:

> You do not have any benefit from what you eat
> except that is how you defecate
> and that which you give to the poor –
> that is what will remain for you. (Ḥadīth)

What will remain for you is what you offer to the poor to build schools and hospitals to serve humanity. That is what will remain for you. But everything else...by Allāh, if you filled this whole room with gold, you would not be able to eat except that which your stomach could bear. Then you would not take this food and these clothes with you to the grave. So think carefully.

What will remain for you is your good words and your good actions, the help you provided to those who are deprived across the earth. There are billions of people who cannot find enough food or water, who are afflicted with diseases. There are women who are screaming and cannot find shelter.

I went to many countries and have seen people in Africa, Asia, Europe, and the Holy Land. I have seen children screaming, hungry and homeless. I have seen women without supporters or husbands. I have seen people with chronic diseases that have no cure. Why is this? Is it the message of Allāh for us to leave them like that?

No, people claim that we are this or that, but they murder people; they destroy their houses; they let people suffer from diseases. How do they belong to humanity? They claim that they are followers of a message, be it 'Īsā' message or Muḥammad's message – what message? They are carrying one message and one messenger, the message of Iblīs. They are his children because they deviated from the teaching of the Prophet and the Messenger, from Allāh's way.

We are carrying the message of unity, the message of Allāh that brings happiness to people. It is the message of peace and love and justice and equality for all people without discrimination. This is the Ṣūfī message, the pure message you are carrying, and that all of the prophets and messengers carried before us. This morning I talked about the reality of the human being, how to become a true human being, and I want to repeat more about this message, to emphasize it.

And I ask Allāh, glory be to Him, to open your hearts and your spirits.

May He heal all of the sick people who are suffering across the earth.
May He heal and help those who are suffering across the earth.
May He satisfy the hunger of all those across the earth.
May He achieve peace for all people, no matter where they are.

This is the way Allāh wanted for us, to live in peace and to help each other and to cooperate with one another. He wants us to be like brothers and sisters, all of us, without making separation and discrimination. May He push envy, jealousy, arrogance and conceit away from us. May He return us to our original essence of humanity. Excuse me that I spoke long but now we will start reading.

"I am Traveling to My Lord" on page 1 of *He Who Knows Himself Knows His Lord* is read from page 13 to page 14 until, "Aṭ-Ṭibb ar-Rūḥ: Know that to the people of Ṣūfism, spiritual medicine involves knowledge of the agitations by which the spiritual heart preserves health and balance, and this can be practiced only by the one who possesses the knowledge of what returns health and balance to the spiritual heart. The self, the nafs struggles..."

It is not possible for the spiritual physician to have the qualities of arrogance or love of his own individual self, the ego. It is also impossible for him to love leadership, to love to appear better than everyone else, or to love the material pleasures of the lower realm. The evil one cannot be a spiritual physician. It does not have to do with how big or how wealthy or how powerful you are.

The true spiritual physician must have a pure heart full of love and mercy and wisdom. He must have direct connection and communication with Allāh. He must be obedient, to Allāh; he must not be a thief, murderer or backbiter. He must not violate people or describe people by what they hate. He must be full of beauty. He must be really polite, courteous and have good manners. He does not fight with people. He does not curse them. He does not backbite them or talk badly about them because Allāh says:

> And when they hear vanity, they withdraw from it and say:
> "To us our deeds, and to you your deeds. peace be to you.
> We seek not the ignorant." (Qur'ān 28:55)

They do not respond in the same way. That is why the Prophet, ʿalayhi as-salātu as-salām, said:

> The best of the best has the loftiest ethics (Ḥadīth)

And Allāh described the Messenger as having the greatest, loftiest ethics.

The Prophet also said:

> You cannot contain people with your wealth or power.
> You can contain people with your love. (Ḥadīth)

This is the original way. This is the foundation that Allāh showed us through the tongues of His messengers, ṣalla-llāhu ʿalayhi wa sallam, showing us how to be happy ourselves and to make others happy. It is not as with those who claim to be Ṣūfīs but who act in a way that is not the way of the Ṣūfīs. What you say must be translated into action on this earth. We need to look at you to see how you are behaving to know if you are a Ṣūfī. Are you a polite person? Do you have good manners? Do you have courteous manners? Are you earth for all your brothers, sisters and family?

If you are a mechanic, it will appear on your uniform because you have oil stains. If you are selling oil, evidence will show that you are an oil seller. This is a simple example. Even if you have grown a beard and you have this and that, it is not worth anything in Allāh's eyes. As big as you think you are, your head is up to the belly button of Iblīs.

So who do you think you are? Do you think you can really deceive people? "I pretend that I am praying in the synagogue or a church or the mosque, but then I go and steal or spread corruption or treat people with arrogance?" What kind of prayer is this? This is the prayer of Iblīs and his followers. Allāh never commands us to do this. Allāh commands us to be merciful.

It was narrated by our master guide, the Prophet Muḥammad, ʿalayhi as-salātu as-salām, that a woman entered the Hellfire because of a cat—because she tied up and imprisoned the cat. She did not offer it food and drink and she did not let the cat search for its own food and drink, so the cat died and the woman was immediately in the Hellfire. How about those who hurt thousands of humans, destroying their houses and taking their wells and property. Are they not true murderers, rebellious against

Allāh? How about those who create discrimination against people and say, "Oh this is rich and this is poor; this is black and this is white; this is a man and this is a woman." They are in deviation of the natural law of Allāh, the law of unity. May Allāh protect you from this.

The reading continues to the top of page 15, "He must attain knowledge to an extent that allows him to treat diseases within the souls of the seekers who seek to arrive at Allāh..."

It is a must that he has knowledge of those treatments...

The reading continues, "...which are not in conformity with the secret of existence, with the spiritual spirit and the singular heart. Instead they lead to..."

Our Master Messenger, our beloved Muḥammad, said to all people and to all prophets that:

> The poor people will govern on the Day of Judgment,
> so have a place with the poor people. (Ḥadīth̲)

What does this mean? It means to offer good to poor people. Do not make separation between you and them, but share everything. They are the people who are helping the poor across the world, and they will have the upper hand on the Day of Judgment. The upper hand will not be for the rich people. We are talking about the poor saints who live in service to others. They do not own anything. They live in service to all others, including the poor and the needy. That is what "Have a place with the poor people," the saints.

The reading continues until, "...the spiritual physician is the gnostic s̲hayk̲h̲ who knows the one able to perfect, guide and lead toward spiritual maturity..."

But the one who claims he is a guide, or claims that he is a k̲halīfa, a vicegerent... The real k̲halīfa is the servant of all of the poor people. The true k̲halīfa is the one who has no trace of arrogance; he does not show any arrogance. The true guide is the one who washes the feet of the poor and has love for them and mercy for them and feels happy for their happiness and feels sad for their sadness. If someone feels sick, he feels sick, too. If he is not like that, he is not a guide, he is not a vicegerent, a kẖalīfa, and he is a liar. He must become earth to become the true guide.

This is the condition for becoming an inheritor of the Prophet, carrying the praiseworthy qualities. He is always happy to serve others. He lives with them with his breath, no matter where they are—not in this country only. No matter where he is and they are, he lives with them with his breath. If my child in Africa is in pain, I feel the pain like he does and I cry for him. I cry day and night because of what I see and hear, and I pray for him. When I see people are hungry and in pain and I see orphans and those without shelter, I cry for them; I pray for them; I help and serve them.

Allāh enabled me with the help of all of you to actually build a school for the orphans in the Holy Land. This school serves one hundred and twenty orphans, and it offers them meals and clothes as well. And we have fifteen teachers to teach them. They teach them English, Arabic and Hebrew without discrimination. We accept everyone so that the Christian, the Jew and the Muslim come to know each other, to know that there is no difference between any of us.

Allāh created us this way and our school has all types of people. I have three black people—I brought them from Africa. They are my daughters, they teach in the school there. They are all happy to serve in this way. This is true Ṣūfism, the way of purity—bringing people together as one heart, one hand, and one spirit. If you are able to do this, then you are the true guide.

Many of the beloveds here helped and offered their sacrifices, and through them I built that school. It was my duty. Allāh granted me success in doing it. Also the sacrifices that we collect went to Darfur to help those who are hungry and homeless. Many of them went to help them. Some of it also went to Uganda in Africa, and many other poor countries.

This is the way of purity, of Ṣūfism. It is not that you sit, teach and you speak. No, the true, pure way, the Ṣūfī way, is a way of action that works to serve and to preserve humanity. We are strong by Allāh, only by Allāh.

We are poor; we are always in need of Allāh. Without Allāh we cannot do anything, but with Him we become rich and we distribute His wealth to the poor. The Ṣūfī way is not as some crazy people claim.

I hope that many of you saw the pictures of the school on the internet. We posted some information on the internet, and I hope all of you will have a look at it.[21] And I ask Allāh to help me to build the second floor so it can contain many of the orphans, needy and poor, those who cannot find a father or food.

This is the true way of Ṣūfism—the way of love, the way of mercy, the way of beauty. Not by words, but by actions. Words are not enough. They must be actualized in action on the earth. This is the truth.

We do not believe in politics. We do not believe in government. We believe in Allāh, our Lord, and we treat people who are poor like we treat ourselves. They are our beloveds. This is our way and we will keep our promise to Allāh.

We gave our promise to Allāh to be servants. We promised Allāh to become servants for orphans, for widows, for those in need, for those who are sick and in hospitals. This is our message, the message of Allāh. We are carrying it and we promise to fulfill it. We are not talking about the message of words, of those who are murderers and thieves. I ask Allāh to grant you success.

Now, is time to offer a gift for you to open the way for protection, to gain protection for yourselves, for your children and to gain protection for yourselves from diseases...

Sidi gives the promise.

[21] An Arabic site with information on the school is http://www.el-quds.org.

The Human Being's Nature and Form

"O Human Being! Who Are You"

From *He Who Knows Himself Knows His Lord*

Lā ʾilāha ʾilla-llāāāāāāh, Lā ʾilāha ʾilla-llāāāāāh, Lā ʾilāha ʾilla-llāāāāāh
Muḥammad rasūlu-llāh, Ibrāhīm rasūlu-llāh, Mūsā rasūlu-llāh,
ʿĪsā rasūlu-llāh ʿalayhim ṣalātu-llāh.

Allāhumma anta-s-salām wa minka-s-salām
wa ilayka yaʻūdu-s-salām
tabārakta rabbanā
ya ḏha-l-jalāli wa-l-'ikrām

As-salāmu ʿalaykum wa raḥmatu-llāh wa bārakatuhu.

May the peace and blessing of Allāh be upon you. I praise Allāh, glory be to Him, that he made it possible for me to come here to you. He provided me with the strength to come and be with you. It is a great honor for me to be a servant to whomever loves Allāh and His Messenger, and to whomever is carrying the message of unity, which is the message of peace and love and mercy and justice. It is an honor for any person to carry this message and convey it to those who have no knowledge of it.

When people carry this message, all of them, regardless of their differences, man or woman, without making separation between black and white, rich or poor, without making any separation between oneself and what Allāh created... One should be in unity with all of the other nations and all of the creation, whether these creatures are jinn, human, animals or plants, whether they are visible or invisible, because it is all the creation of Allāh, glory be to Him. They are nations like ours.

Allāh says in the Qurʾān:

> Everything in creation knows its prayer and glorification of Allāh. (see Qurʾān 24:41)

You cannot understand their languages, but Allāh gave that special gift of understanding to some of His prophets, messengers, saints and "āwliya, the friends of Allāh. They hear and they understand what the animal is saying and what the birds are saying to Allāh. As we know, from the story of our master guide Sulayman (Solomon), ʾālayhi as-salām:

> Until when they came to the valley of the ants,
> one of the ants said: "Oh ants! Enter your dwellings,
> lest Sulayman and his hosts crush you,
> while they perceive us not." (Qurʾān 2:18)

Sulayman heard her and he smiled. That means he understood the ant's language; he knew what she said. There is also the hoopoe. He also understood and communicated with Prophet Sulayman.

When Sulayman, ʾālayhi as-salām, was looking out for those under his authority, those that he governed, some of them were animals, some were jinn, some were birds. He used to check on them every morning because he took care of them. He looked to see: was any creature hungry, any creature sad, any creature sick? He took care of them.

Allāh put him in charge of governing their affairs, but he was not a governor like the governors of today. They eat the money of people; they murder people, and they violate their rights. No, he used to visit poor people and look at all the animals and birds, and look at what this animal needed; he looked at what that bird needed, what that fish needed, what that tree and plant needed. If he saw some thirsty trees he would say, "Oh these trees are thirsty; let me give them some water," and he would water them. He looked after women and children and saw to their needs.

This is an example for the governors today to see how to be, how to govern, because Sulayman was a godly man. The prophets were godly men; they were the heirs of the praiseworthy qualities. They felt the pain of humanity and they felt happy when they saw people happy.

Story of Sulayman and the Hoopoe

When Sulayman was checking on the birds one day, he did not see the hoopoe. He said, "Where is the hoopoe? Is he absent? Why is he not here in his place? (Qurʾān 27:20)" He wanted to hear from him. The hoopoe was the king of the birds. So he said, "How come the king of the birds has left the rest of the birds? He is responsible for them."

So he was wondering why the hoopoe was absent from his duty of taking care of the other birds. He said, "When I see him come back, I will question him. I will take him into accountability about why he left those birds who are under his authority. (Qur'ān 27:21)" It is not like those governors who leave people to get hungry and to suffer, who violate people's rights and steal from them. They do not ask the people under their authority, "What did you do to fulfill your responsibility?"

So the hoopoe came and Sulayman asked him, putting him on trial, "Where were you? Why were you absent from your duty?" Look at the teachings and divine instructions, because Sulayman did not just take it as something of no importance. No, Allāh put him in a position of responsibility to look after the creation, so he had to question the hoopoe.

So the hoopoe was brave. Look at how brave he was. He answered him, because he was the king of the birds. He was a king. He said, "In my travels, I found a lady, a lady who governs people (Bilqīs). She has a great throne and authority and she has been given a lot of riches (Qur'ān 27:23), but she and her nation are prostrating to the sun instead of to Allāh the Creator. They do not worship Allāh the Creator. (Qur'ān 27:24)"

So Sulayman said, "We will see if you really brought accurate news. (Qur'ān 27:27)" He has to verify it for himself. He just does not listen. He has to verify to see the truth of the news he is hearing. Sulayman used to judge all the jinn and creatures because he was responsible for their affairs. So he asked all the creatures, "Who will bring her throne right now in front of me before they come in submission and surrender in front of me, the representative of God? (Qur'ān 27:38)"

This is how he judges people, he wants to verify the news he hears to see if the governor is a murderer or a thief, so he wanted to question that queen and verify what the hoopoe said. So a very strong and mighty jinn said, "I can bring her throne to you before you stand up, I can bring the throne to you here. (Qur'ān 27:39)"

This was something very powerful but Sulayman was not satisfied. So another jinn, a faithful and believing jinn said, "I will bring her throne to you in the twinkle of an eye," and he brought the throne before Sulayman within the twinkle of an eye (Qur'ān 27:40). This was faster than the rockets and spaceships that are talked about now. It was faster than airplanes and all of that. That happened four thousand years ago.

A throne, can you imagine? The great throne of a queen is bigger than this building by ten times. He brought it exactly as it was without anything falling. He carried it within a twinkle of an eye and brought it immediately to the man. Do you know the distance that he carried it within the twinkle of an eye? It was six thousand miles within the twinkle of an eye. This is the glory of Allāh, Who can allow a creature to do such a thing. Do not think it is impossible. Do you not see with your naked eyes, how, within the twinkle of an eye...?

Two years ago you saw something, you saw the tsunami in Asia – it happened in twelve seconds. Allāh moved the water. He ordered an angel to move the water and it happened within the twinkle of an eye. What happened was very grave for humanity. What happened a year ago in South Mexico? It took only five seconds. What could people do to stop it from happening? Nothing, they could do nothing. Do you not see many other things happening? If Allāh wants something to be, He says to it, "Be," and it is. Volcanoes that emerge from the bottom of the ocean...it can happen in a second.

When the throne with the queen on top of it, and also her helpers and ministers were brought to Sulayman, they supported and defended her, but they prostrate to the sun instead of to Allāh. They were all brought within the twinkle of an eye. But before he did that powerful action, Sulayman sent her a message. (Qur'ān 27:28)

It is not the habit of a prophet to deal with people first. No, first they send a messenger. He sent her a message which started with, "In the name of Allāh, the Universally Merciful, the Singularly Compassionate, this is from Sulayman. (Qur'ān 27:30)" He did not say it was from the prime minister or the king or from the president of such and such. No, he just said, "This is from Sulayman the poor slave servant of Allāh to you."

He said, "I heard that you and your nation are prostrating to the sun, worshiping the sun. How is it that you do so when there is a Creator beyond that, Who created everything?" If you do not have faith and believe that there is a Creator, Allāh, then I am warning you. You must contemplate the matter more deeply. I am giving you some time to contemplate this matter. If you are convinced that there is a Creator and you are His creation, and you acknowledge that you are His worshipper, you should worship Him alone."

When they refused, they were brought within the twinkle of an eye, she and her throne and her helpers around her.

This is to know that Sulayman was the messenger of Allāh, not a king. He was a servant and a slave of Allāh and he brought her to know that. These are divine images, examples that were given from Allāh through His messengers to show people His power. These examples are not brought to an end, but are still going on, because Allāh says:

> We will show them Our Signs in the universe,
> and in their own selves,
> until it becomes manifest to them that He is the Truth.
> (Qur᾽ān 41:53)

He is saying, "We will show them Our signs in the horizons around them and within themselves so that they may come to understand, comprehend and intellectualize the message."

From this story, we will enter now a state where we try to understand the human being's nature. We say, "How were you created, oh human? How did you come here? Who are you? Are you just a physical human being?" No, you are something different. Allāh, glory be to Him, said in His speech to the angels before the creation of the human:

> I will be creating a human being out of mud.
> When I finish forming him and fashioning him and breathe into him out of My spirit, prostrate yourselves to him.
> (Qur᾽ān 38:71)

The angels, all of them, prostrated to the human being.

> And (remember) when your Lord said to the angels:
> "Truly, I am going to place on earth generation after generation (of humans)."
> They said: "Will You put there those who will make mischief and shed blood, while we glorify You with praises and thanks and sanctify You?"
> He said: "I know that which you do not know."(Qur᾽ān 2:30)

He ordered them:

> I have fashioned him completely
> and breathed into him from My spirit

> then fall down prostrating yourselves unto him.
> (Qur'ān 15:29, 38:72)

In reality, they did not prostrate to the rude human. No, they did not prostrate to that one. To the murderer, the cruel one, or to the one who spread corruption on earth? No, they did not prostrate to those. Allāh, glory be to Him, sent down two books at the same time. He sent an animal human and a godly human in the same form. So that human is carrying two aspects or two images – one is the animal aspect or image and the other is the godly image, a godly human. Allāh says:

> I created Ādam in My image. He is My mirror. (Ḥadīth Qudsī)

This divine image carries all of the qualities of Allāh because he carries a luminous, godly light. A human in His reality is a divine mirror, because Allāh wants to see His reflection, His image in that mirror. This human, godly image is the reflection of Allāh in which He sees His own Self. So the angels prostrated to Ādam, not to the animal Ādam, but to the godly human in whom Allāh put all of His names and qualities. Allāh says in the Qur'ān:

> He taught Ādam the Names – all of them. (Qur'ān 2:31)

This means that He gave Ādam all the divine qualities, which are ninety-nine in number. Some of them are ar-Raḥmān (Universally Merciful), ar-Raḥīm (the Singularly Compassionate), al-Quddūs (the Holy), and they are all full of light. They are luminous. Angels prostrated to these names, not to the animal form. Allāh put them in the lofty station of the human being. He put His name, Allāh, in the loftiest aspect of the human being.

Look at her [Sidi is looking at his hand]. What do you see {He is forming the "Hand of Allāh" with his hand, as seen below]. You see Allāh's name. This shape forms the name Allāh in the Arabic language. Do you see it? Do you understand?

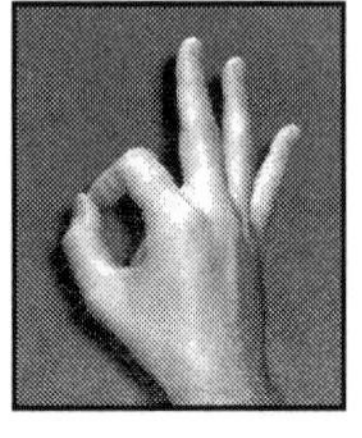

It is the name of Allāh. Imagine how the glorious name of Allāh is within you. He also put the quality of hearing and the quality of seeing and before all of that, He put inside you, "the living" (al-Ḥayy). All of these divine qualities, Allāh put within the human being.

So the angels' prostration was not to the animal form, but to the godly qualities which are within the human. Allāh said to the angels, "Prostrate yourselves to Ādam, so all the angels prostrated. He never told them, "Stand up from your prostration." They are still prostrating now.

But again, the prostration is not to the human animal. It is to the godly human who is carrying and representing all of the godly qualities and ethics. Not to the human who murders, who commits adultery and cheats and kills and spreads corruption across the earth. Allāh wants us to be holy. You are holy. You are as Allāh said, He said:

> I was a hidden treasure and I wanted to be known
> so I created people. By Me they knew Me. (Ḥadīth Qudsī)

How do you know Allāh? It is through the qualities He gave you. If you know these qualities, you will never diminish; you will never annihilate. There is the body that goes back to the earth, but there is also a Reality that will never cease to exist.

So by this you only transform from one realm to another realm, another dimension, because Allāh never goes away. So this human body transforms from one form to another. Go back to one thousand years ago and look. How many people has Allāh created since then? Billions of people, but where are they? They were created out of dust and they went back to dust.

We are talking about the bodies, but the godly human being continued to live, he never died. Because Allāh said that He breathed into him out of His own spirit (Qur'ān 15:29, 38:72), so how can he die? It is impossible for the spirit of Allāh to vanish from existence; it is impossible.

If we want to live a peaceful life, a fulfilled life, a loving life, a merciful life, a life full of justice and spirit, then let us carry the message of Allāh, the message of unity, the message of oneness. Because all people and the whole creation were created from the spirit of Allāh, from one spirit. This is why Allāh said in the Qur'ān:

> If anyone kills a person, or spreads mischief in the land
> it would be as if he killed all humankind,
> and if anyone saves a life, it would be as if
> he saved the life of all humankind. (Qur'ān 5:32)

This is the reality. It is the reality of the human being in a simple explanation. If you continue to live in your animal human physical life, which is full of dirt and pollution and misery... You have to get rid of that. You have to live in the godly human being.

What is the difference between a human who passed away three days ago and the corpse of a donkey? What is the difference between the two? Both bodies stink the same way. The human can even stink worse than what he did during his life. Look at the corpse of a president or a king and the corpse of the poorest man. Is there any difference? There is no difference. Even if he is king of the most powerful nation, can people keep his corpse in their house for three days? They will not be able to; it will stink.

It is as if a donkey were killed in front of your house. Can you just leave it? No, you must move it and bury it. So, tell me, what is the difference between the two bodies – the human animal body and the donkey body?

If we look at the essence in the essence of the human being who continued his whole life to represent and abide by the commands of Allāh, full of love, full of mercy and justice for all, carrying the lofty noble ethics of Allāh. That one, if you smell his corpse, will smell better than musk and better than all of the perfumes.

When the pious and the righteous people are put in their graves you will smell the musk of the grave, because their grave will be like a meadow in the Garden, full of flowers and full of beauty. But those who kept abiding and preserving the noble and lofty divine ethics and kept on believing in the unity of Allāh without associating any partner with Him, will have graves like the meadow in a garden, because that is what the Prophet said. He said:

> Their graves will be like either a meadow in the Garden or a
> hole in the Hellfire. (Ḥadīth̲)

The way of the messengers and the prophets was to never burn the corpse of a human who has passed away. Since the time of Ādam,

Ibrāhīm (Abraham), Mūsā (Moses), ʿĪsā (Jesus), and Muḥammad, ṣalla-llāhu ʿalayhim wa sallam, the bodies of those who have passed away have never been burned. Whoever did that or was part of that knew that the person who was burned will continue to suffer, and also the one who did it will continue to suffer, because the human body is holy.

We should never burn it. We should return it to its natural place. Know that the human, the real essence of the human, transforms to another realm, and in that realm those who believed in unity and had divine ethics will never suffer from anything they used to suffer from in this lower realm we are living in. They will transform to a world that is better.

You must preserve the human form that Allāh gave you. You should not violate its rights, because Allāh created it holy. Why do you violate it? Why do you kill another human? To kill a human is like killing the whole of humanity. We must respect the human body and the human form, and we must preserve its purity and the ethics; preserve the loftiest ethics.

Allāh said that He sent down two books—the visible book, which you are looking at with your own eyes, and the hidden book. The hidden book is known to the godly human. He reads it day and night, because it was sent down from the preserved tablet. Who can read this hidden, inner book? The godly human being who is following the message of Allāh.

Allāh said He sent that hidden, inner book, part by part, to Ādam, Ibrāhīm, Mūsā, Nūh (Noah), Isḥāq (Issac), ʿĪsā, and finally to Muḥammad, ṣalla-llāhu ʿalayhim wa sallam. The hidden book is the collective of all of these books. Allāh said in the Qurʾān:

> Indeed, there has come to you from Allāh a light and a clear book. (Qurʾān 5:15)

Allāh says this in the Qurʾān. He sent a luminous book; it is what is between the lines. What is visible is what you can see with your own eyes. That is what is apparent. But there are other eyes you can look with, the heart's eyes, and there are the heavenly eyes, the divine, godly eyes. You also see the earth. You walk and you see the animal kingdom do you not? And you look at the sky and you see the heavenly realm, the sky, the stars and creatures. Allāh created a thousand more realms than what you see and what you know.

To Allāh belongs many worlds. There are many suns, more than the one we can see, but those are all like a drop in the ocean of Allāh's creation. Some people try to ascend into space and go to other planets, Mercury, the moon or this or that. They imagine it as if they are traveling from one country to another, and they think, "Let us see if there is life there," They go and it seems like another land. And they saw only what? They saw a few things around the earth, a tiny thing. But there is a huge creation, something the animal human cannot see with his physical eyes.

Look at the oceans. The oceans are so great that the land is only a quarter in proportion to the water on earth, and the depth of the oceans can reach to one thousand miles or more. It has marvelous creatures and creatures that humans have no knowledge of. But all of that is like a tiny drop of the other worlds. And what is perplexing is that all of the kings and presidents and governors fight about his tiny thing, the earth. Moreover, they will not stay on it, they will pass away, but they are still fighting over this tiny thing.

They are not eternal here; they are travelers. They will travel. They will pass away, leaving their palaces, their weapons, and their rockets. They will leave everything. All of it will vanish. Is this not the truth? Is this not the reality?

We are just explaining a little bit about the world's formation and giving a little hint about the other realms. Excuse me for not talking more about that; I just wanted to give you a hint so that you may understand that the physical realm is just a drop, in reality. This is the truth, it is the reality, and we cannot deny it. If a person denies this, let him show us he can be eternal. If he has knowledge about this, then he can be eternal here and possess the earth. Let him say it to us. How could he do that? Let him show us that his ancestor, his father, his grandfather is still alive and possessing the earth.

Is there anyone who can claim to stay here for eternity and possess the earth? Is there anyone who dies and can bring himself back to life? I am very certain that he cannot even revive a dead ant, or he is really disabled. But those crazy people still think they can possess the earth. The mentally ill are better off than they are. This is why we must fully surrender to the fact that Allāh is One and follow His laws, His commands, and unify with Him. We have to look with the eyes of unity, and only through that do we see that people are one, equal and the same, and that they are the children of Allāh. Allāh and the Prophet, ṣalla-llāhu ʿalayhi wa sallam, said:

> All people are the children of Allāh.
> The one who is most beloved of Allāh
> is the one who is most beneficial to others. (Ḥadīth̲)

This is the teaching of all the prophets, ṣalla-llāhu ʿalayhim wa sallam. Let me give you just a little example of politeness, the manners of our Master Prophet, ṣalla-llāhu ʿalayhi wa sallam. Let us look at the courteous and good manners of those messengers.

I will give you an example. I give it first to men, whom Allāh willed to become men in this world. This is a picture, a picture and no more. But in the world of Allāh, he created only one: a human being. When he created the first human He said, "Ādam," which means, "from the mud of the earth." He did not say, "I am creating a man." He did not say that. He said, "I am creating a human being." A pure, clean, human being who is without faults in his initial creation.

Back to our example. The human, whether man or woman, came from parents, It is only a picture, an image they took of a woman or a man. But Allāh wants to represent His image in all of His creation, so He created the form of woman and the form of man. He and the Prophet, ṣalla-llāhu ʿalayhi wa sallam, said:

> All people are the children of Allāh.
> The one who is most beloved of Allāh
> is the one who is most beneficial to others. (Ḥadīth̲)

He means those who are the most loving to others, those who carry justice, peace, piety and mercy to all people.

In Allāh's world there is no discrimination, no separation, There are no differences. He created everything in the best way. Our most beloved Prophet, ṣalla-llāhu ʿalayhi wa sallam, whenever he visited his wives and his daughters was polite and would ask permission before entering the house. Not only did he have this polite way of being with his wives, but all of the other messengers would ask permission to enter the places where their wives were. And when they were given permission and entered they would say, "Peace be upon you beloved one, sweetheart."

This is how they talked. These are the good, courteous manners that men should use. Women should use the same courteous manners.

It is not permitted for anyone to break another's heart. A man should never break the heart of his wife, daughter, sister or mother. The woman, too, must never break the heart of her brother, beloved, father or son, because Allāh is Love. Allāh is Love and He wants in life nothing but love, to see love between people and to see people peaceful and happy. This is something brief of the meaning of the formation of the human form. This is just a simple hint. Now I will speak with your language so that you may be able to understand more.

"O Human Being! Who Are You" on page 135 of *He Who Knows Himself Knows His Lord* is read from the beginning until, "We have no knowledge other than what You have taught us. Truly You are the All-Knowing, the All-Wise. So He said, "Oh Ādam, tell them their names..."

After Allāh taught Ādam He said, "Tell the angels the names," because Ādam was a godly human being. He was not the animal human. He was the pure mirror, the divine mirror, and he was from the Light of Allāh.

The reading continues until the middle of page 137, "By existence of the insān al-kāmil, the purpose of the accidental cosmos was actualized by Allāh. If the accidental cosmos manifests upon the image of the pre-eternal existence..."

There is a difference between walking, tasting and witnessing. There is a big difference. A lot of people claim, "I see," but they are not really seeing and witnessing and tasting. Do you not hear the sound of the donkey? It does not mean that he understands. The sound of the donkey tells you he is a donkey. You know how to distinguish it. We will be able to distinguish the human who talks like that, too, because he says, "I am so and so, I am, I am."

Many people shout. They shout across the world. They shout and they make speeches. But there is a difference between the one who talks gently, full of love and peace and politeness and divine ethics, and the one who shouts and yells and says, "I am." Allāh says that these people are like animals; they are even more confused than animals. It is not permissible for any human to claim in his reality that he is what he is not.

Understand that in reality, you are nothing. If you are looking from the human, animal form, you are nothing. But when you look with the divine eye, the godly eye, we are talking about something else. There is nothing loftier than you are or more beautiful than you are or more pure than you are. All the divine pictures exist within you. Do you think of yourself as a small star? Within you the whole universe is contained. Allāh says that:

> My heavens and My earth could not contain Me,
> but the heart of My faithful believer,
> My beloved has been containing Me. (Ḥadīth Qudsī)

We are talking about those whose hearts are full of Allāh. They talk by Allāh; they hear by Allāh; they see by Allāh; they walk by Allāh. They do everything for the sake of Allāh. Allāh says:

> When I love him I am
> his hearing with which he hears,
> his seeing with which he sees,
> his hand with which he strikes and
> his foot with which he walks.
>
> Were he to ask (something) of Me,
> I would surely give it to him,
> and were he to ask Me for refuge,
> I would surely grant him it.
> [If he says, "Be," then it is.] (Ḥadīth Qudsī)

But that human would never say he did this, because Allāh is the Doer through him. He would not say, "I am, I am." He does not know the pictures. The one who says, "I saw Allāh," or, "I heard Allāh," is not actually one who sees or hears Allāh. When does he see Allāh and hear Allāh? When he represents His ethics.

When he adorns himself with the lofty ethics of Allāh and becomes obedient to Allāh, following His natural law and abiding by His commands. So the one who claims "Oh Allāh told me that, showed me that. I heard that. I heard Allāh say that," and is not praying, giving charity, fasting or doing any spiritual practice, or deceives people and whose hand commits murder and theft and who is impolite with people is a liar.

Allāh said on the tongue of our most beloved Prophet, ṣalla-llāhu ʿalayhi wa sallam:

> Whenever a group of people gather to remember Him and contemplate Him, Allāh will mention them to His high assembly of angels and spirits. (Ḥadīth Qudsī)

Angels come and visit these particular people so, right now, angels are here. I see them with my eyes and I feel their presence with my very being, because we are here to remember Allāh, to pray for guidance and to contemplate Allāh. What gathered you here? It is your love for knowledge, to know God, to know Allāh. So you are in worship already and that is why angels come all the time. They have been coming, surrounding you. There are not only two or one hundred, there are a thousand, and they see your light and they pray for you.

The one who is faithful in his worship will see; he will see Allāh's Light through the angels, because the angels are made of Allāh's Light. Allāh says, "Here I am, My servant. What do you want?" When he becomes a godly worshiper, he says to something, "Be," and it becomes.

In a holy conversation that the Prophet had with his Lord, he said that some man could be very poor, have ragged old clothes and be very poor, walking on the street and when he meets people, they do not even look at him. Or this could also be a woman, we are not talking about men only, like Rābiʿa al-Adawiyya. She was poor. She lived in a poor state and when she would ask Allāh, "Oh Allāh..." then it happened. Whatever she asked for, it happened. Because such a servant and slave of Allāh is annihilated in his worship of Allāh, and he becomes a godly human being, a godly representative. He is not an animal monster; he is not an animal human.

An animal human is worse than an animal. Animals are better than he is and are loftier in their behavior than he is. This is the truth. This is the reality. I seek refuge in Allāh for you, and I pray for Him to preserve you in the way that He wants you to be.

The reading continues, "This presence cannot be fully actualized in any of His creation except in that reflective image which is none but the perfect man and this is why he is named the perfect human...subjugated to him and that includes the human animal."

Too many claim this. They say, "I am so, I know so, I am, I am." Do not look at these people. Do not pay attention. Look at their essence, their states, their behavior. How are they? How do they deal with people? Are they really poor to Allāh? The one who is poor in spirit is a servant for all the creation. He never says, "I, I," and he does not show signs of anger, because his ethics are godly ethics.

The one who claims so, even if he has a long beard and he looks pious in his outer appearance, may not be such. Do you know Iblīs? He has his beard up to here. But this is not a sign, because Allāh does not look at your pictures and your wealth. He looks at your actions, at your heart, at your hands. The godly slave and servant of Allāh is a servant of the people. The guide is a servant and he washes the feet of his pupils. That is the true spiritual guide. All the prophets and messengers were like this – servants. Throw your shoes at the one who makes claims and is not this. Do not be shy to do so because Iblīs is even loftier than he is in his state. This is reality; this is the truth.

He must be a slave and a servant for the poor, for all people without discrimination. He must be a servant for all without discrimination, without making separation between black and white, rich and poor. He must treat everyone the same. Why? Because he sees Allāh's reflection in them, Allāh's image. So his realm is a realm of beauty. He sees only beauty. He knows only beauty.

Our master guide, ʿĪsā, ʿĪsā, may the peace and blessing of Allāh be upon him, was full of peace and love. He is the king of peace and love and beauty. That is his name, the king of peace and love and beauty, to the people who have knowledge of Allāh. This is true knowledge, the king of peace and love and mercy. People know him by the name ʿĪsā but he is known to us as the king of peace, mercy, beauty and love. His message will come and it will be fulfilled on the earth. I am carrying it, thanks be to Allāh, and it will be fulfilled on earth.

We get consumed in Allāh, get annihilated in Allāh, more than those who claim they are the followers of ʿĪsā. We love him fully and he is never absent from us. He is always with us; his spirit is with us. He always orders us to spread peace, love, mercy and beauty, because he is the king of this message. And that is why we say we are the people of unity, carrying the message of unity. Our Master Prophet Muḥammad also came with this message. He represented it and actualized it on earth. Allāh said about Prophet Muḥammad in the Qur'ān:

> We have not sent you but as a mercy for all the worlds.
> (Qur'ān 21:107)

He did not say, "We have sent you to be a murderer or a destroyer." So, whoever claims to be a Muslim but murders people, steals and violates people's rights, is not truly a Muslim. He is not a follower of Muḥammad. The one who claims to be a Christian and does these things is not a follower of ʿĪsā, ʾālayhi as-salām.

The one who carries the message of peace and mercy is the follower of ʿĪsā and Muḥammad, ṣalla-llāhu ʿalayhim wa sallam. I kiss the feet of these people and I wash their feet because I am a servant, just as ʿĪsā and Muḥammad were, ʿalayhim as-salātu as-salām.

Story of ʿĪsā and the Dead Donkey with Beautiful Teeth

Our master guide ʿĪsā used to walk in Jerusalem, where I live, actually at a place very close to my house. This is where he used to walk. One day he was walking with some of his disciples and he saw a dead donkey, the corpse of a donkey that was inflated with time. Look what Messiah ʿĪsā said, because he is the master of love and beauty. What happens after a donkey dies? After three days he is inflated, he stinks, and all of that. Is this not the truth? So ʿĪsā said, "What do you think of this corpse?" When he looked at the dead donkey, he said, "Look at the beloved, at the lover."

Look what he said. He first asked people, "What do you think of this donkey?" When people looked at it, they were like, "Ooh, it stinks," and they did not want to look at it. They avoided it. But he looked at it and he said to his disciples, "What do you think of this? Is it not beautiful?" That is what he said. He said, "This is beautiful." What is beautiful in that? Do you know? Imagine what he is saying. He is saying this is something beautiful while he is looking at the donkey corpse.

The disciples said, "This is the worst thing we have seen," but ʿĪsā, ʾālayhi as-salām, smiled and because he is looking with Allāh's eyes said to them, "Look at his beautiful teeth." He could see only beauty.

The human can be the worst of the worst, but the godly human is full of peace, he sees only beauty in everything because his eyes can see only his Beloved. He said to his disciples, "Who created that donkey? Who can create something as beautiful as this?" He did not stop with the picture. He went beyond with the One Who Created the picture. He went beyond, with the One Who Fashioned the picture and looked with His eyes, with Allāh's eyes that are full of mercy and love. He did not belittle the donkey. He did not look at it as something insignificant. He looked at it as something beautiful, a creation of Allāh.

This is something we see and we follow. We are the followers of the message of unity and love, the followers of ʿĪsā. We are not of the ones who talk and say, "Oh we are followers of ʿĪsā," and then do corrupt deeds. They claim that they are kings and they help people, they rescue them, they do this and that, but they are liars. And their actions show they are liars. They murder people; they destroy. Those who do not look with the eyes of Allāh and adorn themselves with His ethics are just liars.

But the matter will end as Allāh wanted it to. His message has been fulfilled, the message that was brought by His lovers, Mūsā, Ibrāhīm, Muḥammad and ʿĪsā, ṣalla-llāhu ʿalayhim wa sallam. It will happen soon and I am certain that you will be the ones who are carrying it, fulfilling it. I ask Allāh to protect your hearing, your seeing, and your hearts, and to protect you and your children and loved ones and your houses. Āmīn.

I think our time is over, but there is no end to time. The metaphorical time has come to an end now, but the true time belongs to Allāh; there is no end to time. Now I would like to open the door to you to give a promise.

Sidi gives the promise.

Pope Valley Sufi School West

Allāh wants you to use all of this in your original, pure state.
You are glorious.
You think of yourself as a tiny microcosm
while within you is the magnificent macrocosm.
You have all the qualities of creation, from the beginning to the end.

~~~~~~~~

If you know your own reality you will know the reality of Allāh.
Allāh will make you see yourself as an essence,
and that you are not established but by Allāh.
You are not seeing, acting or hearing but by Allāh.

Then
your walking becomes worship,
your sleep, worship
your standing, worship
your sitting, worship
your eating, worship.
Allāh will never be absent from you, even for just the twinkle of an eye.

From "Realities of Being Human"
~~~~~~~~

Special Tawba
"The Commanding Nafs"
from *He Who Knows Himself Knows His Lord*

Lā ʾilāha ʾilla-llāāāāāāh, Lā ʾilāha ʾilla-llāāāāāh, Lā ʾilāha ʾilla-llāāāāāh
Muḥammad rasūlu-llāh, Ibrāhīm rasūlu-llāh, Mūsā rasūlu-llāh,
ʿĪsā rasūlu-llāh ʿalayhim ṣalātu-llāh.

Allāhumma anta-s-salām wa minka-s-salām
wa ilayka ya'ūdu-s-salām
tabārakta rabbanā
ya dha-l-jalāli wa-l-'ikrām

As-salāmu ʿalaykum wa raḥmatu-llāh wa bārakatuhu.

I praise Allāh, glory be to Him that He made us living so that we can survive the blessed month of Ramaḍan and get the blessing of it. This is the month of the holy Prophet, ṣalla-llāhu ʿalayhi wa sallam. It is a great month for those who are pious and righteous—for the gnostics who have direct knowledge of Allāh.

It is a month of fasting and a month of staying up all night for Allāh, and it is a month of prayer. It is a month of seeking forgiveness; it is a month of remembrance; it is the month of prostrating to Allāh; it is the month of humbling ourselves to Him and staying all night and worshiping Him; it is the month of forgiveness; it is the month of mercy; it is the month of saving us from the Hellfire.

It is good news and glad tidings for those who are present now and who are observing and experiencing it – especially for those who are fasting the month, if they are able to do so. But if the person is sick, and cannot fast at all, then it is okay, but for every day he breaks his fast, every day that he is not fasting, he must feed a poor person two meals a day. The two meals are worth approximately $30.00, and anyone fasting eats two meals – the meal that breaks the fast and suhūr, the meal before dawn.

Fasting for us, the people of Allāh, is divided into three categories. There is the fasting of the common people – what is that? You do not eat and drink and sleep with your wife during that month in the morning. It is forbidden because your whole direction should be toward Allāh. Do you know that even animals fast? Animals fast. They do not eat or drink at certain periods and they do not sleep, either. This is the fasting of the common people.

There is another category of fasting—the fasting of the pious, the righteous people. In this category the limbs fast. How do the limbs fast? It means that the person's tongue will never backbite or speak hateful or envious words. He never does this because he knows that he will be brought to reckoning, and that there are two watchers over him observing what his tongue says. When you fast, you must never backbite or speak badly about others, or hurt another's feelings. You must never injure a heart with your words.

Your hearing should also fast. It is not permissible to spy and try to listen to what you should not be listening to. Also, your eyes must fast. You must never look at that which is not permissible for you to look at. It is not permissible. It is not permissible, no matter what the case. If your eyes look at what is not permissible you become an adulterer—your eyes commit adultery. Also, you should not be spying, looking at what that person is doing. No, you should not be spying with your eyes.

There is also the fasting of the self, the nafs, which means: if you find something good with your brother or sister, do not envy them. You do not envy and feel jealous of them. You do not act arrogantly with your brother. This is the fasting of the limbs. It is in addition to abstaining from food and drink; you are abstaining from all of these actions.

This is the fasting of the righteous people, of the pious people. If they do something against this and get involved in these types of actions [the wrong types described in the previous paragraphs], then their fasting is null, corrupted.

Whoever wants to sit here must open his eyes and his heart - he must not close his eyes.

There is also the fasting of the abrār, those who excel in good—which means to fast from everything except Allāh; to abstain from everything except Allāh. This is the fasting of the ones brought to divine proximity, al-muqqarabin, the ones who excel in good, and Allāh is not absent from them for even the twinkle of an eye. Whenever [the one who excels in good] goes anywhere he says, "Allāh is watching me, He is hearing me,

He is seeing me." Whenever he stands up he says, "Allāh is moving me, Allāh is watching me, He is seeing me, He is hearing me." He does not stand but by Allāh's command. He does not move or go anywhere except by Allāh's command. That does not mean that Allāh is incarnate in him, no. But it means that his direction is fully toward Allāh. He is devoted to Allāh. He does not ask [anyone] but Allāh. He does not pray but to Allāh. This is because Allāh says:

> And when My slaves ask you concerning Me,
> then [answer them], I am indeed near.
> I respond to prayers when they call upon Me. (Qur'ān 2:186)

For this reason do not go to anyone, a s̲hayk̲h̲ or a guru or whoever, to ask them things. Ask Allāh directly, because He is not far away. He is closer to you than your jugular vein (Qur'ān 50:16), so why are you going to anyone else? If you have a special father, a guide, a s̲hayk̲h̲, you can ask him to pray for you, but it does not mean that you do not ask Allāh and that you depend upon the other person to pray for you. No, you can have both. You just ask the person to pray for you. This is not ḥarām, it is not forbidden.

But do not think that the s̲hayk̲h̲ can ask on your behalf and you can go and forget about Allāh. No, because the s̲hayk̲h̲ is just like you. He is a human being like you. He is not more or less than you, but his connection to Allāh might be a little bit closer, or stronger, and he might have a deeper understanding than you, so he prays for you.

And when you ask him (the s̲hayk̲h̲), "Pray for me," he will. He prays for you and that is okay – that is acceptable. But you must also ask Allāh directly and believe that Allāh will respond to you and accept your prayer. He will answer your supplications because He is the one who created you. Why would He abandon you? He cannot abandon His slaves. Because He is your Creator He will never abandon you.

Your spiritual father has a decree or a place with Allāh because the Prophet, ʿalayhi as-salātu as-salām, says:

> There are special people, places and times for Allāh.
> (Ḥadīt̲h̲)

What are they? The month of Ramaḍan is a special time for Allāh. It is a blessed time. The messengers and the prophets and the righteous are not like other people; they are special people. Some places are special for Allāh because they are holy places, or holier than other places, like the Masjid al-Aqṣā or the masjid where the Prophet, ʿalayhi as-salātu as-salām, is buried, or all places of worship. These are blessed places. They are special places because they are distinguished by the remembrance of Allāh.

There is a difference between a place that is full of garbage and a place in which prayer is established and performed, where the remembrance of Allāh is always happening. People prepare these places to worship Allāh and to remember Him, so these are special prayers. Allāh says that He accepts supplications and worship done in these special, blessed places more than in other places.

There are also special people, like the Prophet Ibrāhīm, may the peace of Allāh be upon him, and the Prophet ʿĪsā (Jesus) They are also special to Allāh because Allāh sent them as messengers, carrying His own message. Prophet Muḥammad, ʿalayhi as-salātu as-salām, and Prophet Mūsā, ʿalayhi as-salām—are special to Allāh.

Those who follow them and take them as role models and follow their ways are also special and blessed. Also, the ʾāwliya, the friends of Allāh or the loyal allies of Allāh, the close ones to Allāh, the ones who inherited praiseworthy qualities who are carrying the reality and who are carrying the truth are also special because they know the reality of things from Allāh. Allāh says in the Qurʾān:

> He has taught you what you did not know [before].
> (Qurʾān 2:239)

And His favor upon you is great. Those who are carrying the message of Allāh are special. They are not equal to the ones who do not have anything to carry to people. They are special people. Allāh gives them this special goodness, this special gift. This is why sitting with them is good. Talking with them is good because they have understanding of the message of Allāh and they are carrying it. Allāh asked us to sit with those people and to take from them their teaching and their advice. Allāh says in the Qurʾān:

> Truly, the ʾāwliya, no fear will come upon them
> nor will they grieve (Qurʾān 10:62)

The Prophet, ʿalayhi as-salātu as-salām, said there are two poison thorns:

1. First, do not talk badly about the saints (ʾāwliya). Do not backbite them, and do not hurt them. They are the saints of Allāh, the friends of Allāh.
2. Also, do not do this to the people of the household of the Prophet, ṣalla-llāhu ʿalayhi wa sallam.

These are the two poison thorns, which means that if you carry enmity for them, or try to hurt them, you will be hurt. Those who do will be afflicted with great affliction if they have enmity toward them. Many tried to hurt them—even governors and rulers. They tried to get me or hurt me, but they could not. Some of them were killed or died or got hurt in the course of trying to hurt me. I am just a poor person, a poor person and no more.

But I cannot but speak the truth. In the face of any oppressor or tyrant I have spoken the truth, and they tried to hurt me and harm me but they could not. I am here and I am moving freely, and they cannot hurt me. It is a favor from Allāh, it is not from myself. I am nothing. I am just a poor slave of Allāh and He is the One Who Protects me.

This is why I tell you my children, my beloveds, that this Ramaḍan is a blessed Ramaḍan. It is the Ramaḍan of pure goodness, and it is the Ramaḍan of forgiveness, mercy and being saved from the Hellfire. In Ramaḍan no supplication is turned back. Everything asked is answered. Allāh accepts our prayers and responds to our supplications and invocations, and He is the Healer and the One Who Gives us well being. But we must come to Allāh with our whole heart—our whole and full heart.

We should never let s̲hayṭān live in our hearts or enter our hearts. We should never let the lower desires enter our hearts. The one whose heart is still full of the lower realm, full of love of it and its lower pleasures, is full of sins. And I say to him, to whoever has committed this sin, do not stop seeking forgiveness. Keep asking for forgiveness.

If anyone commits a sin, and in Ramaḍan sits in regret, feels sorrow that he did it, asks for forgiveness and comes wholeheartedly to Allāh with his own soul and spirit, Allāh will look at him.

But you must fast for the sake of Allāh. Before you seek the reconciliation and the forgiveness of Allāh, you must repent from that sin. Before you ask anything from Allāh, you must seek repentance. You must renew your repentance first. It does not matter how great you are. Do not keep saying, “I am so good now, I am great.” No, do not say that. Say, “I am a poor slave of Allāh,” and humble yourself to His majesty, because you are between His hands and He is the One Who is In Control of your affairs.

You must know that Allāh, glory be to Him, accepts repentance and He is the Forgiver, but He also is Severe in Punishment. He said in His Holy Book to us:

> The one who comes with repentance and a full heart,
> I will transform their bad deeds into good deeds
> and rectify their deeds and his affairs. (Qur’ān 5:39)

This is something important no matter how old you are or whether you are a man or a woman—it applies to everyone. Everyone must seek the forgiveness of Allāh and repent and ask forgiveness for every sin that he or she committed. I ask acceptance from Allāh for you. May Allāh accept your repentance and open your hearts. May He remind you of Himself. May He make you truthful and sincere and honest.

“Tawba is from Allāh’s Wisdom“ on page 34 of *The Religion of Unity* is read from the beginning until:

“For this reason water is a symbol of love. He says, ‘And We have made from water, every living thing.’ Can any of you live without water? Can anyone live without water? All of humanity – can it live without water? Can animals or plants?”

Is there anyone who can live without water? If there is, let him come and say, “I can.” Then we will say, “You are a liar.”

The reading continues until, “Even mountains cannot live without water...And this is why Allāh says that His Name breaks rocks and water gushes forth from them. For Allāh says in the Qur’ān, ‘And indeed there are stones out of which rivers gush forth.’ ”

There are rocks that cry and there are mountains that are complaining. They are complaining and crying because of the sins people are committing. They seek the forgiveness of Allāh, glory be to Him, and return to Him and seek refuge in Him, and ask Him to forgive people because of their ignorance. This is why you see water gushing from stones and rocks. How it explodes and the rocks crack and fall down and break, because it tries to wash the sins of the sinners. It tries to wash the pain and the mourning of those who are suffering.

This is what happens. This water is the weeping of the mountains. It is a mercy for mankind. It is a mercy for the oppressed and for those who are suffering around the earth. The mountains turn to Allāh, asking Him to wash the sins of the sinners and to wash the pain of those who are suffering.

People do not understand this, but Allāh says:

> And indeed, there are stones out of which rivers gush forth and indeed, there are of them [stones] which split asunder so that water flows from them (Qur'ān 2:74)

The water is the weeping of the rocks, the tears of the stones that people break. But Allāh is the one who pardons and bestows His mercy upon all of creation.

The reading continues, "This means we must use water in the way we are commanded to use it. We must preserve it in its original condition as Allāh created it."

We must use water in a good way and in the right way – not in the wrong way.

The reading continues, "We should not transform it with poison or do evil or harmful things with it..."

This is what people do. Not all people, but those who are oppressors and the enemies of humanity.

The reading continues until, "What happens when someone returns and repents? Allāh will rectify his deeds. This means that you must come. Do not give up. Even if you are full of sins He will accept you. So just come. Do you see any solution, any door but Allāh?"

He is the Merciful, the Compassionate. He described Himself as the Universally Merciful, the Singularly Compassionate. He does not disappoint anyone who knocks on His door. There is nothing in Allāh's realm but acceptance, and there is nothing in Allāh's realm but peace. Allāh does not know anything but acceptance. And He says to us:

> Say: "Oh My slaves who have transgressed against themselves!
> Do not despair of Allāh's mercy.
> Truly, Allāh forgives all sins.
> Truly, He is Oft-Forgiving, Most Merciful." (Qur'ān 39:53)

He is the Forgiving, the Merciful, the Compassionate. He is not one who imprisons others. He is not one who murders others. He is not one who hates people. No, beauty and purity are Him and they are from Him. Come to Him wholeheartedly. Come to Him with love. The one who comes with a full heart is accepted. If your heart is broken and is afraid of Him, know that Allāh is full of peace and love and mercy and He will accept you. Do not be afraid. Come wholeheartedly to Him, even if your heart is broken.

We care about you more than you care for yourself, and will take care of you more than you will take care of yourself. Do not be afraid and do not be ashamed and do not let anyone prevent you from visiting us. Come to us and we will open the door for you. The door is open for you. Why are you delaying? Why are you not coming? We are calling you. Do not be afraid of the sins you have done, because He is the One Who always Accepts Repentance, but He is also Severe in Punishment.

Oh Allāh, we ask You for a sincere repentance.

Understand that there is a condition [for your repentance to be accepted]—you must never go back and commit the same sins again. After you regret [your misdeeds], that is it. Do not commit them again and feel regret again. Do not think, "Oh, I will repent now, but I think I will go back and do it again." No. Many people think like that. They say, "I cannot stop now but I will stop tomorrow." I know there are many people like that.

There are many people whose coffins are being prepared right now, and they are unconscious of it. They think that they have tomorrow, yet their coffin is being prepared now. There are many people who do not know if they will live to see the next dawn, because life and death is not by your hand. This is why you cannot say, "Tomorrow I will stop."

Come in haste, come and hurry and rush to repent before it is too late and your appointed time comes. You must come and declare your repentance now. I open the door for you now. This is the repentance of Ramaḍan. Come to me now and declare your repentance. It is the repentance of Ramaḍan. It is Ramaḍan's repentance because Ramaḍan's repentance is a repentance of forgiveness. It is a repentance that will lead to healing from every disease. It will lead to the healing of every disease whether that disease is a disease of the heart, a disease of the self, or a disease of the spirit. It will be healed if you repent sincerely.

You must be truthful and sincere in your repentance. You must direct your heart fully toward Allāh and stretch your hand toward Allāh. Do not look at me as a human being—look at me with the eyes of your Protector so that He may protect you.

Do not hesitate to offer your most sincere repentance now. If you are not fully confident that you are repenting, then Allāh will not accept your repentance. Be confident that Allāh is watching you, protecting you and healing you. Be confident that He will accept your repentance. Stretch your hand, my son. Stretch your hand, my daughter. Seek forgiveness from your sins. Cry and weep for your sins, because tears erase sins. Tears wash away sins. They wash the heart and clean it. As our Most Beloved said:

> Whoever transgressed the limits
> and crossed the boundaries and then came back,
> weeping and regretting and feeling sorry,
> his tears will wash away his sins
> just as pure water cleans all the dirt and garbage. (Ḥadīth̲)

Sidi gives the tawba promise.

Do not think that this teaching is like all other sessions. It is not. It is a special session in the name of the month of fasting, the month of Ramaḍan, which is the month of repentance. Do not go far away. Take your share of the blessings of this month. Look seriously at it. We used to sit with our master guide, our s̲hayk̲h̲, weeping, and we never let that chance go to waste. We always took our share of blessings from it.

This is the truth. This is the clear reality. The one who comes to Allāh, wholeheartedly, which means with sincere repentance...the beginning of Ramaḍan is forgiveness; and the middle of Ramaḍan is mercy; and the end of Ramaḍan is being saved from the Hellfire. Blessed is the one who fasts in the beginning and seeks His forgiveness, and blessed is the one who fasts in the middle and receives the mercy, and blessed is the one who keeps fasting until the end and is saved from the Hellfire. You must read some Qur'ān as I explain it in my new book. It is entitled *He Who Knows Himself, Knows His Lord.*

I wrote it in six years and it is very deep. You must write it word for word and understand it in a deep way. Do not just read it and understand its surface meaning. Try to understand its deeper meaning. It has deep words, and no one comprehends it except those with deep hearts. I will continue to interpret it—not by the tongue. This knowledge is not to be taken from the tongue or from words. No, it is to be taken by tasting. This knowledge is divine knowledge. It is to be comprehended by the spirit. It must be looked upon by the heart from where it was written. It must be written only by clean hands, by purified hands. You must be truthful and sincere when you are writing holy words. You are writing a precious thing.

I will recite some poetry about this. Whoever wants to marry a beautiful woman does not feel it is hard to pay a precious dowry. He will pay it. That means he will pay [by giving] his full heart to her so that she can accept him. Then why do you want Allāh, yet you do not want to give Him everything? If you want His love, give Him everything. You cannot take anything from Him unless you give everything. Give just a little bit. Try and you will see that He gives to you abundantly. But do not give Him false words - do not pretend. You must give Him truthful words. Give Him sincere and honest words that are full of love, full of mercy.

We are in need of a cup that is full of love, mercy, peace and beauty. We are not in need of the afflictions being sent down to earth. Do you see how afflictions and disasters are affecting people everywhere, people who do not need them? Do you observe and are you conscious of the wrath of Allāh? The climate is changing, the desert is changing, and water is changing, taking people over.[22] Water is also becoming less

[22] "Taking people over" indicates that these issues are overtaking people, overwhelming people. They are on a scale individual people cannot control.

abundant. Have you noticed that floods and earthquakes are increasing everywhere? All of this is happening without stop these days. It does not stop. Do not think, "Oh we are secure here." No, Allāh can reach you anywhere. It has reached this land. It has reached everywhere—Indonesia, India, Africa. It reaches everywhere because Allāh warns of Himself, He warns you in His Qur'ān. These disasters even reach to Britain. Sixty years ago there were no floods and nothing like that in Britain. Now, they are experiencing it. Why is this? Because of what your hands earned against yourself. And Allāh pardons many of these sins (Qur'ān 42:30).

Do not say, "Oh it is Allāh who is doing this." No, it is a natural response to what [the oppressors'] hands have earned (Qur'ān 42:30). Allāh gave you gifts but you did not preserve them, and that is the reason for these afflictions. Did Allāh ever tell you to pollute the water? Did Allāh ever tell you to make air pollution, cut trees, and all other actions that have changed the climate? Allāh never ordered this. Return to Allāh, glory be to Him, to be saved. This book [*He Who Knows Himself Knows His Lord*] speaks of this, if you read and understand its deeper meaning.

Fasting in Ramadan

Lā ʾilāha ʾilla-llāāāāāāh, Lā ʾilāha ʾilla-llāāāāāh, Lā ʾilāha ʾilla-llāāāāāh
Muḥammad rasūlu-llāh, Ibrāhīm rasūlu-llāh, Mūsā rasūlu-llāh,
ʿĪsā rasūlu-llāh ʿalayhim ṣalātu-llāh.

Allāhumma anta-s-salām wa minka-s-salām
wa ilayka ya'ūdu-s-salām
tabārakta rabbanā
ya ḏha-l-jalāli wa-l-'ikrām

As-salāmu ʿalaykum wa raḥmatu-llāh wa bārakatuhu.

After we have entered into the blessed month of Ramaḍan, we must explain in detail that Ramaḍan has its manners, its divine politeness and ʾadab. Allāh made fasting obligatory upon us as He made it obligatory upon all nations before us. He made it obligatory upon Ibrāhīm (Abraham), Mūsā (Moses), ʿĪsā (Jesus), ʾālayhi as-salām and his nation, for Yaḥyā (John the Baptist), for Ismāʿīl (Ishmael), and all of the prophets, ʿalayhim as-salām. So fasting is obligatory for every individual who is an adult, man or a woman. Whoever is able to fast, must fast.

Starting from age fifteen everyone must fast unless he cannot for a health reason. For example, if he has a disease that prevents him from fasting. Allāh says in His Qurʾān:

> The month of Ramaḍan in which was revealed the Qurʾān,
> a guidance for humankind
> and clear proofs for the guidance and the criterion.
> So whoever of you sights the month
> must fast during that month
> and whoever is ill or on a journey,
> [you may not fast but you must later fast]
> the same number of days. (Qurʾān 2:185)

He must fast the days he missed when he is well and not traveling. So it is not permissible that we break our fast without reason. If a person is really sick and that sickness is chronic or difficult to treat and he cannot compensate the days, if he cannot fast at all, then he can break the fast. But if he is able financially, he must feed a poor person two meals a day for every day he breaks his fast—the breaking of the fast meal and the suhūr, the before the dawn meal.

The food must be the same as what you eat in amount and quality; it cannot be less than what you feed yourself and his family. And it is estimated that each meal is $30. So whoever cannot fast, be it a woman or a man, because of sickness, chronic sickness or being old–(elderly people cannot fast either), these people must spend their money to compensate the days that they cannot fast. But the one who occasionally gets a disease in Ramaḍan, he can fast later, during the days after Ramaḍan when he is well. He should not be feeding others; he should be fasting because he is able to fast.

Also, the ladies when they get their monthly periods should break the fast. They should not be fasting during that time, but then she can fast these days later when she is not having her menses.

Also, a pregnant woman cannot fast because it is feared that that will affect her child or affect her health. Then the husband or the father of the coming child must feed the poor on her behalf, because she probably is not able to work and earn money and she is not able to fast, so it is the duty of the father to pay two meals per day for the poor.

Also, it is permissible for the nursing woman not to fast because she gives her child and she must feed herself well. But the father must feed poor people on her behalf.

The one who breaks his fast or does not fast without any acceptable excuse, then he is breaking his the covenant he took with Allāh. This is a serious thing. If such a person fasted all of his life, it would not compensate for the days he broke his vow with Allāh. He must then have double the compensation that he should give. So instead of feeding thirty people two meals a day, he must actually feed sixty people and he must seek Allāh's forgiveness, because he did not transgress the limits only against Allāh, but he transgressed the limits against all the messengers and the prophets.

So he must also fast two months consecutively without a break and if he cannot for some reason, then he must feed sixty people. If he does not do so, he will have to answer, be questioned and face the reckoning of Allāh.

And he will be questioned and brought to accountability, because fasting is a serious matter; it is something very glorious.

Fasting means to fast from all of your sins, as we explained this morning. The true meaning of fasting is to fast from all sins, but if the person is old, and cannot really fast, if he or she has money, then he must feed the poor as explained—and that is that. But those who did not fast intentionally, without any excuse, but were ignorant regarding these rules, they must offer a sacrifice instead on behalf of the previous year that they did not fast. This is because they were ignorant of the rules, so they must only pay for the previous year.

If any of you did not fast last year without any excuse, he must pay what is equivalent to feeding a poor person two meals a day. I ask Allāh to bestow His forgiveness on him and accept his repentance, but the one who says, "I did not know, I was ignorant," and neglected seeking knowledge of the rules must pay what he should pay. Because he knows that fasting is obligatory and is ordained for everyone carrying the message of unity, and that he will be questioned by Allāh, glory be to Him, on the day when all the physical bodies and souls and innermost secrets and spirits will be demonstrated between the hands of Allāh.

That is why I invite my children, my daughters and sons, whoever did not fast last year to pay the charity as explained. They should do it immediately and not delay it so that Allāh forgives and protects them and protects their bodies.

The chosen Messenger said:

> Fasting is self-care, so fast and you will have good health. (Ḥadīth̲)

It is like caring for yourself. Because the human body is like a machine, like an instrument that must rest. Because the human body is always working, day and night, it does not stop. So it is from Allāh's wisdom that He ordained fasting for us so we can rest this machine. You do not want to rest, but Allāh, the Great Creator cares for you more than you care for yourself. He is so merciful to you, more than you are merciful to yourself. That is why He gave you fasting. So, as the Prophet said:

> The one who fasts will have good health and will gain health.
> (Ḥadīth̲)

Those who deviate from the command of Allāh are afflicted with many things. Recent scientific research has proven that fasting is a healing for more than fifty diseases. They researched it and modern science proved it to be true. This is why Allāh ordained fasting. He made it obligatory. Our most beloved guide the Prophet Muḥammad said:

> The human being does not fill any worse container
> than his own stomach.
> It is the worst container to fill.
> But if you must eat, let one-third be for food,
> one-third for fluids, and one-third for air. (Ḥadīth)

But what if the human being did not listen to this teaching and filled it to its brim? Then he cannot breathe and he cannot drink. Then he accumulates fat and accumulates things in his body, and what emerges from that are diseases and harmful things.

Even your own bones, eventually, will not be able to carry you if you do not listen to the teaching. Because the bones are created to carry, for example, seventy kilos of something, but then you put double that amount on them so that the bones cannot carry it and will become affected. The arteries, the veins and everything will become affected because it is not created to function like that, and the diseases will afflict you and your heart.

This is what happens, is it not so? And then we say, "What happened to me? Why is my heart not feeling well? Why is my back aching, my head?" We start to complain. Why do we complain like this? It is because of what our hands have earned (Qur'ān 42:30). Ask yourself and question yourself, why? What did I do to get that or to earn this disease? Your stomach does not hold more than two liters, but you sometimes fill it with five liters. This is from you. It is your own behavior. You are the one who is responsible for your own disease. Is this not so?

Allāh cares about you. Allāh wants you to have a healthy body. He wants you to have a sound intellect, a whole heart, a healthy spirit and a beautiful body. He does not want you to carry a diseased body, a sick body. No, it is by your own hands that you are lead to this result. So fasting has wisdom in it. That is why Allāh ordained it for us. If you count Allāh's gifts to you, you would not be able to count them [because they are so numerous]. But because the human's nature is to be an oppressor, he denies this truth. But understand that Allāh is fair and just, and He knows the secret and the most concealed secret of secrets. Nothing is concealed from Him at all, and He did not create a disease but that He also created its cure. It might well be that your healing is in fasting. So why do you refuse to fast?

There are very subtle things that modern medicine has started to know and apply, but if we had been following what the Messenger taught us, then we would not need this medicine because he said:

> We are a group of people that do not eat until we are hungry and when we eat, we do not fill our stomach to fullness. (Ḥadīt͟h)

This is the healthy way, and if we follow it we will not need any physicians. Why? Because there will not be any disease. We will be healthy.

The Bedouin who lives in the desert and is raised there do not have the diseases we have. It is very rare, Why? Because they live in a natural way. They are always in the fresh air, and they eat what they plant by their hands. They are simple and natural and they live a long life because of this. Many of them live beyond one hundred years. I know many of them. I know not less than one hundred people that are not less than one hundred years old. I know them one by one.

Those are from the spiritual guide, the s͟hayk͟h of the Bedouin. They eat very little and they eat only what they make by their hands and what they plant in the land by their hands, in the natural way. They do not have the desires that we do. They do not invent things. They walk a lot of long distances. They do not use cars and airplanes; they walk a lot. But if it is a very, very long distance they ride a donkey or a horse.

This does not mean that I am saying not to ride in a car or an airplane. No, because Allāh, glory be to Him, said:

> Say: "Who has forbidden the adoration with clothes
> given by Allāh, which He has produced for his slaves,
> and all kinds of wholesome food?" (Qur'ān 7:32)

Allāh gave us an intellect, and so we must act accordingly to discern what is good and what is not, what is in balance and what is not. Look at what the human being has made. The human has invented cars, but look how much pollution and gases cars emit into the air, and how they fill the atmosphere around them with all of this pollution. They say, "This is the civilized way," and, "This is what comes with civilization," and then it gives us diseases.

Because with all that we invented we have to deal with the gas and the pollution... And in every household you can find three, four, or even five cars. Look when you are here, there are not too many cars and you smell fresh air, but go into a crowded area in the city and you will see what you smell. You will experience that.

Our Prophet told us that every human being must preserve his body, his intellect, his breath, and his spirit because he does not own any of them; it is Allāh who owns them. He gave them to you as a trust. He gave you the body as a trust and the intellect as a trust. You will be questioned, "How did you use your body? How did you use your intellect, your heart and your spirit?" You will be questioned about that.

He facilitated the way for you to have your medicine and your healing whenever you stray from the way, because He said in the Qur'ān:

> Oh you who believe! Fasting is prescribed for you
> as it was prescribed for those before you,
> so that you may become the pious. (Qur'ān 2:183)

Why? Because fasting is healing and worship at the same time. It is a form of worship, as prayer is. As you pray, you must also fast. But it is also healing for the body.

I repeat again: oh you who are in debt to Allāh, who owe Allāh a debt because you did not fast without excuse last year, you must offer charity instead of these days being wasted and you did not fast. You must do it immediately, now, and do not delay it until tomorrow.

For the thirty days you broke your fast or for any days you broke your fast you must pay that in charity so that Allāh may accept your repentance, protect you and forgive you. And do not listen to those who oppress themselves and others.

Do not listen to your own selves, because your own self will say, "This is too much. Do not do this and do not do that. It is not important to do this." This is Iblīs whispering to your self, to your ego. You must always disobey your nafs, you must always disobey your nafs and s̲hayṭān and listen to those who give you good advice. Disobey your self, your ego.

And I want to open the door for you. Whoever wants to pay that charity, the door is open for him.

Allāh also ordained the giving of zakāh, the obligatory charity during this month. So everyone must give this obligatory annual charity in this month. Allāh says in the Qur'ān:

> And those who hoard up gold and silver
> and spend it not in the way of Allāh,
> announce unto them a painful torment
> [it becomes like fuel for the fire by which their own skin,
> backs and face will be burned]. (Qur'ān 9:34)

And it will be said to them on that Day, "This is what you accumulated; this is what you accumulated; it will burn you."

Everyone must give the annual obligatory charity in full without reducing it by a penny, because you will be questioned about that. You will be questioned in front of all people on the Day of Judgment. This is why I encourage you to pay your annual obligatory charity in the month of Ramaḍan. I ask Allāh to accept our repentance and bestow upon us the gift of repenting.

The husband must pay on behalf of his wife; in the law of Allāh, he must. That is the authentic and the right way. The woman should not pay her own charity. It is the responsibility of the husband to pay on her behalf. This is the law of Allāh and the law of His Messenger, ṣalla-llāhu ʿalayhi wa sallam. Allāh put him in charge of that. Allāh put it as a duty upon him to do so in the religion of Ibrāhīm, Mūsā, ʿĪsā and all the prophets, ʿalayhim as-salām. This is the way.

That is enough teaching for today, you can go. So it is $30 per day if you broke your fast or you cannot fast. You must pay $15 per meal, which is $30 per day, because you must feed the poor person two meals. So anyone who broke one day must pay $30. Is that clear? If they have the money.

Defeating the Commanding Self

"The Commanding Nafs"

from *He Who Knows Himself Knows His Lord*

Lā ʾilāha ʾilla-llāāāāāāh, Lā ʾilāha ʾilla-llāāāāāh, Lā ʾilāha ʾilla-llāāāāāh
Muḥammad rasūlu-llāh, Ibrāhīm rasūlu-llāh, Mūsā rasūlu-llāh,
ʿĪsā rasūlu-llāh ʿalayhim ṣalātu-llāh.

Allāhumma anta-s-salām wa minka-s-salām
wa ilayka ya'ūdu-s-salām
tabārakta rabbanā
ya dha-l-jalāli wa-l-'ikrām

As-salāmu ʿalaykum wa raḥmatu-llāh wa bārakatuhu. Al-ḥamdu li-llāh.

Allāh has created us the way that He willed, and He did not create us the way we want, because He is the Wise and He is the All-Knowing. He knows that we are weak and that we do not know what is good for us—that we cannot manage our own affairs. So He inspires us. He inspired us, taught us, ordained things for us, and sent down holy books to us through His messengers to teach us how to walk in this life.

If we follow what the messengers, the teachers of this world, taught and the ways in which they were guided by Allāh, we will be saved from the suffering we cause ourselves. If we do not walk on the straight path, the right path, then we fall into faults and wrongdoings and we become miserable by what our own hands earn. This happens when we do not follow what the guides taught us and what the All-Knowing taught and showed us.

The human who commits sins and is at fault cannot blame Allāh – he cannot say, "Allāh willed it." We also cannot claim our physical diseases are from Allāh, because Allāh never commands what offends. He never commands what is wrong. Offenses, wrongdoings, and faults come from the human being.

Allāh says in the Qurʾān:

> Whatever of good reaches you, is from Allāh, but
> whatever of evil befalls you, is from yourself. (Qurʾān 4:79)

Because Allāh showed us, He clarified for us how to discern wrong from right and good from evil. He prohibited us from evil and said, "Do not approach it—avoid it." He says, for example, "Do not kill," but we do kill. He says, "Do not steal," but we commit theft. He says, "Do not deceive others," but we do deceive others. He never tells us to be arrogant, full of conceit, or to become envious and jealous of others. On the contrary, He says to us, "Do not be envious," but in deviation from His commands, we envy each other.

He says to us, "Be polite and have good manners," but we lose our manners and we are not polite. He commands us to do good, but we do not do good. He orders us with pure goodness, but we do follow. He prohibits us from all evil, but we deviate from His commands. He tells us that those who use drugs like marijuana, cocaine, and alcohol, and all of that, are destroying us. He says using drugs is prohibited because you use your money towards your own destruction and for the sake of s̲hayṭān. But people do take drugs and let their own children take them.

Once your child reaches eighteen, according to the law parents cannot tell them, "Do this" or "Do not do that." They can take us to court—all in the name of freedom. But it is a false freedom that young men and women use in the wrong way. They use it to harm. Freedom must be used in the right way. The right kind of freedom brings them pure goodness.

Freedom is not to go wherever you want and do whatever you want. A young lady or man who goes and does whatever he desires in deviation to good manners and politeness and of the natural law of Allāh—all in the name of freedom...What kind of freedom destroys families? What kind of freedom separates children from their parents? What kind of freedom is that? This is not from Allāh.

When they fall sick many people say, "Allāh made me sick. He brought this illness to me." And if the people did something corrupt they say, "Allāh led me to do this." No, this is not from Allāh, this is from your own self. It is from the ego that commands you to evil; what is ruling you is the commanding ego, an-nafs al-amārra. The commanding ego belongs more to the animal kingdom, and who is her guide? It is not the human being any more. Her guide becomes the s̲hayṭān.

This type of egoistic self lives in darkness. If she commands you to do something, you need to dispute with her. For example, if you command her to something good, she will tell you, "No, you do not have to do this," or, "You do not have to do that." This is the commanding ego, the self that commands your ego, and it lives for wrong, because it does not live within divine boundaries and natural law. It deviates from goodness. Because it is ruling people now, corruption is spread across the earth resulting in evil, destruction, and murder. Doing good becomes something uncommon and abnormal. The egoistic self has become what rules the human being and governs his life.

What is even more harmful are liars and deceivers who claim that they have knowledge of how to heal this. Because people listen to those liars, they get more caught in the egoistic self. They stray from Allāh's commands and engage in His prohibitions, and they live in illusion and imagination with pictures that the egoistic self beautifies and projects for them. The ego-self projects pictures and illusions to them, making them think that what they do is good and what they accumulate is good, and in this way they stray far from Allāh's ways. In this way the egoistic self leads them to a great fall.

The Prophet Yūsuf, ʿalayhi-s-salām, describes the egoistic self in his saying:

> And I blame myself.
> Truly, the self is inclined to evil,
> except when My Lord bestows His Mercy. (Qurʾān 12:53)

We must strive against the ego that commands us to evil. We must break its grip and move to the first station in our walking. Because the commanding ego will let its possessor live only in darkness, and the one in darkness may claim, "I have arrived."

We want to know exactly where you are. Are you polite? Do you exhibit divine politeness? Are you devoid of selfishness, arrogance, and conceit? Are you truly pure? Do you backbite, do you jinx people, do you envy people, do you have hate in your heart? Are you generous? Do you carry the divine attributes and qualities Allāh commanded you to carry? Or are you carrying a human personality full of darkness and dirt, and are you more eager to possess the lower realm and its pleasures than anything else? If you had one mountain of gold, you would wish for another mountain of gold. Are you like that?

These are the qualities of the commanding ego, the lower self. Did you help people you saw crying and suffering in pain? Did you stretch the hand of help to them? Or are you with murderers, liars, those who deceive people, and those who are far away from divine manners and politeness? If you belong to the envious people who are full of dirt and human sickness, then you are truly one of the people who live in the level of the commanding ego.

When you hear the call to prayer do you find yourself standing and going forth to pray, or do you find yourself busy with something else, saying that you will go and pray later? The one who is possessed by the commanding ego is like a deaf person when he hears the call to prayer or the words of Allāh. There is something in his ear that prevents him from hearing, and when he talks he speaks only evil. This is the one who possesses the commanding ego.

How can we heal this ego? How can we heal this type of self? It is not by writing and reading that you can think, "I am already done with this station. I am beyond it." It is not through reading and writing. You need to understand what the commanding ego is and how to discern it. What is its realm, what is its locus, how to heal it, how to get rid of it. You must read and write, but also understand. You must try to comprehend and avoid its faults and mistakes. When you reach this point Allāh will substitute the commanding ego with another self that is better.

The commanding ego is the first station [of the nafs], and I have explained everything about it. I have explained how to travel from this station and ascend to the next one, how to travel from the realm of the creation to the realm of the Creator. I take your hand and I want you to transform the metaphorical realm into the realm of the Reality. I say, "This is you and you must follow the way."

Let us assume that there is a lady and her house is full of dirt, dust, and accumulation. Can she live in this house? Can anyone live in it anymore? No, she must sweep it, clean it, and purify it so that people can live in it, so that she can live in it. This is an example, but it is a fact in our lives that we can see. I ask Allāh to take our hands to help us.

This is the beginning, but I also want to remind you of what I said yesterday. We are in the beginning of Ramaḍan, and before we read about the station I just described I want to remind you of something I talked about yesterday. Fasting is for Allāh, glory be to Him, and He said to us:

> Fasting is Mine and it I reward it directly. (Ḥadīth Qudsī)

The reward for fasting is the Garden. This is as long as one is fasting purely for Allāh, and so we must perform fasting in the right way and we must purify it. We must perform it by continuous remembrance of Allāh, by seeking forgiveness, and by praying. We must be polite. We are in Allāh's presence and we must be polite with Him at all times.

Here you are, and you are with your Lord. I say: here you are with your Lord. I do not say: here you are with your son or wife. I say: here you are and your Lord. Because Allāh says:

> Fasting is Mine and it I reward it directly. (Ḥadīth Qudsī)

and He says:

> And We are nearer to him [the human] than his jugular vein. (Qur'ān 50:16)

This is why I would like to repeat for you again, that those who did not fast last year must spend in charity in compensation for every day they did not fast. They must feed a poor person two meals for each day they did not fast. One must calculate how many days he broke his fast and he must feed the poor people in accordance with what I explained.

If he did not pay his tax for last year, his fasting this year will not be accepted. He must offer what he needs to offer for the last year. Otherwise, fasting will be harmed; it will not work. I ask Allāh to accept your fasting this year and to protect you from everything.

"The Commanding Nafs" on page 62 of *He Who Knows Himself Knows His Lord* is read from the beginning until:

"You know from the previous explanation that the seven selves of souls are one thing and are named by seven different names according to its qualities. So there is the commanding self, the reproachful self, the inspired self, the secure tranquil self, the satisfied self, the pleased self and the perfect self."

These stations carry different names but they all name one thing. Sometimes we call it "heart," we call it "self," we call it "spirit," we call it "secret," and we call it "most concealed secret" and at the end we call it "secret essence."

To move through these stations we must use practices and exercises to train our selves. We are not talking about the heart as a piece of flesh, we are talking about the heart as our innermost being. Flesh is a picture, the heart is a picture. We are talking about another realm in which the heart means the innermost being. It is not a dense realm, it is a subtle realm. We are not talking about the body and the physical realm which is dense, because this is a metaphorical life, it is not a real life. This life is an illusion because it will come to an end. The human body will vanish, but the human will become a subtle human and transfer to another realm.

There is the animal human and there is the godly human, and I want to transform you from the animal human to the godly human—the godly human is that which Allāh created Ādam as his reflection, His own image. The human being is the divine mirror in which Allāh sees His own image, His own reflection. I am not talking about the picture of the donkey or the picture of the camel or the cat. I am talking about the godly human being, the subtle human who is carrying lofty divine ethics and values. Allāh does not want you to live as animals who are not polite and do not know politeness. Allāh wants you to live a divine life.

The reading continues until, "In this station, let your dẖikr be: *Lā 'ilāha 'illa-llāh* while prolonging the *Lā* and emphasizing the hamza of *'il* in *'ilāha*. And beware of pronouncing the hamzah in *'ilāha* lightly because if you do, it will turn out as 'yā' and the word will become 'lāyilāha 'illa-llāh' and this is not the true word of unification, or tawhid, and there is no benefit in its repetition."

If you see the picture of the one you love, you will follow Him anywhere, because He is the One Who Bestowed Love upon you, and you cannot live without love. Will you then be polite with Him and have good manners, or not? Of course, you must be polite with Him because you want His love, and love is the secret of your life.

We are not talking about human love, we are talking about divine love. No one can comprehend that love and taste it except the one who experiences it, who truly tastes it. Words are many. Many people talk, words are many and speeches can be longwinded, but there is a difference between saying and walking/tasting.

> Once, the Prophet, ʿalayhi as-salātu as-salām, took a jar of honey to Abu Bakr, raḍiya-llāhu ʿanhu, and asked,
>
> "What is this?"
>
> Abu Bakr replied, "It is honey."
>
> Then he took it to Omar, raḍiya-llāhu ʿanhu, and asked him, "What is this?"
> ʿUmar said, "It is honey."
>
> Finally he gave it to ʿAlī, raḍiya-llāhu ʿanhu, and asked him, "What is this?"
>
> ʿAlī said, "Give me the cup, please."
> ʿAlī tasted it and then answered, "Yes, it is honey."
>
> The Prophet said, "The one who tastes is the one who truly knows." (Ḥadīth)

Without tasting it, how can you claim that you know love? We are not talking about the love of an animal, the cattle. We are not talking about love of the vanishing humanity. We are talking about the eternal love that never dies. It is the love that transforms you from the world of annihilation to the love of eternity—divine eternity in which there is no death, no annihilation.

If you taste it now, in this life, you do not wait until you die. If you taste it later, it is not worth as much as it is worth here. It is required that you taste it here. We want to fly out of the world of suffering, affliction, and disasters; it is not worth anything compared to the realm of divine eternity. I am talking to you about another world, different from the one you are living in now.

Rābiʿa, raḍiya-llāhu ʿanhu, said to the Beloved:

> I love You with two types of love –
> the love of desire and passion
> and another type of love that You ought to be loved.

> The love that I tasted, know, live with, and cannot live without,
> the divine love, is the love with which You ought to be loved.
> I love You because You ought to be loved.
> You are the secret of my life, and so I love You.

Do you love your own spouses, husbands, and wives that way? Men, do you love your wives that way? Women, do you love your husbands that way? Search. Look deeply. Do you find that love in your life? I think you still cannot find that love in your life, because when someone finds that love, he annihilates, he dissolves and is consumed in his beloved. Then, there is no anger, no problem, no jealousy, no envy. Everyone will be living with his mirror, with his own reality, with his own reflection, with his real mirror—and he cannot hit or cause any harm to that mirror to break it. The mirror is transparent so he cannot break it, because if you break it you have broken yourself. Our way is to transform you from the dark, dense realm to the subtle, luminous realm which will exist for eternity.

Your job here is to transform from one station to another. To rid yourself of the commanding self, the commanding ego that commands you to evil, is the first step. I give to you little by little so you can absorb.

The reading continues until, "He [the Prophet], ṣalla-llāhu ʿalayhi wa sallam, also said, 'Renew your faith.' When it was asked, 'How can we renew our faith?' he replied, 'Repeat the saying *Lā 'ilāha 'illa-llāh* because saying it removes any sin, and there is no action equal to reciting it, for there is no veil between it and Allāh, and it reaches Him alone.' "

Never leave Allāh. Always say, "Lā ʾilāha ʾilla-llāh." This is the only song full of what you need. Do not look at anything except Allāh. Do not look at pictures. You are carrying His reflection, His image. You are His mirror. How glorious you are. How beautiful you are. You have the secret of divine majesty and beauty because you are a reflection of the beloved. Do you not want to be that way? Do you not want to be His reflection? He wants you to remember Him. He wants you to be conscious of Him. Imagine that you love someone—would you ever be able to forget his or her name? No, only the crazy one forgets the name of his beloved. Our most beloved one is Allāh, and nothing else, no one else.

Allāh, subḥānahu wa taʾālā, says through the tongue of the Prophet in Ḥadīth Qudsī:

> I am with the good that My slave thinks of Me,
> and I am with him as long as he remembers Me.
> If he mentions Me to himself, I mention him within Myself,
> and if he mentions Me in a group,
> I mention him in a group better than his.

Also, the Messenger of Allāh, ṣalla-llāhu ʿalayhi wa sallam, said:

> There is no charity better than remembrance of Allāh (Ḥadīth)

and he said:

> Should I inform you about what is the best of deeds,
> the loftiest in degree and better for you than
> silver and gold?"
>
> They said, "Yes, please do."
> And he said, "The remembrance of Allāh."
>
> He added, "When you pass by the meadows of the Garden, ascend."
> They asked, "Oh Messenger of Allāh, what are the meadows of the Garden?"
> He replied, "The circles of remembrance."

Do you see? This is the truth, this is Reality. You are in a garden from the Gardens of Allāh when you sit and remember Allāh, glory be to Him.

The reading continues until, "You have to know the principals of the creed, such as, what is obligatory and commanded by Allāh and what is prohibited. You must not busy yourself with more knowledge than these basics before you purify yourself—before you purify your nafs and clean your heart. In the beginning, your need is to free yourself from the prison of your nature..."

You must release yourself from the prison in which you put yourself. Before you come and walk further you must destroy the chains that you put around yourself. You must travel from the human realm to the godly realm, the divine realm.

The reading continues, "In the beginning, your need is to free yourself from the prison of your nature and polish the mirror of your heart and to remove its diseases, which prevent it from comprehending the realities

of things and from understanding the subtle sciences. This is because in this station, your mirror is rusted by the rust of arrogance, conceit, boasting, hate, desire, greed and envy, and other blameworthy qualities that you do not recognize in yourself."

This is something very important for walking and for ascending toward Allāh.

The reading continues, "So the most important duty in this station is to rid the self of these impurities which prevent the heart from witnessing the unseen."

You must feel ashamed before Allāh when you are claiming something and in fact you are nothing. When you truly become something, you will not need to say, "I," because Allāh knows you without your needing to say, "I."

The reading continues until, "This station, and I mean the first station, in which the soul is called 'the commanding nafs' is referred to in the Qur'ān as 'nature's prison' and 'the lowest of the low.' So freeing one's self from this station is very important."

Where are you then? If you have not yet gone beyond this station, where are you then? You are in the lowest of the low, the most dirty places, and you see yourself as something. When in fact, you are carrying burdens of sins and wrongdoings. You claim you are a lover, and you are devoid of love. The gnostic poet said, "Everyone claims love for Laylā," but who is the true lover? He has not approached Laylā at all, but he lies. He says, "I arrived at Laylā, I am with Laylā." He must walk in the way that Allāh wants him to walk before he can say, "I have arrived." This is the true way that one starts to become ashamed of all the wrongdoings he has committed with his eyes, ears, and hands.

Some people are still full of dirt and they claim they have arrived. Such people must clean themselves and wash this dirt. They must leave no trace of this worldly, low dirt. They must wash themselves really well from the lower realms and evil, lower desires.

As long as a person says, "I," it means that he is still suffering and still in that lower realm. But when he takes off his shoes—this is how Allāh commanded Mūsā to take off his shoes. He said:

> Take off your shoes for you are standing in the holy valley of Tuwa. (Qur'ān 20:12)

Allāh said that to Mūsā when Mūsā left his shoes. When Mūsā left Mūsā, then Mūsā knew who was speaking to him and who brought him to life. When Allāh manifested Himself in an epiphany to Mūsā, Mūsā was not there anymore. Mūsā was gone. Mūsā was gone completely from his human pictures, and after he came back from this vision and witnessing, he said, "glory be to You, I was one of those who oppressed themselves." Mūsā said, "Oh Allāh, I am always poor and in need of You, in spite of all the bounties You send me."

When you are with Allāh you are self-sufficient. You are absolutely sufficient and rich. You know everything, you understand everything. When you are with Allāh you become the secret of beauty, and the secret of beauty is within you. But if you leave Allāh then you are the loser, the failure. Oh Allāh, we ask You to keep us always in Your presence, with You, conscious of You, witnessing You. Please protect us from afflictions and disasters, oh Allāh.

The reading continues until, "His Lord allows his prayer and direction to influence His determined decree, and allows it to revoke affliction, and to be of avail for those calamities and afflictions that are sent down. Prayers are so honored by Allāh that He becomes wrathful when a person refrains from praying. He made it the essence of worship."

Anyone who loses this, loses everything. Let him search. Let him search where he is. He is worthy of nothing. But if he walks in this way, and follows what he hears, then he comes to be with Allāh and in Allāh and it becomes his garden, the Garden of love and beauty and mercy. He becomes something very glorious. Do you think of yourself as a microcosm when within you is the entire macrocosm?

The reading continues until, "Be alert my beloved, and wake up from your heedlessness, which is causing your ruin and which abases and belittles you. Come forward to the One Whom you cannot be sufficient without. Come forward before you are led by the chains of trial..."

The door is open and the One has opened the gate. Everything you want and everything you need is there. So enter through the gate, secure and safe.

The reading continues until it is finished.

This is a clear explanation for the first station, which is the station of the commanding ego, and I explained how to pass through this station. Not through illusion, not by claims and words, but by striving. We must strive and we must be sincere and truthful and not allow pictures and illusions and imagination to enter into it. Because if you rid yourself of this egoistic self and pass through the first station, you become secure and safe and you will enter the second station.

Do not claim that you passed through the first station of the commanding ego, then the second station (the reproaching station), and the blessed station, and the satisfactory station...and you claim you arrived. No, it is not by saying [you have done so that you arrive], we must strive. Striving is a must. People say a lot of words. There are too many words. But action must manifest on the earth. And I ask Allāh to grant you success and to help and support you.

Now I open a door to divine protection for you, which Allāh gave us permission to open for you. It is a door granted divine protection. This door is needed by anyone who has shortcomings with his Lord and who has committed sins in the past and fell into the hands of his enemy - s̱hayṭān, desire and his egoistic self. Sayyid Yūsuf said:

> Truly, the self is inclined to evil (Qur'ān 12:53)

The person in this station will also have a lot of diseases—physical, psychological, and spiritual. These afflictions are known and experienced by miserable human beings who became caught by the devils, lower desires and commanding ego. Whoever wants to rid himself of the world of illusion and the world of the commanding ego in the way that you have just heard must come and rid yourself of your world of pictures, illusion and imagination. You must come to Allāh through walking, real walking, not illusionary walking.

You must learn how to come to Allāh. You must know how to cross the distance of the first station. To do so you must offer a sacrifice for Allāh. This sacrifice is a protection for you, and it will open the door of divine protection. It is a ransom, it ransoms you from what you used to do, from your past sins. Come and take your chance, you might not have this opportunity to do this with me again. Travel with your whole being and with everything you have to Allāh. This is why I want you to repeat after me...

Sidi gives the promise

You cannot go away from Us. Then come, there is no other choice for you. Where else will you go? We created you and we trained you, and no one can contain you but Us. Seek refuge in Us. This is why our Prophet, ṣalla-llāhu ʿalayhi wa sallam, said to escape to Allāh. Escape to Allāh, He is your true protector. He is Real. He is the Truth. He is Allāh.

Sidi begins reciting poetry:

Who is in His unseen but Him?
Who are you, you human?
Do you have any choice in existence?
You are nothing but Him.

I am the door, so take me.
There is nothing in existence for me but Him.
I am Your scene that You have pointed to.
Take from me anything that crosses my mind except You,
for I am the very essence of love, and I am All.

I am the essence of All,
I am Everything.
Nothing but Him.

If you truly see,
then watch me and be absent from your self,
and you will see Him.
Glory be to You, Allāh, my creator,
the one who originated me from nothing.

Whoever points to other than you is a polytheist.
consumed with the world of separation and polytheism.

May the peace and blessings of Allāh be upon you all.

Defeating the Blaming Self

"The Blaming Self"

from *He Who Knows Himself Knows His Lord*

Lā ʾilāha ʾilla-llāāāāāāh, Lā ʾilāha ʾilla-llāāāāāh, Lā ʾilāha ʾilla-llāāāāāh
Muḥammad rasūlu-llāh, Ibrāhīm rasūlu-llāh, Mūsā rasūlu-llāh,
ʿĪsā rasūlu-llāh ʿalayhim ṣalātu-llāh.

Allāhumma anta-s-salām wa minka-s-salām
wa ilayka yaʻūdu-s-salām
tabārakta rabbanā
ya dẖa-l-jalāli wa-l-ʾikrām

As-salāmu ʿalaykum wa raḥmatu-llāh wa bārakatuhu.

On this blessed day, which is my second day with you, while we are here in this blessed land, we remember Allāh, glory be to Him. We translate His names and we live with His qualities, High is He. We have started to explain the stations of the self, the nafs. The self has seven stations and these stations have different names. The first station is called the station of the nafs, al-amārra, the commanding self. Then there is the reproaching self, or the blaming self.

This morning we explained some aspects of the commanding self, which is like a snake in the human being. It is not faithful to the human, it is not sincere with him, and it does not show him what is good. It always shows him bad desires like boasting, arrogance, racism, hate, and envy and it inclines him toward the lower realm which is dangerous, and it takes him away from Allāh.

This self is described by Allāh as:

> Truly, the self is inclined to evil,
> except when My Lord bestows His Mercy. (Qurʾān 12:53)

Our Master Messenger, ṣalla-llāhu ʿalayhi wa sallam, said:

> Your worst enemy is your own self
> that is between your sides. (Ḥadītẖ)

It is like a snake alive in your body, in your heart. If you are not alert, then it bites you. It always leads you to the lower desires, to lose yourself, your true essence. It leads to you hate and envy and other lower qualities.

This is because she listens always to Iblīs. Her father is Iblīs. Iblīs put her inside the human. But Iblīs will flee when you mention Allāh's glorious name. If you say, "ya Allāh," then this aspect of yourself will not move, but will be still and will not dispute with you. This is why I explained why it is important to remember Allāh and to say it in the right way, "Allāh." Do not mention Allāh's name in an incorrect way. Allāh says in the Qur'ān:

> Truly the Muslim men and women,
> the believing men and women
> the men and the women who are obedient,
> the men and women who are truthful,
> the men and the women who are patient,
> the men and the women who are humble,
> the men and the women who give alms (ṣadaqah)
> the men and the women who fast (ṣawm)
> the men and the women who guard their chastity
> and the men and the women who remember Allāh much with their hearts and tongues
> Allāh has prepared for them forgiveness and a great reward. (Qur'ān 33:35)

This is why the human being must never abandon the remembrance of Allāh.

Allāh, Most High and Glorious is He, gave us His attentive care and He guided us. He says:

> Remember Me and I will remember you.
> And thank Me and I will protect you. (Qur'ān 2:152)

If you remember Allāh, Allāh will protect you. If you thank Him, He will give you more. After you have a deep understanding you will find yourself between two aspects of the nafs, a pushing one and another one that submits. One aspect is satisfied and happy, and another one disputes with you.

[The disputatious one] argues with you and says, "Why did you give that much charity to the poor? Perhaps you gave too much. You are too polite, maybe that is not so good. Why do you not show them who you really are and boast about yourself a little bit? Maybe you are better than this and that." The nafs blames you by saying, "Look at what so and so is doing. Why do you not behave like him? Look how rich he became, whether through theft or whatever." Or it will say, "Look at how big he is, how great he is." Iblīs whispers to the [disputatious] nafs. It listens to Iblīs and blames the human if he does not obey it.

Actually it is a great s̲hayṭān, more than the original s̲hayṭān. Because it comes looking beautiful, and it acts as if it is jealous for you, and as if it cares about you. But in reality, it carries a hidden poison or venom. If you listen to or take in that venom it will destroy you.

This is why you have to understand that the blaming self still has some aspects of the commanding self. This is why it blames you in the wrong way—it advises you with things that apparently glitter, but it does not tell you the truth. It deceives you. It wears a beautiful garment and praises you for everything you do, even though what you are doing is not really praiseworthy and does not deserve it. Even if in reality evil is in what you are doing, still, it praises you.

[At this point audio is lost for a few lines.]

...because they lie to you, the s̲hayṭān and the ego lie to you, and lead you to the darkness, the complete darkness. One can escape this trap by not listening to them and by doing dh̲ikr and remembrance of Allāh and performing prayers when you are standing or sitting. You say, "Lā ʾilāha ʾilla-llāh" one hundred times.

You listen to your self lying [to you when] it says, "That is too much, why one hundred times?" Your self tells you that you are getting tired. It says, "Maybe it is enough to mention thirty times." It says to you, "You see you are tired, your feet are hurting now, and your legs are weak. And oh, you are so tired and exhausted, maybe you should have some sleep. And maybe you just sit and have a cup of coffee, or go to a coffee shop and have a relaxing time." It beautifies for you everything it desires. That is its nature. That is its nature.

It will whisper to you, "Instead of remembering Allāh why do you not go watch this movie?" Or it says, "Oh, these practices are old-fashioned, you need to follow new things." It is not true that she whispers these things to you? Look and listen. Then you look and all of your friends and neighbors went to go have fun, and you are here doing these practices. The self says, "Do not do these practices." This aspect of the self also makes neighbor go against neighbor. It says, "Go to this neighbor, see what is going on with her. She is doing these weird practices, you must advise her." It is a war, a battle between you and the self that does not stop.

And then the self whispers to a woman, "Look how pretty that other lady is. She is so pretty and she dresses so beautifully. She is better than you. Why do you not also go and buy something good for yourself and make yourself appear as beautiful?" Why does the self of the woman [in our example] whisper these things? Because it wants to corrupt the relationship between her and her husband, because maybe her husband is miserable because he does not have enough money to buy her these things. But the nafs whisper to him.

This nafs is s̲hayṭān. (Amany notes that Sidi is using the feminine version of the word s̲hayṭān here). She calls her and she says, "Go call and ask him for some money," even though she knows that he has no money. "Go and buy something beautiful for yourself, you deserve it." And then a dispute happens between the husband and the wife and then the nafs is so satisfied, she is pleased.

These methods of the egoistic self happen. It does these things, and it makes problems between husbands and wives. It commands evil things and it whispers evil things to the person.

"The Blaming Self" on page 69 of *He Who Knows Himself Knows His Lord* is read from the beginning until page 70, "Acting for the sake of being praised by others is a hidden idolatry that is totally condemned. Beloveds know that if you are in this station, you are in the second station and your soul is called 'the blaming one.' The possessors of this station are never safe from danger..."

He is still in affliction. He must rid himself of it. He must walk the path that Allāh guided him to and showed him. That means to walk within

Allāh's commands and boundaries and avoid His prohibitions, as explained and taught to us by His prophets and messengers.

The reading continues until, "So they are commanded to die before their time; their Master, Allāh, says to them, 'Die before you die.' So they strive to die the death of the self with discipline and purification."

You must die and cause to die that which Allāh does not like in your existence. Cause it to die and revise everything that is for the sake of Allāh, that Allāh loves. By your obedience to Allāh you revive, and by your disobedience to Allāh you court death. If you obey the nafs you are destroying yourself and if you obey Allāh you are reviving your life.

The reading continues until the bottom of the page, "Now that 'the ones brought near' do not stop at this station because of its great danger; they continue to strive for its highest degree, which is the degree of 'sincerity and faith.' But the sincere ones are in danger and they cannot free themselves from the danger except by annihilating..."

Faith and sincerity are the foundation of the path. To have faith and be sincere you have to do that for the sake of Allāh and not for the sake of serving yourself. The Messenger said:

> People are destroyed except for those who know.
> The ones who know are destroyed except for those who work with what they know,
> and they are destroyed except for those who have sincerity,
> and the workers who have sincerity are in grave danger. (Ḥadīth)

Why? Because Allāh will question them about their degree of sincerity. Did they do for Allāh's sake or in obedience to the self and s̲hayṭān? This is the foundation to let your action be for Allāh only. Not for the sake of the lower realm. Not for the sake of being famous or a leader. It has to be purely for Allāh's sake. This is the Truth. This is the Reality.

The reading continues to page 71, "Their situation reaches the extent that even if they entered a locked garden, Allāh would decree someone inside to harm them. This is because they still have some human nature which demands boasting, conceit, envy, rancor, bad manners, enmity, hatred, and indulgence in seeking provision, etc. All of these yield weariness and struggle."

Like to be very, very careful, to have a very sharp life—this is what you need. To not listen for those. Listen for Allāh, He protects you. Allāhu akbar.

The reading continues to the bottom of page 71, "Some people arrive and proceed to cut the branches, but they do not uproot the tree nor cut its water source so that they could be rid of it. In the end, they are not completely rid of the poisons, because they cut what does not grow by itself, and the original source of growth, which is the tree, remains."

It is like a snake that fakes its death, but once you touch her, she gets you. So be careful of it. This is you! We are talking about you! Where is this snake, where is this nafs? Is it not within you? You must discipline it. Just as you discipline your child, you must discipline yourself. If you do not discipline your child, he will hit you one day. So you have to discipline your self or it will hit you. You have to discipline your nafs every hour.

It is not something to neglect, because every hour it will hit you, every hour it will beat you up. And then you will scream, you will cry, "What happened? What is happening in my life?" It is by what your own hands earned (Qur'ān 42:30). Search, search for the cause—you will find it in your self.

Where is the house of the nafs? It is in your own garment. This is if it has a little bit of discipline and it is polite. But the evil one, the evil nafs, lives in your own heart and it takes over. On your heart's doorstep, it is there. But if it hears dẖikr coming from the heart, then it escapes, it runs away. This is what Allāh says. This is why Allāh says in the Qur'ān:

> Remember Me and I will remember you. (Qur'ān 2:152)

And the Prophet, ṣalla-llāhu ʿalayhi wa sallam, said:

> Remember Allāh as much as you remember your parents or even more. (Ḥadīṯẖ)

He also said:

> The best of what I, and all the other prophets before me, said is that this [remembrance] is the fortress, the shelter in which you seek refuge, and nothing can harm you in it. (Ḥadīṯẖ)

The reading continues until, "If he must eat, then let one third of his stomach be for his food, one third for his drink, and one third for this breath..."

This is why the stomach is most beloved to the nafs, the self. Why? Because the stomach obeys the nafs blindly. The human could be full already but someone says to him, "Try this, it tastes good. This tastes better. This is an appetizer." And then the human starts to listen and fill his stomach and his belly becomes so big—bigger than a donkey's belly. Why do you eat so much? It is not right. Wisdom is what the Prophet, ṣalla-llāhu ʿalayhi wa sallam, said. He said:

> The worst container that a human can fill is his stomach.
> If he must eat to live, let one-third of the stomach size be for his food and one-third for his drink and one-third for his breath. (Ḥadīth̲)

If he does not eat so much, then he will not have high cholesterol, he will not have diseases, and he will not have all the problems that this eating brings.

The mistake that the human being falls into is that when he gets sick he says, "Oh, this is from Allāh." But no, it is not from Allāh; it is by your own hands. You did this to yourself. The Qurʾān says:

> Whatever of good reaches you, is from Allāh, but
> whatever of evil befalls you, is from yourself. (Qurʾān 4:79)

If he disputes with the nafs, then he will be fine. Nothing will harm him. He must abide by listening to the commands of the Wise, the All-Knowing. Let me give you an example that actually happened to me.

Story of Sidi's Companion who Overate

One day I was riding a donkey. The donkey was walking and I was with another dervish friend who was also riding a donkey. We boys were invited to a house of one of our brothers in the way, and we were going there. I was in my second or third year of walking this path towards Allāh and my s̲hayk̲h̲ used to say, "Be on alert, be careful of your nafs. If you listen to it, it will destroy you; it will kill you. Do not listen to it." I asked to whom I should listen, and he said, "Listen to the Messenger of Allāh. Listen to him and follow him and disobey your nafs."

We followed the invitation and we arrived at our host's house. The host offered us food. I ate a little piece in accordance with what the Prophet ṣalla-llāhu ʿalayhi wa sallam, taught and so I kept within the limits of one-third for food, one-third drink, one-third left for air and breath. I praised Allāh and my friend started to eat. He continued to eat and eat and he ate what five men would eat.

It is our tradition as Arabs to always invite people to eat and whenever they stop we say, "Take more!" So whenever he finished eating the host would say, "Take more!" And he listened and took more. He had six servings and he was unable to breathe after that. He took too much. And I said, "Let us go home now."

After our visit we went on our way. Along the way he became so heavy for the donkey that the donkey could not walk anymore. How miserable was that poor donkey! I felt sad for him and I started to invoke Allāh for the donkey. Oh please, rid the donkey of that human who is making him suffer. So my companion fell off the back of the donkey and started to throw up everything he ate. So I said, "Let's see who has better understanding, you or the donkey." He said, "Are you crazy, what are you talking about?" I said, "I am serious. Let's test that."

We arrived at a well and we wanted to get some water. I took the bucket and put it in the well to get some water, took it to his donkey, and gave him some water from the bucket. The donkey did not drink all of it. He drank some and satisfied his thirst. Then I held the donkey's ear and said to him, "You are the donkey of so and so – drink more, drink more!!" I even forced his head into the bucket and said, "Drink more! Drink more!" so that my friend would know who had better understanding.

The donkey did not drink, of course, so then I asked my friend, "Who has better understanding—you or the donkey?" The donkey refused to take more than what satisfied him, but many of the children of Ādam behave like donkeys. Donkeys are even more intelligent than them because the donkey refuses to take more than what he needs.

Allāh is truthful, He says the truth when He says that people that they are sometimes like animals, or even worse than animals. Who causes the human to transgress limits like that? It is the nafs, the self, the ego. When the human obeys the desiring, commanding ego, he falls into disease and sickness and suffering and pain and afflictions and he is full of hate and envy and he goes far from the way of Allāh. That is why you must cut your food and drink and obey the teachings of the Messenger, ṣalla-llāhu ʿalayhi wa sallam. These are some stories I said as examples to show you your reality. Allāh creates similitudes for people so that they can know and understand that behind every word there is wisdom.

All animals are nations like us (Qurʾān 6:38). They also remember Allāh and they know Allāh, but the animal does not take more than he needs—ever. He never eats more than his need. Look at the chicken, if you give them more they do not eat more than they need. But the human is like a monster. He is not disciplined. He takes more than what he needs. Animals know what their duty is—what they need, what they should take, and what they should leave, but the human does not.

Our master guide Muḥyi-ḍ-dīn ibn al-ʿArabī taught us, saying, "Learn how to walk to Allāh through watching the dog." We asked him, "Why especially the dog?" He said, "Because the dog has seven good qualities. If one of these qualities is within you, then you can arrive through it. They are:

1. The dog is disciplined. He knows how to go against his self, his nafs, because he has patience.
2. He is honest and He is sincere
3. He is faithful
4. He submits
5. He likes friendship and companionship.
6. He is also jealous, a good jealousy, a protective jealousy for his house and for his friends—he has this protective quality.
7. He has love on a great level. His love is so subtle and so transparent and so sincere, and it continues until death takes him from his friends.

This is a quality, an aspect of some animals. This is why we must wake up, advance in our walking and obey Allāh's commands and avoid His prohibitions.

The reading continues until page 73, "They decrease their food and drink, and reduce the amount of time that they sleep, and their talking decreases because one who is hungry and tired does not desire talking."

He cannot talk, so hunger zips his mouth as if you are...hunger disciplines him. When he is hungry he also remembers the poor and the ones in need and the unfortunate ones.

The reading continues to the end.

Now, we will end at this point and I open for you the door for protection so that you may be able to protect yourself, your children, your houses and your loved ones. You will even be able to protect your parents who have passed away. It is also to protect your walking. Especially since we are in the month of Ramaḍan and Allāh put within it a great blessing and pure goodness.

So whoever would like to take this chance to come forward and come to Allāh, let him do that and help himself in his walking toward Allāh. That will help him overcome his self and his ego that is commanding him and also the reproaching self. He will be able to overcome both aspects of the nafs, the commanding and the reproaching, and this self will submit to him with the help of Allāh. This lower self does not want to give so when you want to overcome it, you must give, you must oppose it and give. When you give and oppose it, then you overcome it and you do what you are worthy of doing, and you obey Allāh and you abort your nafs by doing so.

Sidi gives the promise.

Realities of Being Human

"O Human Being! Who Are You?"
from *He Who Knows Himself Knows His Lord*

Lā 'ilāha 'illa-llāāāāāāh, Lā 'ilāha 'illa-llāāāāāh, Lā 'ilāha 'illa-llāāāāāh
Muḥammad rasūlu-llāh, Ibrāhīm rasūlu-llāh, Mūsā rasūlu-llāh,
'Īsā rasūlu-llāh 'alayhim ṣalātu-llāh.

Allāhumma anta-s-salām wa minka-s-salām
wa ilayka ya'ūdu-s-salām
tabārakta rabbanā
ya dẖa-l-jalāli wa-l-'ikrām

As-salāmu 'alaykum wa raḥmatu-llāh wa bārakatuhu.

Praise be to Allāh
and may the peace and blessings of Allāh be upon our Messenger
and all the other messengers and prophets
and all the beloveds of Allāh
and all the saints and gnostics
and those who are walking on the path to Allāh
and those who are trying to actualize the message
of unity, justice, freedom, peace, mercy, and divine beauty
to free the suffering human from the consequences of separation.
I ask Allāh to provide humanity with good life that is created by Allāh
as He wants it to be, not the life of animals that we are living today.

The human is confused. He does not know bad from good. He cannot discern anymore between what is good and beneficial [versus] what is harmful, detrimental and evil. He will be able to discern if only he listens to the commands of Allāh that came through the angels and prophets and the Messenger. The human must remember his true essence and hold to the human values, because the human in his true essence is pure and purified. He carries the names of the divine beauty and the divine wisdom. He carries the divine wisdom that Allāh deposited within him. By this wisdom Allāh made the godly human being to carry His lofty ethics and actualize them.

Allāh, glory be to Him, Most High, said, "I created Ādam as my reflection, after my own image. I chose him to be my viceregenton this earth and to apply and actualize my ruling and my law the way I wanted it, not the way that the human may want." But the human became rebellious against the divine commands and laws. He thought of himself as the Creator, as the one in control, as the manager who controls everything through his hands. He does not understand anything in the Reality. He can only understand this through Allāh, the true Creator. Allāh put within him lofty ethics and gave him gnostic, divine knowledge. Without that the human would not be able to see life, or to experience it, or to hear or to do anything in it.

On this good morning I will start to explain something about the reality of the human being and to clarify for you who you are, oh human, and why you were created, and what you are carrying in this lower life. Are you just an atom of dust that will go without any meaning or purpose, without any deep meaning or essence? Or are you the one who is carrying the message that reflects all of the lofty ethics of knowledge of beauty and mercy?

Allāh has qualities with limits that the human being cannot reach because He has the absolute beautiful qualities, but He gave the human being some gifts of His qualities. He adorned the human being with lofty ethics and made him as a divine mirror, pure and clear. If the human continues in his divine giving he will continue to live in a most high and lofty garden full of fruits. The Prophet, ʿalayhi as-salātu as-salām, said:

> The one who believes in me today is in the Garden today, not tomorrow. (Ḥadīth̲)

What does it mean to believe in him [the Prophet, ṣalla-llāhu ʿalayhi wa sallam]? It means to know him and to follow his teaching and his example, to taste like he tasted, because tasting is the foundation of knowing. We are not talking about the physical sense of tasting because this is how an animal tastes. We are talking about a subtle human tasting that is full of beauty, full of perfection, full of rest and ease and tranquility. That subtle tasting is a tree that is never cut and never dies; it is always supplying him. It is a power by which Allāh provides people with life, a life that is devoid of all distress and affliction and disaster, a peaceful, tranquil life.

"Oh Human Being! Who Are You?" on page 134 of *He Who Knows Himself Knows His Lord* is read from the beginning until, " 'Tell me the names of

these if you are truthful.' They said, 'Glory be to You. We have no knowledge other than what You have taught us. Truly, You are the All-Knowing, the All-Wise.' "

People ask, "Who are the angels?" and "Who is the human being?" Are we talking about you or are we talking about something else? We are talking about something else. We are talking about the subtle human who is devoid of lower desires, who is devoid of racism and hate and all of the negative qualities. We are talking about the pure, perfect human. We are not talking about the human living with his low and selfish desires or the human who has the qualities of being a deceitful liar, a thief. We are talking about the ideal human that Allāh created as His reflection because Allāh would never order the angels to prostrate to a dirty human being who is full of dirt. The prostration of the angels was to the ideal of the most beautiful and perfect human being whom Allāh cast with His own hands. He says:

> I have fashioned him and I have breathed into him
> from My spirit. (Qur'ān 15:29, 38:72)

That means that the human is created from the spirit of Allāh, not from dirt that is full of hate and envy.

The human who is living today is the one who changed that which Allāh deposited within him, the human who accumulated dirt and enmity. He became the enemy of his brother and sister. He became unable to discern between what is good and evil. He became a destructive monster. Do you see how he violates his brother and sister, how he does not believe in the human beauties that Allāh created in His own image, and how he abuses these beauties and violates them?

How beautiful is the image that Allāh created by His own hands and breathed His own spirit into! How can we equate the lower life with the subtle realm in which the original, eternal human lives? The human contained all the lofty ethics of love, mercy and sensitivity. He was devoid of hate. He never knew enmity. Allāh says:

> I have fashioned him and I have breathed into him
> from My spirit. (Qur'ān 15:29, 38:72)

The human is from the spirit of Allāh. Every human is from the spirit of Allāh. There is no one who came from somewhere else. Allāh says:

> Remember when your Lord said to the angels: "Truly, I am going to create man from clay."
> "So when I have fashioned him and breathed into him [his] soul created by Me, then you fall down prostrate to him." (Qur'ān 38:71-38:72)

When Allāh created the human being He said:

> Humankind is created in My image [it is a divine mirror]. (Ḥadīth Qudsī)

You must then preserve it. Allāh said to the angels, "Prostrate" to this human image which Allāh called [in the Arabic language] "ins." "Ins" in Arabic means "affable" and "courteous." So it is to that image that the angels prostrate; i.e., to the one who has a friendly attitude and affability.

There is a subtle meaning here which commands us to live with such a friendly, courteous manner and affability. The human cannot be described as "ins" unless he adorns himself with these qualities of love and mercy and beauty. His heart must be devoid of hate. With that he lives. If these lofty ethics are lost and go far away from the divine human, then he becomes like a destructive monster. He abuses others and he violates their rights. That is happening today. Look with the divine eyes of Allāh and see what is happening in our world today. It is like battles between two monsters. This is what is happening today.

What are people fighting for? They are fighting for materialistic things, for leadership, and for things like that. They do not care for the life of the human being. They do not care for the justice and mercy. They do not apply these lofty ethics. The divine image means love, it means subtlety, gentleness, kindness. It means that the person looks and sees only Allāh. To be with Allāh is to return to the state where you know who you are. Know who you are. Know who you must be. Know who you were originally and preserve that essence.

Look with the eye that is full of love and mercy. When you talk you must talk with the tongue that is full of love, politeness, and courteous manners. In that state you will be manifesting the divine qualities that Allāh commanded you to manifest. When you see a helpless person you stretch your hand to help him. But whose hand are you stretching? Is it truly your hand? No, it is not your hand. It is the hand Allāh made for you and the hand that he subjugated to be merciful for the poor and helpless and those people in need. This hand would never dare to violate, abuse, or kill anyone. It was not created for this. It was created to distribute mercy, love, and peace, and never to break a heart.

Also, the eyes that Allāh created so beautifully! How glorious and pretty the eye is! Allāh created it to see only beauty and to look only with love. The eye should never look with an attitude of envy or jealousy because it was made as a divine eye. It can only bless. The godly eyes always look with mercy and kindness. They always give love and distribute peace.

How about the ears? They belong to Allāh as well. They should be godly ears. If you are pure and devoid of the pollution and dirt that the human accumulates, you will open your eyes in the morning and the first thing you will listen to is the chanting of the birds and the wind passing through the trees. You will hear only beauty. This is the godly hearing by which you hear only what is good. You will even hear the rivers chanting the glory of Allāh and praying. You will hear the birds chanting dẖikr (remembrance) of Allāh, praising and glorifying Him.

If you want to understand the language of the world and creation, return to the original purity in which Allāh created you, and do not take your senses to something else, away from the purities that Allāh originally created. You were originally pure, so return to your original purity.

Have you not seen that Allāh said to the angels:

> And He taught Ādam the names of everything, then He showed them to the angels and said, "Tell Me the names of these if you are truthful."
>
> They said: "Glory be to You, we have no knowledge except what you have taught us. Verily, it is You [who is], the All-Knower, the All-Wise."
>
> He said: "Oh Ādam! Tell them their names." (Qur'ān 2:31-2:33)

What are the names we are talking about? The names are all the sciences, all the qualities that Allāh created – everything that Allāh created in its original reality.

> He said: "Oh Ādam! Inform them of their names."
> (Qur'ān 2:33)

[He was referring to] the names of everything beautiful. Inform them of the names of love, peace, mercy, and justice. Inform them about all the lofty ethics. Tell them the secrets of this world.

We are not talking about the physical, animal human. We are talking about the subtle human. We are not talking about the physical human because in that state he just acts like an animal. He eats, sleeps, drinks, and has sexual intercourse like any other animal. Allāh gave him these desires but He wants the human to be pure and healthy and to be full of the meaning of love, mercy, and justice.

Allāh wants you to use all of this in your original, pure state. You are glorious. You think of yourself as a tiny microcosm while within you is the magnificent macrocosm. You have all the qualities of creation, from the beginning to the end. It all belongs to Allāh. Allāh created you originally pure as a manifest sign of beauty and perfection. Why then do you destroy that beauty, purity and perfection? Why do you make it dirty? You are destroying yourself.

You made yourself an idol and asked others to prostrate themselves to you. How can they prostrate to you when you are full of dirt and enmity, when you violate the rights of others? Why do you ask others to prostrate to you? You do not deserve their prostration. You want people to prostrate to you because of the power of your weapons and the destructive power of your rockets and airplanes. Prostration cannot happen that way. People will not love you that way because love comes from the heart. The heart is the house of the Lord. People prostrate only to love.

Allāh says:

> My heavens and My earth cannot contain Me.
> Only the heart of My faithful servant contains Me.
> (Ḥadīth Qudsī)

If you want people to prostrate to that love, then be polite with others, have courteous manners with others, and carry lofty, godly ethics. It is not through illusions, pictures, and imagination. No! You must be pure. You must be in the pure and straight way Allāh ordered you to be.

Allāh said, "Be," and you became. You were originally His reflection, full of beauty. Why do you not preserve that? Why do you deface that? It is not permissible for you to deface your original holy image. Do not get confused. Do not point out "This one is evil; this one is good."

We are not talking about metaphorical things. We are talking about the pure and transparent human being that Allāh ordered the angels to prostrate to. Allāh never ordered the angels to prostrate to someone who is full of dirt, pollution and evil. Allāh ordered the angels to prostrate to the godly human being who is the divine reflection in which the divine qualities are actualized and manifest. That means he is full of true knowledge and absolute perfection, beauty and excellence. He is full of goodness, mercy and love. That is the one who is carrying the godly qualities.

I want to ask here, "Who are you, oh human?" Do not think of yourself as someone who is trivial. If you want to transform yourself into an animal in your own way, be as you want. You have free choice, but then know that you will not be happy. You will have a miserable life. You will suffer and be in pain. You will have suffering from your own arrogance and conceit.

We must search for the realty of everything Allāh created. We must return to it and to preserve it to be able to achieve and attain happiness. How can we attain happiness? By following His commands. If Allāh gives us a command we say, "We hear and we obey. We surrender. To You is the final return." We should never transform the words [of Allāh] to suit our own egos, or interpret things our own selfish way. We must always accompany the holy ones. If Allāh orders us to obey, then we obey. If He prohibits us from something then we must avoid it. We should never interpret things in accordance with our ego.

The prophets did not order us from their own selves. They took the orders from Allāh. They speak by the tongue of Allāh. If they order us to do something then we do it. They are honest and sincere. They just convey the message. But for us to interpret things the way we want, to turn ourselves into something, to tailor everything to suit our own ego, is not permissible.

In reality we are nothing, but we become everything by Allāh. By Him we see. By Him we act. By Him we stand up. By Him we live. By Him we can see and hear. Without Allāh we are nothing. In reality we are nothing. We became something only by him. That is why we must prostrate to Allāh. We must listen to Allāh because we are nothing. You may live fifty or sixty or one hundred years, but eventually you will go. You will be buried in the dust.

Are you eternal in this physical life? No, you are not eternal here. You are nothing. It is not up to you. Your eternity belongs to Allāh. What will remain for you? What remains for you is to see by Allāh, act by Allāh, hear by Allāh. Be full of divine beauty, ethics, love, justice and peace. You must be chanting the true song of peace and tranquility. This is your eternity.

The reading continues, "He said, 'Oh Ādam, tell them their names.' "

Who is Ādam? We are talking about the Ādam who carries the divine qualities Allāh gave to him.

The reading continues to the bottom of page 136, "To the spirit, 'imagination' comes from the essence of the individual qualities or from [phantoms], and not from the essence of the immortal qualities."

There is a big difference between existing and witnessing. Existing can be divided into two [types]:

1. The first type is "illusive existence," or "your existence." "Your" existence is illusion.
2. The second type, "metaphorical existence," is higher. You see the imagination. It is as if you are standing on the sun and seeing your shadow. You cannot grasp that shadow, can you? But it does exist! But it is a metaphorical existence because it will also disappear.

So what is your existence? You are a temporary mirror. It has a beginning and an end. Allāh wants you not to get attached to this phantom and illusory existence. Do not worship it and hold it really tightly, because it is like a simple, tiny toy that is very beautiful and attractive that you give to your son or daughter. When you give him/her this toy the child is so happy to have it. For the child the toy becomes a real thing. You are the same. You are a child to God. Allāh gives you this thing that you live with. You live with the pictures, but in Reality these things disappear and you also will disappear.

This means that this existence is illusory. It is not of Reality. If it were of Reality it would stay. What is of the Reality remains. These pictures disappear, so they are illusion. Allāh wants you to transform to the witnessing of the world of eternal existence. When you are witnessing you see that you are a servant and slave worshipper of Allāh.

You are the human the angels prostrated to because you are so pure and clean. That is why the gnostic tells you, "Do not be like the donkey who is going in circles [around the millstone]." Do not keep going around yourself. Transform from the realm of creation to the realm of the Creator. This means travel to your Reality. Do not tire yourself by traveling in circles and not moving from your own place.

Is this not your case? Have you ever stopped going in circles? You work, you eat, you drink, you sleep, and you work again. Are not those the facts you live? If this is your reality then why are you arrogant, boastful? You are nothing. Allāh is fair, just. He says in the Qur'ān:

> Say: "Who has forbidden the adoration with clothes
> given by Allāh, which He has produced for his slaves,
> and all kinds of wholesome food?" (Qur'ān 7:32)

Yes, He gave all these things to you to use, but use them in a balanced way, within the boundaries He has set. Use them in a pure and good way. Be polite. Live in this lower realm in the way He wants you to live.

If you disobey and deviate from the way of Allāh, then you tire yourself. You become miserable. It is not Allāh who makes you miserable and tired. It is you. Do not say, "Allāh made me so sick. Allāh made me so tired. Allāh made me miserable in life." No, you earned that by you own hand (Qur'ān 42:30).

Allāh created you subtle, pure and perfect. You have full perfection and subtlety. How perfect you are! How glorious you are! He gave you this existence. He said, "This is your garden. Do with it as I want you to." But you corrupted it. You damaged it. Allāh gave you complete freedom when He said, "Here it is. Do with it what you want."

The reading continues to the top of page 138, "The Messenger of Allāh, ṣalla-llāhu 'alayhi wa sallam, said, 'Many men have been perfected, but among women, only Mary and Āsiya and 'Ā'isha.' By perfection he means, knowing themselves. Knowing your self is the essence of knowing your Lord."

How can you know your reality if you do not have an image, a reflection? This is why Allāh gave us the perfect men and women as examples. She must be the mirror of his essence and he also should be the mirror for her. That should be pure, clean, perfect love. When a man loves a woman it mirrors for him his essence. So love must be pure and clean. It should never be betrayed, as many people do in this world today. Love must be very pure. Can you drink dirty water? Are you willing to drink water full of pollution? No, but in fact he [the human] is drinking that, and worse than that! Allāh made something so pure, so subtle, so gentle. Why do you pollute it and make it so dirty?

You who betray and destroy the love, know that the love is holy and sacred but you crush it with your feet. We are talking about the divine, godly love that came through the godly mirror of women. The word "woman" is from the Arabic word "imra'ah," which shares the same root verb with the word "mirāh," which means the English word "mirror." This is the deep meaning, the true meaning of women. If a woman is pure then she reflects the divine picture. If the woman is dark and has accumulated rust and dust, will you be able to see your image in her? The human is a criminal because he did not preserve the holy, sacred picture of the woman. So man became dirty and woman did, also.

Imagine having in your home [drinking] glasses that are so pure and beautiful. And then imagine hitting them and pushing them. This would not be using common sense, it would not make sense! It would not be acceptable. It is the same with people. People destroy the pure image of love for both men and women. They destroy themselves because they have not been surrendering to the lofty values and high ethics on which love is built. They become like animals. What are you searching for? You are lost. You lost these gems that Allāh gave to you. You caused them to be wasted, they slipped through your hands. This is why many families are now destroyed, by destroying the heart, which is the house of Allāh.

Allāh says there are houses which He ordered to be raised above all others:

> In houses [mosques], which Allāh has ordered to be raised,
> in them His Name is glorified in the mornings
> and in the afternoons or the evenings (Qur'ān 24:36)

These are the houses where Allāh is remembered, where the chanting of His glory and praise is established. These are the houses of divine gnosis and divine qualities. When you clean these houses and listen to the commands of Allāh and the teachings of His Messenger, then you enjoy these houses that are full of love and beauty. Then you arrive at the station of witnessing. You will not see anything but Allāh. You will only talk with Allāh. You will not hear but by Allāh.

You cannot claim to talk with Allāh while you are still full of dirt. You cannot say, "I am listening to Allāh," while you are still full of sins. You cannot say, "I see Allāh." I say that you are a liar. You have not seen Him yet because you are in opposition to the teachings of Allāh. Your character and attributes show that you are far from Allāh. The person must listen to his loved ones because they see his actions. He sees them, too. They must listen to each other. They are mirrors for each other. Then he will no longer be veiled when he listens to his loved ones.

You are the one who is actually veiled. Allāh is the Manifest. He is the Apparent. Who can hide Allāh? Allāh is manifest in everything. If you look deeply you see Allāh in everything, including in him and in her. If you have the divine insight, then your sight becomes sharp like iron, so clear. You will start to see now, not tomorrow. You cannot claim to be seeing [with the divine sight] if you are not yet in complete surrender to the commands of Allāh.

The servant can be veiled, but Allāh can never be veiled. He is the Manifest. He is manifesting in everything. That is why you must be polite with Allāh and ask Him for provision, help and support. I ask Him to help you and make you understand and open your hearts. [I ask Him] to make you of the sincere and the truthful ones so that you may arrive at what you really wish.

This is something very brief. I wanted to tell you about who you are, oh human.

Do not think that you are a small star.
Do not think of yourself as one from the realm of forgetfulness.

You can always be in the station of excellence and beauty.
Do not think you are lost.
Within you are all the real meanings.
Look at your heart.
You will not find anything but Him.
He is the One Talking.
He is always talking to you through every tongue
that is talking to you.
He is the One Speaking everywhere and always.

Know that Allāh is the secret of clarification. He is the One Who is Always There, in every time and in all places. May the peace and blessing be upon Muḥammad and his family, followers and companions. Everything I see is Allāh, at every time and everywhere.

I ask Allāh to give you safety and security. May He bestow His goodness upon all of you. Whoever wants to ascend from this lower realm that is full of dirt and illusion, anyone who wants to walk to arrive at the secret of gnosis and true knowledge, let him come to me in this blessed moment in which I open the door of gnosis for you. I open the door of rain, the godly divine rain that is now showering upon you, to be able to understand your own reality.

If you know your own reality you will know the reality of Allāh. Allāh will make you see yourself as an essence, and that you are not established but by Allāh. You are not seeing, acting or hearing but by Allāh.

Then
your walking becomes worship,
your sleep, worship
your standing, worship
your sitting, worship
your eating, worship.
Allāh will never be absent from you, even for just the twinkle of an eye.

Then you enter into the station of witnessing. The foundation, the original principle, is to be in the foundation of witnessing, not in the station of the worshipped. Be in the station of witnessing because He is your Most Beloved. Then you will see Him. Do not say that you have a beloved other than Allāh. Allāh is the Beloved. If you love something else then you do not have any knowledge. Look at me with my eyes [of gnosis] because your eyes are the locus of divine epiphany. So look at me with your insight.

Claiming "I, I" is polytheism. It is associating a partner with Allāh.

Stop doing that.
Throw it in the ocean.
Bury it under the earth.
Crush it with your feet.
Never look at it again.

This is an aspect of the Reality that I am ordered to speak to you about so excuse me, my children and my beloveds. I was ordered to speak like that and to explain the Realities to you. I want you to promise me to walk in accordance to the teachings that you heard so that you can attain what you promised, what you heard. I ask Allāh to help you. This is the promise of the spirit. This is the promise of the divine secret, to be His beloveds and lovers, under His majesty, humbling yourselves.

Sidi gives the promise.

This is a very blessed gathering and meeting in which Allāh gave us a gift. He sent His angels upon us and bestowed gifts upon us. He is accepting your coming to Him. He knows that your hearts are calling for Him, coming to Him, and He will not turn anyone away disappointed, because He is the One Who Answers Prayer. He is the Responder. Āmīn. Āmīn. Āmīn.

Farm of Peace Sufi School East

A true Ṣūfī is a unifier.
He is in unity.
He unifies.
He worships Allāh only,
and does not know anything but Allāh.
He does not rely and depend upon anything but Allāh.
He does not surrender to anything but Allāh's order and command.

From "True Fasting"

True Fasting

Lā ʾilāha ʾilla-llāāāāāāh, Lā ʾilāha ʾilla-llāāāāāh, Lā ʾilāha ʾilla-llāāāāāh
Muḥammad rasūlu-llāh, Ibrāhīm rasūlu-llāh, Mūsā rasūlu-llāh,
ʿĪsā rasūlu-llāh ʿalayhim ṣalātu-llāh.

Allāhumma anta-s-salām wa minka-s-salām
wa ilayka ya'ūdu-s-salām
tabārakta rabbanā
ya dha-l-jalāli wa-l-'ikrām

As-salāmu ʿalaykum wa raḥmatu-llāh wa bārakatuhu.

Alḥamdu li-llāh! May the peace and the blessing of Allāh be upon our Master Prophet Muḥammad and all of the other messengers. May the peace and blessing of Allāh be upon the saints and those who are carrying the message of knowledge and unity, who are remembering Allāh while standing and sitting and as they lay on their sides and they contemplate the heavens and the earth. They say, "Oh Allāh, that cannot be created for falsehood, but it is created by the truth." May the peace and the blessing of Allāh be upon all of you.

From the bottom of my heart and my spirit, I praise Allāh, Most High, that He carried me to you and helped me to be here with you. It is a great honor for me to carry the message of Allāh to you and to all who love Allāh. Those who love humanity and love the happiness of humanity, carry for humanity the message of love and peace and mercy and justice and freedom for the whole world.

Those people who are suffering and screaming from pain across the world and stretching out their hands and their hearts, praying for peace and justice, are praying so that their suffering can be lifted. This suffering humanity, I pray for them. I pray for those people, for humanity. You are here, too, to carry this message, the great message, and to pray for them. This is the message of humanity that Allāh ordered His prophets and messengers to carry and to convey to people and to apply, so that people can apply it in their relationships with each other.

Do not forget that this month is the month of worship. It is the glorious month of Allāh, It is the month of Allāh, Most High, in which Allāh is very generous to us. It is the month of misery, but it is the month of empathy as well because we feel the pain and then we help those who are suffering across the earth. It is the great wisdom of Allāh that He made fasting obligatory for all nations, since the time of Ādam to, Ibrāhīm (Abraham), to Mūsā (Moses), and to ʿĪsā (Jesus), ʿalayhim as-salām. It was made obligatory for us, for Muslims who follow the message of Muḥammad, ʿalayhi as-salātu as-salām. This message is for everyone. It is a message of mercy as Allāh said in the Qurʾān to His Prophet,

> We have not sent you but as a mercy for all the worlds.
> (Qurʾān 21:107)

This month is the month of fasting. Fasting is something great. It is made to discipline the selves and to train the hearts and the spirits. It means to prevent oneself from eating and drinking and from having intimate relations with one's wife or husband during the day. This is the outer practice and meaning of it, but there is something deeper and more beautiful if we look at it. It means that the soul itself must fast because the soul has a commanding ego, and it must fast.

This self is the commanding ego that orders you to do evil or bad deeds, and it whispers to you day and night. It whispers to you because behind it is Iblīs—s̱hayṭān. Behind it is the devil whispering, supervising and commanding the self to do that, which is evil and not good. If your self desires what Iblīs is saying to her, she follows him and obeys him and it is called, at that level, the commanding ego. Why is it called commanding? Because it commands the person to do what is evil. Because the commands that she orders you with are deviating from Allāh's way—they are in Iblīs' way, the devil's way.

This self must fast, but we know that all the human's senses must fast to discipline this soul. For this reason we will look at every sense—first, the sense of human sight. The eyes look and they carry great power. They carries the energy of evil or of good because you can look at someone with an envious eye, wishing to have whatever he has, or you can envy him and feel jealous because of his rank or because of the ethics he is exhibiting. That envious one wishes to have these things for himself only. Then he starts to look at his neighbors to wish to have everything they have, and he looks at married couples and he envies them and wishes that they will become separated and he will have relationship only for himself. For this reason fasting is mandatory for the eyes. The major sins start with the eyes.

The eyes lead to the Hellfire, which actually starts with a little spark of fire. How many stares would destroy the person from inside, because the eyes shoot arrows even without having the arrow and the bow; they still have an effect. This is the envious eye that envies others. Our chosen Prophet, ʿalayhi as-salātu as-salām, said,

> The envious eye is real. (Ḥadīth̲)

It can actually cause the death of a person. It can bury men in graves and it can bury the gifts of Allāh in graves. May we seek refuge with Allāh from this envious eye and its afflictions.

This is why when the human looks at something he admires he must say, "mā sh̲āʿa-llāh," this is Allāh's will, because this statement is the treatment for the envious eye. It is the healing, so it can treat his envy. He says, "mā sh̲āʿa-llāh," this is what Allāh willed for that person and may the peace and blessings of Allāh be upon the Messenger and all the prophets and all the saints. If he says this, then he is protecting the other person from being affected by this envy. When anyone looks at something he admires, he must say these words.

Now, let us look at the ears, the human ears. The eye is the servant of the ear. When the ear hears, it looks. The eye will look, following it. It is like the ear is commanding—look at this, look at this. When you even hear with your ear that so and so is successful, that he achieved that much success in his job or whatever he is doing, your nafs start to say, "Why did he achieve that? He does not really deserve it. He is not worthy of it." In this way the ear envies as well, and it orders the eye to look, so the eye is the servant of the ear.

But Allāh did not create the eyes and the ears to look at people in this way. He created them and ordered them by the tongue of his prophets, ʾalayhīm as-salām, to look with love, with mercy and in peace at others, and to feel happy. As the eye sees people happy, it should be happy, and as it sees them suffering, it feels their pain and rushes to them to help them and support them. This is why Allāh made fasting mandatory for the senses.

What is the meaning of fasting, then? It is not to envy and it is not to look with an evil eye. It does not mean that you do not eat and drink while at the same time you wish harm for others and are envious of others and the gifts Allāh gave them. That is not fasting. It is hunger; it is thirst; it is like the animals when they feel hungry and thirsty—there is no difference. This is not fasting. This is not true worship. The true fasting is to praise Allāh, to be in a state of gratitude, and to thank Allāh for everything He has given you and given others.

The heart must also fast. The heart is the king of the body because the Prophet, ʿalayhi as-salātu as-salām, said,

> There is a piece of flesh in the body.
> If it is well, then the whole body is well
> and if it is corrupted, then the whole body is corrupted. (Ḥadīth)

If the heart is devoid of disease and blemishes, like envy, arrogance, selfishness, self-righteousness, boasting about oneself, that "I, I, I..." No, know that you are like everyone else. You are equal. Allāh did not create you out of gold or silver and create others out of chalk. He created all of us from the same thing, from mud. But what distinguishes a human from others is his good deeds. By his good works and good actions he is distinguished from others. That is what makes him distinct from others. Our Master Prophet said:

> You will never be distinguished over others
> by your wealth or what you look like,
> but you will be distinguished
> by your special, beautiful ethics and good actions and words,
> by having complete politeness with Allāh
> and courteous manners with people. (Ḥadīth)

The heart, then, must be pure, devoid of all disease - all envy, all hate. What is the locus of envy? It is the heart. What is the locus of hate? It is inside the heart. Racism and all other evil qualities exist in the heart, so the heart must be pure and devoid of these qualities. Rather, it should be full of love and mercy.

We are talking about the fasting of the senses. If you achieve that, you are like an angel walking across the earth. It does not mean just to abstain from food and drink. It means you feel the hunger of the homeless, the thirst and suffering of the one in pain, and the suffering of the poor people. You must offer them what you can. Fasting is something great. Everything you do is for your own self, but fasting, as Allāh said:

> Fasting is for Me alone, and I reward it directly. (Ḥadīth Qudsī)

Allāh will reward you for fasting—fasting is for the people of the path of Ṣūfism, the path of purification. Fast from everything else except Allāh.

Our hearing must become divine, our tongue must be godly and divine, and every sense must become of God. It means to obey Him only and not to look at anything but Him. It means to be pure and full love, and to be for Him. He becomes our Beloved in existence, and we see Him in every manifestation. We witness Him in all of creation. We must not stay in the station of existence, but we must emigrate to the station of witnessing in which Allāh will not seem absent for even the twinkle of an eye, because your Beloved is never away from you. You see Him day and night. You see Him in your food; you see Him in your work; you see Him in your marriage.

There is nothing but Allāh. He is the One Who Causes Life and Death and He provides for you. You should not see anything but Him, and that means you must surrender to Him. Are you ready to live like the animals live? This is something else then. And it is your choice—you can choose for yourself. If you knock on the door of my Lord and you understand that you should move from the station of existence that is full of suffering and move to the station of witnessing...

Allāh says in the Qur'ān to escape to Him, to seek refuge in Him, because He is your True Protector. Because of this you must surrender, surrender completely, to His commands. What does it mean to escape to Him or seek refuge in Him? It is to surrender to His commands. Your religion must be the religion of unity, you must unify anything that is other than Him, and you must submit all of your affairs to Him because He ordered you to do so. I ask my sons and daughters, please, fast in the best way you can and beware of your commanding ego. Do not turn to it.

People must fast the way Allāh ordered them to fast. The tongue must fast. The tongue must fast from everything that Allāh did not order us to do, because Allāh says:

> Anything the human utters is recorded by two mighty angels—
> a watcher and a recorder. (Qur'ān 50:17)

And what leads people to the Hellfire more than the tongue? It is the fruits of their tongues, the harvest of their tongues, which leads them straight to the Hellfire. It is the Hellfire that Allāh prepared for those rebellious people, because the tongue has a great effect. It has an influence on others. This is why the tongue must never talk about one's brother or sister in a bad way, in backbiting. Because if the tongue starts to backbite or talk badly about a sister or a brother, then the fasting is broken, the fasting is nullified. All of the sins that the senses participate in actually nullify fasting. Do you not see then, that you must control the senses so that they do not disobey, so that you can preserve your relationship with Allāh, Most High?

That is why I say to my children here, upon whom Allāh bestowed His mercy, to my children who have started to know Allāh through this path and have become the children of this way, you must fast. Because you know Allāh now, so you must fast.

Those who did not start to fast last year or this year are not fasting. They must spend for the sake of Allāh in compensation for the days they did not fast. They must spend for the sake of Allāh from their wealth to compensate for the days they did not fast. How much should they pay? Whatever their average meals cost. For example, for some people two meals, lunch and dinner, costs $30. For others it costs $20. That is how they eat in their average daily life. The person must spend the charity in compensation for the days he did not fast last year or this year, and he must offer this charity to the poor. He must spend the equivalent of two meals for each day he broke the fast.

A person who is sick with a chronic disease and cannot make up the days later, can break the fast. He should not be fasting, but he still must feed two meals a day to a person unable to feed himself.

Also, women during their menses should not fast, but if they are able, they should compensate for these days later. After Ramaḍan they should fast to make up for the days they had their menses.

The one who falls sick occasionally for two days during Ramaḍan can break his fast, but he must compensate for these days and make them up later, after Ramaḍan. One must abide by this law between him and Allāh, because you know what you did and Allāh knows, so you must follow the law of Allāh.

Know, my beloveds, that in the month of Ramaḍan the beginning is for forgiveness, the middle is for mercy, and the end is for being saved from the Hellfire. It is a month of worship and it is the month in which one is in retreat with Allāh, Most High. It is a month of retreat, the month of the kẖalwa with Allāh. Let the one who is establishing it in the right way have good news. Let him continue to recite the Qur'ān, remember Allāh, and be with Allāh all through the month. Let him turn away from everything bad that people are doing and be in continuous worship of Allāh.

One must renew his repentance – he should make a special repentance in Ramaḍan because the Messenger of Allāh and all the other messengers ordered and commanded their followers to renew their repentance and make a special repentance during this month, during fasting. This is so that Allāh might accept your fasting and worship. He, Most High, is not pleased with you until you become pure, truthful and sincere in what you do. May He accept your efforts and may He bless you and forgive you all this month. In this month, Allāh can forgive all the sins of the one who repents sincerely and starts to do good deeds, because Allāh says in the Qur'ān:

> Oh My *slaves* who have transgressed against themselves!
> Despair not of Allāh's mercy,
> verily Allāh *forgives* all sins.
> Truly, He is Oft-Forgiving, Most Merciful. (Qur'ān 39:53)

But know that this special repentance in the month of Ramaḍan is so great. It is especially great, and to Allāh belong all spirits and everything. He is able to Accept Repentance and Forgive all sins.

"Introduction to the Meaning of Sūfism" on page 69 of *Religion of the Unity* is read from the beginning until the middle of page 70, "Allāh created people so that they could get to know and to love each other. People should know each other person to person, cooperate with each other, have mercy upon each other, and be compassionate with each other."

The origin of anything in existence is One, without partner. Allāh created this existence and ordered it into being so that everything would come into unity and unify with Him. He is the One in Command. He is the Great Creator and He is the One in Control of this World, and so we must submit to only His command, to His way. Anyone who claims otherwise is a liar and he is expelled from the mercy of Allāh, glory be to Him.

Allāh is not a material thing, and He is not the image that crosses your mind. There is nothing like unto Him, and He is the All-Hearing, the One Full of Knowledge, and He is the Creator and the Originator and He is excellent, He is perfection. He does not accept separation, discrimination, envy or hate. It is not in Allāh's creed to discriminate between people or to separate them, because He created all of us from one soul (Qur'ān 7:189) and within that soul He put His own divine spirit (Qur'ān 38:72). That is why we must surrender to His commands, His laws.

If you surrender to His commands
you will feel secure
you will feel at ease and at rest
and you will feel that way for eternity.

Your original state will return to you and
the door of eternity will open to you.

You will leave this world
which is full of dirt, pollution, diseases, hate and envy
and you will move to the divine world
which is full of love and light and which exists for eternity.

In this realm of Allāh, there is no discrimination, no multiplicity; there is only unity, so seek this. What are you seeking? While you are in your human garment, what are you seeking? Are you seeking yourself? If you are seeking yourself truly, then do it, but with a divine eye, a divine heart and a divine spirit. What I mean by that is to seek, considering the fact that you are a godly human being. You are a divine being. You are not a "normal" or common creation. You are a special creation, because Allāh gave you divine hearing, godly hearing, and godly sight. He gave you all of these beautiful qualities, so you must hear Him and be able to see Him and become a godly human being, a slave to Allāh and a servant.

Allāh said through the tongue of the Prophet, ṣalla-llāhu 'alayhi wa sallam:

My servant does not draw near to Me with
anything more beloved by Me than the religious duties I have enjoined upon him,
and My servant continues to draw near to Me with
voluntary works so that I will love him.

When I love him I am
his hearing with which he hears,
his seeing with which he sees,
his hand with which he strikes and
his foot with which he walks. (Ḥadīth Qudsī)

That person comes into the station of witnessing, he is not in the station of just eating and drinking and doing the things that all animals do. He is not hurting others, acting with cruelty, and becoming a monster as his ego and the s̲hayṭān command him. The secret of unity means to become Allāh's true worshipper, His lover, so that you become a mirror in which He sees you and you see Him. This is the principal of fasting—to fast from all the pictures and to see only Allāh in everything.

This is why it is forbidden for anyone to kill his brother, steal from him, destroy his house, cut down trees, pollute oceans and seas, or invent weapons of destruction. These things are not in the way of Allāh; they are not the creed of any religion—whatever that religion might be. Our master Ibrāhīm, the father of all the religions, came with a message to destroy all idols...

[the recording is lost for a few minutes]

...submission to Allāh that all of the prophets, ʿalayhim as-salām, brought. All the prophets came with the same message, Ādam, Ibrāhīm, ʿĪsā, Mūsā, Muḥammad, ṣalla-llāhu ʿalayhim wa sallam. They are all messengers of God and beloved to Him, and they all came to say, "We are carrying the message of unity. We want to make people one nation."

Allāh, glory be to Him, created you from a single soul (Qurʾān 7:189), and out of it He created Ādam's spouse, and then He created many men and women from a single pair, male and female (Qurʾān 49:13). This means that each human is the brother or sister of every other human. There is no discrimination between yellow, black and white, male and female, because in the message of Allāh, all people are one. There is no discrimination between one human and another; there is no difference. All people are equal...

When people looked and saw that they were diverse in their colors and races and ethnic groups and they started to differentiate and make themselves into groups, they did not surrender and follow the commands of Allāh. Allāh let go of them, so they went into suffering. The greatest sin that humanity committed is losing unity, because they started to command separation; they started to worship people or different aspects of the creation, and did not worship Allāh directly. So they created discrimination and separation. But Allāh said:

> And when My slaves ask you concerning Me,
> then [answer them], I am indeed near.
> I respond to prayers when they call upon Me. (Qur'ān 2:186)

So we must not worship others or ask them instead of Allāh.

Allāh said, "If you do not surrender to My commands and return to the unity and the station of witnessing, and if you do not stop all the things you are doing and all of your disobedience to the natural law of Allāh, then go ahead, see if you can find another Lord." And may Allāh forbid, there is no other Lord, so where will you go? There is only Allāh, so where will you escape? There is no escape. That is why Allāh made fasting mandatory for us, for all people. He said, "Oh you who believe, fasting is written upon you just as it was written upon all of the people who came before you."

Fasting in its true meaning has a condition. What is the condition? It is to keep oneself from everything that Allāh prohibits and to not look to the existence, to the sensual existence. Look to the station of witnessing and look from there, because when you look at that station you see only Allāh; you see that Allāh is in control. If you are seeing that other people are in control then you are in polytheism. You are committing the sin of associating a partner with Allāh and you are not being in His way. If you start to see yourself as in control, as someone better than others, then you are also associating a partner with Allāh and you are not being in His way.

This is why I say, your existence, your very existence is polytheism, and it is not equal to any other sin because you are associating a partner with

Allāh if you see yourself as someone greater than others. You will become great only if you surrender completely to Allāh, submit to Him and abide by following His commands. Then you become something worthy of it.

Otherwise, the tiny insect is better than you. Why? Because such an insect does not claim to be something other than what it is. It accepts its state. That tiny insect knows who and where she is and accepts her state. Be like this. Be a true slave and servant of Allāh, then you will become great. Witness Allāh. Be in the station of witnessing and you become great, but only by Allāh. You become noble by Allāh. You become powerful by Allāh. You become a lover of Allāh. This is the origin of the message.

The reading All people are equal. Humankind is not peculiar to a man or to a woman. Both are humankind. They both share humanity, for Allāh said in the Qur'ān, "We created humans in the best mold." He did not say, "I created men in the best mold or I created women in the best form (Qur'ān 95:4)." He said that in general He created humans in the best form. The names that humans give each other are just names. Our ancestors came up with these. But the reality is, that a human is a human...

[the audio cuts out for a little here]

...what does it mean to adorn yourself? You adorn yourself with all the beautiful attributes by following the commands of Allāh. You adorn yourself, you beautify yourself with the beautiful attributes so that none of your organs, hands or feet, will do evil deeds like killing or stealing or violating people's rights or being an oppressor. Instead you beautify yourself by surrendering to the commands of Allāh. It does not befit someone to claim, "I am a Ṣūfī, I am a pure one," while not following the commands of Allāh—not praying as Allāh commanded him to pray.

Such a person is a liar. You cannot drink water if it is full of dirt. Purity means to fully surrender to the commands of Allāh. You must be in surrender and submit to every single command that Allāh ordered. Allāh established these orders for us and prohibited certain things, and He said, "Listen and obey." Whoever obeys Allāh and His Messenger will be successful. The one who obeys the Messenger is actually obeying Allāh. Obey all of the messengers and all of the prophets. Allāh sent them as a mercy for us because they show us how to arrive at His presence. But the one who says, "I am a Ṣūfī," and does not pray the true prayer; and at the same time he lies and kills and spreads corruption around the earth, and then says, "Allāh commanded me to do these harmful things," is a liar, because Allāh never commands to evil.

The one who takes people's money wrongfully and deceives them and discriminates between them and also makes himself better than others and looks down on others as if they were his slaves, is not truly pure. He is not a Ṣūfī. If he does not love for others what he loves for himself, he is not pure, he is not a Ṣūfī. Because the Ṣūfī, the true pure one, is full of mercy and devoid of envy and hate and discrimination. He is unity. He is a unifier. He loves people and serves them and does what is good. So if such a person who spreads corruption and separation is asked what his religion is and he says, "I am a Ṣūfī," I say he is a liar and an evil one. He is not a pure one. He is not a Ṣūfī.

Your religion is unity—it is to unify with Allāh. This means to surrender to His law and His commands and to not cause separation and not discriminate between people. You should be carrying the message of unity, love and mercy and justice and believe in all the messengers without creating separation and discrimination between any of the prophets. Listen to the message of the prophets, apply it, follow it and surrender to its instructions.

There is no religion that is called Ṣūfism. It is not that. It is not a name. It is a creed—a creed of unity. It is to be in that state and to believe the way Ibrāhīm believed, the way Mūsā believed, the way ʿĪsā believed, the way Muḥammad believed. They believed that the Lord is one and so their creed was one, their beliefs were the same. It is the belief in the unity. But the one who claims otherwise, his actions claim otherwise; he is a liar and is outside the range of the true religion of unity.

I ask you: how can you arrive at this true station of purity? You can arrive through discipline and training the self, through purifying the self. So purification has two aspects—to renounce negative things and to adorn and beautify yourself with beautiful things. To renounce everything that Allāh prohibited for you, and then adorn and beautify yourself with everything Allāh wants for you. So this is our religion. It is one and the same religion carried by all the prophets. That is why we say the father of all the prophets, Ibrāhīm, carried the message of pure intuition of unity. His creed, his belief, was belief in the unity of Allāh and the unification of people.

But the one who does otherwise is just a deceiver. He is a liar. He is in sin. He claims to be something he is not.

A true Ṣūfī is a unifier.
He is in unity.
He unifies.
He worships Allāh only,
and does not know anything but Allāh.
He does not rely and depend upon anything but Allāh.
He does not surrender to anything but Allāh's order and command.

Because your Lord is One, your God is One. He is the Creator, Most High, glory be to Him. He said to Mūsā, "It is Me; I am Allāh. I am Allāh and there is no God but Me so worship Me and establish regular prayer for Me." He said to Ibrāhīm, "There is no god but Me. Worship Me and establish prayer to remember Me." He also said this ʿĪsā.

The first thing, the first word that ʿĪsā uttered was "Allāh." When his mother brought him to her people and the people said, "How did you become pregnant with that child?"

> Then she [Maryam] pointed to him [ʿĪsā].
>
> They said, "How can we talk to a child in the cradle?"
>
> He [ʿĪsā] said, "Truly! I am a slave of Allāh,
> He has given me the Scripture and made me a Prophet.
> And He has made me blessed wheresoever I be,
> and has enjoined on me prayer, and zakāh, as long as I live.
> And dutiful to my mother, and made me not arrogant, unblest." (Qurʾān 19:29 – 19:32)

ʿĪsā talked in his cradle and said, "I am the slave and servant of Allāh. I am the slave and servant and of Allāh." He did not say, "I am the son of Allāh." He said, "I am the slave and servant of Allāh and my mother is truthful."

These are the prophets of Allāh, the states of the prophets. They said, "We are slaves and servants." They did not say, "I," "I." But what about you? You claim that, "I, I and," but in our creed we are the children of this way, the children of purity, the people who discipline themselves and purify themselves. They believe only that Allāh is One. We believe that Allāh is One and we believe there is no mediation between you and Allāh. You have a direct relationship with Allāh. We tell you, "Here you are with your Lord, with a direct relationship. You can move right to Him. You can reach Him directly, without any mediation."

People asked the Messenger of Allāh, "Where is Allāh, how can we reach Him?" Allāh replied:

> And when My slaves ask you concerning Me,
> then [answer them], I am indeed near.
> I respond to prayers when they call upon Me. (Qur'ān 2:186)

He responds to you directly, without any mediation. So you do not want to put something in the middle between you and Allāh—you do not want to talk to the guide and say, "Oh, please ask Allāh for me." No, you should not be putting an idol between you and Allāh. Ask Allāh directly.

But you can look for a guide who guides you to what is good, who advises you, who shows you the good way and teaches you how to discipline yourself and walk to Allāh. This is something else. It is not as you believe, that he has power. He is like you. He is poor, just as you are, and he needs Allāh all the time just as you do. So he is equal to you. Many seekers are truthful and they arrive because of their truthfulness and sincerity in seeking Allāh, Most High, and so this is the origin of the message.

The reading continues until page 75, "This is why we tell you that the message of Ṣūfism, of purity, is not achieved by the one who makes claims like, "I am a Muslim," "I am a Jew," and, "I am a Christian," while he murders people, steals from people, does not do good deeds, and violates people's rights. Those are the ones who deviate from Heavenly instructions."

This is the time. It is the blessed month of Ramaḍan in which I open for you the door of special repentance, the repentance of Ramaḍan. Everyone must come to it and actualize it, embody it. After I explained the true meaning of repentance and what its rights over you are, that you must observe, you must come and repent fully. You should repent every month and keep renewing your repentance, because humans are full of sins. There is not a day that goes by that he does not fall into fault, make mistakes and commit sins.

If you want to be pure and clean, make use of this blessed month in which Allāh opened the door to repentance. He opened the door of repentance in Ramaḍan by saying:

> In the beginning of Ramaḍan there is forgiveness,
> in the middle there is mercy
> and at the end there is saving from the Hellfire. (Ḥadīth)

Do not let anyone claim that he repents if he then returns, after Ramaḍan, to committing the same sins. The one who returns to commit the same sins is a liar against himself. He lies to himself. He lies to his very existence and even graver than that, he lies to Allāh. But Allāh knows; He knows what is hidden. He knows everything, and nothing in the heavens and the earth is concealed from Him. So everyone who commits sins—sins against himself first and then against his family—come and repent.

Do not keep yourself from repentance. Do not stop from coming and returning to Allāh so that Allāh may accept you and purify you. I hope you are sincere and honest in your repentance, because your sincerity and repentance are not for me. I ask you to be sincere and honest for Allāh, Most High, and to come to Allāh, because I am only a slave and servant. I cannot give you forgiveness. I can ask Allāh for you on your behalf, to accept your repentance and prayers and to make you one of His worshippers and slaves and servants.

Sidi gives the promise.

The Inspired Soul: The Third Station

"The Inspired Self"

From *He Who Knows Himself Knows His Lord*

Lā 'ilāha 'illa-llāāāāāāh, Lā 'ilāha 'illa-llāāāāāh, Lā 'ilāha 'illa-llāāāāāh
Muḥammad rasūlu-llāh, Ibrāhīm rasūlu-llāh, Mūsā rasūlu-llāh,
'Īsā rasūlu-llāh 'alayhim ṣalātu-llāh.

Allāhumma anta-s-salām wa minka-s-salām
wa ilayka ya'ūdu-s-salām
tabārakta rabbanā
ya ḏha-l-jalāli wa-l-'ikrām

As-salāmu 'alaykum wa raḥmatu-llāh wa bārakatuhu. Al-ḥamdu li-llāh.

May the peace and blessings be upon our Messenger and all the messengers and prophets of Allāh, ṣalla-llāhu 'alayhim wa sallam, the gnostics, saints, and all those who are on the path of Allāh, raḍiya-llāhu 'anhum.

I praise Allāh, Most High, for bringing me here to you tonight to show you how to walk to Allāh, not in an illusory or imaginary way. Those who are subjected to pictures and illusions think they are with Allāh. They see and they hear and their state is never equal to the state of the gnostics. They are walking, and the reality with which they walk and what they see and comprehend is not real. It is illusion. One can claim, "I passed the station of the commanding ego and the reproaching self. I passed these levels and I have already arrived at the station of the inspired soul, the pleased soul. I have reached to the perfect soul."

Rely on Allāh and it is better for you. You would not be able to bear that wind if Allāh really brought it. So what if it truly happened and a severe storm came? What would you do? This government which is illusive and thinks that it is in control, what would it do then? They cannot prevent water from coming from the sea. Why do they claim to be in control? When you realize your helplessness and disabilities, then you actually have knowledge of that truth of Reality. So those who boast and are arrogant, know that your reality is one of helplessness, and you cannot withstand the wind.

We are talking today about the station of the inspired soul. Know that there is also the station of the egoistic self, the commanding ego, and the reproaching soul. Did you already pass through them? Understand that they are all names for one thing, but the soul wears different garments.

Imagine a woman who wears seven garments, and each dress is a different color. The woman dresses differently each time, but she is a single woman, only one woman. She lies about her beauty to her metaphorical beloved. She dresses in these beautiful garments to claim beauty and deceive her lover. So she deceives and seduces him by wearing a different dress every time. She has not changed. It is only the outer dress that changes. She gives him a different color so that she can sell her goods and receive what she wants. However, she is deceptive and a liar, and she plays with seven traps that she prepares.

You must be intelligent and know it is the same soul, metaphorically. She is the same woman with only one color, and these outer dresses are not a reality. You must be conscious and have sound comprehension and understanding. Do not listen to her even if she screams loudly. Just ignore her until her voice disappears. Let her take off her garments one after the other until she takes off all seven of her garments. You will find she is one and the same without any different pictures. It is one and she is carrying seven names.

The first level of the soul is the commanding ego, and we have explained it. It is a must to understand her and to understand her voice, her qualities, and description. You must understand at each level the locus of that soul, its realm, its qualities, and what the healing is for it. You must understand why she comes now with a white dress. Why she comes next with a red dress or with a yellow or green dress. Why she comes in different colors.

We are talking about the human self that colors herself with a different garment. One time she dresses with the garment of envy. Another time she dresses with the garment of hatred, power, killing, or harm. Sometimes she comes with a nice, subtle, beautiful garment. In her outer appearance, she is carrying good food, but inside that food could be poison. Be careful, oh miserable one, because if you eat from her food, and listen to her, she may give you enthusiasm. She may whisper to you that you are the best teacher now. You are the one who has passed through all the stations, and you understand and are deserving of this level or station.

You seek her but you cannot find her. "Where are you, the one who is guiding me?" She will answer you, "I went away and I left you lonely to suffer." She says, "Do not listen to me. Why do you listen? Listen to the One and only, because I do not remain here for you. I will travel and go far away from you today or tomorrow but the One Who remains is the only One, Allāh." The people who hang onto these deceptive qualities are not truly seekers, pursuing the path of Allāh.

Walking and leaving behind that level of the soul is very important. The next station will never be open unless one is truly sincere and truthful and does not look to the right or the left or to pictures, illusions, or imagination. He does not stop even with the subtle, high images. He will always say, "Only Allāh. I am not satisfied with these pictures. I am only satisfied and inspired by Allāh."

The true seeker must say, "I am never opening my eyes to illusion, pictures and things that will annihilate. I open my vision only to the One Who created me in excellence and perfection. I look only at Him, because He is my Creator and Provider. He is the One Who takes my hand and helps me, the One Who Bestows His Gifts upon me. It is not permissible for me to look at any other but Him." To whom do you look if not to Allāh? Do you look to illusion, to something that does not exist?

"Oh, wherever I look, Laylā you are my compass, my focal point. Oh Allāh, there is nothing in my existence but You. You are the witness of humans. And oh Allāh, You are the witnessed. There is no third."

Allāh says in the Qur'ān that there is the one who witnesses and the one who is witnessed (Qur'ān 85:3). Is there not always a couple, a bride and a groom in your metaphorical realm? This is your world. It is an illusory, metaphorical world. Each woman is awaiting a groom and each man is awaiting a bride. However, this is all illusion. You are truly waiting for the One Who Created and Inspires you. He is your Originator and He provides for you. This is the One you should be waiting for. Why do you travel and emigrate to pictures, illusions and the imagination while Allāh is saying, "Escape to Allāh. Seek refuge in Allāh. Do not look at anyone but Me."

So when you open your vision, oh seeker, open your eyes to look at Allāh only and nothing else. This means you look at the Truth, the Reality. This truth is in everything, every creature. This is what you should be looking at, the Truth and Reality within creation, beyond the outer appearances.

Allāh sent down two books, one book which is written and one book which is to be seen. The visible book is you. It is every creation. Allāh manifested Himself within you and within all of His creation. When you look you are seeing the Reality, so you must see the Truth in every creation. You are holy and pure in your essence. You cannot be just a metaphorical picture; you are in truth a mirror in which Allāh manifests Himself. Do you not feel ashamed, then, to claim another lord or an idol beside him? You must walk honestly and directly toward Him, because when you know His Reality He will make you have faith in Him. He will provide for you faith that was absent from you before.

You must leave all illusions and pictures. Through your sincerity and honesty and by fully directing yourself toward Allāh, you will find the Truth, because you are looking for the True Beloved. You are a lover and as long as you are a lover, you need a Beloved. Who is the one whom you love? Do you love the lower realm? Do you love illusions and pictures? Do you love the afflictions of this lower realm? Allāh says that the true believers are the ones whom He loves and then they love Him. He put in His love in you first. He loved you before you loved Him.

In the world we call to Him and say, "I love you," and everything in creation will hear the command of our Beloved. Why? Because you are the beloved, and when you dress in the garment of love, you actualize that love to the One Who is beloved. This is the One Who is Manifesting within your own self, the One Who created you and loves you. Allāh is the origin of beauty and beauty comes from Him. This is the Beloved whom you love. Therefore love whomever you want and you love Him, if you understand deeply.

Story of a Man Who Didn't Know Love

One day a man came to my master guide and said to him, "Oh Sidi, I want to take the promise with you. So my guide asked, "Do you know love? Did you ever love someone?" "No not yet, Sidi." So he said, "Go and love anybody, even go and love a donkey, and then come to me. How can you walk in the path of the people of love when you have not tasted love yet?" I heard this conversation and I was young, seventeen or eighteen years old, and I was wondering what my master guide was saying. Was He saying, "Go and love a donkey?" It was something beyond me at that time. He was one of the gnostics.

He took my hand and said to me, "My son, there is a difference between saying, walking, tasting and experiencing. You must taste and experience. If you do not taste, then you are a liar, and you are not straightforward. When you taste the real taste of love, and you become sincere and honest in your love for Him, then you will not see anything but Him. There will be no deception coming out of you. There will be no harm to others, nothing, but you will walk straight forward. When you treat anyone, you will know that you are treating Allāh. You will treat them in the way of Allāh. You will not hate anyone. You will love everyone, and you come into the true station of love. In this is a reminder to anyone who possesses a true heart and can hear.

The lover does not know hatred, destruction or harm. He knows only Allāh and he respects everyone. He respects all of creation and he cannot hurt even an ant or a honeybee. He cannot hurt any of Allāh's creation because he becomes and actualizes love. The truthful and sincere lover walking in the first steps of the station of the inspired soul must walk full of love. The seeker will be well-established in the station of the inspired soul when he can bring that full love to all people without discrimination, boasting or being arrogant. Without hatred or envy, he carries only pure goodness for everyone.

This means that he is just starting to taste, because when he hears the call he asks, "Who is calling me? Is this the voice of my Beloved, my Lord? What is my Lord saying? Would my Lord ever say to hate people? No. Would my Lord say to assault this one, cut off this one, or to envy that one?" No. He would say, "That cannot be the voice of my Lord," because he tastes love. The taste of love will not make you hate people. His whole reality and creed becomes one which is pure unity. He loves only one, therefore he loves all.

Have you ever seen a heart that was able to love more than one beloved at a time? Would you be able to love more than one man at a time? Allāh says in the Qur'ān that he did not put two hearts in one man. He gave the man only one heart, so he loves only one. Who is capable of loving two at the same time? If you are capable, then raise your finger; tell us now. Is there anyone who is capable of sincerely loving two at the same time?

If you are truthful and sincere then walk with truthfulness and sincerity with Allāh so that people may love you. If you become sincere, purify your religion for Him, obey His commands and avoid His prohibitions. Then you enter into His Realm. If Allāh tells you to fast then you must fast. You must preserve the essence of fasting, because it is a command from your Beloved and you want to please your Beloved. The gnostic said that the lover is always obedient to his Beloved, and always wants to please Him. Do you accept any beloved beside Allāh? Always remaining with you, He is the Absolute Beloved and the Lover. Would you love someone or something that passes away and no longer exists?

Understand that when you die and leave your body you will travel to another realm. Over there you will meet Allāh and you want Him to open His arms and embrace you, saying, "Welcome, My beloved. You are the one who kept My promise and kept the covenant of love with Me. Welcome to you, oh one who obeyed Me and trusted My command and avoided My prohibitions."

This is the first station of testing. In this station, you have passed away from your existence. Your witnessing is what remains. You no longer need to look behind anymore. You must look only straight and walk forward to Allāh. This is something brief that I wanted to hint about regarding the station of the inspired soul. The words in Arabic are deeper than this English language. I heard it but did not hear the music of Allāh. Read, Bismi-llāh.

"The Inspired Self" on page 90 of *He Who Knows Himself Knows His Lord* is read from the beginning to "In this station, its walking is upon Allāh, which means that the wayfarer does not open his eyes except to look at Allāh, the Exalted, because the manifestation of the reality of faith has permeated his inner being..."

This is the state of the one who is full of attachment to Allāh. He has transitioned into the other realm and the spirit of the lover merges with the Beloved, and only One remains. Your spirit is incarnate in your body, but it is able to transfer to the other realm. Rābiʿa, raḍiya-llāhu ʿanha, said:

> Oh Allāh, I love You with two types of love.
> There is the love of passion and
> The love by which You ought to be loved.

> It is impossible for me to see anything but You
> in all of Your outer creation.

In this station you do not know anything but Allāh, and you walk directly toward Allāh. This does not mean that you allow others to insult you or take advantage of you. Allāh wants you to be intelligent, with a sound intellect and comprehension. Allāh never tells you to be foolish. He wants you to be conscious and of sound comprehension, putting everything in its rightful place. It says in the Fātiḥa:

> Guide us to the straight path. (Qur'ān 1:6)

The one who walks in the way of Allāh is most intelligent, beautiful and pure, with sound judgment. The Ṣūfī, the pure one, is not lazy, deceptive or a liar. His qualities become divine, godly. He is shy, modest, intelligent and active in work.

The reading continues to page 91, "Its qualities are generosity, satisfaction..."

The seeker in this station must have knowledge, generosity, humbleness and politeness. These are the characteristics of arrival at this station.

The reading continues until, "Among some of the qualities of the inspired soul are yearning, bewilderment, weeping..."

The qualities of the inspired soul are yearning and bewilderment before Allāh, with regret and sorrow for any shortcomings he may have had in the past. He weeps for the days that he wasted playing games, lying, deceiving and participating in illusion and imagination. This weeping is beautiful and good because it washes him and shows his sincerity and regret. The ones who weep a lot are beloved to Allāh because they confess their guilt and sins. Whoever repents, Allāh welcomes and accepts them. He promised to forgive the one who repents and rectifies his past deeds (Qur'ān 5:39).

The Prophet, ʿalayhi as-salātu as-salām, said that there are two types of eyes which will not be touched on the Day of Judgment:

1. **The first are the eyes that remember Allāh and cry from the sorrow and regret from having looked at something other than Allāh.** It is the eye that cries for any shortcomings. The person

with this type of eye will not be harmed by the Hellfire on the Day of Judgment.

2. **The second eye is in the person who gave everything that was precious in his life to Allāh.** This is the eye of the person who renewed his covenant with Allāh. We are not talking about the promise of the body, soul, and heart. We are talking about the promise of the inspired spirit with a heart that has nothing else in it but Allāh. She takes a promise that it will never scratch or crack this heart.

The reading continues down the page, "The inspired soul is called thus because the Real inspires it with both righteousness and corruption, and it has begun to hear, without intermediary, the whisperings of the angel and those of the s̲hayṭān, whereas in the previous station it heard nothing..."

In the previous station, there was no discernment between the voice of the Most Merciful and the voice of the s̲hayṭān. However in the inspired soul, the soul starts to listen. Allāh opens the door for you and makes you enter through that door. He says, "Rely on Me and listen." The soul starts to hear and is able to discern the two voices at this time. This is the truth, the reality of that state. I gave you a brief introduction to what I wanted to explain to you today. Tomorrow we will continue and expand our explanation. I ask Allāh to take your hand and help you to walk to Him.

Now I would like to open the door for you to renew your promise of the heart and the soul in order to continue your walking to Allāh. Whoever is ready with a pure and sincere intention, let them come now and rely on Allāh. This promise is not one for the physical body that will be forgotten later. It is for the heart and soul to continue walking toward Allāh. If you give this promise with pure intention it will help you move from the station of the reproaching self to the inspired self.

I ask that you do not postpone this chance. Make use of this time and take this promise, because it is good and will help you in your walking. The promise that you are giving is to be sincere and truthful with Allāh. If you are sure that you are truthful, honest, and sincere, and not deceiving or lying to yourself, then come take the promise. We will return the promise to you so that you can reach Allāh with your whole heart, and He will return to you as well. Stretch your hand and do not postpone this step. This chance may not come again.

Sidi gives the promise for the heart and soul.

Listen and Let Go

"The Inspired Self"

From *He Who Knows Himself Knows His Lord*

Lā ʾilāha ʾilla-llāāāāāāh, Lā ʾilāha ʾilla-llāāāāāh, Lā ʾilāha ʾilla-llāāāāāh
Muḥammad rasūlu-llāh, Ibrāhīm rasūlu-llāh, Mūsā rasūlu-llāh,
ʿĪsā rasūlu-llāh ʿalayhim ṣalātu-llāh.

Allāhumma anta-s-salām wa minka-s-salām
wa ilayka ya'ūdu-s-salām
tabārakta rabbanā
ya dha-l-jalāli wa-l-'ikrām

As-salāmu ʿalaykum wa raḥmatu-llāh wa bārakatuhu.

On this blessed day, which is the second day since I have arrived, I send my greetings to your physical beings, souls, hearts and spirits, with the loftiest signs of love and mercy. I wish for you to remain in a life which is pure and good. This life is one in which you have knowledge and gnosis that will transform your souls from one station to the next, from the station of the commanding ego, to the reproaching self, on to the inspired self. Allāh wants the soul to become more and more transparent and sensitive. He wants the soul to transform from the animal life to another life in which there is full and complete love, beauty, and gnosis. In this realm, the soul takes directly from Allāh, and not from his desires or the shayṭān.

There is no real taking from illusion, pictures or imagination. She washes and reconciles with Allāh, getting rid of the blemishes, pain and suffering of the lower world. There is a cleansing from diseases of the cheap life for which the human fights. This causes him to abandon his travel to Allāh. The human has settled into the station of the lower desires, falling down to the lowest animal life. Allāh does not want this type of life for us because He honors the children of humanity. He said:

> And undoubtedly We have honored the children of Ādam
> and We have carried them on land and sea. (Qurʾān 17:70)

This means He carried the children of Ādam from the station of the land, to the station of the sea, to the station of heaven. Do not take this literally. The station I am talking about is this realm of the lower life, which is the station of land. In this realm, there is no difference between the human and the animal that walks on four legs.

However, the human being is different than this. Allāh made him a king, the viceregent of himself on earth. Allāh decreed this life for him. Allāh says in the Qurʾān:

> Truly, We did offer the trust
> to the heavens and the earth, and the mountains,
> but they declined to bear it and were afraid of it.
> But man bore it. (Qurʾān 33:72)

The human being carries that trust because of the ignorance and oppression within himself. He oppresses himself. Allāh says, "Blame yourself, because you wanted to carry it. You made that choice. You chose what you chose and We gave you what you chose. You accepted the trial because you were arrogant and not so intelligent. You were in the realm of your desire and you did not recognize that the One Who is testing you is your Lord."

He presented the trust to you and asked if you were Ibrāhīmic or Mūsāic. Are you like Mūsā (Moses), Muḥammad, or ʿĪsā (Jesus), ṣalla-llāhu ʿalayhim wa sallam? Are you one of them? Are you able to carry the trust? Choose for yourself what you like. Become the Ibrāhīmic slave; be a servant like Ibrāhīm (Abraham). Ibrāhīm said:

> I will emigrate for the sake of my Lord
> [i.e. I am performing my pilgrimage to my Lord.]
> (Qurʾān 29:26)

He submitted to Allāh, surrendering completely with his whole self, his world, his soul and everything belonging to him. He rid himself of his human soul. He did not want to become just the human self; therefore, he divorced this self without any intention of returning to it. He washed himself with godly water and drank from godly love. He is one of those who tasted, and whoever tastes knows (Ḥadīth). When he tasted the true taste of divine love, beauty and life, his spirit became godly, divine.

There is no room for change from this state, because it is the station of Ibrāhīm. Allāh bestowed his gift upon the children of Ibrāhīm, to the special ones among them who were truthful and sincere. This station is vast, limitless. It has no beginning and no end. It is vast enough to contain millions and millions of humans.

The Ibrāhīmic station was named after him. His name has two syllables: "Ibrā" and "hīm." What does this mean? It means that when you heal from all of the diseases of the self and move through the stations of the soul, then you become One in the eternal realm. In this realm there is no death and no annihilation. You will just taste the first death in order to pass from here to the next realm.

The one who possesses this station was asleep, but when Allāh put him on trial he submitted to Allāh fully. The submission to Allāh is the recognition that there is no power or strength except Allāh. It also means surrendering to Allāh's commands and avoiding His prohibitions, and not allowing the ego or s̲hayṭān to take hold. The realm of the egos or individual selves is the realm of illusion. You made it. However, the human is something so great. Look at yourself carefully. When you sit, your imagination runs wild. You build palaces and you think of yourself as a great this and that. But within a twinkle of an eye...

In the Qur'ān they ask you about the mountains. Allāh will bring the mountains to dust within a twinkle of an eye (Qur'ān 20:105). Humans build high buildings, travel to space, and invent what they want while they fight and dispute without end. His life transforms into an animal life, and even worse than that to a monster life in which there is no mercy, love or peace. The family of Allāh who are the Ibrāhīmic people have moved to the other realm while still in this lower realm. They transformed this life into gardens and meadows full of beauty, love, godly subtleness and gentleness. They divorce everything of which Allāh does not approve.

Allāh approves of two things only:

1. He approves of the eternal life that is without end and
2. He approves of annihilating everything except Allāh and merging with Him.

While walking on the path you have a certain name, but your fragrance will be smelled from miles away. It would be so beautiful to become a slave and a servant who is full of Allāh's love. You wash yourself with the eternal godly water. Your world then becomes very different from all others. You become something else. You become different from the humanity which is in disobedience to the divine natural law. This is the station of the spirit which is transformed from the soul station, the self station, to the spiritual station. In that station your heart will be full of the meaning of true knowledge. You will be new people given a new birth. This is the realm of the heart. The heart becomes more alive. Allāh says:

> My heavens and earth cannot contain Me
> but the hearts of My faithful believers have been containing Me. (Ḥadīth Qudsī)

The heart cannot contain Allāh in a literal way, but this means it has full knowledge of Allāh. It surrenders, obeys, and listens to only Allāh. It annihilates everything except Allāh. Then he hears and sees through Him. He stands up with Him and has knowledge through Him. The divine attentive care surrounds him. The heart becomes so vast, because it contains the One Beloved that you see. You see Him and you accept Him as your Beloved. You accept yourself as His lover.

This life I am talking about is real if you annihilate everything except Allāh. When you become the godly servant and slave, surrendering to the divine commands of Allāh, you become more glorious than the angels. The angels prostrated to your father Ādam. You can become this station also, and the angels will prostrate to you.

Have you not heard that when Allāh asked the angels to prostrate to Ādam, He did not mean to the Ādam that is full of dirt, envy and hatred; not to prostrate to the one who kills and steals. We are talking about the Ādam who annihilates everything that is not Allāh. He lives with Allāh only, following His commands and avoiding His prohibitions. Allāh's love is marvelous. His taking of you is by force.

Reconcile with Allāh. His reconciliation can happen within a twinkle of an eye. Live all your life with Him and in His presence. Why do you show people how to live in dirty places and then state that you are in this station or that station? Who gave you permission to do this while you are deviating from Allāh's divine law? Know that Allāh is nearer to you than your jugular vein (Qur'ān 50:16). He is very close to everyone, and He sends you noble, honorable messengers to teach you. You can learn directly from their teachings and follow their instructions.

Then you become the leader of the guidance, the imām al-ḥuda. This means your sight, healing, and hand become divine. Everything becomes godly in you, because you annihilated everything that was not Allāh. You listen to and do things only by Allāh. You follow Him, and you are in the station of witnessing Him always.

So where are you when you are in this station? Where is so and so? You are not, because you have annihilated in everything that Allāh commanded. Therefore, there is nothing else but Allāh in His realm. You are with Allāh in every breath, because you cannot utter a word without the permission of your Lord. "Oh our God, it is You Whom we worship. It is through You that we ask guidance to the straight path." Do you not say this in your daily prayer?

Allāh is your straight path so be with Him. Say, "Oh Allāh, let me be in Your heart. Let me be in Your eyes so I can look with Your eyes and become the godly slave and servant who always obeys You. I can only see You because You are my witnessed Beloved. You are everything in my life."

This is a very good morning because Allāh bestowed knowledge of Him upon us, and made us listen to His sayings and his words. I ask Allāh to bestow understanding and comprehension of His words upon you, and the ability to look at Him. I ask Allāh to make us see the Reality and Truth in our realm.

This is just a brief introduction in which Allāh permitted me to talk and reveal the secrets of your reality. This is because you are beloveds and you are my children. I care about you. I would be questioned by Him if I did not say what I have said to you. I would like for you to live by this teaching and for this teaching and to be as the Prophet, ʿalayhi as-salātu as-salām said:

> The one who believes in Me is in the Garden today. (Ḥadīth)

This is the saying of Allāh. He wants you to be in the Garden now. He does not want you to suffer in pain, to struggle and argue. Live with Him always, because the godly life has no beginning and no end. There is a big difference between a life that is full of pain and suffering and an eternal life that is full of purity. The godly life has everything the souls might crave and all that has not been seen by the eye or been heard by the ear.

"The Inspired Self" on page 90 of *He Who Knows Himself Knows His Lord* is read from page 91, "In this station, the traveler's state is weak and cannot distinguish between beauty and majesty, nor between what the angels suggests to him and what s̲hayṭān insinuates.

Here I would like to remind you that this book has many marvelous secrets and deep meanings. These meanings cannot be comprehended except by the one to whom Allāh chooses to reveal them.

This is why I recommend that you buy it before it is sold out. Also I recommend that you write it. Do not just put it on the shelf. You must read and write it with your hands repeatedly, until you know who you are. The one who knows himself knows his Lord. The veil will be removed from you and Him if you understand this book. I ask Allāh to allow this to happen.

If I wanted to really explain every word in it, then it would have taken me thousands of pages. However I tried to be brief and I put it in this form so that you might understand. Days and nights pass away until you see what you see, and then ins̲hā'allāh you will see me again and I will explain more.

The sentence above is re-read.

I am here between your hands. I came to take your hand and take you to your Lord. Why are you hesitant to listen to me and to take it to heart? The goods of Allāh are between your hands. So buy them! I show you what will never be harmful to you in this life or the next. This life is not worth anything. How many years are you going to live? Sixty, seventy, eighty, or maybe ninety years. You will pass away. You are a traveler on a journey; I met you and I will show you the way. So why do you not take my hand and travel to Allāh? Take yourself to Allāh. I will show you how to walk. Listen to my words and sayings because it is good for you.

The reading continues, "This may corrupt his faith and he may abandon obedience and commit sins, and then still claim that he is a main of the unity to whom things have been unveiled and he may claim that others who strive in obedience are veiled from this witnessing."

Many people are like this. They claim things but they are at the bottom of the sea. Even the fish at the bottom of the sea know more than they do and unify with Allāh better than they do. Fish have intelligence and Allāh says that they know when an enemy is present. Take as much as you can from me, because you cannot take all that I carry. Why not become the godly fish in His ocean? This is your state in reality.

The reading continues to page 92, "Satanic imaginations flash to him in glimmering ways and he takes them for Compassionate epiphanies..."

Allāh, we seek refuge in You from this state. Please move us with Your knowledge to Your vast garden.

The reading continues, "On the other hand, his reduced fear does not encourage him to follow the Law. This is why it is said, 'O beloved, you must follow the guide who helps you...' "

Give everything to Allāh and you can take everything from Allāh. He gives you everything in creation in one moment.

The reading continues, "You also must make it an obligation upon yourself to recite your al-awrād (pl. of wird) and restrain yourself with the binding of the ṭarīqa. This may become difficult for the soul because it is in a station in which it inclines to irresponsible liberty, making excuses, and carelessness."

Then you begin to scream and cry. There will be no end to this screaming, exactly as it is with Iblīs. He is still screaming since disobeying Allāh.

The reading continues to page 93, "O seeker of perfection! Rise up and abandon the frivolities..."

LISTEN...LISTEN...LISTEN...to what the Real is telling you!

The reading continues, "Free yourself from this danger and your revelation will continue."

You were created absolutely free. Therefore, why would you enslave yourself to desires? Why surrender yourself to anything else other than Allāh? Your Lord is the Real Who wants you to be absolutely free, living an honorable, noble, and eternal life. Why do you want to descend to the lower life?

He created you to fly, remembering and chanting in a beautiful and godly voice. He created you to sing godly love and pray godly prayers with all the angels. The angels will even be jealous of you, because of your love for Allāh. The angels are still prostrating in this station which you can attain. Allāh said, "Prostrate to Ādam," and they have been prostrating since then. There are no other Qur'ānic 'ayah that inform us that Allāh told them to stand up from their prostration. If you truly rid yourself of this human picture and transform to the godly realm, you will live witnessing the angels prostrating to you. You will transform from the temporary life to the eternal life which is endless.

This physical body transforms from one state to another. The spirit transforms to another realm. This is the creation of Allāh, the Maker of Perfection. He started the creation of the human being from mud, and it will return to mud. However, the spirit is something different. It is said in the Qur'ān:

> I have fashioned him and I have breathed into him
> from My spirit. (Qur'ān 15:29, 38:72)

This is something godly and eternal. He wants you to annihilate everything that is not Him and be in this station of annihilation. This is the station of the obedient ones who submit and surrender totally to His commands. They are the people who do not allow the lower realm to enter their hearts. They live in this life with politeness and godly manners. Their special, unique lives are full of love, mercy and divine meanings even though they still carry the human form and the physical body. They are pure and clean and carry the loftiest of ethics given by Allāh.

Such a person knows that this is a temporary journey of traveling from one station to another until he attains the eternal life, which is what will remain.

The reading continues to page 95, "So his evil continues to overcome his good, and he becomes a zindīq—one who rejects religion, and does not distinguish between human and animal. I will strike an example..."

The reason that I am giving you this example is to make you understand, to take your hand and bring you to Allāh. I am warning you to not get lost in the mazes. Allāh does not want you to do this. I have tried to mention this in detail for you. Pay attention, listen and follow these words so that you may be saved. It may be one word heard that reaches your heart, while you are in a sincere and truthful state. This one word could benefit you greatly. I am certain that you will benefit from what you are listening to now, inshā'allāh.

I do not want you to be in prison. I want you to free yourself from the shayṭān, your individual ego, and the lower realm in order to be in the eternal life with Allāh. This is the path to Allāh in which you attain absolute freedom and the eternal life which is full of beauty, peace and love. Āmīn.

The shayṭān is weak. If your breath is pure and supported by Allāh then the shayṭān cannot harm you. He will escape and seek refuge hundreds and thousands of miles away. You will not experience any jinn or shayṭān. Nothing can approach you. There is no jinn or shayṭān that can stand in front of the truthful and sincere one who is walking to Allāh. He escapes from him because the fragrance of the people of Allāh is stronger than any other and it drives them away. Allāh says in the Qur'ān:

> Certainly, you [Iblīs] will have no authority over My slaves,
> except those who follow you of the astray ones. (Qur'ān 15:42)

He has no power over them. The shayṭān cannot stand in front of you if you become the slave and servant of Allāh. Therefore, do not say it was the shayṭān who whispered and made me do this. Understand that his cunning blood is weak and it cannot have an effect on you if you say, "Bismi-llāh, in the name of Allāh." It will have no effect on you.

The reading continues to page 97, "their assets are humiliation and poverty and manifesting their helplessness, indigence and slavehood to Allāh, their Beloved and Creator."

Now I give you what Allāh has bestowed upon me and has asked me to give to you. I pray to Allāh that He allows you to understand this station. This is the station for which Allāh has bestowed upon us an explanation to give to you. I would like you to follow it, and I hope that Allāh grants you success in your walking toward it. Now I open the door to give the promise of that station of the spirit and the secret in order for you to continue your walking toward Allāh, and to help you in the understanding of what I have said to you. May you attain what you want.

This promise is different from all the others. The first promise you give is for your physical being. Then there is the promise for your soul/self. However this promise is different. It is a promise for the spirit and the secret. I have explained to you how to reach to this station, and if you give this promise with sincerity then you will reach this station and understand the meanings as Allāh wants you to. Do not prevent yourself from taking this opportunity. It is also in the blessed month of Ramaḍan, which is the month of giving. It is the month of secrets and blessings. I ask Allāh to help you in this blessed month to arrive at the stations your souls wish for.

Sidi gives the promise for the spirit and secret.

You Are Ready—Do Not Look Back

"The Inspired Self"

From *He Who Knows Himself Knows His Lord*

Lā ʾilāha ʾilla-llāāāāāāh, Lā ʾilāha ʾilla-llāāāāāh, Lā ʾilāha ʾilla-llāāāāāh
Muḥammad rasūlu-llāh, Ibrāhīm rasūlu-llāh, Mūsā rasūlu-llāh,
ʿĪsā rasūlu-llāh ʿalayhim ṣalātu-llāh.

Allāhumma anta-s-salām wa minka-s-salām
wa ilayka yaʿūdu-s-salām
tabārakta rabbanā
ya d̲ha-l-jalāli wa-l-'ikrām

As-salāmu ʿalaykum wa raḥmatu-llāh wa bārakatuhu. Al-ḥamdu li-llāh.

All praises to Allāh
and may the peace and blessings of Allāh be upon our beloved Messenger
and may the peace and the blessings of Allāh be upon
all the prophets and messengers and guides and beloveds of Allāh
and all those who are following them
and the companions of the Prophet
and the heir of the Prophet
and those who are polite and who are walking on the path of Allāh
carrying the message of the truth
those who are carrying the quality of the truth and who are polite
the same politeness that the people of Allāh have
those who have divorced their egos, their selfish selves
and all that is evil and that does not surrender to Allāh's commands
and that treats the beloveds of Allāh in an impolite way
and that which stops those reciting and remembering Allāh in a foolish way
those who are standing on the boundaries of Allāh
and are impolite with Allāh and impolite with Allāh's creation
who are going out of the natural laws of Allāh
and are not guided by the commands of Allāh
those who make people bear more than they can.

Worship should not be for repetition; the practice of the remembrance of Allāh and recitation should not be to gain repetitions. It should be for self-discipline and training to abide by the limits that Allāh has set. It is a duty. One must never go beyond these limits and become impolite. I send my peace and blessings upon the Messenger.

Oh Allāh, we seek refuge in You from those who are looking for people's faults. We seek refuge in You from those who seek the victory of their individual selfish selves. May Allāh provide us with the strength and power to stay within His limits and be polite with everyone in His creation.

Allāh, glory be to Him, Most High, ordered us to have wisdom and to advise people with courteous manners. Allāh says in the Qur'ān:

> Invite people to the path of Allāh with wisdom and with courteous manners.

Every human is full of faults, full of mistakes from his accumulating dirt and disobedience and rebellion against Allāh. That is why discipline is very important. The murāqaba—watching oneself all the time—is very important; it is important to watch the commanding ego that is always in opposition to the seeker. So one must watch that commanding ego and stop it if it wants to commit anything that deviates from Allāh's natural law and His commands.

The guide of the commanding ego is Iblīs. He is waiting for a chance to see the seeker deviate from Allāh's law. He will get the seeker angry for himself [i.e. feeling victimized], urge him to jump and do things in that deviate from Allāh's way. It corrupts the seeker's walking, because it whispers the self saying to speak according to personal or selfish desires, and not for the sake of Allāh. He forgets that he is weak and he has just fallen into Iblīs' trap. He destroys what he has already achieved. That is why Allāh says, "Beware of the self that deviates from His commands."

To give advice is a great thing. It is a true way in this path. So, we should advise each other with the right thing. But the one who is giving advice for people to obey the divine commands must advise in the polite way. This is because we fall into the habit of advising people in an impolite way and with the motive of the self, seeking victory for itself. So the person, even though he wants to go on the straight path and advise people, is still in the habit of obeying the commanding ego and acts from that perspective. But the messenger should just convey the message politely. He cannot force someone to do anything or fight with them to do anything.

The Messenger of Allāh used to do that—to convey the message to people—because he had mercy for the people, not because he was angry with them. The one who stops with his commanding ego, is free to do what he wants, but this is not the true way. It is not from our courteous manners to push people or force them and to cause disputes between people, even though that which we want may be right.

That is why I ask Allāh to provide all of us with the attitude of politeness and good courteous manners so we can treat everyone in the right way, in the way of the Messenger of Allāh. I do not want to keep mentioning that more than I should, but I want to alert people that our way is the way we were commanded to have.

So we must abide with the awrād (plural of "wird"), the recitation that is prescribed by the guide. All of the awrād comes from Allāh, not from people. We took it from our guides who are the heirs of the Prophet Muḥammad, ʿalayhi as-salātu as-salām. We must abide by following them as I explained yesterday. If someone does not want to follow the guidance, as I said, he is free.

In the S̲h̲ād̲h̲iliyya ṭarīqa we abide by the awrād of Abu-l-Ḥasan as̲h̲-S̲h̲ādhilī and not any other wird. We abide by that wird. Whoever believes us, let him believe and have faith in us. Whoever wants to cover up the truth, he is free too. But we ask that person to respect our way. The wird we recite morning and evening is a true wird that our guide inherited. He took it from his guide, ʿAbd as-Salām ibn Mas̲h̲īs̲h̲. That chain goes back, so it is a constant and real, authentic wird in the S̲h̲ād̲h̲iliyya ṭarīqa right up until today.

It was the gnostic people who advised us to recite it. They had wisdom behind this—they did not want to make the seekers bear more than they could. They have mercy for people and they do not make people abide by something beyond their abilities and capacities. They know what the seeker needs and what he can bear, what he can carry. I can carry ten pounds for example. I cannot carry more than that; I cannot carry fifteen pounds. So the seeker can get confused if he can bear only ten pounds and I give him fifteen pounds. I am responsible for every seeker and every thought that crosses his mind because of the guidance I receive. I feel every seeker, and I know what the seekers need. So when I advise something, I am not saying it from my own self. It is not my own command, my own order that I am giving.

This is a very subtle and accurate matter and we should not interfere in the divine commands. For example, Allāh tells us to pray four rakāh at ḏ̣huhr prayer. We cannot go ahead and say it is better to pray five rakāh. We cannot change that. We cannot say, we will pray seven or twelve because praying more is better. No, it is not correct to do it that way. We must abide and surrender to what Allāh commanded us to do.

Our guides took commands from Allāh when they advised us to recite this awrād. Maybe our master guide wrote twenty books. Of course, it is good to read them if we can. But he recommended something for us to read daily and give it more attention and abide by it, because it will lead us to understand the way and comprehend it. So, he gives his recommendation by divine command, not from himself to help the seekers understand more and walk more. I ask Allāh to forgive everyone.

We ask Allāh also to forgive those who tried to advise in an impolite way and I ask Allāh to provide such person with politeness and conscious manners with everyone, in the way of Allāh in the true way, and not in the way that the self will claim. We are polite people and our world the earth. So we are earth; we bear what others do. We show love to everyone who comes to this path. We love everyone who comes to us with the word, "Lā ʾilāha ʾilla-llāh."

Allāh says in the Qurʾān that the believers are brothers and sisters to each other. Your brother is your brother. The one who has no brother will fall into the Hellfire. Have you not heard the saying of Allāh to Mūsā? Mūsā said to his Lord as it is quoted in the Qurʾān:

> And my breast tightens, and my tongue expresses not well
> [Make him a support to me. Let him comprehend what I say.]
> So send for Harūn [Aaron] [to come along with me]. (Qurʾān 26:13)

You cannot easily find a brother in the way of Allāh or a sister that is walking in the path of Allāh—you cannot find that easily. You cannot go to the market and find one and buy her or him.

So the brother in the way of Allāh cannot be bought. It is something so precious, because it cannot be found easily. It is like a precious gem. You cannot go and buy a sister, who serves you in the way of Allāh, who loves you in the way of Allāh, who advises you in the way of Allāh. So, you treat each other as one. You are she and she is you. So be careful and do not look at your brother or sister in a selfish way, in a jealous way, but look with love, look with peace, look with unity. Because Allāh said,

> And hold fast, all of you together, to the rope of Allāh.
> (Qur'ān 3:103)

Be under the umbrella of Allāh, together.

We have to understand we still are holding onto our old habits because we are raised in ways that give us the selfishness and all the blemishes of the self. But here, the soul starts to drink the taste of love and to drink the water of love and peace. But if you are still seeking leadership or being higher than another, and are seeking a high rank and all of that, then you are falling actually into Hellfire. This is not the way.

I am willing to carry everything upon my head. As long as Allāh is pleased with that, then I bear people. These are the lofty ethics of the seeker. Not the ethics of the arrogant, the people who want to possess the lower realm and have diseased souls. I ask Allāh to protect all of you from these sicknesses.

These fights about rank and leadership are not in the way of Allāh. But I want to clarify them so we will not fall into our mistakes again. You are a glorious one; you are great, as long as you are a servant to all the beloveds of Allāh. You are great as long as you are polite and have courteous manners with all the seekers. Would you like to really know if you have actually passed by all the stations and arrived? Then this is how you will know.

Story of Sidi Meeting His Second Guide

My master guide told me once when I came to him—my first guide took me to my second guide and said, "This is your guide now." I was twenty-two years old at that time and he told me, "This is your guide now." I said, "I love my first guide so much..." What could I tell him? I cannot disobey him. My first guide was forty-five years old and my new guide, may Allāh sanctify his secret, was one hundred and nine years old. So I asked, "What is that [that he is so old]?"

The human self that is her nature was whispering to me, "What is that?" She said, "That is a very old man. What can he teach? He is already lost his mind." This is what my self, my ego, told me. This shows that I was ignorant of what my first guide knew. My new guide said, "Welcome to you my son. I have been waiting for you for a long time—even before your mother carried you, I was waiting for you, and now it is your time." And I had no idea what he would do with me.

He said to me, "This is your place, here." What was that place? It was the place where all of my beloved brothers and sisters put their shoes. He said, "This is your duty, to take care of all the shoes. This is your first walking." I had to say yes. I did not object, because the original principal in walking to Allāh is to follow the guide's orders in everything, little or big. If you object, you fall. Whenever you object to your guide, you fall. If he said, "This is your place," you stand in your place.

It is not like even the military order. It is stricter, because it is a divine order. So I stayed in that place for 6 months, arranging the shoes, and I was outside, far away from the guide, but I listened still to what he said in the teachings. And I never forgot what I was listening to - not any word of it. When he passed by me I would look at his eyes, I would look at how his eyes were moving. If he opened his eyes, I would look at his eyes and I would see the whole of existence in them. We can grab people by our sight - by looking at them. So, what if someone is playing? Let him play. Let him play. But we know how to get him when it is time.

After six months my guide called me, "Oh Muḥammad, come here now; sit beside me." That was an order also. The two orders were equal to me. The two orders were equal to me. Whether I was standing with the shoes or sitting beside him, it was one and the same. I remember, he put his hand on my back and he said, "You have passed the test." It was a divine command.

What is the benefit of this story? What is the benefit of what he did to me? It was to kill the self, the ego, and make the ego descend to its place because you came here rebellious. You came here arrogant and we disciplined you and taught you that you are human and you are ready to carry everything without objection—to serve. You must understand that the command you take from me is not from me but it is from Allāh.

See how I left a younger guide and went to an older guide? It was very strong for me to bear that, because the commanding ego does not accept being a servant and having to clean the shoes but I had to discipline her and make her surrender. This is the true essence of the matter because our guides taught us how to kill the diseased souls that are rebellious and in disobedience to Allāh's law. In that way we can carry the message of truth and become servants to all our beloved brothers and sisters and all people. This is why the Messenger of Allāh was humble; he had the quality of gentleness, mercy and humbleness. Allāh says to him in the Qur'ān:

> And had you been severe and harsh hearted,
> they would have broken away from about you. (Qur'ān 3:159)

That is why you must carry these beautiful qualities, because Allāh saved these treasures for you.

The stations of the journey, as we explained before, have characteristics. The most dense station is the commanding ego, because it is destructive. This commanding ego is destructive and evil. You must just treat it as a little child who knows nothing. Otherwise, it can possess a person and pushed him to do evil.

This is not an easy thing. It requires patience and persistence because it is a rebellious self. And Iblīs is with that commanding ego. Are you allowing Iblīs to order you around? If you allow him to do that, he will ride you. You become his ride. We must discipline our selves in an accurate way, following Allāh's orders in an accurate way. And if the self becomes rebellious and wants to eat or desires this or that, I say, "no". You must discipline her.

My guide Muḥammad, the S̲hād̲hiliyya guide said...He was a man of good health and he was handsome. He used to dress really nicely in elegant clothes, and he really did not pay attention to anyone. He was working with Allāh, completely absent from the world. He was in full absence and in the divine rapture, and wherever he looked he saw Allāh in everything. He used to have a long mustache and a long beard and he had a good build. He carried with him a whip and he would walk on the street every morning and Allāh's epiphany upon him was really irresistible; it was powerful. So his first duty was to walk on the street as if he were a policeman. And he walked the streets in the morning and watched the salesmen. If he saw any salesmen in a mess and doing a terrible job, he gave him a strike. But none of them used to object. They use to say, "Yes, Sidi," because they knew who he was. They understood that he was teaching them and disciplining them. And they saw the mercy even in his whip. Because he was not violent in the way he did it; he was just alerting them. His way was marvelous.

Story of the Seeker Who Wanted Fish

One of the seekers...we say here that you must not obey your ego, you must discipline yourself, you must teach yourself how to be humble, how to recite the awrād in accordance with the guidance you are given. You teach yourself how to be merciful with the poor and polite with everyone. In that way, we do not give her, our self, room to be rebellious and disobedient. So, this seeker I am talking about once said, "Oh, my self, I do not want you to feed yourself, to feed me anything." Well, that seeker once desired to eat fish. So he said to himself, "This self wants to eat fish, but I am not giving her the fish. Never. I will not listen to her and give her the fish. I would rather, instead of giving her the fish, go to Sidi Muḥammad," the guide we were talking about earlier, "and take a lashing from him." So, he said, "After I take this lashing from Sidi, I am going to feed her."

So he went to the market and he found Sidi Muḥammad walking on the street with his strong, long mustache. But the seeker did not really know the guide, what he looked like, but he was looking for someone who appeared strong to give him that lashing. So, he found Sidi Muḥammad walking and he was a strong man. So he said, "How can I make him strike me? I must do something to bother him, to annoy him." So he said, "The best way may be to pretend that I am walking and then just bump into him." He came running from far away but before he bumped into him, Sidi Muḥammad held him like a bird in his hand. He said, "Oh foolish one, go and feed her the fish." So I say to those who are still sick, who are still carrying the sickness of selfishness and are seeking leadership and are descending from their station, "Go, feed yourself the fish."

The human is sick when he obeys his self and does not obey his Lord. The one who wants to be a slave to his ego, is free to do so, but he will lose this life and the next. If that human desires leadership, let him lead himself first and feed himself the fish first; let him be the guide for the fish.

The reading "The Inspired Self" on page 90 of *He Who Knows Himself Knows His Lord* begins on page 97 and goes through to page 98, "So know, my beloveds, that one of the conditions of love is to surrender to the demands of the one who is loved and this is why one of the lovers said..."

The condition of true friendship and walking to Allāh is to be gentle and easy to be with and to communicate and to show people your love. Those people who know the true meaning of love must be sought for companionship and friendship because you cannot attain that station unless you become ready to receive from them and learn from them. How can you attain Laylā's love when you are still not carrying any of her qualities? You must become a true lover, pure, preserving Allāh's commands, following them and abiding by the awrād that Allāh gave to you. You must also carry all the gentle and subtle qualities, the lofty godly ethics. But if you do not have these godly ethics and if you are not carrying the divine beauty in talking to others, then you are not yet in that station. To be in that station you have to have all the godly qualities, which are all lofty qualities.

You must have love, mercy, peace, beauty, gentleness, support for others. You must be intelligent, wise and manage all affairs in the best way. You must be strong. You should not be weak. That means you must carry the true qualities of the real human being and you must be able to discern the bad or evil from the good. Everyone can discern between the harmful and the beneficial, even if he is still a little child. Everyone has this capacity. Give a sweet date to a child, and he will eat it. Give him something hot like a stone of fire, he will reject it, naturally. Because he knows what is harmful and what is beneficial.

So you seeker, you are able to discern between the good and evil, between the harmful and the beneficial and you know how to walk to Allāh and in the way of Allāh. If you know your true healing, not the illusory healing, you must know the true healing of your self's diseases, not the illusory healing that stops with the pictures and the imagination and illusions. These illusions come from Iblīs. He projects them to you. He gives you imaginings and pictures that come to you. Be careful not to think they are from Allāh. You are able to discern what is and what is not from Allāh. Know that these illusions come from s̲hayṭān. If you are walking a true walking, abiding by the divine, lordly commands, then these illusions will not come to you. The s̲hayṭān cannot project his illusions and pictures on you. This is the weapon of s̲hayṭān—to project on you all of these illusory pictures. This is his weapon.

The reading continues, "...and they abandon the ritual praying and the fast and they do not give charity. Instead, they follow their appetites and they act in disagreeable ways and in spite of this they claim to be the people of tawhid..."

As long as you are the slave and servant of the Lord and you are dressed in the divine garments which are the garments of unity and gnosis, then preserve that. Hold tight to that. Listen only to this gnosis because this knowledge is the foundation, is the principle of the walking. Do not listen to any other illusions. In this station you are in the station in which the luminous divine inspirations come to you. But understand that it is as it was explained before, deeds are judged by the intentions behind them. Understand that you are traveling to Allāh. If you travel to Allāh and you listen only to the words of Allāh, then you become like Ibrāhīm. Ibrāhīm said:

> I will emigrate for the sake of my Lord. (Qur'ān 29:26)
> It is He Who guides me (Qur'ān 26:78)

Allāh will never abandon a slave and a worshipper who is coming to Him, who is walking in His way. Allāh will never not listen to someone who is calling Him and invoking Him because He says in the Qur'ān:

> And when My slaves ask you concerning Me,
> then [answer them], I am indeed near.
> I respond to prayers when they call upon Me. (Qur'ān 2:186)

That means to ask Allāh directly, to seek His help directly, to understand that He is the One Who is Beneficial, and to listen to only Him and accept what He is teaching.

Is there anyone else to ask, by Allāh? If there is anyone else in existence, show him to me so I can ask him, too. There is nothing in absolute existence except Allāh; then ask Allāh; do not ask another. The one who knocks on a door other than Allāh's door is foolish, because all the other doors are broken. But the door of Allāh is the true gate because Allāh is the One Who gave you life, power, intellect, strength. He is the One Who gives you politeness, beauty, humbleness. So, surrender to Him, and you will have everything and everything will then disappear. Only the face of Allāh will remain. Then seek refuge in Allāh. He is your True Protector.

"Except for Us, Here Is the Cow Market"

One day I was walking in Damascus with one of my brothers in the way of Allāh, forty or fifty years ago. He was also an elder, but he was one of the gnostics who knew Allāh directly. He was a tall man, two meters or more, and I was a short man beside him. I was holding his hand because he was an old man, over one hundred years old and his sight was effected a little bit. So I was holding his hand and helping him.

I was on his right side, holding his hand and we were walking and he was telling me, "You are my beloved and I do not see but you."

And I said, "Me, too. I do not see but for you."

Then he said, "Then we are in agreement."

That means it was a sign of unity. We were both seeing the same thing. So I said, "All right, I will continue walking with you."

The people of Damascus like to interfere in people's affairs. They see two people walking together and they say, "Why are you walking with that man?" That is their way; they are curious.

I heard one saying to his friend while we were walking, "Go to this guide, the older guide, and ask him where the market of the cows is." But the guide actually understood what he meant. I understood too what he wanted.

So the man came and said, "Oh S̲hayk̲h."

So my S̲hayk̲h responded, "What is it, impolite man? What do you want?"

He said, "Where is the cow market?"

He said, "Except for the two of us, here is the market."

That meant that all of them were cows because they did not understand about Allāh.

The people of Allāh cannot be objected to because when they walk in the street they are with Allāh. Like I am here now but my heart is in another realm. My eyes are opened but my eyes are crying in another realm. This is our world and our life. We live with Allāh but we live also with the creation of Allāh, and we feel the pain of people and we feel sad because they are sad. That is our way. Our most beloved Allāh said to His Messenger:

> We have not sent you but as a mercy for all the world.
> (Qur'ān 21:107)

If anyone accepts becoming a lover of Allāh, and accepts this way, he must become a mercy for all people wherever he is. Despite their beliefs or their different states, he has mercy for them.

No country or land is empty of the lovers of Allāh, but sometimes they do not manifest, they do not appear to people; they do not make themselves known. Because through them Allāh bestows His mercy to people. Because they always pray for others and ask goodness for people. This is why the gnostic poet said, "Do not belittle the stone because it is part of the mountain." There are many hidden people of Allāh so be polite with everyone so Allāh will treat you the same way. This is the foundation of discipline, the principle of discipline, of having the divine qualities. It teaches you how to move from station to station, from the station of the commanding ego to the reproachful self to the inspired self.

Why do we call that soul in the third station the inspired soul? Because the soul is ready at that time to receive true understanding. So the soul becomes ready in this third station to give and take. Allāh provided that soul with the ability to discern between evil and good. Allāh made everything clear but gave her free will. Allāh showed the nafs in this station, "This is the evil and this is the good, and you have free will." She knows. She can discern in this station the evil from the good. So Allāh says now, "You are in the realm of comprehension."

So do not look back at the other stations that have desires and temptations and envy and hate and enmity and all of these qualities like racism and hate. So now in this station you have some understanding. You can discern between evil and good. You know what rights you have and what responsibilities you have toward others.

We have been teaching you, disciplining you, to reach this station. If we say you are a teacher and you are giving classes and you are teaching, that means it is because we see that you have understanding. But you have to teach according to people's levels and if someone cannot understand yet, you give him according to his level. When you feel he has completely comprehended what you say, then you can give him a little bit more. It is a simple example.

When the seeker of Allāh becomes obedient and abides by Allāh's commands, then through this obedience, he can actually move through the stations until the highest station. Then the seeker may start to claim, "Oh, now I have attained this high station, the inspired station." But then we put him on trial. We put the teachers to a test. Because he sees and he knows where he is but we put him to a test because we know where he is, and Allāh teaches him.

We test him by giving him a little bit of disease and we see how patient he will be. What will he do then? He will not have reconciliation. We can give him like a test, for instance, that he will not be able to stop going to the bathroom, and then he starts to scream. What happened to you? What did you do? Then he says, "I need medicine," and he starts to seek a physician and looks here and there for help because he is humbled. There is no way but for him to seek help. Do you remember now that you are weak? That is good. Why did you not remember before that you are truly weak and helpless? Remember what you did. It is from what your hands earned, but Allāh pardons and overlooks many of your mistakes (Qur'ān 42:30).

With this disease, can we claim that it is from Allāh? Many foolish people say, "Yes, these diseases came from Allāh." No, it came by what your hands earned. But Allāh actually overlooks and pardons a lot of your mistakes (Qur'ān 42:30). It could be that you just ate rotten food. Or you were asleep in a place where weather was cold, or it could be that during your work you did something not right because you felt angry and you had distress that shook your whole body; then you fell sick.

There are many causes. Everything good comes from Allāh but everything bad comes to us because of what our hands earn. Allāh does only what is good and gives us what is good and He overlooks many of our mistakes. Then go ahead and take your medicine. You are still not going to heal because you still have not understood how to correct yourself and rectify your behavior. If the car stops working, you must see what is wrong with it, what the cause is, and fix it. Do you not go to someone who is an expert in how to fix cars? But your heart is not to be healed except by your Lord, and your self is not to be healed except by your Lord, which means you must listen to His words. Follow His teachings and all of what He says.

And you must never listen to the s̱hayṭān, the lower desires and the commanding ego. Listen to Allāh and look to His wisdom and use everything in its right place as Allāh created it. Because when you do that, the s̱hayṭān will have no power or control or influence over you. So there is no way for you in this world but to be a divine slave, to be the Lord's slave and servant. Allāh says in His Ḥadīt̲h̲ Qudsī:

> My worshipper continues to approach me by voluntary actions
> until I become the eyes by which he sees,
> the ears by which he hears,
> the hands by which he works,
> the feet by which he walks.
> He becomes a truly godly slave and servant,
> and at that point when he says to something "Be," it is. It happens.

So I tell you, annihilate, destroy everything that is not Allāh. Destroy all the illusions, the pictures and the imaginings, and then you will join. Join whom? Join your most beloved, who is Allāh. The most beloved is Allāh; the most beloved is Allāh. May He protect you and us and may He make the Garden your final abode.

Allāh, Lord of the Worlds, please forgive our sins and protect us and help and cover up our faults and correct them and help them. This is the end of the teaching session I give you this morning and I open now the door for protection.

Before we start I would like to tell you something my beloveds. Do not think that the spiritual healing is enough. The University of Spiritual Healing and Ṣūfism teaches how to heal oneself and move from station to station, and it teaches the healing, the spiritual healing. So the university is teaching the healing and it is part of the Ṣūfī path, the Ṣūfī school and they are joined together. You must also go to the university and take your chance to learn more, because those who are leading it are my beloveds and my children and they teach in accordance with what Allāh taught them, so joining the university is a must. So the Ṣūfī school is not enough. The university will give you more.

So join the university because they are joined together to achieve the same goal. No one should be saying, "This is better than that," because the issue here is to learn, and learning is everlasting, is limitless. We all need to learn more and more, so I do recommend that you go to the university. I ask you to go and I pray to Allāh to help you understand and take His teaching from Him. I am always with you and I would also like you to know that there is now a book, which is about healing. It took me six years to write it and it includes remedies for eighty-nine diseases. It is a very beneficial book.

Pope Valley Ramadan Retreat

Important to know,
she is your mom,
your sister,
she is every woman.

Everything is contained in the woman and Islām.
He care about her.
I ask you to be conscious of Allāh while dealing with women,
to treat them good
and to guard yourselves against evil when you deal with them,
to have taqwa.

Because the woman in our way,
as explained by the Prophet Muḥammad,
is a holy being.
She is a queen in her house and she is protected,
her honor is protected
and her heart must never be broken.

Those who are confused and who went astray from Allāh's true religion
do not understand this.
The woman in Allāh's way and the religion is a gem,
she is a precious jewel that must be protected.
That is why you must understand
it is a serious covenant
and the one who breaks this covenant
is breaking his covenant with Allāh
and he becomes the enemy of Allāh, Most High, glory be to Him.
So keep this promise so that Allāh may keep you.

From "Laylāt al-Qadr"

Bowing to Allāh, Most High
Ṣalāt al-Jumʿa

First Kẖuṭba

Lā ʾilāha ʾilla-llāh, al-ḥamdu li-llāh, praise be to Allāh and may the peace and blessings of Allāh be upon our master, guide and prophet, Muḥammad, ʿalayhi as-salātu as-salām, praise be to Allāh, who guided us to this. We would not have been guided except that Allāh has guided us. We ask Him to help us and forgive us and we seek refuge in Him from the worst of our deeds and from the evil of our selves. Whoever is guided by Allāh is the one who has true guidance, and whoever is left to stray by Allāh cannot find a guide.

Allāh, glory be to Him, said that Allāh and His angels pray and send their peace upon the Prophet, ṣalla-llāhu ʿalayhi wa sallam. All of you who believe, send your peace upon the Prophet, ʿalayhi as-salātu as-salām. May the peace and the blessings of Allāh be upon our master guide Muḥammad and the other prophets Ibrāhīm (Abraham), Mūsā (Moses) and ʿĪsā (Jesus), ʿalayhim as-salām, and all the other prophets and messengers of Allāh. May Allāh be pleased with all the followers in their footsteps to our beloved Allāh. May the peace and blessings of Allāh be upon all of you. Allāh, Most High, glory be to Him, says:

> Truly the Muslim men and women,
> the believing men and women
> the men and the women who are obedient,
> the men and women who are truthful,
> the men and the women who are patient,
> the men and the women who are humble,
> the men and the women who give alms (ṣadaqah)
> the men and the women who fast (ṣawm)
> the men and the women who guard their chastity
> and the men and the women who remember Allāh much with their hearts and tongues
> Allāh has prepared for them forgiveness and a great reward. (Qurʾān 33:35)

This is the month of Ramaḍan, and it is the month of blessing and repentance. It is the month of forgiveness and mercy, and the month with which Allāh is pleased. This is the month that can save us, the worshippers, from the Hellfire.

This month is coming to an end, so all my beloveds, my beloved men and my beloved women...

Did you ask yourself?
Did you truly take this chance to become closer to Him?
Did you take this chance to be with Him and in Him
in continuous worship and remembrance of Him,
always conscious of Him,
being with the closest angels chanting hymns of His praise and glorifying Him?

Are you seeking Allāh's forgiveness in the early morning before dawn?
Are you glorifying and praising Allāh early in the morning and late at night?
Are you one of those who fasted and who truly cared for His fasting,
and fulfilled its conditions completely and fully without any shortcomings?

Did your tongue truly fast?
Did your eyes truly fast?
Did your hands truly fast?
Did your feet truly fast?

Or were you rebellious and stubborn?
Did you continue to backbite others without listening to Allāh?

There is no word uttered by the human except that an angel records what he uttered. There is an angel recording every good word you say and every evil word you say (Qur'ān 50:17). Were you conscious of your tongue when you were talking? Did you use your tongue in obedience, in worship? Did you use this tongue to seek forgiveness? Did you use this tongue to recite the Qur'ān, the word of Allāh, the Book of Allāh? Because Allāh said in the Qur'ān:

> Recite of the Qur'ān as much as is easy for you (Qur'ān 73:20)

The Prophet, ʿalayhi as-salātu as-salām, said:

> I do not say that alif lām mīm are one letter,
> but alif is a letter, lām is a letter and mīm is a letter.
> With each letter you recite, you will have ten rewards. (Ḥadīth)

Reading one letter of the Qur'ān sent down to our Prophet Muḥammad, ṣalla-llāhu 'alayhi wa sallam, brings ten-fold blessings. Did you recite Qur'ān or did you use your tongue for hours in backbiting others or speaking vain words that are not pleasing to Allāh and His Messenger?

Oh human being, do you know the affliction that Allāh has prepared for you if you deviate from His way and if you become rebellious against His commands? Ramaḍan is almost saying farewell to you and you do not really know if you will be alive next Ramaḍan. How many people are there whose coffins are being created now and they are unconscious of it? People do not even know if they will live to see the coming dawn.

Did you prepare for this journey,
this difficult journey you are going to have after you pass away?
Did you prepare with your repentance?
Did you prepare by doing good deeds?
Did you prepare by fasting and prayer?
Was your fasting true fasting
or was your fasting just to be hungry and thirsty,
and on the other hand your tongue was as sharp as a knife
backbiting people and speaking badly of them?
Did you accuse others who were innocent of what you were accusing
them of, or did you spy on people and try to listen to their private
affairs?
Did your ear commit this sin?

All that is left of Ramaḍan are a few days that you can count on one hand. This is a month of weeping and a month of worship. It is a month where the human being should feel sorrow and regret for his transgressions of the limits set by Allāh. Did you give your charity in full? Allāh says about that those who give charity in Ramaḍan without any delay are the ones who will find success.

Give your zakāh, especially in these last ten days of Ramaḍan. Zakāt al-Fitr, the charity at the end of Ramaḍan, is the charity of fitr, of breaking the fast. You have to give it for yourself and for everyone under your care, on behalf of everyone in your care, because it is a zakāh, a charity that will bring you protection. It will keep you and protect you, your children, and your wife or your husband in all ways. Also, if you broke your fast for a few days you have to give charity in compensation for these days. You have to give what is enough to feed a person in need two meals, and you must also pay the Zakāt al-Fitr on behalf of those under your care whether it is your parent or your wife, and you must do it right away. You should not delay it.

Some scholars say that it must be paid on the first day of ʿEid, but we say it must be given during the last ten days of Ramaḍan. It is the duty and obligation of every Muslim to give the Zakāt al-Fitr. Zakāt al-Fitr is obligatory for every person: child, woman or man. [If you care for someone who cannot pay] you pay on behalf of those under your care. Allāh will not accept your fasting and bless you unless you pay this zakāh. Zakāt al-Fitr, the charity of breaking the fast and ending the fast, is very important to protect you, your family and your loved ones. This charity goes to those who in need, the poor. It should never go to those who are rich or those who are not in need. It is forbidden and impermissible for them to take it.

Everyone must pay the full charity on his yearly earnings and also the Zakāt al-Fitr.[23] We are talking about two types of charity. I see that some people still have not paid it and I do not know why they have not. Do they have a promise from Allāh that they are going to live to see tomorrow or after tomorrow? Do they really know that? Do not delay it then. You have to pay it right away. I invite you to pay this charity and also the Zakāt al-Fitr later, because it is very important. The Messenger of Allāh, ʿalayhi as-salātu as-salām, gave a ḥadīth about this.

There was a man called ʿAbd Allāh ibn Salām. ʿAbd Allāh ibn Salām was a great man from the Jewish people, and he was one of the beloveds of Allāh. Once the Prophet, ʿalayhi as-salātu as-salām, came to the city of Medina this man came to the Prophet, believed in him, and took s̲hahādah.[24] He said, "I bear witness that Allāh is God and that you, Muḥammad, are His noble prophet, messenger, slave and servant."

---

[23] There are three types of fasting Sidi discusses in this chapter:
1. Zakāt al-Māl: each year a Muslim is required to give 2.5% of his or her net wealth as charity, and it should be paid as early in the month of Ramaḍan as possible.
2. Zakāh al-Fitr: is paid at the end of Ramaḍan (Sidi is saying to pay it during the last 10 days). In the U.S. it usually costs $20-$40 ($5-$10 per person in your family).
3. If you miss fasting days during Ramaḍan you can make up the days either by fasting them after the month is over, or by offering zakāh to those in need. You give an amount equal to what it would cost to feed a person two meals.

[24] The first of the five pillars of Islām is to bear witness that there is no god but Allāh, and Muḥammad is His messenger. Bearing witness in this way is known as

> ʿAbd Allāh ibn Salām narrated that he asked the Messenger of Allāh, ʿalayhi as-salātu as-salām, "What is the way to reach the Garden [i.e. Paradise]."
>
> This was the answer the Prophet gave, "Feed people and spread peace and the greeting of peace; then you will enter the Garden in peace."[25]

This was the answer of the Messenger, the Messenger of peace, mercy, justice and love. He said, "Oh ʿAbd Allāh, slave and servant of Allāh, feed people; feed those who are hungry and spread peace and the greeting of peace all over the world. Reconcile those who are fighting; mediate between your brothers and sisters who are fighting."

This is the Messenger of Allāh, the messenger of peace, justice and mercy. He called us to this because he is the message of peace, love, mercy and justice. He said:

> Whoever invites people to this way will enter the Garden. (Ḥadīt͟h)

I say this and I seek forgiveness for myself, so please seek forgiveness for yourself as well.

Praise be to Allāh,
may the peace and blessings of Allāh be upon our Master, our Guide,
Muḥammad, ʿalayhi as-salātu as-salām.

We ask You by Your Majestic Essence, by the truth of Your Messenger,
not to let any one of us be deprived, but give him what he needs.

We send our blessings upon our Master, our Prophet Muḥammad,
and all the other messengers and prophets, Ibrāhīm, Mūsā, and ʿĪsā.

We send a continuous prayer and a continuous blessing
that will never end until the Day of Judgment.

"taking s͟hahādah." To take s͟hahādah repeat, "Lā ʾilāha ʾilla-llāh Muḥammadan rasūlu-llāh" three times in front of two witnesses.

[25] The greeting of peace is, "As-salāmu ʿalaykum," which translates as, "Peace be upon you."

Allāh says in the Qur'ān:

> Those who believe faithfully are the ones who are going to prosper, they are the ones who are going to attain success.
> (Qur'ān 33:35 and tafsir)

Who are those who believe? Who are those who will be granted success and prosperity? They are the ones who will be acceptable to Allāh. Allāh explains it in the Qur'ān. He says:

> Those who humble themselves in their prayers
> and those who keep the prayer and do not abandon it.
> (Qur'ān 33:35 and tafsir)

Those who neglect the prayer and are forgetful of it are not acceptable to Allāh. Those who pray sometimes and not at other times are not acceptable to Allāh.

The Messenger of Allāh, 'alayhi as-salātu as-salām, said the covenant between us and people is the prayer [ṣalāh]. Whoever abandons the prayer abandons the way. The one who does not pray is the one who is in disobedience to the Messenger of Allāh and is not accepted by Allāh. Allāh will discharge him from receiving His mercy and forgiveness. But the true faithful believer, the truthful one, is the one who will be granted success and prosperity.

How can the mu'minīn, the believers, be granted success and prosperity? By being humble and being in humility during prayer. Those who are really feeling the presence of Allāh in their prayer, who know that Allāh is seeing them and hearing them, and their hearts are with Allāh will be successful. They are not the ones praying in body only, or thinking about what they are going to do later at work or at home or of other concerns. We are talking about a prayer where the person is fully devoted to Allāh.

When you begin the ṣalāh you say, "Allāhu Akbar," "Allāh is the Greatest." It means that Allāh is the Greatest. It means that you say goodbye to the lower realm and all of the concerns that busy you in the lower realm. You are directly in Allāh's presence; you dwell in Allāh's presence.

Imagine yourself standing in the presence of a king or governor—you stand politely. You stand with full concentration, alert. Why do you not do that with Allāh? Allāh is the Creator of everything, the King of Kings. You must be polite with Allāh. You must be present in your reading [recitation of the Qur'ān].

When you recite the opening sūra, al-Fātiḥa, you contemplate the meaning of the words. You are conscious that you are speaking directly with Allāh. You bring yourself to consciousness and presence. Those who turn away from Allāh get involved with vain chatter that is not useful. It is not useful for them, for others, for the believers, or for any human being because it tends to corrupt those who listen to it. The words you hear on television, for example, are of that kind of talk. It is vain talk; there is nothing useful in most of it. It is not useful for the body, the heart, the spirit, or the intellect. It does not mean that our religion, our way, prevents us from listening to television. No, we can listen to what is useful and take what is useful for us, and we must always keep company with good people and listen to good things that will benefit us.

Allāh says in the Qur'ān that those who will be granted success and prosperity are the ones who give charity, the zakāh. They give zakāh because their hearts are with Allāh and with poor people. They feel their pain. They feel sad when the poor are sad, and they feel joy when they see them joyful. These are the qualities of the faithful believer. But the one who does not give zakāh, may Allāh grant us refuge from that, will not be granted success and prosperity. Allāh also says that characteristic of faithful believers is chastity, those who keep and protect their private parts. They protect themselves and are faithful to only their wives and husbands. They do not betray them or look at any other with lust. They are pure and they keep themselves pure.

I ask Allāh to forgive me and you.
I ask Allāh and His angels to send His blessings upon the Prophet,
'alayhi as-salātu as-salām.

Send your peace and blessings upon the Prophet, oh faithful believers.
May Allāh be pleased with the companions of the Prophet,
his followers, the four rightly guided caliphs and all of their followers.[26]

Oh Allāh, please be pleased with all of them and all of those prophets
and messengers and their followers until the Day of Judgment.

---

[26] The four rightly guided caliphs were Abu Bakr, Omar, 'Ālī, and Uthman.

May Allāh be pleased with all the scholars and beloveds
who follow this way.

Oh please, Allāh, forgive our sins and cover our faults,
and take our souls out of this life while You are satisfied and pleased with us,
and do not let any need of ours remain,
but fulfill it as long as it is pleasing to you.
Please fulfill our needs, if it is pleasing to you,
our needs for this lower realm and the next life.

Please Allāh, overwhelm the oppressors and tyrants and
grant victory to the poor, needy and weak
who are oppressed across the earth.

Please grant victory to those whom You love,
those who carry the message of unity,
the message of Lā ʾilāha ʾilla-llāh and Muḥammad rasūlu-llāh.

Please Allāh grant victory and support to the ones who carry the
message of peace and love and mercy and justice to the whole world.

Please overwhelm the tyrants, oppressors, murderers and thieves,
those who are corrupting the earth and everything green,
and who are corrupting people.

Establish prayer, and prevent people from doing what Allāh forbids.
Allāhu Akbar. Allāhu Akbar.

Second Kh̲uṭba

I ask Allāh for you to have really listened. I hope that you have really listened to the first kh̲uṭba in Jumʿah, the Friday speech, and that you really understand your duties. Do not violate Allāh's rights [over you]. I hope you will follow the teaching you have just heard because Allāh will bring every human to reckoning. Turn back to Allāh before it is too late because no human knows if he will live for the next hour, the next day, or the next two days. Know that the lower realm, the life of this world, is just a traveling station. The real abode is the final life, the next life. No matter how many years you stay in this life, in the end you will pass away; you will pass away from this life and Allāh will bring you to reckoning. He will question you. He will ask you, "What did you do with the teachings I sent through My messengers and prophets, like Ibrāhīm, Mūsā, ʿĪsā, Muḥammad, and Nūḥ (Noah)?" These are the people of unity. Allāh will ask you what you did with the teaching you received. Did you hear the teaching that came from Allāh directly? Or, did you listen to the teaching of s̲hayāṭīn, to illusion and imagination?

You know now with certainty what the real message is. Now you can—you must—follow the teaching of this message before it is too late. Otherwise, you will be standing between Allāh's hands and you will be questioned about every major and minor thing you did. Do not think that when life ends everything will end. This is the life that some people who are ignorant understand. They think that they will live only 60 years, for example, and it will come to an end. Such a person does not comprehend, does not understand, that he will live a next life, another life, and that he will stand in front of Allāh, between His hands, and that he will be questioned. I do not want to mention many details about that now, but by Allāh's will, tomorrow I will give you another teaching. The next teaching will be about the day of standing between Allāh's hands to be questioned, when your actions will be demonstrated before Him.

Be prepared for that day, the day of paying your debt with Allāh. On that day no wealth, no children, no supporters, nothing will benefit you. It will not benefit you if you are strong or tall or have wealth or are healthy; nothing will benefit you. Nothing will benefit you because every human will go singly and stand between Allāh's hands to be questioned. I ask Allāh to grant you success and happiness in this world and in the next, because He is the One Who Responds to Prayer. But whoever would like now to pay Zakāt al-Fitr, the charity of breaking the fast, can come now and give it to Ṣāliḥ Cotten. Whoever also is ready to give the charity for his wealth, Zakāt al-Māl?, can come now. There are two zakāhs—the Zakāt al-Fitr (for the breaking the fast at the end of Ramaḍan) and the Zakāt al-Māl (for all of your wealth and assets).

The Zakāt al-Fitr, the zakāh for breaking the fast, is paid on behalf of yourself and everyone under your care. For every person give $20. If you are single with no one under your care you give $20. If you are responsible for a family, you give $20 for each member of your family.

Zakāt al-Fitr is a way of begging Allāh to accept your fasting, to purify your fasting even more, and to let your fasting be acceptable. It means,

"Oh Allāh, I fasted for You. Please accept it and purify my fasting if it was not perfectly pure, because none of our fasting is pure. Please Allāh, accept and purify our fasting. I obey You. Please accept this and give it to the poor and needy." This is the meaning of Zakāt al-Fitr. It is different from the zakāh you give if you miss a day of fasting during Ramaḍan because you are traveling or sick. This is for the end of the fast.

There is the other type of zakāh—the zakāh you pay on all of your wealth. If you saved money paid annually, you pay for that too. It is recommended you pay this during Ramaḍan. These are the three types of zakāh.

Allāh says in the Qur'ān:

> And those who hoard up gold and silver,
> and spend it not in the way of Allāh,
> announce unto them a painful torment. (Qur'ān 9:34)

It will be said to them, "Taste what you did."

There is a reason, a wisdom in paying the Zakāt al-Fitr—the zakāh of the end of fasting during the last ten days of Ramaḍan. In the last ten days there is a feast coming, which means if that if this zakāh reaches the poor early enough, they can celebrate 'Eid. Otherwise, they will not feel the 'Eid, because they do not have the funds to pay for a good meal, new clothes for their children, or toys. This is why it is recommended that you pay the Zakāt al-Fitr in the last ten days. This gives the poor people a chance to prepare meals, pay for clothes, buy things for their children, and celebrate 'Eid with everyone else, not later than everyone else. This is the divine wisdom behind paying it in the last ten days.

Allāh is pure goodness, and so He is the One Who Commands Pure Goodness. He is the peace and the beauty and the mercy. Allāh wants peace and mercy and love and beauty for the whole earth, for everyone, for all people. For this reason give zakāh for the sake of Allāh, purely for the sake of Allāh. Everyone can now pay Zakāt al-Māl on all of his wealth, the annual zakāh. He can also pay the Zakāh al-Fitr, and he can pay the zakāh if he has broken his fast during Ramaḍan and has not fasted those days. These are three types of charity. It is better to pay it as soon as you can. Do you take for granted that you will live to compensate for the missed days? It is better to pay now just in case. Then you can compensate for the days with fasting if you can, because that is better.

I will leave you now to rest because we are approaching a night that will be full of prayer and remembrance and spiritual practices. You are in need of rest now to be ready for tonight, and I will be with you from now until the end of Laylāt al-Qadr—the Night of Power. I will be with you all of this time, so be prepared for the blessed hours coming up. Take your chance, the opportunity to benefit from the blessings of these coming hours and from the Night of Power, because Allāh says it is peaceful until the dawn. It is the night of peace and the night of souls being saved from the Hellfire. By Allāh's will, I will be with you in every major and minor thing.

Spend these coming days reciting the Qur'ān, because for each letter you recite from the Qur'ān you receive ten blessings, ten-fold the normal blessings. This is what the Messenger of Allāh said. This is why I recite the whole Qur'ān about five times in the month of Ramaḍan when I am here, but when I am back in Masjid al-Aqṣā I read it, the whole Qur'ān, fifteen times during Ramaḍan. I do not read it for myself, I recite on behalf of everyone, for everyone asking Allāh to send peace and blessings upon the poor, the sick, and those who are suffering across the earth. I recite it and I weep, I weep bitterly and I pray to Allāh to lift the wars, suffering, disease, and destruction from people. May He grant us peace, and may we achieve it across the world for all people.

This is how I spend my time. Also, when I am in this country I spend it in this way. My whole life is a retreat, especially at night. All my nights are retreats. I am with Allāh in the night and in the morning I am with Allāh, as well. I ask Allāh to accept you and to accept from you. I am certain that Allāh will accept you because you are very fine people. I love you a lot because you are sincere and truthful with Allāh, and honest with Allāh, and you are fully devoted and directed toward Allāh, and Allāh will not turn you away disappointed. Allāh never, ever turns away His beloved from His door disappointed, because He is the Merciful and the Compassionate. Āmīn. Āmīn. Āmīn.

Prepare for the Day of Reckoning
Ramaḍan is the Door to the Garden

Lā ʾilāha ʾilla-llāāāāāāh, Lā ʾilāha ʾilla-llāāāāāh, Lā ʾilāha ʾilla-llāāāāāh
Muḥammad rasūlu-llāh, Ibrāhīm rasūlu-llāh, Mūsā rasūlu-llāh,
ʿĪsā rasūlu-llāh ʿalayhim ṣalātu-llāh.

Allāhumma anta-s-salām wa minka-s-salām
wa ilayka ya'ūdu-s-salām
tabārakta rabbanā
ya ḏha-l-jalāli wa-l-'ikrām

As-salāmu ʿalaykum wa raḥmatu-llāh wa bārakatuhu.

This day is a glorious day. It is one of the days of Allāh. It is not one of the days that are known to people. I direct myself fully towards Allāh, Most High, by the truth of this day, the day we are living in now. This is the day of forgiveness, the day of repentance, the day to be granted forgiveness. This is linked to another glorious day of Allāh.

Let us explain to you the meaning of this day that the whole world is waiting for. All people await the day when they will be raised up as butterflies, all together. Allāh mentioned it in His Qurʾān. He did not hide it from us. I would like to explain to you about that glorious day when all people, from the first one to the last one, young and old, will be assembled together. The criminal and the pious—everyone will be assembled together. Starting from the Pharaoh to the least known people. We are talking about the Day of Resurrection, the Day of Standing for Judgment. On that day Allāh will come and the angels will come lined up according to their ranks.

Before this day comes there are a lot of signs that indicate the day is approaching. Allāh says in the beginning of this noble 'ayah of the Qurʾān:

> Oh you who believe!
> Fear Allāh as He should be feared, and die not except as Muslims. (Qur'ān 3:102)

On the Day of Standing [of the resurrection] the heaven and earth will be folded together at His feet. glory be to Him, He is beyond anything they attribute to Him. On that day the trumpet will blow and everything alive will be made dead with a thunderbolt. After a second blow everything will be resurrected—alive again.

Let us stop a little bit at these two 'ayah. We have not appraised Allāh as He ought to be appraised. We do not truly know Allāh. Those people with all of their differences: race, age, rich or poor, women or men, king or un-kind people. We are talking also about those who carried the true message, who were truthful and sincere.

We are talking at the same time about the criminals, murderers, liars, robbers, corrupters, and tyrants who destroyed everything and stepped on humanity. They did not pay any care for the poor, the miserable, and the helpless. They did not turn to the poor and the needy to help them. They were never afraid of Allāh because they did not know who Allāh was. They did not think a Day of Reckoning would come for them. They think there will be an exception [made] for them, and that they will not be brought to accountability. They broke people's hearts and they did not imagine that they too would be brought to the Day of Reckoning like everyone else.

Allāh says to those people, "You did not estimate Allāh as He should be estimated. You did not realize that you were going to return to Me and that I was the one who will question you and bring you to accountability for every major and minor actions you did." So Allāh addresses the rebellious people, the criminals, the monsters. Allāh is addressing them and asking them, "Where are your weapons and your airplanes now? Where are your atomic bombs? Where are the palaces you used to live in? Where is the money and wealth you stole from the people? Bring it with you!" Allāh will challenge them. "Bring it with you." They did not estimate Allāh as He ought to be estimated. They did not respect Allāh. "You did not realize that you would be brought to Me for judgment."

How many people stole from the people and did not pay their share of charity. You were born screaming, "Oh, we have nothing!" You were born helpless, screaming for help. Nothing was with you. But you grew up and assembled this wealth. You became a tyrant and an oppressor of others. Those who do these types of actions do not estimate Allāh well. Allāh warns them in the Qur'ān about the coming day. They did not estimate Allāh. We have to feel Allāh while living in this lower realm, because Allāh informs us of what will happen on Judgment Day.

With the first blow of the trumpet the entire earth and all of its living creatures will perish (Qur'ān 39:68); the whole earth will actually perish with all its inhabitants and everything alive there will also perish, creatures that we know and creatures that we do not know. In every heaven there are creatures that exceed [in number] the creatures of this earth by a hundred times. Everything will be assembled.

Allāh created seven earths. The distance between each earth and the next earth is equal to five hundred years of Allāh's years. One day of Allāh is like a thousand years here on earth. So who are we? We are a tiny drop in a huge magnificent ocean. But look at us, with all of our tyranny and all of these things that we think are great. What are these things we think are great? They are nothing. They are just like an atom.

There are seven heavens in Allāh's grasp. There are also seven earths with other features. There are humans, animals, and jinn. Everything will be assembled together to come to Allāh. Oh ignorant one who does not know what will happen, you are talking now, but do you not know that you will pass away sooner or later? Did you not hear Allāh saying in the Qur'ān:

> Every soul will taste death,
> and then you will be returned to Me [brought to accountability
> at the Day of Resurrection and Standing for Judgment]
> (Qur'ān 29:57)

Know that no matter how long you live you will die, and you will be brought to accountability. Are you ready for this questioning? Oh foolish one, do you give charity thinking, "Oh, I am giving from my own money?" Do you have this attitude while giving? Know that all wealth, everything belongs to Allāh, because when you were created you were helpless and nothing was with you.

That is why Allāh says, "My slave and servant, be generous and kind and noble and share what I gave to you with the poor and the needy. Do not accumulate it in treasures and wealth and hide it from others thinking that you will live forever with this wealth." (Qur'ān 104:3 and tafsir)

Think of that coming Day. Allāh warned you in the Qur'ān that those who accumulate silver and gold and do not spend it for the sake of Allāh will receive severe suffering as a consequence of their actions. They will be burned by this very same wealth in the Hellfire. Their faces and their backs and their hands will be burned. (Qur'ān 9:34-9:35)

It will be said to them:

> This is the treasure which you hoarded for yourselves.
> Now taste of what you used to hoard. (Qur'ān 9:35)

See how it will benefit you [the hoarder] now. You have accumulated thousands and thousands and you are giving hundreds and you think that, "I am giving of myself" while you hide what you actually have and you do not pay your charity. In front of Allāh there will be no room for lying, concealment, or hiding. Allāh says that the poor and the needy have a right to your wealth (Qur'ān 17:26). You are not giving of yourself. It is their right.

So we go back to this ayah again where Allāh says to give Allāh His real estimation because everything in the heaven and the earth will be folded in His grasp at the end on that Day. What will happen that Day? The earth will have a great earthquake. All of its burdens will come out (Qur'ān 99:2). The people will come out and exclaim, "What is happening!" The earth will explain that Allāh inspired her to do that.

It will happen as great ships are sailing on the ocean, airplanes are flying, and palaces are well established. And then it will happen – the great earthquake. We are not talking about the common type of earthquake people have experienced so far. We are talking about something great, something never experienced before: a great earthquake where all buildings will fall down in a twinkle of an eye. They will all come to dust, as if they had never existed before. This is the beginning of the earthquake. It will be like a great warning.

Then other things will happen. The trumpet will be blown and everything will be thunderstruck. Everything will die. The angel of the air, Isrāfīl, will be ordered to blow a special instrument that was created by Allāh. I want you to know that Isrāfīl has five hundred wings, and each single wing is as vast as the heaven and the earth. It can reach through all of the seven earths and seven heavens. That angel of air, Isrāfīl, will carry this instrument and blow it. It will be a severe sound that none of these huge buildings can stand. There will be people dancing at that time, unconscious. There will be people asleep. There will be people trading in the market. There will be people traveling in airplanes that will all just fall at once. Everything will be brought to dust.

What more will happen? The oceans and seas will boil with fire. All of the bodies of water will be fire because all of the oil underneath will be lit with fire. Earthquakes will happen. What will the miserable, helpless human do at that time? The only escape and refuge is Allāh. He is our only refuge. Everything in the heavens and the earth will be stricken with a thunderbolt and made dead, except a few people. Who are these people? They will be the messengers, the prophets, the martyrs, the saints, the friends (ʾāwliya), and the followers of Allāh [those who are carrying the Message of Allāh, the message of unity, peace, justice and mercy in the way of the prophets]. Everything else will perish and die. Also, the angels who are carrying the throne of Allāh will not perish. They are exempt. They will be left standing.

Then a second blow from the trumpet will happen and everything will resurrect. All people will be resurrected to life again. It will be as if they went to sleep and then woke up. People will think, "Oh, I have just been asleep for a day." However, it is another life. At that time Allāh will be present and everyone will be conscious of His presence. All of the angels will be brought into lines in accordance with their ranks. Oh Allāh, nothing is like You. You are far more glorious than anything here. You are far transcendent. On that Day everything will be shaken.

People will then come back to life by the command of Allāh. Their actions will be demonstrated in front of Allāh. They will come out of their graves a new creation. They will stand between Allāh's hands in front of Him to be judged and for their actions to be demonstrated. So the one who stole will be brought to reckoning. The murderer will be brought to reckoning. Everything a human committed, whether major or minor, will be questioned. He will be judged. Are you prepared for that Day? Do you realize that this Day will come and must come? Do you realize that for posterity you will stand between Allāh's hands for that reckoning?

Allāh then says that after all of this happens the earth will be illuminated by the light of its Lord. There is a divine light—I marvel at how some people fall asleep now while I am talking, while a reminder of Allāh is being recited! On that day the earth will be illuminated by the light of its Lord and Allāh will judge people in accordance with the Realty, in accordance with the Truth. They will never be oppressed by the weight of even an atom.

All the oppressors will be standing in front of Allāh. The women who fell into abusive relationships where their husbands threw you into the street, took all your rights, and violated your rights...And also you men if your wives have violated your rights. Know that these people will be brought to accountability and be judged fairly.

The one given his book of recorded actions in his right hand will have a light, merciful reckoning. Allāh, Most High, glory be to Him, says that our beloved Messenger once asked people:

> The Messenger asked, "Do you know who is in bankruptcy?"
>
> The people answered, "The one who lost all his money, the one who does not have a dirham."
>
> He said, "No. The one who is in true bankruptcy is the one who comes to the standing of the Day of Judgment with this in his record: that he backbit, that he stole, that he beat others, that he cursed others, that he oppressed others and violated their rights. All of his good deeds will be given to the ones whom he violated. (Ḥadīth)

Those who had been oppressed by that person will come and say, "That person violated my rights. That person backbit me. That person oppressed me. That person broke my heart. That person cursed me." Everyone will complain to Allāh, "That person did this and that to us." [In this way] the blessings of his good deeds will go to those people instead of going to him. He will be in bankruptcy because he will lose all of the blessings from the good actions he did.

These people will still have rights over him. If all of his good deeds are gone, then their bad deeds will fall upon him and he will be punished for the bad deeds of those whom he oppressed. Then he will come into true bankruptcy. So the one who is in true bankruptcy is not the one who has no wealth. No. The one in true bankruptcy is the one who does not have enough good deeds as credit.

Allāh, the Almighty, will say, "Light the Hellfire." Allāh ordered the angels to guard it and keep the fuel going. This fire is different from physical fire we know in this world. It is more severe by tenfold or more. The Day of Reckoning will come and everyone will be brought to accountability. Are you prepared? Are you ready to be questioned? Do you know that you will pass away for sure and that you will travel to the other realm for this reckoning?

Suppose you live a hundred years. You will pass away after that. You will travel to the other realm. Did you create yourself? No, you were brought here, and then you will be taken from this world. Allāh is the one who fashioned you in the first place and wants you to follow His guidance and His rules and to not spread corruption across the earth.

All of the prophets and angels and messengers and martyrs and saints and loyal followers of Allāh will be brought back to Allāh, and they will be given their rights. They will say, "Oh Allāh, we surrendered to Your commands and we served You." Who are you following? You are a follower of the Prophet Muḥammad, ṣalla-llāhu ʿalayhi wa sallam. Do you know how the mother guards and protects her children? The Messenger of Allāh, Muḥammad, will also embrace those who followed him and carried the message of unity in a merciful way. He is the one who has the right of intercession with Allāh and he will intercede on behalf of his followers, may the peace and blessings of Allāh be upon him and all of the messengers and saints.

Everyone will receive his book of records, his scrolls. The ones who will be given their book of records in their right hands will have light, merciful judgment. These are the people who were kind and who tried as much as they could. They were the followers who tried to walk straight to Allāh. Allāh will water them with the water of life, purity and light. This is because they walked straight, carrying the message of true unity. They will be the ones who will be saved. Those are the ones who believed and carried the true message of Allāh, the message of unity. They will walk in joy toward Allāh, thanking Him for His favor upon them.

Every soul will be given the consequences of her deeds in full. The one who does an iota of good will receive its reward, and the one who does an atom's weight of evil will also receive its consequences (Qurʾān 99:7). What will the state of people be after the reckoning? There will be those who are saved from the punishment of Allāh, from the severe suffering.

They are the ones who established regular prayer, who were completely obedient to Allāh, who never lied to Allāh, who never lied to people, and who did not stop with pictures and imagination but held to the truth of the Reality.

But those who stopped with the s̲hayṭān, who obeyed their selves and their evil desires, those people will end up where? Allāh says those who covered up the truth, those who denied the Reality will be led by the angels to the Hellfire that was prepared by Allāh. Oh beloved, save yourself before it is too late. The time is coming and there is no doubt about it. So hurry up. Prepare yourself for this difficult journey to the next life. Have good provision for this journey.

The people who covered up the truth and denied the Reality will be led to the Hellfire. Those criminals, oppressors, and tyrants will be led to the Hellfire. The pictures of those actions will come with them and will be projected back to them. The gates of the Hellfire will be open to such people.

The guardians of the Hellfire will ask the people who covered up the truth and denied the Reality, "Did you not receive messengers who warned you against this Day and told you about Allāh and His path?" They will say, "Yes. A messenger came to us and informed us about that Day." The guardians will say, "So the messengers came to you and warned you about that Day?" They will say, "Yes. The messengers came to us and warned us. We were rebellious and did not listen to them. We actually harmed some of those messengers. We actually killed some of them. We turned our backs to them. We slept as drunk people who were perplexed and confused."

It will be said to them, "Because you have now confessed that you were rebellious against Allāh and His message you deserve the Hellfire, the consequences of your own actions. It is what your hands earned. But Allāh pardons more and more of what you did (Qur'ān 42:30).

If the criminal is not brought to accountability and judgment, he just continues his tyranny. The arrogant one who treated people with arrogance and thought of himself as a glorious one who was better than others will be taken by force. So who are you? You are nothing. The ant is even better than you if you are in such a state, because Allāh is

Almighty, the Powerful, and He does not like the arrogant or people who boast and like to appear better than others.

Allāh, Most High, glory be to Him, says the Hellfire is the worst abode. It is the abode of the arrogant ones, the possessors of the Hellfire, the ones for whom Allāh has prepared a great suffering because of their arrogance and violations of other people's rights. They did not prepare for the abode that would sustain them and provide a good provision for them. The angels at that time will say to those people, "Dwell then in the gates of the Hellfire because this is the worst abode that is prepared for the arrogant ones."[27]

On the other hand, those who were conscious of Allāh, those who guarded themselves against evil and fought against evil, will be led to the Garden. Who are these people? These people are the ones who followed and carried the message of unity, who had kind hearts, and listened to and actualized the message of peace and love and mercy for all people; they are the people who surrendered to Allāh's commands. Their quality was mercy and they sacrificed themselves for the sake of Allāh. They devoted themselves to Allāh and to serving others and to serving humanity with good action. They carried a difficult message and burden, but they sacrificed themselves for the sake of Allāh, for the poor and needy, helpless and weak.

These are the messengers of Allāh who carry pure goodness and do not spread corruption across the earth. Allāh says that the people who are conscious of Allāh and who guard themselves against evil from within and from without will be led to the Garden. The angels will say:

> "Salāmun ʿAlaykum [peace be upon you]!
> You have done well
> [You have been merciful and now you will be granted mercy],
> so enter here to abide therein." (Qurʾān 39:73)

These are the patient ones who rush to help those who are suffering across the earth, the sick people who are in pain and cannot have medicine. They rush to the hungry, the homeless, and the needy. They are the ones who always speak the truth and stand for justice without being afraid of anyone but Allāh.

---

[27] Allāh says in His Qurʾān that nineteen angels will preside as the guardians of hell (Qurʾān 74:31)

When they arrive at the gates of the Garden what will happen? It will automatically open for them without any questioning. Then the angels will chant for them a beautiful song saying, "Welcome to you beloveds of Allāh, followers of the messages of the prophets who obeyed your Lord. Welcome to you. This is your Final Abode. May you rejoice in what you did."

One of Allāh's qualities is justice. He is Justice. He says:

> Whoever does an atom's weight of good will receive the consequences,
> Whoever does an atom's weight of evil will receive the consequences. (Qur'ān 99:7-99:8)

All the messengers and prophets had followers and beloveds. Every messenger cares about his followers and disciples. You must hold tight to the message of the Prophet, ṣalla-llāhu ʿalayhi wa sallam, and do not let it go.

The people who followed the true message will dwell in the Garden with their spouses and children. These people will say:

> Praise be to Allāh Who fulfilled His promise to us.
> (Qur'ān 39:74)

Allāh promises you that if you follow the message of unity, love, justice, and mercy, and if you apply and actualize this message, you will receive this reward. He will fulfill His promise. He knows the human being. He knows everything, and that is His decree—that the person who carries this message will dwell in the Garden.

What will be in the garden? It has what no eyes have ever seen and no ears have ever heard. It has beauty. What should we do here, while living in this lower realm, to attain the Garden? Allāh gave us a gift. He gave us the month of Ramaḍan. This is a door, a gate He opened to us for repentance. Annually this month comes and these gates of repentance are opened. Allāh says about this special month that in the beginning of it there is forgiveness, which means that in the beginning of Ramaḍan the gates of repentance are open to you. So why do you not repent to be granted the mercy of Allāh, as you have heard now in the Qur'ān? Why do you not want to receive this mercy and be accepted by Allāh through repenting?

Allāh says about the month of Ramaḍan that it has forgiveness in its beginning. In its middle there is mercy. The reward for this repentance will be mercy. We have past that middle so repent now so that you can be granted that mercy. For the last ten days of Ramaḍan there will be the "saving from the Hellfire" so why do you not repent? Why do you not consider every month a Ramaḍan for you, as every month you seek repentance? Weep to Allāh. Ask Him for forgiveness. I want a repentance in which you weep, and you sincerely weep out of sorrow and regret for what you have done, for all the sins you have done, and for all your delay in being totally devoted and obedient to Allāh.

Allāh, Most High, glory be to Him, says:

> The one who comes with repentance and a full heart,
> I will transform their bad deeds into good deeds
> and rectify their deeds and his affairs. (Qur'ān 5:39)

Allāh also says:

> Say: "Oh My slaves who have transgressed against themselves!
> Do not despair of Allāh's mercy.
> Truly, Allāh forgives all sins.
> Truly, He is Oft-Forgiving, Most Merciful." (Qur'ān 39:53)

Are you ready to seek repentance, to be granted forgiveness and mercy and to be saved from the Hellfire? I ask you to seek forgiveness for yourselves and I will seek forgiveness for myself. Whoever wants to repent now for all past things, let him weep and come to me now, asking Allāh in sincere repentance for mercy and to be saved from the Hellfire. The doors are open now. Let every slave and servant of Allāh come and be granted this blessing. This hand is stretched to you from Allāh. Allāh wants to save us from the suffering that is prepared as a consequence for the oppressors and the tyrants. Allāh will never punish those who are fasting, and those who pray, prostrate, and bow down to Allāh. So do not delay your repentance. Come now because the doors are open in this blessed moment Allāh is giving us. His mercy will be granted to the one who repents and rectifies his deeds. Allāh will accept such a person (Qur'ān 5:39).

Sidi prays for the people present:

Oh Allāh,
[He] who knows the reality of repentance,
I ask You on behalf of my beloveds who come confessing their sins
and acknowledging You as the only God
and acknowledging that Muḥammad is Your only slave and messenger,
and that all of the faithful believers are their brothers and sisters.
They come in repentance directing their hearts fully toward You
and asking for forgiveness for all their sins.

They are weeping.
They are sincere.
They are asking for Your help.
They are honest and truthful
so please accept them.

Oh Allāh, please forgive their sins and relieve their burdens
and make them among the truly repentant during this blessed month.
Grant them forgiveness.
Pardon them.
Hide their faults.

Oh Allāh, the One Who Raises His Servants,
please raise us and do not turn us away from Your doors disappointed.
These are Your sinful slaves and servants.
They come in obedience to You.
They come asking You because they know
that You are the Kind, the Merciful, and the Gentle.
They come to be granted Your pleasure.
They want You to be pleased with them
so please give them the joy of being granted your mercy.

Oh Allāh, You are the Most Powerful, and there is no other deity but You.
Please forgive all of us. Āmīn. Āmīn. Āmīn.

Sidi then gives the promise of repentance.

We All Need the Mercy of Allāh, Most High

Lā ʾilāha ʾilla-llāāāāāāh, Lā ʾilāha ʾilla-llāāāāāh, Lā ʾilāha ʾilla-llāāāāāh
Muḥammad rasūlu-llāh, Ibrāhīm rasūlu-llāh, Mūsā rasūlu-llāh,
ʿĪsā rasūlu-llāh ʿalayhim ṣalātu-llāh.

Allāhumma anta-s-salām wa minka-s-salām
wa ilayka ya'ūdu-s-salām
tabārakta rabbanā
ya dha-l-jalāli wa-l-'ikrām

As-salāmu ʿalaykum wa raḥmatu-llāh wa bārakatuhu.

May the peace and blessings of Allāh be upon all the prophets and messengers, all beloved to Allāh. May the peace and blessings of Allāh be upon our Master Guide, Ibrāhīm (Abraham), and Master Guides, Mūsā (Moses), ʿĪsā (Jesus), and Muḥammad.

This morning, we gave a divine warning for those who are heedless of what is going to happen; those who are unconscious of why the human being was created. Allāh says in the Qurʾān:

> Do you think [that We created you as a game]
> and that you will never return to Us?" (Qurʾān 28:39)

Glory be to Allāh, the True King, Most High. He is the True King and there is no other god but Him. He is the Lord of the glorious Throne.

Many people say, "Oh we just live this life and nothing will happen afterwards. We will just perish in time, and there is no life after death." Many people think that way. They deny or reject the idea that Allāh created them, and He is the One Who Gives them Provision. They think that their physical life is all that there is. They just live and die. These are the people who do not understand the reality of the matter. They do not have sound intellect because they have to think with common sense; like the physical thing does not create itself. This is not true? Can a materialistic thing create itself? We want to search with you in a scientific way.

Actually, the true guide is not the one who knows only religious things, but the one who is knowledgeable in mathematics, science, biology, and every other science that humans know. The gnostics knew these sciences even from long ago, even before science came to people in that form. If the human looks at the smallest atom in existence, you know that the atom has two parts; the positive and the negative charge. The atom has the positive neutron and the negative electrons. It is very well-structured and the electrons always circulate. It is always in circulation without stopping. If it stops, then the great event will happen. The great disaster will happen. This is how crazy people thought of the atomic bombs and weapons. Because they did that, they stopped the motion, and used the atomic bomb.

We knew that before them and we are able to do it. But Allāh put within us, the gnostics, mercy for all human beings, and we know that we will be questioned about every minor thing we do. Our masters, the beloved prophets, told us that Allāh will have mercy upon those who are merciful to others. The saying goes:

> Have mercy on the people on earth
> so that the One in heaven will grant you mercy. (Ḥadīth)

The agents of Iblīs are the ones who make and use destructive weapons. They think that they can destroy the world for their own benefit. But in reality they are so helpless; even more than the tiny fly. They cannot do anything.

The whole structure of the world will continue, and the whole destruction of the world will result in a new world that will have gardens and meadows and everything beautiful. Allāh will transform the evil world into something good. This is the promise of Allāh and the promise of all the prophets and messengers.

Our Master Prophet, ṣalla-llāhu ʿalayhi wa sallam, said that there are sciences for the approach of the Last Hour. After the Last Hour the world will continue to be in peace, justice, mercy and love. The human will know nothing but love. But there are sciences that will come before that, and the messengers and prophets informed us with these sciences. In our Qur'ān that Allāh sent down Allāh says that He will send people. He named them by name. In Arabic they are known as Ya'gūg and Ma'gūg. These people will spread corruption on earth. They are like monsters and they think that they are able to control humanity. But Allāh, the Most Merciful, will send an affliction on them, a disaster from among themselves that will destroy them. This type of person does not pass a place without causing corruption and destruction in it.

For example, [Ghengis Khan] is one of the people mentioned in history. Whoever has studied will know the name, probably you pronounce it differently. [Ghengis Khan] came out of China and he was a tyrant. He spread destruction on the earth and he invaded many countries until he reached Europe and the Middle East and destroyed many people. But at the end, what happened? Allāh sent to him true believers, faithful believers who actually isolated him, removed him from the place, and ended his oppression.

This is what happens to the tyrants who spread corruption and destruction across the earth. No matter what they claim, and no matter how strong they are, and how many weapons they have, Allāh is able to stop them. Within the twinkle of an eye, He can actually destroy them. And also, within the twinkle of an eye, reconciliation can happen between the Lord and the slave, or between the slave and his Lord. So, Allāh certainly will rectify their affairs. The one who is ready to receive correction, will be corrected. Otherwise, Allāh will take him by force from the world for his tyranny. glory be to Him, He promised the faithful believers who are carrying the message of peace, and mercy, and justice, and love; He promised them great goodness as a reward for them.

I want to give you a hint here that the one who is the heir of the Prophet Muḥammad, is ready to appear, to manifest. Everything has a time. And his message is the message of peace, love, mercy, justice, and freedom for all people. He will gather all people under one flag; the flag of unity, and [certify] that there is no other god but Allāh. Allāh wants all goodness for people. He wants mercy for them, not corruption, destruction and harm.

We ask Allāh to make us one of His beloveds, and make you one of His beloveds and one of those who will carry the message of unity, peace, love, mercy, and justice for all people. And Allāh is the Responder to our prayers. Let me remind those who are arrogant, those who are working for the lower realms, for the gains of the lower realms. Let me remind them why Allāh created you, oh human. Why did Allāh create you; just to eat, drink, sleep, and marry? Or did He create you to carry a message, to make good use of the land that Allāh created for you, and to preserve what Allāh has given you? He wanted you to live the good life that He wanted you to live. He does not want you to live a life full of disasters, afflictions, destruction, fights, harm, and all of that.

His Name is the Universally Merciful, the Singularly Compassionate. How can these be His Names if He wills you otherwise? Would He ever will for His creatures to live in suffering, disease, affliction, and disaster? No. So what happens in the world now is because of what your hands have earned; that which comes to you, your hands earned (Qur'ān 42:30). We want to purify our hands and purify our dirty tongues that say dirty words and backbite people. We want to purify ears that only listen to evil. Our message is of true unity that Allāh sent down to our most beloved guide, the Prophet Muḥammad, 'alayhi as-salātu as-salām. We want to be Allāh's tools, we want Allāh to use us, and to be His true worshippers. Allāh wants to remind us, and to remind also the evil people, and those who are arrogant and those who are stubborn.

Allāh says in His Holy Book:

> Oh people, be conscious of your Lord
> and guard yourselves for Him against evil people.
>
> [Remember that]
> He is Allāh, the Creator, the Inventor of all things
> [with complete command of the matter in My hand],
> the Bestower of forms
> [The Bestower of gifts]
> [The Healer]
> [The one who Suffices]
> [The Irresistible]
> To Him belong the best Names [all the beautiful Names].
> (Qur'ān 59:24 with tafsir)

Allāh manifested all His beautiful Names through His creation and through His people.

> Therefore remember Me. I will remember you,
> and be grateful to Me
> and never be ungrateful to Me. (Qur'ān 2:152)

Allāh says in the Qur'ān, "Oh people." To whom? To the people, especially to the beloveds who acknowledge that He is the One Creator, He created you in the excellent and perfect form, and created everything with accuracy, perfection and beauty. Allāh says:

> ...you (humankind) are poor (Qur'ān 47:38)

We are talking about the one who is poor in the way of Allāh. He is actually the one who is rich, or sufficed by Allāh. And Allāh says to serve the people, and you always stay in need of Him.

This came also on the tongue of His Prophet Mūsā, 'alayhi-s-salām, who said:

> I am always in need of You, even though I acknowledge all the richness and all the provision that You have given me.

So ask yourself, who gave you two eyes, who gave you a tongue, who gave you your provision, who gave you your life, your very life? It is He. He is the Self-Sufficient and you are the poor, always in need of Him. If a person came to you and said, "Give me your eye and I will give you millions and millions of dollars," would you give your eye to him? No, you would not sell your eye. But my Lord gave you this eye that is priceless, without any price. Did He not give you a tongue? Would you sell this tongue for anything? You cannot even do that. Even the cat will refuse to sell her tongue to any other creature.

This is why we really have to feel the value and estimate the value of what Allāh has given us; and to be thankful to Him, to be grateful, and to always praise Him. Then we must never violate someone else's rights and what Allāh has given them. Allāh wants to remind us and He says to us in this blessed month, most of it has already passed. Remember our beloved Prophet has said, "The beginning of it [Ramaḍan] is forgiveness, the middle of it is repentance." You repent to be granted mercy. Because in the middle of it; mercy is granted. Who will receive this mercy? Who will be granted mercy? It is not granted to the one who repented with his tongue only. Allāh wants you to hold tight to it by your hands, your actions, all of your affairs, in your daily life. Allāh says to us that the earthquake, the commotion of the earth in the Last Hour will be tremendous. And it is coming without doubt.

We are talking about the last earthquake that will come before the Day of Judgment and the resurrection. What will happen? Cars will be driving, airplanes flying, buses driving on bridges, merchants in the markets trading, people working, other people in entertainment; some are standing some are sitting, or sleeping. Allāh says that earthquake of the Last Hour will be something tremendous. We are not talking about common earthquakes that you have heard about or experienced. This will happen within the twinkle of an eye. It will shake the oceans, it will shake the land under the oceans, and the bodies of water will start to boil with fire. The mountains will be destroyed and everything will come to dust. Allāh says that it will be tremendous. Allāh says to us, on that Day, we will see that, experience that.

What will happen at that Day? When you will see or experience it the nursing mother will forget her child. She will be nursing her child and because of the terror and the horror and the fear she feels, she will throw her baby away. And every pregnant woman will have a miscarriage. From the horror, from the terror, from the fear that she will have, she will have an immediate miscarriage. You will see people deathly that feel drunk out of fear, like they are drunk because they cannot believe what is happening.

Do you know how the one who drinks, who is intoxicated, how they feel? This is another type of intoxication that will make the mind absent. You will see people drunk in that way, but they are not really drunk, they are actually living and experiencing a reality. This must happen; it will happen with certainty.

> And Allāh's punishment is severe. (many places in the Qur'ān)

At that time, one must be ready for the reckoning; the reckoning that I talked about this morning. So prepare for the Day of Resurrection, for the Day of Standing for Judgment, the Day of Sorrow and the Day of Regret; where regret and sorrow will not benefit anyone. Nothing will benefit the person except his good deeds and his full heart that devoted to Allāh.

Allāh says that some people argue about that matter and they deny it; they reject that and they think that it will never happen (Qur'ān 25:11 and others). But it will happen, whether they believe it or not, because the Creator informed us of that. Allāh says in the Qur'ān,

> And some people argue about this matter of Allāh
> without having true knowledge. (Qur'ān 6:25)

Because they do not have true knowledge—they just follow the sẖayṭān's whispers.

But, oh our Lord
our God,
our Creator
our Protector
our Gentle Lord
our Merciful One
we believe what You say.
we believe in Your Words
and we are helpless people.
We are in need of You and we ask for Your mercy.
We ask You to grant Your mercy to us
and bestow Your compassion upon us
and guide us to the way of safety and security.
Please give us true knowledge of Yourself, grant us gnosis.
Please treat us with Your qualities, not with our qualities.
Please, Allāh, do not humiliate us, do not destroy us
make us happy and make us safe and secure,
in our bodies and in our spirits, in our hearts, and our land.
And make us one of those who unify You.

The Prophet, ʿalayhi as-salātu as-salām, said that the Last Hour will not be established as long as there is a person on the earth who still says, "Lā ʾilāha ʾilla-llāh," who still witnesses that. As long as there is someone who is witnessing that there is no god but Allāh, and Muḥammad is His slave and Messenger, then the Last Hour will not come. And this is the meaning of Allāh's saying,

> We have not sent you but as a mercy for all the world.
> (Qurʾān 21:107)

Muḥammad is a human being, but he is a gem, a pure gem. He is a gift of mercy that was sent down to the earth. This is not human mercy. It is Divine mercy from the Universally Merciful, the Singularly Compassionate. So, all you who love Allāh, and love the Messenger of Allāh, do not be afraid of that Day. You who are carrying the message of majesty and unity and beauty and justice; you who are chanting the glory of Allāh and the praises of Allāh, do not fear.

Allāh says in Ḥadīth Qudsī:

> No group of people will gather to remember Him,
> but the angels will come, surrounding them from all over.

We are in need of this mercy. Are you not in need of mercy? We are in the month of mercy. Allāh says:

> My Mercy is vast enough to contain everything,
> but My special Mercy will be to those faithful believers.
>
> [i.e., Neither the heavens nor the earth can contain Me, only the heart of My faithful slave contains Me. (Ḥadīth Qudsī]

We are weak and helpless and we only have our Protector to suffice us. But the other group of people who do not rely on Allāh, who do not surrender to Allāh's commands and natural law, and who do not fast, do not do the divine obligations, and do not keep their prayers and do not give their charity for the annual money they accumulate, the zakāh; they are the enemies of humanity and the enemies of the prophets and the messengers. Allāh warns those people of a severe punishment, as a consequence from what they did.

But this blessed month, Allāh loves it. We are in need of His mercy this month because Allāh promised that in the beginning of the month, He will grant forgiveness, in the middle, He will grant mercy. Are you not in need of this mercy? If you are truly in need of this mercy, and you love this mercy, then why do you not come, if you are truly in need of this mercy? Come to me and promise Allāh, promise Allāh that you are repenting to be granted this mercy. If you come for the repentance asking for mercy and forgiveness, then I am certain that Allāh will accept you, will take your hands to Him, and will bestow upon you a great mercy from Himself. Mercy comes directly from Allāh. Because Allāh says:

> My Mercy is vast enough to contain everything.
> It contains everything, but
> My special mercy will be given to My faithful believer
> who believed in Me,
> who believed in My Prophets and Messengers
> because those are My true beloveds.

So true beloveds, oh true beloveds, if you want, come and give this promise of repentance asking to be granted the mercy, the special mercy of Allāh. I am sure and certain that He will bestow His Mercy upon you because you are standing at His door, and knocking on His door asking

Him to accept you. Oh Allāh, please accept them because You have power over everything.

Guarding the Self for Allah, Most High

"The Tranquil, Secure Soul"
from *He Who Knows Himself Knows His Lord*

Lā ʾilāha ʾilla-llāāāāāāh, Lā ʾilāha ʾilla-llāāāāāh, Lā ʾilāha ʾilla-llāāāāāh
Muḥammad rasūlu-llāh, Ibrāhīm rasūlu-llāh, Mūsā rasūlu-llāh,
ʿĪsā rasūlu-llāh ʿalayhim ṣalātu-llāh.

Allāhumma anta-s-salām wa minka-s-salām
wa ilayka yaʿūdu-s-salām
tabārakta rabbanā
ya dha-l-jalāli wa-l-'ikrām

As-salāmu ʿalaykum wa raḥmatu-llāh wa bārakatuhu.

Today is the twenty-fifth day of the blessed month of Ramaḍan, the month of repentance, the month of forgiveness, the month in which people are saved from the Hellfire. This is a great month and it is coming to an end quickly. I say, "Have glad tidings. Good news for you, oh one who really fasted the month, and stayed up at night praying, and really was conscious of what is prohibited in fasting, the one who really fasted with his heart, and soul and spirit, and was present in that month wholeheartedly. He did not just come to eat and drink after he was hungry and thirsty."

All the angels who are close to Allāh were present in this month. The one who really was truthful and sincere and honest in his worship and fasting during this month, I am certain that Allāh has granted him or her mercy and forgiveness, and He will relieve his difficulties and pain, and will bestow His mercy upon him, because Allāh was with you all the way.

The Prophet, ṣalla-llāhu ʿalayhi wa sallam, said:

> Allāh, Most High, glory be to Him,
> descended and manifested Himself in the last third of the night into the lower realm.
> He asked, "Is there anyone asking for forgiveness
> so I can grant him forgiveness?
> Is there anyone who is sick asking for healing so I can heal him?

> Is there anyone in need of help and support so I can bestow My help and support to him?" (Ḥadīth̲ Qudsī?)

This happens in Ramaḍan. Divine mercy descends on the people who are awake at that time and worshipping Allāh. This is a divine gift that Allāh sent, greater than the table that was sent down to ʿĪsā (Jesus), ʿalayhi-s-salām, and his disciples. Congratulations to those who sat around the divine table each night. They were Allāh's guests and Allāh was the host. Allāh accepted them.

However, those who did not fast purposely without excuse and those who did not pay the zakāh are not accepted. Those who did not pay their zakāh, their fasting will not be accepted because they were not fully truthful, sincere, and honest in worship. You still have a chance until the end of the month. If you have not yet paid the zakāh, you must pay the zakāh so your fasting and worship can be accepted. Otherwise it will go to waste. You will lose everything you did.

Allāh says:

> Whatever of good reaches you, is from Allāh, but
> whatever of evil befalls you, is from yourself.
> And Allāh pardons much. (Qurʾān 42:30)

Allāh, of course, will pardon the one who does not have means and does not have enough money. There is no zakāh for that person; but those who are wealthy and able to pay the zakāh and do not do it, they must do it; otherwise it will be too late for them. This is my advice to you, my beloveds, my brothers and sisters and sons and daughters.

Now we are approaching the end of Ramaḍan and I explained to you yesterday about the Day of Judgment and Resurrection, which is coming for certain without doubt, and I explained how there will be a final judgment and reckoning and punishment and reward as consequences of people's deeds in this lower realm. I explained to you that everyone will be questioned about his prayer, his fasting, and how he obeyed or disobeyed the commands of Allāh.

The faithful believer must be truthful, sincere, honest, loving, fair, and merciful. These are the divine qualities that the faithful believer must have. Those who lie, deceive, murder, and steal, these are not the divine qualities, and common sense rejects all these qualities. They are not acceptable to anyone. I ask Allāh to protect you from these qualities and to protect your hearts and to turn you away from all these horrible deeds and actions that are not in conformity with Allāh's way.

Now we will talk again about the subject of the stations. We will read today about the fourth station, which is the station of an-nafs al-muṭma'inna, which is the secure and tranquil self.

"The Tranquil, Secure Self" on page 111 of *He Who Knows Himself Knows His Lord* is read from the beginning until the top of page 114, "In this station, you may also experience the desire for leadership and fame and your ego will whisper to you that you are able to guide others to spiritual maturity..."

It is something that actually happens to many crazy people. Many crazy people think that they can become s̱haykẖs like that, out from the street becoming a s̱haykẖ all of a sudden. They want to collect money, and the money cuts them off from their Lord because it becomes their occupation. They are occupied with how to get money. They appear as if they are higher than others, and they belittle others. They become arrogant and far away from Allāh, forgetting that they are only human from flesh and blood and bones, and they are not worthy of anything. In truth they are carrying and accumulating all dirt. First the nose is carrying dirt and the mouth also carries dirt, even the stomach is like a small box carrying a lot of dirt. They forget that they are an insignificant drop and their end is a dirty corpse. They carry within them rotten stuff. If they really knew about their body, they would be disgusted by it.

Are you like that? Yes, you are like that! You cannot actually argue and say, "No, I do not have this!" Why then do you become arrogant and think of yourself as better than others and belittle them? Yes, you worked hard and Allāh provided you with good wealth, money, but that does not mean you can be arrogant, because the wealth came from Allāh. All that you really should own is what you eat because you cannot eat more than your stomach can take. You eat and then you defecate. You wear clothes, but then they wear out with time, and then what remains for you is really the charity you give. What food you get, you defecate, and you wear clothes and they wear out with time. They are not something that will remain for you. If you give charity to the poor and the needy and do good and serve the people, that will remain for you.

If you dwell in the ways the s̲hayṭān projects onto you, then you will lose. If s̲hayṭān becomes your companion in your life, whispering to you, saying to you, "You do not have to give all of this money. Maybe you should keep that, and you will become rich and great. When you have that, you will become like a great businessman." He promises you that you will become great if you collect a few million, and build palaces or houses and get an airplane. However, remember, are you going to take all of that with you when you pass away, when you die?

I am certain that if you are that rich, your children will wish you would die so they can inherit that from you. For the people who have lost love from their hearts because their father did not raise them in a divine way, that will be their case; they will wish that the father would actually die so that they can inherit the material wealth. But if he raised them in the divine way, they will wish better for him. They will wish that he become healthier and richer. But those other people who are not raised in the way of Allāh but in the way of the s̲hayṭān, they will wish bad for their father. They will say, "Oh, we wish he would go to Jahannam, the Hellfire, and we will just take the money. We do not care about him." They were not raised in the divine way, in the godly way. When the children are raised in the divine way, in the godly way, they wish good for their parents, they give to their parents, they have love in their hearts for them.

Allāh in the Qur'ān commanded children to take care of their parents when they become old. Allāh decreed that you worship only Him and you excel in doing good to your parents. When they become old, you do not say, "oof" to them. You should not say that (Qur'ān 17:23). You think of this little word as nothing, but it is something great. Suppose your mother is calling you and you say, "Oh, she is calling me again. I do not want to hear her voice."

Do you not remember when you were a little child and you used to cry, she would rush to you; she would be almost crying as well. She cried for you. When you wept, she wept. When you were sick, she stayed beside you. Do you not remember that? Do you not remember when you fell sick one time and your dad was so worried, standing wondering what he could do, taking you to the doctor, and to another doctor, and getting you the medicine? Why does the father do all of this? Because his child is a piece of himself. Allāh knows this. He knows with the knowledge of certainty how some children become rebellious against their parents.

That is why He commanded us in the Qur'ān to excel in doing good to our parents.

> One day, the Prophet, ṣalla-llāhu 'alayhi wa sallam,
> went on the platform to deliver his speech.
> He went one step. Then he started to say, "'Āmīn."
> Then he went another step and he said, "'Āmīn." Again.
> Then the third time he said, "'Āmīn."
> Then the companions asked him,
> "Why did you say "'Āmīn" three times?
> He said, "Because Jibrīl was sent down to me and said,
> 'Miserable and a failure is the one who is still present in life
> while his parents become old
> and he is rebellious and does not care for his parents.' "

That will make him miserable and a failure, and Allāh will let him go to the Hellfire. He is a failure because the Hellfire is his final abode. The second 'Āmīn was because Jibrīl said to the Prophet, "Whoever was present in the month of Ramaḍan and did not take his chance and was not forgiving, is also miserable and a failure because he was in deviation of the divine command." This is something very deep. The third step on which he said "Āmīn" was because Jibrīl informed him that the one who did not surrender to his Lord's commands will have his final abode in the Hellfire. So we are talking about three things.

Open your eyes and ears and heart. Do not close your eyes! Open your heart because Allāh is watching you. He is watching you and He feels angry if you fall asleep.

There are also some people who are crazy about leadership and about becoming s̲haykh̲s, leaders and guides. They are so obsessed with the idea. The one who is walking toward Allāh should focus his goal on Allāh, not leadership. He wants to arrive at Allāh, he wants to have Allāh's love. He wants to have the joy of being close to Allāh in His presence. He wants his Creator to be pleased with him. For your Creator to be pleased with you is the greatest grace.

I say, let Allāh take from me all my wealth, all my health, anything belonging to me, so that only His love remains for me. That is the only thing I care about. That is why I speak poetry:

If all was taken from me and
He did not leave for me anything but His love,
then I am richer than any other rich one,
because I was granted His love and pleasure
and He is the very essence of my life.
[It is] enough for me [to have] a piece of clothing
to cover my body from the cold weather or the hot weather.
That is enough.

Do you not observe that the bird is better than the human by a thousand times? Look at the bird. Allāh says in the Qur᾿ān:

> If you truly depend on Allāh and rely on Him fully,
> then Allāh will provide for you as He provides for the birds.

The birds go out in the morning hungry; they return full. See this beautiful bird? He flies in the morning and his stomach is empty. He does not have food in his house in storage. You hear him chanting his prayer. He is hungry but he is chanting. He first prays and then he asks Allāh. He says, "Allāh, I am your slave. You created me, so please provide for me." And he flies searching and he finds his food. He takes what is enough for him and returns home to his nest. In the evening he puts his head under his wing and sits on top of the branch of the tree and he sleeps at peace. He is not worried about anything. Do you not think he is happy? Who is happier—the bird or the human who keeps struggling to accumulate and collect money? I am certain that the bird is happier.

These are examples Allāh gives to us. Look, the bird has no storage full of food. Go look at the nest. Does he store food there? He is actually free, at peace, and loving. Do you not see how he loves his Beloved and gets annihilated in His love? He does not worry about anything or anyone. This is because he is fully directed towards Allāh. The crazy man, why does not he learn something from that bird? That bird is teaching him how to love, how to give and how to rely on Allāh. These are the birds. All the animals are like that. They take what is enough for them and do not search for more. They look for peace and they search for love and for true freedom.

This means that everything in creation is loftier in its state than the human being. Supposedly the human should be the loftiest creature on the earth. We are talking about the human who will truly give his rights to Allāh, and give his body and his heart and his spirit. He would become the loftiest creature. Allāh honored you with that station. No matter how you struggle to accumulate things, your end is to Allāh.

Allāh created you to worship Him, which means to know Him and to walk in accordance with His guidance. He did not create you to murder and destroy and steal and break hearts, oh crazy ones who are lost in the realm of desires. Why do you reject love and live in a state of misery? People look for money, leadership, and fame. Why are they looking for these things? The ones who are at the bottom rank of humanity are such people. Allāh chooses you to support people, to care for them, and to prepare for them the way for justice and to serve them in every way. This is something great and an honor from Allāh to you that makes you a servant to Allāh. Allāh did not create you to send the children to die, or to steal the money from people for your own sake. The one who really cares about people and their children, becomes the servant of those people.

One of the truly guided k̲h̲alīfa, ʿUmar ibn al-K̲h̲aṭṭāb, the successor of the Prophet, ṣalla-llāhu ʿalayhi wa sallam, was the prince of all of the faithful believers. He used to take his men and go in the streets at night after all the people were asleep, and he looked and listened: Is there anyone in pain? Is there anyone crying who is hungry? That is what he used to do.

Story of ʿUmar ibn al-K̲h̲aṭṭāb holding himself responsible for the health and well-being of his community

One day he heard a child crying in the night; he could not sleep. This k̲h̲alīfa, the successor to the Prophet, ṣalla-llāhu ʿalayhi wa sallam, would never sleep until he made sure everyone was okay.

He knocked on the door to see why the child was crying.

The mother said, "Who?"

He said, "I am the slave and servant of Allāh."
He did not say, "I am the prince or the president."
He said, "I am the servant of Allāh."

She said, "What do you want now?"

He said, “I would like to ask you why your child is crying.”
He did not tell her “I am Omar.”

She said, “May Allāh forgive Omar because he is the governor and he left my children hungry. I put a pot on the stove and I put some stones in it to pretend that it is food, so they can drink the water and think that it is food or something.”

He said, “Would you please give me permission to come in?”

She said, “No, I will not let you in. I do not know who you are.”

He said, “You are a truthful, sincere and honest woman.”
So he went and brought some food and carried it by himself on his back, and he knocked on her door again.

She said, “Who?”

He said, “One who is carrying food for you.”
He still did not say his name.

She said, “I will look at who you truly are.”
So she looked a little bit and she found that he was truly carrying food.
She said, “Ok. I will open for you.”

So she opened the door and he brought a lot of food for her and her children. He took off the pot that was full of stones, and instead put on the food and cooked it himself. They used to blow on the fire to keep it going, and he did that himself. The smoke was going through his long beard and he could feel the heat, but he was in total joy because he was serving someone.

The lady kept saying, “May Allāh forgive Omar. May Allāh forgive Omar.”

He said, “Oh, slave of Allāh.”

She said, “How does Omar know about you? Why do you think Omar knows about you?”

She said, "Why did he accept to be the governor who is responsible for me and my children and he does not know me. He is responsible for knowing me. He is responsible for every child in this community."

This is how it used to be. The governors who were the successors of the Prophet used to ask for the orphans, for the single women with children, for the older men. They used to look after them because they used to know the true meaning of the relation of Islām, which means the governor becomes the servant of all people. If he is not a servant, he is not eligible to become a governor, president or leader. Whoever is ready to be a servant, welcome for him; but whoever wants to sit on the throne and take people's money, then he does not deserve to be the leader.

Leadership is not for the evil ones. The way of Allāh is that the one who is responsible and in the position of leadership should care for everyone in the community. This is how people used to live. These governors, the well guided kẖalīfas, lived in service to people and cared for every orphan and child, for the weak people, and all the poor.

I ask Allāh to grant all people true leaders who care for people, who carry the peace and justice and freedom and mercy for all people without discrimination. This is Allāh's creed. This is what Allāh wants for us. This is the way that leads to Allāh.

The reading continues until, "if Allāh...causes you to become known, and clothes you with the garment of a sẖaykẖ...And also that, when you look within yourself you do not see any distinction between you and them, but perceive them as better than you because you are indebted to them for their belief that they are lower and for their respect for you."

What really destroys the human being is envy. Why is this one richer than me? Why is he better than me? Why has he more fame than me? Why does he dress better than me? Why do you busy yourself with other people? Be busy with yourself! Look at your own blemishes and the evil within yourself! The woman becomes foolish if she busies herself with her neighbor, how she looks, how her house looks. Let her clean her house first, clean herself, and care for her own self first. After that she will be able to cooperate with her neighbor and their relationship will be devoid of envy and hate and jealousy and gossip and backbiting and all of that. This is what influences people and causes fires and fights between them, that they busy themselves with comparison.

The reading continues until, "And if you ever think that they are in your debt, then know that you are not one of the people of this path."

Allāh wants to be generous to you, and He gives to you without your requesting to be a leader. He takes you because of your sincerity and honesty and devotion in serving others; and then He puts you on a chair and starts to guide you and teach you what you have no knowledge of. Then it is a favor from Him. It does not mean you are great.

It is a great test in this station, and a great trial to you, because every action you are doing is watched. Are you really merciful to every one of your children who comes asking you to teach them and guide them to walk toward Allāh? Or do you in this state use your children to become your servant? Do you want your children to kiss your feet and glorify you and use them as you wish? Or do you truly become their servant? For the people of Allāh, they become the servants; they do not use their children. The true s̲hayk̲h̲ is chosen by Allāh to become the servant of people and he has the Godly qualities. He does not know hate or envy, and he becomes earth for everyone to step on in their way to Allāh. He becomes the water from which every seeker drinks. He is full of love, full of humbleness, politeness, and he never raises his head above anyone, a child, or an elderly person.

Who put him in that position? Allāh! Allāh purified him, chose him, and selected him for that mission to serve the people just as Allāh selected the prophets and messengers before him. Allāh chose Mūsā, He chose ʿĪsā (Jesus), He chose Ibrāhīm. He chose them from among the people. Most of them were orphans. Mūsā had no father; he was an orphan. Also, the Prophet Yūnus and the Prophet Muḥammad were orphans. They were raised around the table of Allāh. Allāh raised them; He is the one who took care of them and taught them from His knowledge.

No one can make himself a leader; Allāh must make him a leader. The one who makes himself a leader must never say, "Ha, I am a leader." He should never be arrogant if he is truly chosen. This is the sound of arrogance. The true murrabi, the one who takes care of his community, must be completely polite, full of peace, love, mercy and tranquility. That is why Allāh said to His Messenger Muḥammad:

> And had you been severe and harsh hearted,
> they would have broken away from about you. (Qurʾān 3:159)

The Prophet, ṣalla-llāhu ʿalayhi wa sallam, said,

> The one who taught me politeness is my Lord,
> and He did it in an excellent and perfect way. (Ḥadīt͟h)

So follow the example of the prophets, Mūsā, ʿĪsā, Ibrāhīm, and Muḥammad, because all of them were like that.

If any s͟hayk͟h is boasting and walking in arrogance and you see him like that, you have the right to throw your shoes at him because you want him to leave; he is not a true s͟hayk͟h, a true guide. He is Iblīs who took the picture of a guide, and you have every right to throw stones at him and make him leave, because he is not truly a divine slave and servant.

The divine slave and servant to Allāh is the one who always gives, he does not know hate, he does not know racism, he is humble and polite, and he carries a great burden. The true guide carries a great burden; he has the pain of all of his seekers. All of their difficulties he cares about, and he carries them. Wherever he is and whenever it is, he cares for every minor detail and major detail in their life. It is not because of them. He is always conscious of Allāh and he knows that Allāh will question him for his shortcomings in caring for any seeker.

Any seeker has the right to ask about such a guide on the Day of Judgment and Reckoning, [and to say] that his guide treated me badly. "I asked him and he did not give me the answer. I asked for his help and he did not help me. I asked him for support and guidance and he did not give it to me." It is a great responsibility to be a guide for the people, to be a s͟hayk͟h, because you become responsible for even the ant that is walking, for the animals, for the environment, for everything around you. It is not something simple to be a s͟hayk͟h; it is a great burden and responsibility.

People beware of two mesmerizing trials: wealth or money, and leadership. Those are deadly temptations for people. The one who has love for money and leadership has a great sickness in his heart that is very difficult to cure. He should not desire for people to say, "Oh the s͟hayk͟h came, the s͟hayk͟h left," and refer to him in such way as a great guide. No, the true s͟hayk͟h serves himself and also serves his seekers. He cares about every one of them. This is the original principle of the guide because he is the heir of the Prophet Muḥammad and he inherited all the praiseworthy qualities of the Prophet Muḥammad, the divine qualities.

The reading continues until the bottom of page 115, "Then, forgetfulness of all the things of the world other than Allāh overwhelms you..."

You must rid yourself of everything and forget everything while you are walking to Allāh. You must abandon your egoistic self and surrender completely; become purified and clean, and let your soul, your nafs, surrender to Allāh completely. The soul must leave everything except Allāh, and her heart must be attached only to Allāh, not to any other thing from the lower realm, because in that station Allāh will call such souls saying, as it is stated in the Qur'ān,

> Oh secure, serene tranquil soul,
> return to your Lord pleased and pleasing,
> and enter among My slaves, servants and worshippers
> into My garden. (Qur'ān 89:28)

This is because Allāh will transform you from the material realm to the divine realm of witnessing. At that time your tongue will become the tongue of Allāh, your eyes will become the eyes of Allāh, your ears will become the ears of Allāh. You become truly truthful, sincere, and honest with Allāh. You become a divine servant. You become the Lord's slave. At that point there is no separation, no he or she. He is she and she is he. Nothing else! Only Allāh! Do not say, "I am a man." Or, "I am a woman." Only Allāh! You can be like that. This is the real walking.

What are you searching for? You become rich by Allāh. There is nothing impossible. You must walk and watch yourself, and know that Allāh is watching you in every minor and major action you do. The one who will be granted proximity is the one who never deviates from the divine law and surrenders to Allāh's commands and forgets everything and leaves everything and attaches himself only to Allāh.

I seek forgiveness from Allāh and I repent to Him and I ask Him to protect all of you and grant you success and put pure goodness in you and make you walk straight to Him, for He has power over everything. May He choose you in the way He wants, not in the way you want. Oh Allāh, please make my heart be always with You, and make me a divine slave and servant. Make me a strong slave and servant and worshipper who will never disobey any of Your commands.

In this blessed day I would like to open for you the door to protection, because I want to protect you, your children, your loved ones, your home and all whom you love from the sh̲ayāṭīn of human and jinn and from all harm. Whoever would like that protection, come to me now. In this blessed month I fully direct myself toward Allāh, asking Him to protect you and your wealth and your houses and your children and all of your loved ones. May He protect your parents and all of us from the punishment of Allāh. May He accept your repentance and forgives all the sins you did in this month and before this month. I ask Allāh to give you pure goodness and blessings.

Sidi gives the protection promise.

Women are the Twin Halves of Men

How to Care for Women and Children

Lā ʾilāha ʾilla-llāāāāāāh, Lā ʾilāha ʾilla-llāāāāāh, Lā ʾilāha ʾilla-llāāāāāh
Muḥammad rasūlu-llāh, Ibrāhīm rasūlu-llāh, Mūsā rasūlu-llāh,
ʿĪsā rasūlu-llāh ʿalayhim ṣalātu-llāh.

Allāhumma anta-s-salām wa minka-s-salām
wa ilayka ya'ūdu-s-salām
tabārakta rabbanā
ya dha-l-jalāli wa-l-'ikrām

As-salāmu ʿalaykum wa raḥmatu-llāh wa bārakatuhu.

May the peace and blessing of Allāh be upon the teacher, ṣalla-llāhu ʿalayhi wa sallam, the teacher who taught us the loftiest ethics and made us understand what politeness means, what truthfulness and honesty and sincerity mean. He taught us how to be polite with everything, with everyone. He taught us to be truthful in what we say and what we do. We look now at his ethics.

Let us look, for example, at how he treated children. This illiterate man, who did not go to school, the illiterate prophet, he was unable to read or write, he did not go to school. But Allāh taught him directly, taught him what he did not know. He taught him all the sciences that challenge the whole world now.

One day he was playing with the children. He used to give them one full session to play with them and to teach them at the same time how to be polite. After playing with them, he went to pray. He was the imām, he was the leader of the prayer, leading people in the prayer, and his grandchild, Ḥusayn, came during the prayer and found the Prophet, ʿalayhi as-salātu as-salām, prostrating, and he said, "Wow, what a beautiful ride." So he took a ride on his back. He mounted his back and continued to play and the Prophet, ʿalayhi as-salātu as-salām, kept prostrating, he never yelled at him. I say to those who claim to be scholars, who claim to be the followers of the Prophet, look at how our most beloved prophet used to treat everyone, including children.

Ḥusayn stayed a long time on the ride. Why? Because the ride was very beautiful, was very comfortable. He was very kind and he took his satisfaction from his ride. Only then did he unmount the back of the Prophet, ʿalayhi as-salātu as-salām, and the Prophet, ʿalayhi as-salātu as-salām, continued the prayer. His companions said, "Oh messenger of Allāh, why was the prayer so long? Why was the prostration so long? What happened? Did anything happen during the prostration?" He said, "No, it is something simple. My grandchild mounted me and sat on my neck and I did not want to disturb him. I did not want to annoy him. So he took his satisfaction and then he went away. It is something simple." This is the ethics of prophethood, of the Prophet. These are the loftiest ethics that we learn from the Messenger of Allāh.

When a child comes to a person and starts to yell at her, "Go away from me now!" or things like that, it is not from the loftiest ethics of Islām. It is from the ethics of s̲hayāṭīn, because Allāh, Most High, glory be to Him, says to the Prophet, ʿalayhi as-salātu as-salām:

> And had you been severe and harsh hearted,
> they would have broken away from about you. (Qurʾān 3:159)

And he said:

> My Lord taught me politeness
> and He did it in the perfect way. (Ḥadīt̲h)

He used to kiss all the children and he did it without making any difference between the girls and boys. He kissed all of them treated all of them the same and he used to say to the people:

> Allāh will bring you to accountability,
> even to question you about why you did not kiss your children.
> (Ḥadīt̲h)

If, for example, you have a daughter and a son and you came home once and you gave a kiss to the boy and you did not give a kiss to the girl, Allāh will ask you about that, why you did not kiss the other child. It is something very sensitive but it hurts the heart of the child, it makes him carry this pain, this sadness to carry all his life. These are the ethics of the Prophet, ʿalayhi as-salātu as-salām.

One time a man came to the Prophet, ʿalayhi as-salātu as-salām and said, "Oh messenger of Allāh, I have ten children, daughters and sons and I never kissed any of them." He said, "You are a cursed one. Go away from here. Do not stand in front of me." Allāh does not want this of you. Allāh wants us to be polite, merciful, loving, merciful, full of love. Where does the love come from? It comes from your religion. Your religion is love. Your religion is beauty. Your religion is politeness. And courteous manners, that is your religion.

The child is like an angel; it is like an angel and he comes to you to visit you. You are a strong man, but know that his visit to you is an honor, is a blessing for you. If you just pat his head like that, you will get a great blessing from doing that act of kindness and love. The Prophet, ʿalayhi as-salātu as-salām, used to be like that with the children. He used to observe every family how each family are treating their children. Are they treating their children with love, with good words, with kindness and politeness and respect? We must raise our children in the good way, in the way of Allāh.

Children need our care. They need also discipline. They need guidance to do what is good and how to behave good. We do not just leave them to do whatever they want, we guide them. We guide them and teach them the politeness, rules and the courteous manners that Allāh wants us to have. It is not permissible for us to be harsh with them or rough on them. The child comes to a land like this and he sees the land is so vast he likes to run and jump and he feels it belongs to him too. Why do you yell at him? Why do you suppress him? Just give him some love and mercy and you can guide him. Be polite, do not raise your voice, be careful. Just teach him how to deal with it. Isn't that the truth or the reality that should be?

Also the Prophet's behavior or attitude with his wife used to have the characteristic of loftiest ethics because the wife is a queen. The wife is a queen in her house; she is glorious in her house. She has this position of a queen and the man must be a servant to her. He must treat her with politeness and gentleness and full love. Look at how the Prophet, ʿalayhi as-salātu as-salām, speaks to his companions when they came back from a trip. He advised them:

> Do not come to your wife for intimate relations as a beast. (Ḥadīth)

You must be decent and polite and gentle. You must treat her with gentleness and politeness and love. Do not yell at her like a donkey with a loud voice. This is not permissible. You must talk to her with politeness because she is a human being, she has her own humanity. The Prophet says:

> Women are the twin halves of men. (Ḥadīth)

So she is equal to you. You are not better than her in any way. You are not glorious or greater than her in any way. Allāh says in the Qur'ān:

> So their Lord accepted of them:
> "Never will I allow to be lost the work of any of you,
> be he male or female.
> You are one of another," (Qur'ān 3:195)

This is true whether a male or a female, He will treat you equally.

How did the Prophet behave with his wife or his daughters? When he wanted to visit one of daughters or his wife, he would send someone to receive permission and let them know that he is coming. He would ask, "May I visit? May I come?" And he only came if they gave permission. Otherwise, he would not go.

Also, when he went to his own house, he would knock on the door first, He would say, "Are you ready for me to come visit?" This is the truth, this is the real way it should be because it is a house, but she is the queen of that house and she is the one who is managing the affairs of that house. She cares for the house, and he just wants to go make the house dirty and go out. No, he must never do that. This is not Islām. If he comes to his wife and he receives permission...he knocks on the door and waits to see if she permits him to come.

Whether it is his daughter or his wife, the first thing he used to say was, "Peace be upon you sweetheart, beloved, precious one." And then he went inside his house and greeted them by kissing their foreheads. He asked them to supplicate Allāh on his behalf and then he said, "How you are doing. How was your day? What happened?" And he used to feel happy when they were happy and sad when they were sad. When he visited his wives, he would say, "Peace be upon you, oh most precious ones, beautiful ones, beloveds." These are the loftiest ethics of Islām, the message. This is for those who believe.

This is the ethics of the Muslim husband with his wife, because the wife is a queen and the husband must serve her. He must work and fulfill her needs and she must rest at home. According to Islām she can go to work but she does not have to. He must support the house. He will have to pay for her needs, and that does not mean he will prevent her from working. Her husband says, "It is your choice whether you would like to go out to work or not, but I will continue to support you." He does not say, "All right, give me half of what you earn or you must pay this in the house."

These are not Islāmic ethics. This is not the divine structure for the family. It is s̲hayṭānic. It is from Iblīs. Here the woman works as the man, like machines. Day and night, they both work and she works and she puts her money into the house. Is this from the religion? Is this respecting women? Is this how women take their rights in your society? Where is your right? Your right is to work hard and come home to work more at the house. Is she not a human being that needs support and respect? The Qur'ān and Allāh give her her full rights and give her her right estimation and value and honor her.

I worked as a judge for thirty-six years, and I used to have a stick beside me. Any human who used to violate the rights of his wife, I did not wait for the police to come. I beat him myself. I say, "What are you doing. She is a human being. Why do you treat her like that? You are like a criminal, a monster, why do you treat her that way?" He cannot talk to me and I say, "I will put you in jail for fifteen days." This is what the law gave me as a right, until I called the police and they give him more. So I put him as a judge for fifteen days in jail. And the wife comes and she is so kind, she says, "Please do not put him in jail Sidi, because of my children." And I say, "But he did what he did. He was not polite to you was he? He was impolite. He must take his share." She said, "But Sidi, you already beat him. That is enough." "No, it is not enough. He must learn his lesson really well."

This is Allāh's rule. This is the judgment of Allāh. We must not allow him to abuse her or beat her or harm her. She is not an animal, and you do not even treat an animal like that. The woman is something every holy in our religion, in our way. She is a very holy creature from her toe up to her head. She is holy and she has her full rights. We do not allow, in our religion, that the women should be used as something to be sold and bought, and we do not allow her to be on the streets on her own so that monsters may take advantage of her. True freedom is to preserve the humanity of this beautiful creature, the woman. The woman needs support. When she is thirteen years old she needs more than when she was three years old. She always needs support. Why? Because she is now growing beautiful and monsters on the street would like to take advantage of her, use her for their own pleasure.

In the time of our grandparents it was different. Look at your own families. Long ago, at the time of your grandparents, the family structure was different. The freedom of today is barbaric freedom. It is not true freedom, it is false freedom. We want to go back to our roots, to the law of the divine, to heavenly teachings that command us to preserve the woman and respect her humanity. In this way she keeps herself pure until she finds a husband that can support her, respect her and provide for her. This is the message of Islām, the way of Islām.

This is the message of Muḥammad but also the message of Mūsā and ʿĪsā (Jesus), ʿalayhim as-salām. It is the message of all the prophets. It is the Jewish message. In Judaism the woman is considered a jewel, and also in ʿĪsā's teachings the woman is a jewel. But western ideology is corrupted and ruled by those who want to take advantage of people to use them and benefit from them. They give people sweet words and poison. They try to benefit from them and take advantage of them by selling them the idea of false freedom. But in our way the woman is so precious, the wife is so precious, and love must be mutual between the husband and a wife.

This is metaphorically speaking, but in reality the woman in herself is the mirror because in Arabic, the word "imrāʾa" means "woman." This word in Arabic shares the same root with "mirʾā," the word for "mirror." This is a clear sign that she is a divine mirror. The man is also a divine mirror in which the woman can see herself.

This divine mirror must never be broken. Is it permissible for you to break a divine mirror? It is not permissible. That means that both of you must have mutual understanding, share love, and stop fighting and competing, because the message of Allāh is founded upon love. It is founded upon love and peace and justice and mercy. If you do not have mercy on your beloved, who will have mercy on her? And if you, woman, will not have mercy on the one you love, your beloved husband, who else can give him that?

This is our religion, our way and what we recommend for people. We, the people of the straight path, care very much about the relationship of the man and the woman, and we put it in the right perspective, in the right way so that they may be happy and their children may be happy, as well. Because their children will be raised in a noble household with generous parents full of peace and love so the child grow up full of love as well. Is this not so? This is the message of Allāh and we must care to actualize this message and apply it.

Any young lady must keep herself pure and protect herself and not allow her body to be hurt by monsters of the street who want to take advantage of her and throw her away. She must be patient until she finds someone who truly loves her and will provide for her, she should not give herself to someone for a couple of months, because then he will just leave her and go to another. This is a noble life. She must live this noble life and feel true love and be the beloved. This is our way.

I have one daughter and five sons, but I love her more than I love all my sons. If she asks for my eyes, I will give her my eyes. If she wants my hand, I will give her my hand. I love her intensely and I have never spoken a harsh word to her that will hurt her. Not only with her, but also with her mother before her, before she passed away. I never spoke a harsh word to her. She was sick for thirty years, and I never asked her, "Why did you do this? Why did you not do that?" I was never harsh with her. We must keep hearts whole, because the one who breaks a heart, Allāh will break his heart.

Allāh says:

> I am with those whose hearts are broken for My sake.
> (Ḥadīth̲ Qudsī)

Because the broken heart for the woman, there is no veil between her and Allāh. If she says, "Oh Allāh, please help," He will destroy the one who broke her heart immediately. Immediately Allāh will destroy the one who broke her heart. He can actually get him into a car accident or a thunderbolt or something will actually destroy him, because Allāh answers the pain of the oppressed.

We must then be conscious of Allāh while we are dealing with our children and while we are dealing with ourselves and our husbands and our wives. We must treat our children in a godly way. We must care for their feelings and treat them so that they can preserve the divine essence in them as Allāh wants it to be preserved. Does any of you have no mother? I am sure every one of you had a mother or a sister or a wife or an aunt. We are talking about the divine family the godly family that we want to preserve or care for. We want you to know about his type of family that is full of love and justice and equality. This is the original principle and foundation of our creed, our belief. Our message is for peace and love and justice and mercy and freedom and we must actualize and prove ourselves true. We must never listen to the arrogance the fights and the egos. We must be as Allāh wants us to be. This is Ramaḍan's message that I want to send to every heart.

Now we are almost at the end of Ramaḍan, and our most beloved Prophet explained to us that the beginning of Ramaḍan is a chance for forgiveness, the middle is the bestowal of mercy...and what are the last days? They save you from the Hellfire. How can you save yourself from the Hellfire? Did you truly fast during Ramaḍan? Did you observe all of the conditions, the true conditions of fasting? Did your tongue fast? Did you just stop consuming food and drink, but at the same time hurt people with your tongue or your eye or your ear? Did you steal? Did you cheat? Did you deceive? Did you backbite people?

If you did, know that your fasting was not true, was not authentic. It was just hunger, the hunger of dogs. It was not fasting, it was not true or authentic fasting. It was a lie, because true fasting is to prevent the limbs, the senses, the eyes, the tongue from doing what is not pleasing to Allāh. Did you really observe the fasting in that way? Did you give the zakāh for your fasting? Know that your fasting is hanging between heaven and earth. It is not reaching to heaven and accepted by Allāh until you pay zakāh. Why? Because Zakāh al-Fitr, the zakāh of the end of Ramaḍan, purifies your fasting from the mistakes you might have made, and it purifies the heart and the spirit as well.

There is another aspect of fasting that is even loftier. Did you fast from all otherness and only have Allāh? Did you fast from existence, and witness only Allāh? Was your fasting from love and obedience to Allāh? If your fasting was truly for Allāh as Allāh says in Ḥadīth̲ Qudsī, on the tongue of the Prophet:

> Fasting is Mine and it I reward it directly. (Ḥadīth̲ Qudsī)

I fast from everything except my Beloved. People of intellects know that I am keeping my promise. I cut from everything except Allāh. You fasted to seek forgiveness and I ask Allāh to grant you that forgiveness. You also fasted to be granted the mercy, and if you truly observed the conditions of fasting then Allāh will bestow on you mercy, because He has power over everything.

There is also another kind of fasting: fasting to be saved from the Hellfire. The one who committed the major sins, like killing someone or stealing someone or raping or abusing someone, must come and repent sincerely and honestly from these major sins. The one who committed adultery or raped a woman and she got pregnant and then he denied it, he did not support the child, or the one who betrayed his wife or her husband must repent sincerely. Right now I open for you the door to repent and the chance to truly repent and be saved from the Hellfire and to be forgiven from all of the sins you committed in the past and I ask Allāh to accept your repentance. If you would like, come.

Sidi gives the promise.

Laylat al-Qadr: the Night of Power

"Unity and Divestment" and "Intelligence and Incapacity" from *He Who Knows Himself Knows His Lord*

Lā ʾilāha ʾilla-llāāāāāāh, Lā ʾilāha ʾilla-llāāāāāh, Lā ʾilāha ʾilla-llāāāāāh
Muḥammad rasūlu-llāh, Ibrāhīm rasūlu-llāh, Mūsā rasūlu-llāh,
ʿĪsā rasūlu-llāh ʿalayhim ṣalātu-llāh.

Allāhumma anta-s-salām wa minka-s-salām
wa ilayka ya'ūdu-s-salām
tabārakta rabbanā
ya dha-l-jalāli wa-l-'ikrām

As-salāmu ʿalaykum wa raḥmatu-llāh wa bārakatuhu.

This day is the day that is right before Laylāt al-Qadr. Al the angels are now getting ready in the heavens for the divine wedding, to celebrate with all the people who obey their Lord by fasting the month of Ramaḍan in surrender to Allāh, Most High, glory be to Him. They are awaiting the prize, the divine prize. That prize is so great, it is like someone who had a hard work, was working day and night, and waiting for this, and Allāh gives us the best example. And of course Allāh is greater than any example we set, because He created us without us giving him back anything, and we did not give him anything back for his creation of us. He created us without asking us to give Him anything.

He only asks us for one thing—to worship Him, which mean to know Him, to acknowledge Him. He says, "Have gnosis of Me, and have true knowledge by surrendering to My commands. Preserve the existence I gave you without destroying it. You should obey My commands that I sent through the messengers to preserve your existence that I gave you."

All the prophets and messengers were given divine teachings to help people live and be happy in this world, because when you obey Allāh you find happiness. Allāh does not want anything from us, He is the Self-Sufficient. He does not need anything from us. He is the One Who Created the heavens and the earth. And He gave it as a gift to the human being to do everything he wants with it, but within set boundaries for the human's own safety. He did not give us this gift to corrupt it, to poison us, to destroy it, as even people are doing now. Even the sky is not protected from their evil, they also pollute it, because they started to put destructive materials in airplanes and they throw it, or they go to outer space and pollute it. Allāh says:

> Oh assembly of jinns and men!
> If you have power to pass beyond
> the zones of the heavens and the earth, then pass!
> But you will never be able to pass them without My permission! (Qur᾿ān 55:33)

Human activity must be on earth, the earth that he came from and that he will return to. You cannot bury anyone in heaven, in the sky. He was not created from there. He was created from the earth and his corpse will go to the earth. If he actually falls dead in the sky he will naturally fall to the earth. Where will he be put? He will just be there in a place that is unknown. It is a crazy man who thinks he can possess the world, and he says, "Bury me in such a planet and such a sky." No. The heavens will not accept a dirty man. So it drops him to the earth, and his body gets decomposed to its elemental components on the earth.

And when he dies he is not permitted to stay in his own house that he built. He will be kicked out and carried to the earth. This is the reality of the human being, is it not so? He must then be very polite with himself first, then with all others. And he must not harm himself or another. This is what Allāh commands him to be, to be merciful, to be merciful to himself and others. And to look at the poor and needy among people and help them. Because when he helps them he is helping his own self. When he offers them something he offers it to his own self.

Now we are in a very glorious time of Allāh, because all the pious people do not sleep during these days. In the morning they recite Qur᾿ān and remember Allāh and praise Allāh. They do not waste their time in vain talk and backbiting, speaking badly about others. They spend their time in conversation with Allāh. You can do that by reciting Qur᾿ān, by doing tasbīḥ, or practice the remembrance of Allāh, to glorify and praise Him, These are the types of worship, and through worship you converse with Allāh. Because this worship is what will save the human body, heart and spirit from the Hellfire.

And I have described to you before that after the human passes away from this world he will arrive at Judgment Day. It is a very glorious day, where all the angels will be lined in accordance to their ranks, guarding the heavens. There will be millions of angels, because they outweigh the number of human beings. Mighty angels will surround the ones are rebellious and disobedient. The jinn will also be assembled and judged. Allāh says in the Qur'ān:

> Oh assembly of jinns and men!
> If you have power to pass beyond
> the zones of the heavens and the earth, then pass!
> But you will never be able to pass them without My permission! (Qur'ān 55:33)

There is no one more glorious than another, because everyone will go as a slave and servant to Allāh at the end. They will all be equal. All people will be assembled and they will have nothing with them. They will be in surrender, humility and humbleness, and they will know that they will be questioned about every major and minor action. So how can we face this? Allāh gave us, for example, this noble month, and he gave us a noble life, why cannot we know this nobility in this life and surrender to His commands and care about our selves, our bodies, our actions? He wants us to be active on the earth. He wants us to act with sincerity, with intention and all the beautiful qualities. Allāh says to us to travel in the earth and seek the provision of Allāh, but to know that the final assembly will be to Him

So he wants you to be and build on the earth, but in the right way. He wants you to care for the earth, your children, your daughter and sons, to care for everyone. This is the way of Allāh. He created the earth to give us care and provision, not for destruction. So we must care for our relationship with Allāh. How do we care for it? Through worship. And we should care for our relationships with others. How? By knowing the loftiest ethics in treating others. Then you should also care for yourself. How? By caring for your body, the beautiful body Allāh has given to you. You must surrender to the divine commands to preserve the body and spirit Allāh gave you.

Now we are almost at the end of the month of Ramaḍan, and today is a day of repentance, a day of forgiveness, a day which people can be saved from the Hellfire. Are we prepared? Do we have our accounts ready to review what we did? We have to bring our reports forward and see what we did, and know what was given to you and know what was taken from you. You must bring yourself to accountability. You must ask yourself what you did for Allāh.

Allāh is Self-Sufficient, He does not want anything from you. But what did you do for His sake, to please Him? Allāh only wants you to be straightforward, pure, happy in your life, honest, sincere, pleasing and pleased. Were you generous with the poor? Did you establish your prayer? Were you sincere and honest with Allāh? Because there is a third obstacle these days that you need to cross. There were three obstacles in Ramaḍan—in the first ten days you needed forgiveness, in the second ten days you needed mercy, and in the third ten days you need to cross the Hellfire, to be saved from the Hellfire. I am certain that Allāh, Most High, glory be to Him, has forgiven you and bestowed His mercy upon you. Because He promised us so. He says:

> The one who comes with repentance and a full heart,
> I will transform their bad deeds into good deeds
> and rectify their deeds and his affairs. (Qur'ān 5:39)

Now you are about to face the third obstacle, which is very dangerous. You need to cross the Hellfire. You need to cross this obstacle and be saved from the Hellfire. The human is like a captive to the idea of always doubting himself. "Did I really do my duty well? Did I really help the poor and needy enough? Did I fulfill my obligations in the right way? Did I care for my parents well enough?"

Know that if your parents are unhappy with you then you have a problem, because you will lose, you will be a failure. You must try to gain the pleasure of your parents, so that they are happy and satisfied with you. Do not say that, "My father or mother did this or that to me when I was young." No! Even if he or she did they will be brought to account by Allāh, they will be judged, they will face their reckoning. But not from you—you cannot bring them to reckoning. You must still do your excellent good to them, and you must be very polite with them.

Once someone asked the Prophet, ṣalla-llāhu ʿalayhi wa sallam:

> "Who has the most right over me for companionship?"
>
> The Prophet answered, "Your mother."
>
> "Then, who is next?"

The Prophet answered, "Your mother."

He asked for the third time, "Then, who is next?"

The Prophet answered, "Your mother."

The fourth time the man asked the Prophet said, "Your father." (Ḥadīth)

The one who fasted, prayed, did ḥajj, gave zakāh, but treated his parents badly and did not stay connected to them, all of his actions will go to waste. The rebellious one against his parents can do any good action but it won't be accepted, his prayer, charity, fasting, everything will not be accepted from him if he treated his parents badly. One must always reconcile with his parents. Go visit them, support them, give them the love. Why? Because these people were the source to bring you to this life. They did a lot for you when you were little, they felt sad when you were sad, they felt pain when you had pain. Do you not how the mother is with her little child?

That is why I say to all young women and men, and also to old ones, hurry up and make reconciliation with your parents. Do you excellent good to them. Do not say, "Oh, they did this or that to me when I was young." Because if you do excellent good to them they will return that to you, they will not treat you badly. It is your responsibility and your duty.

What happens now is from the system the human being invented, not from divine law. People claim that under freedom you can do whatever you want, even if your parents do not approve of it, and they destroyed the family structure is now destroyed. Understand that the family is the foundational rock upon which society is built. But they came and said to the daughter and said, "You are free. You do not have to listen to your parents. You can make whatever choices you want." And they said to the son, "If you are eighteen you can do whatever you want." This is dangerous, it is false freedom. The problems you see in today's society come from this system we invented, and we do not follow natural law.

The last step we need to go up is the last one, because tonight is Laylāt al-Qadr. It is actually the night of the twenty-seventh. How do we know? If you read Sūrat-l-Qadr, the Night of Power, in the Qur'ān, and you count the Arabic words (not including, "Bismi-llāhi-r-raḥmāni-r-raḥīm") you will find there are twenty-seven. The sūra contains twenty-seven words.

That is one of the secrets. This holds a marvelous secret. Allāh says to the people, “If you want to live in peace, then search for peace.

So I say to you from the Qur'ān:

> Truly! We have sent it [this Qur'ān] [through the prophets and angels] down in the Night of Power
> Into the earth descended the angels and the Spirit [Jibrīl]
> by Allāh's Permission with all decrees [for the next year]
> (Qur'ān 97:1, 97:4)

On the Night of Power any nation that tried to start a war or something evil, Allāh sends one of those mighty angels and causes it to stop. This is something everyone knows. I have seen with my eyes one night what happens on the Night of Power. On that night and about one thousand people were remembering Allāh. We heard airplanes flying overhead. Sidi said, “Now something bad will happen to the airplanes.” Because this should be the night of peace. They cannot cause any harm on this night. And it did happen. As soon as the airplanes came, they started to collide with each other and destroy each other, and they could not harm the people who were remembering Allāh.

That will happen to those who want to destroy people and humanity. I saw it with my own eyes. It was not a coincidence because this is a blessed month, a noble month that Allāh gave a special blessing. It is a time of forgiveness and mercy, and a time where we should return to our true humanity as Allāh created it. Allāh created humans to be in the realm of peace, to live in the world of perfection and excellence and divine beauty. This is how Allāh created humanity. He did not create us so that we would not know him and start to harm each other.

Ramaḍan teaches us how to be. Ramaḍan teaches us the qualities we should have. People ask, “Why do you fast? Why do you pray?” We say, “For Allāh, for Allāh. We do that to remember and be conscious of Allāh.” But do we do this only in Ramaḍan? No, because the Lord of Ramaḍan is the Lord of Sha'ban, the Lord of all the other months.

This means we must always be conscious of Allāh at all times, not in one month only. Because some people say, “I stop stealing or cheating or backbiting in Ramaḍan.” No, why do you stop stealing in Ramaḍan only? He says, “It is Ramaḍan, it is a special month.” So we start to say, “I will not lie in Ramaḍan,” but after Ramaḍan what do you do? What changed you? I know you are an accursed s̲hayṭān, a thief. Once I asked one of those and he was dressed in an elegant way and he entered the mosque. I said, "What happened to you? You stopped stealing and lying and all of that and you are coming to the mosque, what happened to you?" He said, "Because it is Ramaḍan, Sidi." I said, "You are only here at Ramaḍan? Oh foolish one, this is not the right way."

You must always and continuously fear Allāh. Peace must always be continued. Mercy must always be continued. Gnosis must always be continued. Allāh did not give you life to live only one month. He gave you a long life, and He wants you to live that way your whole life. That is why I want you to return to the month of Ramaḍan always, while you are keeping your promise with Him. I want you to always keep your promise with Allāh all other months, all other days, when you are in your house, when you are in your working place, even when you are asleep. You must always be straightforward and you must care about the relationship with your spouses, children, friends, to keep it and care about it to be in the right way. I ask Allāh to protect you. Now we are about to enter a marvelous station which is the station of divestment and unification and singularity.

"Unity and Divestment" on page 126 of *He Who Knows Himself Knows His Lord* is read from the beginning until, "Unification implies affirmation and detachment implies faith..."

Know that Allāh, glory be to Him, gave the human being three subtle steps.

1. **The first step is to unify Allāh, to know the unity**; to understand that nothing happens except my Allāh's will and that there is no creator but Him. With that step he becomes one of the people of the unity.

2. **Then after that there is divestment or detachment.** He must divest himself from lower desires and his ego and give himself a new birth. He must become a godly human being, a divine being that will never utter a word but from Allāh, and then he reaches the divine gnosis and he will not be talking but godly words and he will not fear anyone but Allāh, Most High, glory be to Him. And no matter how much he worships Allāh, he will always still fear Allāh, but at the same time, he will be certain that Allāh loves him. Because the gnostic once said, "If Allāh had wanted bad of you, He would not have inspired you to believe in the unity and realize

the unity. So He used you to be His servant and slave and worshiper because He loves you more than you love yourself. This is why you must be pure. You must open your heart to Allāh.

Allāh loves you greatly. Do you love Him the same way? Allāh says in the Qur'ān that He loves the believers, and they love Him. So the fist love comes from Him. He loves you first and that is why He made you in an excellent, perfect way. So you must obey Him because if you are truly a lover you must please your Beloved. So if you are looking for a beloved, love Allāh through the mirror that is given to you, which means that you love Him in every manifestation. Any human that came into being, is carrying the divine image, the divine reflection.

Oh Laylā, you are the focal point of prayer because wherever you look, Allāh manifests to you, and everything you see become a mirror to you in which you see the reflection of Allāh. And the godly human being, the slave and servant of Allāh, is the one who understands divine limits and surrenders to these commands. But the one who will disobey Allāh's commands and will not do the spiritual practices like fasting and prayer and will not follow the natural laws... Because understand that mercy has a law, peace has a law, everything has its natural law, divine law and you must understand it and follow that law.

So the first station is the station of unification. How do we reach that state? By seeing Him and witnessing Him in all the manifestations, because when you look with that eye of unity, you see that everything testifies to Him. Because think how the human talks with him tongue, it is because Allāh gave you that ability. Otherwise, it is only a piece of flesh; it has no ability on its own. The tongue is just a piece of flesh. It just cannot do anything unless Allāh manifests upon that tongue with His quality of the one who speaks.

Also, the eye, what is the eye? It is almost all water, but it sees. How does it see? Because Allāh manifests on it by His name al-Baṣīr, the All-Seeing. Also, the ear, when He manifested by His name, as-Sami', the all-Hearing, you had the ability to hear with your ear. So by all of these beautiful names Allāh manifests upon you, which means you only stand by Him, sit by Him, hear by Him, see by Him. Because He manifested His name "the living: (al-Ḥayy) upon you, you have life now. That is why Allāh says:

> If anyone kills a person, or spreads mischief in the land

> it would be as if he killed all humankind,
> and if anyone saves a life, it would be as if
> he saved the life of all humankind. (Qur'ān 5:32)

Violating a human being's rights is like violating Allāh's rights, and reviving one soul is like reviving all of humanity. How can you hurt another human? How can you? It is like fighting with Allāh, and Allāh says:

> The recompense of those who wage war against Allāh
> and His Messenger and do mischief in the land
> is only that they will be killed or crucified
> or their hands and their feet be cut off on the opposite sides,
> or be exiled from the land.
> That is their disgrace in this world,
> and a great torment is theirs in the Hereafter. (Qur'ān 5:33)

But the one who divests himself of all lower desires and the whole world, and is only with Allāh, will be full of love, respecting every form of life, including the lives of animals. Because animals are creatures, and these creatures also carry, some of the names and qualities of Allāh manifesting through them. So such a human, always respects all of life, including animal life. But the human who stays with his lower desires chooses to be an animal human.

It is your free choice. But that is why he is suffering. He is suffering in this world and the next because he wanted to live in the animal kingdom. He did not want to be a true human being, because all of his qualities, his ethics, are like a vicious monster or beast and he violates people's right and breaks their hearts and treats them like animals. That is why we must divest ourselves of all the qualities that do not belong to the divine lofty ethics.

Those who transform themselves from the world of physical existence to the world of witnessing do not see anything but Allāh, and they do not know anything but Allāh, and they do not talk to anyone but Allāh. That is why you find them always polite, full of love and politeness and beauty. Nothing evil ever comes out of them to harm others. But the one who thinks of himself as so great, lies to Allāh, harms others, and does not obey Allāh is deceiving himself. And Allāh will let him suffer the consequences. You must divorce the lower realm and not get attached to it.

The reading continues down the page to, "...one of the brethren asked him, 'what do you want with him?' "

This is a divine scene and it is an image that the people who live with Allāh, see. The one who is absent from everything but Allāh while being present with Allāh, sees that. So listen to what this gnostic said.

The reading continues to the top of page 127, "Had I lost Him for a twinkle of an eye, I would have died an hour ago; and he began to recite, 'The beloved asks his Beloved to be pleased...' "

His beloved is never absent from him, so how can he think of himself as existent? His beloved never leaves Him for even an hour, so he is always living in love with his Beloved, always. Allāh is never absent from you. You become absent. You are actually non-existent. You are absent in your lower realm and your life which is full of pain, but those who are truly present with Allāh do not fear anything, nor are they concerned with anything. Wherever they are, in their workplaces, their factories, their markets, they are always with Allāh because they know they are treating Allāh whenever they treat anyone.

And they are the most intelligent people. If he is a doctor, he is with Allāh. If he is an inventor, he is with Allāh. It is a marvelous realm; the realm of Allāh is something marvelous, it is nothing simple. These are the true kings, princesses and princes. These are the true kings who are doing their work for Allāh; their work is for Allāh and they are transparent, they are beautiful, and they are full of mercy and always stretching their hands to help others. They do this because they see the divine essence in people and they treat them with mercy. Wherever Allāh shows them something it is a glimpse, just a glimpse of His glory. This is just a glimpse of His glory.

The reading continues, "He said to me, 'Since I have known Him, I have never been unaffected by Him.' I asked..."

Can you live without a sincere beloved, and we are talking about a metaphorical beloved here? But you get attached to him and you always want to be with him. What if the love is a godly love, divine love? This is true life, true love, and I want you to live with Allāh in that love.

This is what it means to single out, at-tafrīd. There is no one in existence but my Beloved who lives in me. Do not blame me that I surrender my heart fully to Him. Because He is my whole and I am a glimpse of Him. I cannot say more than this. This is the Truth. This is Reality, and I want you to live with this Truth and Reality to live with Allāh. I want to pull you to Him and show you, "Here, see, He is with you. He is with you wherever you are. He never separates from Him." Do not ever have the illusion that, "Allāh is not with me. I cannot see Him. I cannot feel Him," because He is always with you day and night, in your workplace, in your house, everyday, in every place. He never abandons you. If He had abandoned you, He would not have given you a lot of His qualities. Can you not hear and see and speak?

The reading continues, "the young man asked, 'Since when did you know Him?' Since He put my name among the madmen..."

He is not a madman. Everyone else is actually crazy except for him. These people always hide themselves, but because of them the mercy is sent down upon people. Because when they invoke Allāh, Allāh never turns their supplications away. He always responds to their supplications, so we must be very polite with them.

The reading "Intelligence and Incapacity" on page 127 is read from the beginning to the top of page 128, "So he understands that what is with Allāh cannot be gained except by obedience; when he understands this, illusion departs from him."

It is enough to understand that the divine love never departs from anyone and Allāh is always bestowing His mercy and forgiveness, even if the person feels, "It is too late," or, "I do not feel it," know that Allāh is never abandoning you. But know also, as much as you give Allāh, Allāh will give you ten-fold.

Know that we are in the last days of Ramaḍan and I invite you to give your covenant with Allāh, to give a Ramaḍan covenant, because this is an hour in which Allāh answers prayer. Ask Him to accept your worship and to accept your deeds and to prepare the road for you to ascend to Him. May He open for you, the door of safety and security to be safe from the Hellfire. This is the day of witnessing. This is the day of witnessing, divine witnessing. This is the Night of Power. This is the night of divine witnessing, not the night of the rigid humanity, dense humanity, so try to save yourself from the Hellfire.

It is not a physical fire that burns sometimes; we are talking about being deprived of receiving divine love. This is more intense. The Hellfire of separation is more intense than a real physical fire that burns your skin. If you do not know Allāh, that is a more intense fire than the fire that burns in this world. I say, "Oh Allāh, burn me in the fire of this world, but do not burn me on the pyre of being separated from You. I cannot bear that." If You burn me in the Hellfire of separation, then I have lost everything. My station is within You, with Your love continuously. This is my life, my bowing down and prostration, my absence, so please repeat with me.

Be with me in witnessing Him and existing in Him.

"Oh One and Only,
Oh Singular One,

Oh One Who created Ramaḍan
and created the month of Ramaḍan
and the Night of Power,

Oh One who gave us life, please give us the gift of witnessing You,

give us the gift of witnessing You,
give us the gift of witnessing You,
give us the gift of witnessing You,

And bestow upon us gnosis so we can know You.
Make our existence in Your existence
so we will not do any action except by You.

We return to You.
We repent to You
and we ask for
Your Gentleness,
Your Forgiveness,
Your Pardon,
Your Light,
Your Beauty.

We ask for Your Peace,
Your Mercy,
Your Justice,

Oh Allāh,
Oh One Who is Most Merciful in this lower realm and the next,
please give us and our loved ones a good life
and do not repulse us from Your love.

Make a barrier between me and the lower realm
and make no separation between me and You.

Oh Living One, Eternal One, please accept us Allāh.
Save us from the Hellfire in the month of Ramaḍan.
Save us from the Hellfire in the month of Ramaḍan.

Oh Living One, Eternal One, accept us.
We seek refuge in Your generous Face.

You promised that Your mercy contains everything.
You said, "My mercy contains everything. My mercy contains everything."
So please surround us with Your mercy.
Make our hearts clean and pure and do not accept any but You.

Please protect our children,
our spouses and our loved ones in this blessed month.
Please do not end this month until You are satisfied and pleased with us.
Do not turn us away from Your door disappointed.
Answer our prayers.
You are the Most Merciful.
Please return us to Ramaḍan
and make the whole month of Ramaḍan for us.

Al-Fātiḥa
In the name of God, the Universally Merciful, Singularly Compassionate
Praise belongs to Allāh, Sustaining-Lord of the worlds
the Universally Merciful, Singularly Compassionate
Sovereign of the Day of Judgment
You do we adore, and from You do we seek aid
Guide us to the straight path [the true Ṣūfism and the true Islām]

Not the path of those upon whom is Your wrath
Nor of those You have led astray.

The door to be saved from the Hellfire.
The door to be saved from the Hellfire.
It is the door to be saved from the Hellfire.
We ask Allāh to pardon us
and to forgive us
and to have mercy upon our faults.
He is the One Who Accepts Repentance
and He is the Most Merciful, Most Compassionate."

Sidi in English:

Important to know,
she is your mom,
your sister,
she is every woman.

Everything is contained in the woman and Islām.
He care about her.
I ask you to be conscious of Allāh while dealing with women,
to treat them good
and to guard yourselves against evil when you deal with them,
to have taqwa.

Because the woman in our way,
as explained by the Prophet Muḥammad,
is a holy being.
She is a queen in her house and she is protected,
her honor is protected
and her heart must never be broken.

Those who are confused and who went astray from Allāh's true religion
do not understand this.
The woman in Allāh's way and the religion is a gem,
she is a precious jewel that must be protected.
That is why you must understand
it is a serious covenant
and the one who breaks this covenant

is breaking his covenant with Allāh
and he becomes the enemy of Allāh, Most High, glory be to Him.
So keep this promise so that Allāh may keep you.

Say: I promise Allāh,

Sidi performs a divine wedding.

University of Spiritual Healing and Sufism Years 2-3

The life of love never ends.

This is the way of the ones penetrated with love and with love of Allāh.
They sing the song of love.

Their words are the words of unity
and their walking on earth is one of glorifying Allāh.

They weep from melting in the love.

They are the mercy of Allāh, a gift given to people.
They live for Allāh and for serving his people.

Live day and night in the shadow of the one who loves Allāh
and you will see the light.

This is just a continuous poetry
and I hope that I translated it to the best of my ability.

From "Is There Any Life but Rābiʿa's?

How to Be a True Healer

Lā ʾilāha ʾilla-llāāāāāāh, Lā ʾilāha ʾilla-llāāāāāh, Lā ʾilāha ʾilla-llāāāāāh
Muḥammad rasūlu-llāh, Ibrāhīm rasūlu-llāh, Mūsā rasūlu-llāh,
ʿĪsā rasūlu-llāh ʿalayhim ṣalātu-llāh.

Allāhumma anta-s-salām wa minka-s-salām
wa ilayka ya'ūdu-s-salām
tabārakta rabbanā
ya d̲ha-l-jalāli wa-l-'ikrām

As-salāmu ʿalaykum wa raḥmatu-llāh wa bārakatuhu.

Praise be to Allāh, and may the peace and blessings of Allāh be upon our Master Guide and Messenger Muḥammad, whom Allāh sent with guidance and the religion of truth to be over all other dogmas. May the peace and blessings of Allāh be upon all the messengers and prophets and beloved guides, the people who carried the holy message and were holy themselves. There was no separation between them; they were all followers of the unity and were sent by Allāh.

And there is no partner to Allāh. He is not begotten. He has no son and no wife. He is the Creator, the Worshipped Creator, who created us in the way He wants us to be and He provides us with provision. He created you human beings in the best of molds and fashioned you in the best of images.

Oh Allāh, glory be to You, Most High, You are our Creator and Originator and Protector so please help us to obey You and keep us distant from disobedience. Make us holy people who are carrying the signs of beauty and majesty. Make us signs that carry the beauty and majesty. Make us carry the message of peace and mercy and freedom and justice for all people.

My beloveds, I love you as much as I love myself. I care for your bodies, for your souls, for you hearts, I care for your intellects and I do care that you always be honest and faithful and truthful and be away from illusions and pictures and imaginings. That is why I ask you, please open your hearts, your souls, your ears, because I will recite for you, words that you have never heard before and give you knowledge that no one has had before. This knowledge came through the prophets of Allāh.

I want you to be healers, to be well first, and then to heal. Then you can be healers. I do not want you to stop with imaginings, illusions, and pictures. I want you to be true healers and know who you are. I want you, human, to know who you are. I want you to carry the humane qualities that came to us through the holy message, through the holy physicians like ibn Sīna, known in the west as Avicenna, and ibn Rusẖd (a.k.a. Averroes), and all the other holy physicians who came to us and who know exactly how to heal the human being.

They were inspired through a divine inspiration, and through that they know how to heal the human being. They know how Allāh created the human being. He created the human being pure and noble and clean, and He created him to be in harmony with divine law. That is why the human being is a divine jewel. He has no dirt, no pollution, no poison. He is clean and pure and I want you to be like that, to know who you are and from what you are combined. This is the true divine message that came from the guides who healed bodies, souls and hearts. They heal spirits and intellects, too.

From this point I start. I start in the name of Allāh, asking His help and support and asking the help and support of all the prophets and messengers of Allāh. May He inspire me with only truthful and sincere words, just like the words that came to the Messenger of Allāh, ʿalayhi as-salātu as-salām. From this point I start. Did you open your hearts? Did you open your minds and intellects and souls to me? Because the words that will be spoken now are direct divine words. They do not come from Buddhism or Confucianism or images or illusion, they come purely and directly through the messengers like Mūsā (Moses), Ibrāhīm (Abraham) and ʿĪsā (Jesus), from Allāh to humankind.

Allāh put a condition on us to follow His law, His natural law, His demands. So the true healer does not listen to illusions and pictures. So do not say, "I see, I know," unless you are very sure that Allāh informed you, that Allāh gave you knowledge that you did not have before. Allāh said to our Prophet:

> Has taught man that which he knew not. (Qurʾān 96:5)

He told His messenger:

> Read, read (or Recite).
> He said, "I cannot read."

Allāh said, "Read in the name of your Lord," (Qur'ān 96:1-96:2)

He did not say to read in the name of s̲hayṭān, or in the name of your illusions, or in the name of your pictures. No, he said "Read in the name of your Lord." So, you have to start by reciting the name of Allāh.

Know that the human being can be afflicted with many diseases that I will mention. First, there are kinds of diseases that afflict bodies. Then, there are diseases that can afflict souls. Thirdly, there are the diseases that can afflict the heart, and then the diseases that can affect the spirit.

We would like to start with how to heal diseases of the body. The physical body originated in the best and healthiest way. So, when the mother gives birth to a child, he is pure physically. He is pure at heart. He is pure in his heart and in his spirit. But we have to understand from the perspective of what the human body is made of. What does the human body have?

It is made of four elements. The first element is water. The second element is dust. The third element is air and the fourth element is fire. So you are made of four elements. But all of the elements are equal and pure. There is no separation between them: water, air, dust and fire.

First, we have to understand that the heat of fire is inside you. Inside you humans, there is the heat of fire. How can this fire be inside the human without burning the body? Do you not see when you get a fever, a high temperature, that you feel the heat of the fire more intensely than before? And what happens when you have a fever? It actually melts the fat in your body and it affects your physical being. So do you not see that you have the heat of fire inside you? Can you see that every human being also has electricity inside him? Do you not feel your electricity? This is also part of the heat of fire. Why does it become more intense sometimes? Because in the human body there is a disturbance, so he must use something to turn off the heat of fire, which is water.

Water also exists inside the human being, but it is hidden and it is pure inside the human physical body. It balances.

So, how about dust? The human being also has dust within because dust is made of a lot of elements. Dust is actually what is converted into flesh, and the dust must also contain water.

This physical construction also has air.

Those are the four elements of physical construction. So, as we mentioned, the physical body consists of four elements, but from where do these elements come? They can come from plants or animals or the air we breathe and from water we drink. So we must preserve these elements, balanced and pure, while we partake of these from the outside and preserve them in the original way that they were created by Allāh.

Why did our ancestors live for one thousand years, and now the life span is decreased to less than one hundred years? We have to search to find that out. We know that Prophet Nūh lived almost one thousand years, and Prophet Ibrāhīm lived almost four hundred years. Why did it keep decreasing to less than one hundred and twenty years? I have seen people live up to one hundred and fifty years who were healthy and youthful.

I lived with such a person. He was a farmer. One day I asked him, "How have you lived so long?" He put his axe down and said to me, "My son, I never ate anything but natural foods that I planted it with my own hands, I cared for the plants and I raised animals. Then I ate their meat and I drank only from a well that had pure water that came from rain, and I did not pollute it. Also, whenever I ate, I did not really fill my stomach to its utmost."

This is following the Prophet's saying:

> We are a group of people that do not eat until we are hungry and when we eat, we do not fill our stomach to fullness. (Ḥadītẖ)

This is our state. He also said:

> The worst vessel that a human can fill is his stomach.
> But if he must eat, let him fill one-third with food,
> one-third with drink and one-third, leave for air. (Ḥadītẖ)

So, who inspired the Prophet with this? It was Allāh. Allāh taught him this.

First the Prophet, ʿalayhi as-salātu as-salām, referred to the human body and explained that it has elements that should be preserved in their purity. These elements come mostly from plants, and now modern science knows this, but all the true gnostics knew this before science did. The Prophet said:

> Eat oil and anoint yourself with it, too. (Ḥadīth)

We want to explore this saying carefully. We want to understand what he means so that you do not rush to the market with shampoos and stuff that are full of poisons and fragrances that might not be healthy for you. They do it just to get your money. We want to know what the true healers say about this, not the false healers.

To wash your body you use things. Mostly it is liquids with different fragrances and it makes a lot of foam. They say, "This really cleans the body." But in reality, it kills the body because it takes away the oil and the fat and it effects the body in a bad way.

What is most important to protect and preserve the body is to take the right amount of oxygen. That is very necessary for the body, because if there is a lack of oxygen in the body, what will happen? The bones will be weakened and the skin cells will be destroyed and the liver will also be affected, as well as the kidneys. The intestines will have diseases too. This could be the result of using all of these materials that you wash your body with because they reduce oxygen intake. It has been proven scientifically that the best healing, that compensates the body for what it lacks, is to take the oil of the blessed tree that mentioned in the Qur'ān.

What is the blessed tree that is mentioned in the Qur'ān? It is the olive tree that is neither from the east or the west, and its oil is illuminated without need for fire (Qur'ān 24:35). That means it has a lot of oxygen. This heals the body and keeps it well, and is necessary for the skin.

This is what the Prophet, ʿalayhi as-salātu as-salām, said more than fourteen hundred years ago. He said that it was good for the body and for the health of the intellect to drink the oil of the blessed tree, which is olive oil, early in the morning. Drink two tablespoons first thing in the morning. That will protect your body, providing it with the oxygen it needs, and you will never lose your memory. Your memory will become always sharp, your bones will always be strong, even if you reach one hundred and thirteen years old. And you will never forget. Your brain will continue to function well because the olive oil feeds the arteries with the oxygen necessary for their wellbeing.

That is why ancient people used to plant olive trees by the thousand. They cared for olive trees. Jerusalem is the land of the prophets, and you will find a lot of olive trees there. They planted them because Allāh praised the olive trees in His Holy Book. He mentioned the olive tree in the Torah, the Bible and also in the scrolls of Mūsā and Ibrāhīm, and ultimately, in the Qur'ān.

Allāh told us about how to heal our bodies. This is not from a human who is imagining that this is good or that is good. Fifty years ago they calculated how many olive trees are in the Holy Land, Jerusalem, and they found that it had thirty-five million olive trees. Some of these olive trees go back one thousand years, and have roots three meters wide and three meters deep. They do not die. Why? Because they have the secret from Allāh, He gave it as a healing for people.

What can we do with this olive? Can we do other things with it or just eat it? Do you know that in ancient times they used to eat them raw? They would eat them, not after they heated them, they just ate them with bread. I have inherited this habit from my grandfather who reached more than one hundred years of age. He used to make me drink a half of a cup of olive oil daily, and I would ask him "Why do you make me drink this?" He said, "Because the Prophet, 'alayhi as-salātu as-salām, said, 'Eat the olive oil and anoint yourself with it.' " So, I said, "All right, I know how to eat it, but how can I anoint myself with it?" He had been an Arabian physician, an herbalist. He knew all the herbs and what they could do. He would take me and let me carry a bag and he taught me, "This herb is used for this and that for that." I would collect these herbs and walk beside him.

So, what does it mean to anoint ourselves with it? It means to make soap out of it and not add any other ingredient to it. I know how they used to make the soap out of olive oil. They used to use only natural things. They did not add alcohol or any other things that they use in it now. They did not add fragrance to make it smell strong or good. For fragrance they used rose water or jasmine water, natural things. They did not use its water; they used its oil. It has a very beautiful fragrance and it is very natural.

The best soap is that which is made out of olive oil and it protects us from diseases, eczema and other skin diseases. But these other things that are sold with high price are not good. They can actually cause harm to the skin and what is under the skin, but the healing from these diseases exists. To cure the body's skin, follow Allāh's guidance for you. He taught you how to preserve your skin, to use this tree that grows in the earth. Your body came from the same earth. It is easy for you to learn how to do this and to do this even at your house. You do not have to go to the market and pay a lot of money for this. You can make it in your own home. We are talking about the olive oil that preserves and protects your skin and your physical body.

Also, look at the animals whose meat you eat. Look back at the types of animals and birds that our ancestors, the prophets and the messengers ate. They did not have the types of diseases that we have today. There are new diseases that you did not see in the past. Why is that? Because our ancestors raised these animals by their own hands, cared for them, and fed them only natural herbs, natural things, not with things that are made in factories and have poisonous materials added to them. Now they bring the chicks and the baby animals and they feed them things made in factories that have poisonous things added to them and after one month you find that the animal grows abnormally. Why is that? It did not really grow in a healthy way. It just has nothing healthy in it. But they want money so they want the animal to appear as big as possible. But the food contains killing poisons.

The human beings go to the sea to fish. So, what do the fish eat? The fish eat natural things, the herbs that grow under the sea and other fish and it is all natural. So it is very healthy to eat fish because fish has calcium, iron, a lot of good necessary elements for the body. But what happens if the sea is polluted? Then the fish will contain all poisonous things.

Also look at the cows, how people raise cows now. Cows produce milk from which we make cheese and butter. But is this cheese and butter and milk in the supermarket natural? No, because they feed the cows killing, poisonous things, not natural things that are planted naturally. They do not care about you, whether you will live twenty years, fifty years, or seventy years. They do not care whether you will live these years in suffering.

If you raised ten chickens at your own house, imagine that. You are feeding them natural things. Are you not protecting yourself that way? You will eat fresh, natural, good eggs and meat. You say, "Oh it is something simple to just go and eat this thing from the supermarket." But it is not that simple. Look at our ancestors, how many years they lived and look at us now. So, that means that raising these natural things and eating this natural food is the healthy way. It made them live longer and stronger.

Have you not heard about mad cow disease recently in Britain? I knew a brother from among my beloved children. He lives in London. One day I visited him and I found him feeding the cows with something that he bought at the supermarket. So I took it and I smelled it and I said, "From where did you bring this?" He said, "From the factories, they make it and they put it in the supermarket." So, I smelled it and I smelled the blood in it and I smelled many other bad things and I told him, "Do not feed them this food. It will generate diseases in them and they will be transferred to the human being." This was long before mad cow disease. I told him, "You will know this for certain soon." So he said, "All right," and stopped feeding them this food. He started to feed them natural food.

Then, a few years later, mad cow disease came. The cows became mad, full of poisons and they did what? They burned these farms that had like one hundred and fifty thousand cows. They killed all of those cows. Why did the cows have these diseases? The diseases were from the food that they had been fed. They fed them with deadly substance. In your country you see this as well. You see the little cow grows faster and bigger than usual and he weighs more. But it is not healthy, because if you eat the meat of this animal, these poisons will come to your body and will cause you to have diseases.

Allāh created the human being's body in accuracy and excellence and with love and beauty. All the good qualities that come from the good things that the animals eat should transfer to the human being, so Allāh created everything in that purity. But the human interferes with that and invents things that cause diseases like AIDS and cancer and many other new diseases that were unknown to our ancestors.

There are one hundred and seventy-two types of diseases that have now emerged. And who let those emerge? It is the human being. If we care for our bodies and want our bodies to be healthy, then we must care about our food. What we eat and what we drink, we must care about that. You find a lot of bodies of water and they use filters and try to supply people with this water at their homes. But even though this water could be pure water because it comes from the rain, know that the environment around it is polluted now. That is why when you just filter it and take it to your house, it is not good. Our ancestors used to find wells and take water from those, because this water is pure. Try it. Take some water that is pure from these pure resources and cook with it and taste the food. You will taste the difference because it is pure and has no pollution or poison.

This world is very materialistic now. The people do not care about the human being; they only care about collecting money. They consider humans like a tool in a machine and if a part is broken, that is fine, they can replace it. They do not value the human being. So, the healing of our bodies lies in what we eat. Also, it is affected by the air we breathe. Is the air not polluted? What about this fuel that we burn all the time from factories and cars and all of that. It pollutes the air. How then, can we heal our bodies? There are now one hundred fifty-two thousand diseases in the world. How can we protect ourselves from them? By following the divine commands and the guidance as much as we can. Allāh says in the Qur'ān:

> Truly, We did offer the trust
> to the heavens and the earth, and the mountains,
> but they declined to bear it and were afraid of it.
> But man bore it. (Qur'ān 33:72)

But the human carried that trust because he was an oppressor of himself and others and was ignorant.

You must have caring. You must care for the plants that you plant and water them with pure water. You must care for the animals you raise. If you want to care for your own physical body, and care for its health and wellbeing, then eat only what is natural. The vegetables that you eat, you must care that they are pure vegetables and you must investigate about where they grew. Did they grow by being watered with pure water in a pure environment? You must care for the food that you take into your body.

Also, you must not let your body carry more than it should. Do not eat more than you should. Even the donkey is wiser than you, human being, because he eats only what suffices him. If you put food out for him after he has eaten, he will not touch it. But the human, give him something delicious after he has eaten, and "Oh, I will try this." So be careful of how much food you take in, because where will you put the water? Where will you put the air? This is the heavenly teaching, instruction for you.

Allāh created the stomach with a certain size. Every human has the size of stomach that is necessary for him and he divides this stomach into three parts as the Prophet taught us: one third for food, one-third for water and one third for air. So, you have to learn if you eat, not to eat to your very fullest. And it is a disaster if you eat and go to sleep right away. Many people do that; they eat and then they go to take a nap or go to sleep at night. But the body is a divine instrument. It has its own way to operate. It needs you to walk. Like a machine or an instrument, it needs motion. So you do not go to sleep after you eat. You stay active, because if you go to sleep, then the viruses will have a chance and the bacteria and all of that, to accumulate in your body because the tool will not be operating in the right way.

We are now looking at where these diseases of the body come from. Do you know now how to heal your own body? It is in your own hands. You are the physician of yourself. Know what you are eating. Know what you are drinking. From where do you drink? From where do you eat? Look at the container in which you put the food. Was it clean? Was it healthy? Or was it made out of something that contains lead or something that can be transferred to your body, poisonous things that can cause diseases.

Our ancestors used vessels and plates and containers made from the dust. This is how our ancestors ate. Everything was clean and had natural things. They cooked it in the fire. The clay was prepared in the fire so it was clean. Then they cooked in it, they washed their food in it, they drank from it and they were not afflicted with diseases. Do you know that flies do not come to clay containers? This is something natural; they do not approach it. Things made out of wood are good too; they do not have any pollution or poison in them. So, your food comes from the dust, your plate comes from the dust and what is mixed with that dust? All the oils, the natural oils that your body needs.

This was the way of our true spiritual physicians, our ancestors, the prophets, messengers and guides. They ate following the divine law, the s̲harīʿa, the natural law that Allāh sent upon their hearts to understand

and follow. This happens through divine guidance. Allāh gave them guidance and taught them how to preserve and protect the body from diseases because, as the gnostics said, sound intellect is connected to a healthy body. The healthier your body is, the more sound your intellect.

So if you have healed your body like that you will also be a good healer for others. In my latest book I explain many diseases that afflict the physical bodies, and also diseases that can afflict the hearts and the souls and the intellects and the spirits. And I say to you, this book with its many pages, it contains a lot, has eight-nine diseases. I ask you to read it, understand it and follow it accurately.

It took me almost seven years to write it and I looked into fifteen ancient documents. Some of these documents go back thousands of years. I took from documents from all around the world, from the ancient gnostics. That is why it took me a long time to understand their languages. One page would take me like three days because I read it in other languages, ancient languages, and I had to translate it and understand it from the old Hebrew and the old Arabic, I used a lot of resources to translate it. If you come to my office you will find like one hundred documents at a time to translate just one page.

I praise Allāh that He gave me patience and helped me to write it. I wrote it in Arabic but I also gave permission for it to be translated into Hebrew, English and French. But you, the English-speaking people here, you were second. After I did the Arabic, I ordered it to be translated into English because I love you. I want to give it to you first. I want you to care for yourselves as I care for you. I want you to learn how to heal yourselves.

If you look at any of the diseases that afflict us today, you will find their healing here. Many physicians fall short and are unable to heal some of these diseases. This healing is successful. But it is not enough. You also have to always be following Allāh's commands. Everything is connected to your worship of your Lord. You have to be praying always to follow Allāh's commands. You have to always be in remembrance; otherwise the healing will be delayed. There is no separation between the physical and the spiritual healing and the worship of Allāh; they are connected. How can you be healed when you are not praying or when you are a liar or when you are stealing or when you are polluted and dirty? No, understand that the spiritual and the physical are connected. Listen to what Allāh says, He says:

> My slave worshipper, listen to Me and I will listen to you.
> If you follow My way and My commands,
> I will also fulfill your needs.

That is why I say to you, physical healing will never be fulfilled if the person is in disobedience to Allāh, no matter how many times he recites or any other person recites for him. He must first be in obedience to Allāh. You must first obey Allāh, listen to Allāh, correct yourself and start with the name of Allāh, the Healer, as<u>h</u>-S<u>h</u>āfī.

Our Prophet Ibrāhīm, said:

> And when I am ill, it is He Who cures me. (Qur'ān 26:79-26:80)

He said, "Allāh heals me. He is as<u>h</u>-S<u>h</u>āfī, a healer." But that means you must follow Allāh first, you must know Allāh first and obey Him. How can anyone heal if his own heart has a disease? How can he heal others? How can he heal if his heart is full of the diseases of envy, of jealousy, and hate and his heart is empty of love and peace? How can he heal others? You must believe with sincerity. You must believe that to become pure is part of healing.

I know what I am talking about. You must believe with sincerity in what I am saying—that healing is connected to purifying your soul by listening to Allāh and following His commands and knowing His divine law and following it.

You must first purify your heart. To purify your heart you cannot abandon the s<u>h</u>arī'a. You cannot abandon following the divine law, because Who sent down this divine law? Allāh! Whoever believes in something other than Allāh and strays from His divine law is a rebellious one. Allāh will never send healing through his hand and never heal him that way. But sometimes Allāh can give him a little bit of good and the effect of healing so that he can say, "Look what I can give you; so follow me more." But he must listen to that and appreciate it and follow Him more so he can have the full effect of healing. Then he can heal others.

You must understand that the human physical body has the four elements: dust, water, fire and air. What is the story of fire? What is this fire that Allāh preferred at the end for the rebellious disobedient ones? Those who do not use fire in the right way while in the lower realm, in the way Allāh created it to be used, which means it is to be used for the happiness and in service of humanity, are the ones who will suffer later because they should have used this fire to serve humanity in a good way. As a result of using it in the wrong way, they will be afflicted with diseases. They will get burned by that fire here in this world.

You know that there has never before been something called cancer. It is a new disease. It is a modern disease. Our ancestors ate natural things and drank pure things and breathed pure air. But now, we eat dirty things, drink dirty things and breathe polluted air.

Do not say, "Allāh, caused me to have this disease; Allāh gave me that disease." Allāh always sends what it good. He gave us what is pure and taught us how to preserve that. So it is you who afflicted yourself with the disease, but you are also your own physician. You have the capacity and ability to return to the natural way and heal yourself. Do you not see that Allāh subjugated the fire to you? So if you use the fire with wisdom, it will make you happy. But if you use it unwisely, it will burn you and burn others around you.

Now, many countries use fire to kill other humans. They invent weapons and rockets and things that travel distances to kill others. Those are foolish people. They are stupid. Why do they make these things to kill humanity? Is this their goal? If only 3 of those atomic carrying weapons that travel a long distance, if only three of those exploded, it would destroy the whole of humanity. This is foolishness.

Did Allāh create us to do this? No, Allāh created the human full of beauty, to live happily. He created the human full of love and peace and justice. We do not need this killing fire and weapons that destroy us and destroy our properties and belongings. The fire is something good but why do we use it to burn? Why do we want to create this destruction with it? We want to achieve good with it. We do not want to use it the wrong way so it can spread many new diseases.

When these bombs fall into countries, what happens? It does not cause just immediate destruction and killing but it creates effects that cause many other diseases to animals, plants, air and humans. But we are carrying the message of Allāh, a godly message. We are carrying the message of beauty and majesty of Allāh, the message of love and peace and pure goodness and justice and freedom for all. To carry this message, there is a first step, to carry the message for the body, which means to preserve and protect the body as it was created by Allāh.

Allāh created the human being to carry the message, the godly message, first on the physical level by making it healthy and living happily with it. How? By following the divine instructions that came and were prescribed by the Prophet, the guidance that is given to us by Allāh. He taught the human being all the names (Qur'ān 2:31). He taught us knowledge through the prophets. He taught us all the names, which means everything that can benefit the human, everything that the human needs. He taught us how to make things and protect ourselves and make useful things. He taught the human what is good to use and what is evil and so to avoid what is evil and what it dangerous and harmful. But it is you who goes to the harmful and poisonous things and makes use of them, unwisely. This is the story of fire.

The evil human being started to use fire in an evil way, a wrong way, but he is capable of using fire in the good way to make humanity happy. How can he do this? He has the capacity because Allāh gave him an intellect. If he uses his sound intellect, he will know. The human being now is using only five percent of his brain cells. What would it be like if he used ten percent? Oh, s̲hayṭān would be bigger than Iblīs if he did this, but he will not be able to do this.

I am certain that Allāh will burn the corrupters of the earth and will make those good people, the righteous and the pious have victory over the earth. I am sure that Allāh will make those good, righteous, pious people rule at the end. I ask you, I beg you, weeping in humbleness, to please, follow this prescription of the Prophet. Because I am certain that if you use this, you will be successful in healing yourself and others.

Follow what I wrote to you. I gave you everything in detail. Not only in this book, but in many other books, but this is like the last essence of my books of healing. So, I ask you, please write it, read it, understand it, and follow it and depend and rely only on Allāh.

Do not think of yourselves as healers while you are not praying and not following. The prayer itself is very important. When you do your ablution, do you think you are just cleaning your body, just washing? No. There are conditions. The water must be very pure, to purify you. It must be devoid of all poisons and pollution. You must be certain that you are fully directing your whole self and your heart toward Allāh when you are purifying your hands and your face and your mouth and you say, "Allāh, I am purifying my being because I want to please You, I want to serve You."

You cannot claim to be a healer while you are not praying. I say, "No, you are a liar." Because what happens in prayer? In prayer you ask Allāh to help you. So, when you make ablution and pray and put your hand on someone, it becomes healing and pure because you say, "Oh Allāh, I worship You," in your prayer. And Allāh says, "Be to me as I want and I will be to you as you want. I will fulfill your needs if you follow My ways and fulfill My commands." He said:

> And when My slaves ask you concerning Me,
> then [answer them], I am indeed near.
> I respond to prayers when they call upon Me. (Qur'ān 2:186)

As long as you are pure, obedient, praying and loving Allāh, then Allāh will help you and your hands will become godly hands and healing hands.

I just explained to you the story of fire. How do you really know what the fire is? Do you not read in the Qur'ān? Mūsā says to his family, when he was going back to Egypt, "I have seen a glimpse of fire. Let me bring a flame of it so you can get warm and cook on it."

So what fire are we talking about? We are talking about a godly flame that burns pollution, it burns corruption, and it burns all the evil qualities. This is the fire that Mūsā saw. It is the fire of love. The fire of love is so beautiful. There is nothing more beautiful than the fire of love. It is delicious. There is nothing more delicious than the fire of love. The love of God is the glorious fire that burns all evil and corruption away. If you swim in the ocean of the fire of love, you will find a lot of treasure and you will be able to heal people.

If you want to heal people, heal them with the fire of your love. Use your full love to heal the people. Put your physical body as earth for the people to walk on, toward Allāh. This is the godly command.

A healer or a physician without love equals nothing.
A healer or a physician without divine godly beauty is nothing.

A healer or a physician without peace equals nothing.
A healer or a physician without godly mercy in his heart is nothing.

The true physician is someone who is holy.
He is carrying every divine image and reflection.
When he lays on his hand, he is laying on a godly hand.
He says, "Oh Allāh, heal with Your names and powers." T
his is how we learned it from our prophets and messengers and guides.

So, we just talked about one element in the body, which is the fire and we have been talking only about that element. But if someone falls sick, he gets a fever and he says, "I have a fever; I have a temperature," this is a sign of fire. This fire actually melts the fat in your body; it burns your very flesh. So we know there is fire; just touch a person who has fever. I say to the one who has fever, "Do not fear, if you are truly a believer, I can cure you in five minutes, this fire can be gone." How can it be healed? Mix one-half of a cup of water with one-half of a cup of vinegar and soak a towel in it. Put it on the head and the fever will disappear in five minutes. It works for any age, a child, a woman, a man, an elder. It works, this healing. Vinegar comes from where? It comes from a lot of fruits. I explained here how to make apple cider vinegar. I explained how you can make it at home, here in this book.

I have worked in healing the diseases of the human being for a long time because the human will not have the strength to fully worship and serve Allāh unless he has a healthy body. If he wants to fast and pray and go and serve people, serve Allāh and help the poor and needy and carry the message of Allāh to people, he must have a healthy body to do that. That is why in our field, caring for the physical body is an important part of our beliefs, our creed. It all comes from our pure love for Allāh. We care for the body because we care for Allāh. So, the one who does not love Allāh in that way and does everything for His face, cannot heal any other. You must follow Allāh and obey Him because He is the One Who created you.

We will now talk about the third element, air. Air is divided within the body. For example, there is an odor every human being has. Some have a very offensive odor. For example if you see a rotten chicken, you find it has an offensive odor. So, the human being can also have this offensive odor if he cuts others, if he slanders and spies on people and reveals their secrets and backbites others. He will have a more offensive odor than the corpse of a dead animal. And the flesh of such a human will be more offensive than the taste of a rotten animal because that becomes dirty and it sends dirt and into the human body. But for the godly, the good words are healing. They heal the ones who say them and they heal others.

There is a difference then, when someone comes to you for help and healing and you say, “Oh my God you have a serious disease” and you start to make him feel horrible. No, lifting his spirit and giving him optimism is part of the healing. You have to give him full love and raise his enthusiasm and energy to heal him. These are the good words that you should give him.

Going back to air; air (hawāʾ) comes for the root verb, “hawā,” in Arabic, which means, “falling down.” You can fall down in love or you can fall down into evil. So be among those who fall down in love. Let your hand always be beautiful and good and pure, always carrying love for others. Let it be the tool for happiness of all of humanity. Whoever did not taste the taste of falling in love falls down. Those words come from the same root word in Arabic, to descend. So you can fall in love or you can descend into the lowest of the low.

So the one who does not taste falling in love cannot heal others. He just descends into evil. But the one who falls in love with Allāh can heal by the way he looks at people, by the hand with which he touches people. This love is something marvelous. It is part of the godly love, the divine love. Love is the healer and the healing. It can heal everyone on earth.

Allāh bestows His favor upon the one who does good for himself and others to have this tool of healing, love. The lover devoid of love falls down into the lowest of the low realm of evil and loses everything. Show me, is there anyone who has a heart, who is devoid of love for Allāh? If your heart is devoid of love for Allāh, raise your hand now. There is no one who does not love his Lord. It is something so beautiful. I raise my hand and I say, “I love Allāh only. Nothing but Allāh is in my heart.” I ask Allāh to make you one of those lovers of Him.

So, we now came to talk about this air, hawāʾ in Arabic, which is falling, and I say:

> Oh Allāh, I love You with two types of love.

A love that is falling the desire of love
and the other type of love
is that I know You alone ought to be loved.
(adaptation of Rābiʿa al-Adawiyya's poem)

This is the origin of love. This is the hawāʾ, the air falling in love, the air by which you live. Can you live without air? Air in Arabic is hawāʾ. Hawā is falling in love in Arabic. Can you live without breathing air? You cannot. You have to breathe this hawāʾ, this descending in love. So, preserve this air. Preserve your love for Allāh. Preserve your love for others, because Allāh Most High, glory be to Him, will then take your hand and fulfill your needs and make you His true servant.

So we are still talking about the first type of disease, which are diseases of the physical bodies, and I have explained to you the conclusion of how you can heal your physical bodies before you step into healing others. So I ask you to write the book and absolutely understand every word and apply it, and then you can become a true healer by the permission of Allāh, the will of Allāh.

This is the covenant or the promise of the physical body. If you are able now and you want to take the promise to care for your bodies and to heal your bodies, then come now to me. Whoever wants to be a true healer, to be a true spiritual physician, must come to me now and promise me and give his covenant to Allāh with his full being, truthfully, sincerely and honestly. And the one who feels he cannot wash this way, let him not come, but everyone needs to come. Do not say, "Oh I already did that; I already know that." You must come and surrender to Allāh. Obey Allāh and ask Him to help you and support you because He will provide you with more and support you and help you to heal. But if you become disobedient and rebellious toward Allāh, then you will be forsaken and broken and you will not be qualified to heal. Do not think of how big you have become. So come. Do not postpone your coming. This chance might not come again, so come now and promise Allāh.

Sidi gives the promise.

Travel from al-Mulk to al-Malakut to al-Jabarut

Special Tawba Practice

Lā ʾilāha ʾilla-llāāāāāāh, Lā ʾilāha ʾilla-llāāāāāh, Lā ʾilāha ʾilla-llāāāāāh
Muḥammad rasūlu-llāh, Ibrāhīm rasūlu-llāh, Mūsā rasūlu-llāh,
ʿĪsā rasūlu-llāh ʿalayhim ṣalātu-llāh.

Allāhumma anta-s-salām wa minka-s-salām
wa ilayka ya'ūdu-s-salām
tabārakta rabbanā
ya dha-l-jalāli wa-l-'ikrām

As-salāmu ʿalaykum wa raḥmatu-llāh wa bārakatuhu.

Allāh, please let us live in peace, love, mercy, freedom, justice and beauty. Please keep us in the station where we have everything permissible from You and in the station where we recognize that everything is from Allāh, by Allāh and in Allāh. Whoever arrives at the station of love, reality and truth will arrive at the true essence by which he was created. Our most beloved guide, the Messenger of Allāh, ʾālayhi as-salām, said:

> Every child is given birth with the pure intuition. (Ḥadīth)

He is given everything that Allāh wants of him, meaning that he carries the image of absolute beauty, absolute love, absolute mercy and absolute knowledge.

The child that is given birth is a gnostic. He knows Allāh directly and purely. When the human being is created within the womb of his mother, he is created in the best mold with the best image. Allāh said:

> I created Ādam in My own image [as My own reflection].
> (Ḥadīth Qudsī)

He also said in the Qurʾān that:

> We have certainly created man in the best mold. (Qurʾān 95:4)

This means that he is devoid of darkness in his heart and spirit. His heart and spirit are pure originally, and he is complete and perfect in everything. He does not need anyone to guide him or to help him walk, he is already pure. The proof is that when he comes from the womb, he directly knows his mother and automatically or naturally goes to her breast and feeds. Do you not see this? Does he have the human mind saying, "Oh this is my mother" and recognizing these things or does it just happen intuitively?

I want to explain with subtle accuracy the human nature. Human souls are divided into three parts.

Three Levels of the Human Soul

1. The animal soul
2. The spiritual soul
3. The godly or divine soul

The human lives in the realm of dominion, al-mulk. Al-mulk is the realm of physical and sensual position. This is the first realm, al-mulk. At this level the human is like an animal and lives like an animal. There is blindness in this realm. It cannot comprehend its own nature. The human at this level forgets the realm from which he came; the realm of purity.

He was in this realm of purity as a child. It is full of beauty, purity, perfection and completion. It is a realm of surrender and knowledge, direct knowledge from Allāh. Being in complete surrender, the child desires nothing outside of what Allāh gives him. Allāh assigns someone to take care of him. He assigns two angels to take care of him, one on his right side and one on his left side. These angels are the ones guiding him to feed on his mother's breast.

Being perfect and pure, he immediately has love for his mother. Allāh puts the love of the child into the mother's heart as well, even though she had pain, suffering and difficulties during pregnancy. When the mother conceived the child, she walked away very happy, knowing that she had a child in her womb. She was awaiting something glorious happening within her that would come to life. As she begins to feel the pain of pregnancy and giving birth, she must remember that she chose to be pregnant. She chose that by herself, no one pushed her. She came to the man of her own free will and desire. One must be patient when they are pregnant and bear the consequences of being pregnant.

Would a donkey complain about carrying luggage? He is subjected to that often and he just obeys. In a similar way, a mother is also subjected to carrying a child. When she was single, she said that she wanted a beloved, a husband. This was her free choice that she made for herself. She must be patient with the trial that she is going through. It is a trial. In giving birth, she suffers a lot of pain and at the end she either gets a boy or a girl. At this point of suffering, she just wants anything. She does not care if it is a boy or a girl. She wants to be done with it.

Why does she scream at this point? It is actually a divine prize or gift that He gives her. However she complains and screams, asking to get out of the situation. She can barely bear it. She can start to ask Allāh to support her secret, using him to help her with all the pain.

She will say, "Allāh, Allāh," if she is speaking in the Arabic language. If she is speaking English she will say "Oh God, help me." No matter what language she speaks she will mention God at this point. Even though it happened by her free choice, Allāh does not want her to suffer. If she asks him for help, he will help her. She chose that path, wishing for a beloved, a husband.

It was of her free will that she wished to have a child. Why then does she scream? She must be patient because after a while the little one will come and when he comes, he will know her immediately. He knows his mother immediately because every mother has a special fragrance and he can recognize that fragrance? He goes directly to her. A few hours after giving birth, the milk starts to come especially for him.

This very state can be experienced by every human. According to his understanding, he can grasp the meaning of this thing. Even the animals go through it. You can see that when the cow gives birth and stands on her feet after a maximum of two hours, the baby calf starts to nurse. This is something that happens naturally because of divine attentive care and provision from Him. He gives His love to the little ones and the mother so that she can give him the care he needs. The human being at this level is at the level of a-mulk, the realm of physical position.

This realm is a holy realm. Why do you make it dirty and impure? It is the human being who polluted this beautiful holy realm of physical position. Within the first nine years, the human is actually in the realm of purity. After that Allāh makes him of sound intellect, having the capacity to discern good from evil. Then he gives him free choice.

The little child is a sign of love, mercy, and purity. In children you can see these qualities clearly because they are godly human beings at that age. They are fully divine and godly with the pure intuition that Allāh gave them. This is why they are honest, sincere, and loving. If they weep, their weeping is worship. If they speak, they speak the truth. If they cry, it is a mercy for their parents, a worship, a prayer.

The human must preserve this beautiful nature given to him as a child. The human soul at that childhood age is a humane soul not that of an animal soul. However after desire fills it, it can be at an animal level and become an animal soul. This happens because the parents and society begin to teach the child to change his nature and the child becomes an animal soul. If the parents are good people, then the child will be raised to be a good human, possessing a human soul not an animal soul. If the parents are evil then the child becomes evil.

The milk that comes from the mother affects the child. If the husband truly loves her in a pure way and the mother loves him in a pure way, then the milk is so pure. It will feed the child in the right way. How does this pure love come from the father? Is this a true humane love or an animal love? If the father's soul is truly a human soul then it follows all of the divine commands and the natural laws of Allāh. It follows all the godly commands that Allāh inspired all the prophets and Ādam, the leader of all of humanity, to do.

Allāh taught Ādam all the names. He had no life before and Allāh gave him life. Allāh asked Ādam to inform the angels of the names of all this. Ādam told them right away because Allāh gave him that capacity, that knowledge. The angels prostrated in service to him. Allāh told Ādam to teach them the names of all the things that have been created and that He will make manifest later.

Allāh created the seven heavens and the seven earths in six days, and on the seventh day, He established himself on the Throne of Authority. Ādam informed the angels of the names of all the things that were and will be. He asked the angels the names of all these things. Do you know them? Allāh asked the angels to tell Him about the human soul which comes from his own spirit which is his manifestation in this existence. I am the authority in every manifestation and I am the hidden in everything concealed. He asked the angels to inform Him of these things.

The angels said, "We have no knowledge except what You taught us." Allāh then told Ādam to inform them and Ādam did. Ādam's mud was taken from three places. We are talking about Ādam, the human being. One place was under the holy place in Jerusalem. Another place was under the Kaʿba, and the third place was under the place where the Prophet Muḥammad, ʾālayhi as-salām, was buried. Ādam came out of these three places. This holy mud came from these holy places which the heart's desire and want to visit.

Ibrāhīm, the father of the Prophet asked that the desire be put in people so that they would love and visit these places. This is why the Prophet, ʿalayhi as-salātu as-salām, said that people do not really desire to visit places for holy reasons except for these three places. People go around the Kaʿba sometimes not even knowing what they are doing. They do it because their hearts are called to go and do so. The Prophet Ibrāhīm, ʾālayhi as-salām, asked that the hearts of people be made to desire and wish to visit these holy places and experience this sacredness.

The three places: the Prophets tomb, the Kaʿba sanctuary and the holy place in Jerusalem are the house of Ādam, Ibrāhīm (Abraham), Mūsā (Moses) and ʿĪsā (Jesus). It is the divine Throne, and it is the land where people will be assembled at the end for the gathering on the Day of Resurrection and Judgment. This is the essence or the foundation of the human mosque. It came from these places.

The human soul is innocent, not a monstrous, animal soul. It is the human being himself who made it an animal soul by his actions and his choices. He chose for himself to be an animal that is walking and talking. He speaks the language of the animal and walks like one. We made you a human being with a human soul. Why do you change this and make it lower than that? We gave you a pure, beautiful, loving, merciful soul. Why do you want to change it?

Allāh says:

> Whatever you experience is a result of
> what your hands earned by your actions.
> And I pardon much. (Qurʾān 42:30).

I created you, and I will care, provide and guide you always. Why do you not preserve the purity, perfection, and excellence which I have given you? Instead you follow your lower desires. You change into something lower and become an animal human.

Why do you abandon the divine, godly qualities which distinguish you from the animal kingdom? Allāh, Most High, created the human being in the best mold (Qur'ān 95:4). He is the essence of purity, mercy, love, annihilation and persistence in existence.

You think of yourself as a tiny microcosm while within you is the whole macrocosm. You are a holy being, a holy mirror. It is not permissible to destroy this divine mirror. Why do you not transform from the animal soul which is full of dirt, pollution, ignorance, hatred, jealousy, envy, anger and desire to your human soul which is pure, kind, and loving? Your very essence and life started in the Garden, which is more vast than what the heavens and the earth contain.

When a child screams for the first time after leaving the womb, he is saying, "Aa," which means, "Allāh." The letter "alif" in Arabic, or the letter "a" in English and in all languages, means "Allāh." It calls Allāh. It says, "I am the worshiping slave for the sake of Allāh. I am loving and merciful. I am the divine image. I love everyone."

However the true journey does not start with physical birth. It is very innocent and started in the pre-eternal world. Allāh took from the seeds of the human ancestors and asked, "Am I not your Lord?" They said, "Yes." At that time they did not have their physical senses. However, they had a tongue and could speak. They had consciousness, and in spite of the differences of their languages or what they would be in the world or from which land they came, Allāh asked them at that point:

> "Am I not your Lord?"
> They said: "Yes! We testify,"
> lest you should say on the Day of Resurrection:
> "Truly, we have been unaware of this." (Qur'ān 7:172)

They said, "We worship and serve You. We bear witness that You are the One in control of all affairs." Iblīs and his companions from the jinn did not respond to that divine question. Allāh asks, "Iblīs, why do you not say that you are my worshipping slave?" Oh evil one, murderer, why do you not affirm that Allāh is your Lord? Did anyone push you to not affirm?

No, Allāh gave you free choice and you chose not to say "yes" and affirm that Allāh was your Lord and that you were His slave.

This happened before you, my daughter, gave birth to any sons or daughters in this realm. This happened in the ancient realm of eternity. It is a realm of which none has knowledge of except Allāh and the very close ones that have the divine godly breath. This divine breath has no limitations or boundaries. It is in the divine realm of love. This is not like climbing a mountain. Follow the straight path for it is the direct, straight way to be in the divine presence. Allāh told his messengers, Ibrāhīm, Mūsā, and ʿĪsā, to say, "Allāh."

After giving birth to ʿĪsā, ʾālayhi as-salām, people came to Maryam and asked her where she had brought him from and what she had done.

> Then she [Maryam] pointed to him [ʿĪsā].
>
> They said, "How can we talk to a child in the cradle?"
>
> He [ʿĪsā] said, "Truly! I am a slave of Allāh,
> He has given me the Scripture and made me a Prophet.
> And He has made me blessed wheresoever I be,
> and has enjoined on me prayer, and zakāh, as long as I live.
> And dutiful to my mother, and made me not arrogant, unblest." (Qurʾān 19:29 – 19:32)

He actually could speak and he said, "I am the slave of Allāh. Allāh gave me the Holy Book and made me a messenger."

The man said, "Allāh, who is talking at this point? Is it ʿĪsā, ʾālayhi as-salām?" No, in the realm of Reality it was the tongue of the Truth. Allāh talked to them through ʿĪsā, ʾālayhi as-salām. This is the station of witnessing. Know that the station of existence, like seeing this table or seeing me talking is the realm of witnessing. You witness the Reality, the Truth.

Know that there is no god but Me, and establish your ṣalāh. If you want to be a human soul and not an animal soul, then be My beloved, know that I am Allāh, the One, and establish your prayer regularly for Me. Know that this is the straight path. Do not turn right or left. There is no right or left. There is only Allāh. Say, "Allāh." Repeat the word "Allāh," and establish regular prayers for Me.

This is the realm of position that you are in now. It is a realm of metaphors, imagination, pictures, desires hatred, and envy. It is the realm of physical position, al-mulk. Then there is the realm of the human soul.

Allāh asks, "Do you think that We created you without a purpose? No, I created you to witness Myself in every bowing and prostration. In every prayer and begging, I witness Myself through the mirror of the words through the human being (see Qur'ān 3:191)

Know who you are and how to live in order to get out of this safely. Know how to love and obey Allāh, and know how to love the creation and all people. Where is this love that we are talking about. The love is beauty. Why do you not manifest your beauty then? Where is your beauty?

The gnostic said, "Wherever I look I see You. You are my qibla." Wherever you look you see Allāh. If you touch someone you are touching Allāh. This happens if you are a human soul instead of an animal soul. You are not one of those who lies, steals, murders and destroys. We are the healers so how can our hands be healing? It is only by following Allāh's commands, not by deception and lying to ourselves and to others. We must truly be in the way of Allāh and following His command.

At that point, the realm of physical position transforms to the realm of the true kingdom, the dominion of Allāh. It becomes a garden full of love, mercy, justice and peace. Allāh says:

> The one who believes in Me is in the Garden today. (Ḥadīth)

He does not say that today or tomorrow he will enter the Garden. He says that now he is in the Garden. When he dies this is not death. He transforms to the other realm and continues to be in the Garden.

This is not an end. The human soul just transforms from one realm to the next dimension. The human soul that pierces through the animal realm can transform into the other realm. This is the realm of the divine dominion, al-malakūt. It is the angelic realm, full of angels, purity, righteous and pious people. They walk humbly on this earth, and if someone ignorant attacks them, they say peace to them and leave them. This is our realm.

Our religion is the religion of the Truth. It is the way of Reality, and we surrender totally to the commands of Allāh, and we transform from the animal realm to the dominion, the angelic realm. If we transform to this reality now we become an angel walking on earth. We do not know anything but pure goodness and our hands become healing hands. Our realm becomes one of obedience, not rebelliousness toward Allāh and natural law.

Hands become healing at that point. Allāh showed us the way. He said that this is His straight path and do not turn from it. Direct ourselves fully toward Allāh and he becomes our focal point of prayer. Our walking must be toward the heavens, the angelic realm, al-malakūt, which is the dominion of Allāh. This means that the human soul moved into the spiritual soul.

Allāh says, "Welcome to you, My heaven is open for you now. You know Me. Take this gift of My love, knowledge, and secret. You are now ready to eat."

Allāh gives this to the obedient ones and not to the deceivers, the liars who proclaim but do not truly and fully obey. At this station the soul becomes the spirit and it lives in the realm of the angels, the divine dominion. It is full of gardens and beauty. There is no death in this realm. The human can travel more and transform into something else.

This is not the end. He starts another beautiful journey. The ones who stay with the animal soul, are deprived of this because they are disobedient and rebellious and they cannot arrive at this. Allāh shows everyone what is the good and what is the evil. Allāh never tells you to go and corrupt, steal, lie, destroy, or hate.

Allāh says of the people on the straight path that He loves them and they love Him. The realm is devoid of hate. It does not know hate. This is the nature of the true human soul. Can the human animal heal? No, it is full of thickness. It is an animal full of thickness. However the human soul, the true spiritual soul can heal. The healer must heal himself first to become a true healer. The healing secret lies in truthfulness, sincerity and love.

At that point, he exits the realm of the animal kingdom and he becomes the human soul. The animal human is like a monster and you must rid yourself of the garments of this animal soul. You must be a true human which means to be polite. Do not attack a woman and sleep with her without her permission or in a lawful way. Preserve her purity and yours as well. Allāh gave you this essence of purity. Do not listen to those who corrupt the earth and spread their false claims on the earth.

You must always wash your body and heart and keep it pure and clean as Allāh created it. At that point you become a true human being like an angel walking on the earth. When you are asked who created you, you tell them Allāh. Why not surrender to him and follow his way. Allāh gave you these beautiful qualities. Why do you deviate from these qualities and the way of Allāh? Why do you disobey and rebel? Why do you pollute these beautiful qualities which Allāh gave.

The way of the Jews, Christians, and Muslims is that after you sleep with your wife, you must wash. You think that by washing the body you are pure. No, you must wash with the divine water. It is the godly, unseen water of eternity. Always be present with Allāh and rid yourself of the garment of the animal being, and become a true human being. Return to this purity. Did not Allāh ask the angels to prostrate to your father Ādam? You must return to that purity. When you were a child, the angels still prostrated to you.

Did Allāh order you to go to dirty places? Never, Allāh loves you. He gave you the pure water to purify you. He gives you all good things. Allāh does not push you to go to the dirty places. Allāh says:

> And when My slaves ask you concerning Me,
> then [answer them], I am indeed near.
> I respond to prayers when they call upon Me. (Qur'ān 2:186)

"If you deviate or need help, knock on My door and ask for help. You will be provided for. Know that I will still respond to the prayer even after My slaves spread corruption in My heavens and the earth. I respond to them if they turn to Me."

Are you really satisfied with this narrow physical lower realm in which you live? Are you satisfied with this life or are you looking for another life? The true healer must leave the animal soul. Leave it behind and return to your original human soul. Be a true human being, full of love, beauty, mercy, kindness and gentleness. This is what Allāh wants from you.

Allāh said to the Prophet, "Do not despair or feel sad because I am with you. I will help, support and heal you. I will grant you prosperity and success." If you want anything ask Allāh directly. Remember that Allāh never pushes you into doing evil. Allāh does not want that. It is from your selves; your own nafs do evil. It is the animal soul that pushes you to do evil. Allāh created everything beautiful and in an excellent way. He taught you how to teach and use the animal in a good way. He teaches you how to use everything in the good, right and wise way for your own benefit.

You must travel from the realm of physical position to the angelic realm, the realm of divine dominion. Finally, you reach the realm of al-jabarūt, the divine mind which is the house of Allāh. Allāh says:

> My heaven and My earth cannot contain Me,
> but the heart of My faithful believer
> has been containing Me. (Ḥadīth Qudsī)

Can anyone contain you except your Beloved? The donkey's heart cannot contain you. The heart of the shayṭān cannot contain you. Only the heart of your Beloved can, and Allāh is your Beloved. He is the Compassionate, the Merciful. Follow the Truth, the Real Who is Allāh. Allāh's name is al-Ḥaqq, the Real, the Truth. Follow the way of Reality. The name of Allāh in Hebrew and Arabic is "Allāh." You say, "Allāh-hum" when you invoke Allāh in Hebrew and Arabic. It has one meaning, which is that we are invoking the One Creator Who originated us in the best of molds (Qur'ān 95:4).

We have a duty to arrive at this final realm, this divine potency which is the divine mind, the godly realm. It is a realm full of purity and love. It is not permissible to lie, steal, or deceive. There is no mountain to climb. The door is wide open for you. You can be in the divine presence now. He says:

> My heaven and My earth cannot contain Me,
> but the heart of My faithful believer
> has been containing Me. (Ḥadīth Qudsī)

If this heart is pure and clean and full of the beauty and love, then it is in that divine, godly realm.

Allāh says:

> My servant continues to draw near to Me with
> voluntary works so that I will love him.
>
> When I love him I am
> his hearing with which he hears,
> his seeing with which he sees,
> his hand with which he strikes and
> his foot with which he walks. (Ḥadīth Qudsī)

In this station, you are worshiping Allāh in the right way and following His commands. When you touch someone who is sick and say, "In the name of my Lord, my Master," then Allāh will make the healing be channeled through you and that sick person will be healed.

Allāh knows you at that station. He sees and hears you. Allāh sees the secret and whatever is concealed, more than the sickness.

The Prophet, ʾālayhi as-salām, said that:

> Allāh sees the tiny ant in the dark night under the black stone. (Ḥadīth)

Allāh knows that ant. Be like that ant and say that you know your Lord. I have nothing; I only love my Lord and all of the people. If I had seen anything but my Lord, I would have been destroyed by now. I see only Allāh. It is a must that you wash and purify yourself to transform from the animal realm to the angelic realm. You must repent from all the things you did and realize the godly reality within you. Has anyone here never committed a sin? Show me that person. We have all committed sins. I see, I hear and I know that all of you committed sins. Some of you slept together without being married, or this or that...

I know that you all come to Allāh to repent and be purified. You want to wash and purify your body, soul, and spirit. You want to transform from the realm of the animal soul, to the true human soul and then on to the realm of the godly soul. Are you ready to acknowledge that you committed sins? Are you ready to transform yourself and treat others with love, honesty, sincerity and mercy? Know that Allāh will keep purifying and transforming you from the realm of the animal soul, to the true human soul and to the godly soul. Are you ready to acknowledge your sins and give a promise to Allāh to transform and purify yourselves from all your past sins? Are you ready? Answer me. Yes...

Whoever is ready let them come to me now to promise Allāh to rid themselves of their animal selves and to become true human souls that believe in Allāh and follow his boundaries. They do not cross the boundaries that are set by him. They follow his commands and his prohibitions.

I want you to forget your sins from now on. Do not keep remembering your sins. I see everyone and what sins they committed. I can see it in your eyes. I can tell each of you what sins you committed. I say to conceal that and forget about it. Allāh is the Concealer. He conceals our faults, pardons and forgives us. I do not want you to dwell in the past and keep remembering your sins. Seek his forgiveness. I ask Allāh to forgive you because He is the Most Compassionate and Most Merciful.

Know that this is a very serious promise, a heavy covenant. Whoever is not ready to wash himself with the unseen water, then let him not come. This means that you must be faithful to your husband or wife. You must not sleep together without marriage. Do not steal or lie. You will follow the divine commands and then you can really possess the divine, godly soul. You will be granted success and prosperity in everything you do. At that station He will have no barriers between Him and the people. Know that the reconciliation with your Lord can happen within a twinkle of an eye. Are you ready? Allāh will make you a true healer.

I want to tell you something to help you to move fast and arrive at your Lord. Know that the human self has an animal self and a blaming self. It is all one soul. It just has stations or levels. This repentance that you are doing now has conditions that must be met before it is granted.

Special Tawba Practice[28]

The first condition is to remember Allāh.

1. On the next Thursday, Sunday and Thursday nights, seek forgiveness by saying:

   Astaghfiru-llāh al-'aḍhīm wa atūbu ilayh

   3000 times

   Say this 3000 times, and do this three times (i.e. starting on the next Thursday or Sunday, whichever is sooner, and doing it two more nights on the next Thursday or Sunday.)

2. Then say:

   Lā 'ilāha 'illa-llāh

   3000 times

Recite this holy name 3000 times for the next three holy nights of Sunday, Thursday and Sunday.

3. Conclude by saying:

   allāhumma ṣalli 'alā sayyidinā Muḥammadin wa ālihi wa sallam

   3000 times

   Recite this holy prayer on Thursday, Sunday and Thursday evenings. This will purify and wash you from your past sins.

Allāh sends the Qur'ān in the Arabic language and the language of the Garden is in the Arabic language. Therefore you must say it in Arabic.

---

[28] You must take a special promise with Sidi in order to do this practice; and you must do this practice fully before doing the Special Purification practice revealed in the next teaching. Contact the Shadhiliyya Sufi Center for more detailed information available about this practice.

You have to be certain with this promise. It is not only for the students, it is for the teachers as well. It is for everyone here. I am only the slave of Allāh and I do not bring this of myself. I only ask Allāh to accept it from you.

Please put your hand in my hand and do not delay. Do not wait my sons and daughters. Put your hands on the back of your brothers and sisters and give me your promise. My spirit will reach you by the praise of Allāh. My eyes will see you by the praise of Allāh and my breath will reach you by the praise of Allāh. I came to you in this human form and know that I am nothing. However within me is everything. His hand is above my hand. Know that you are giving the promise to Allāh.

Sidi gives the promise.

Annihilate in Allāh, Most High, and in the Guide

Prayer Practice to Purify the Body, Heart, Soul, Spirit and Intellect

Lā ʾilāha ʾilla-llāāāāāāh, Lā ʾilāha ʾilla-llāāāāāh, Lā ʾilāha ʾilla-llāāāāāh
Muḥammad rasūlu-llāh, Ibrāhīm rasūlu-llāh, Mūsā rasūlu-llāh,
ʿĪsā rasūlu-llāh ʿalayhim ṣalātu-llāh.

Allāhumma anta-s-salām wa minka-s-salām
wa ilayka ya'ūdu-s-salām
tabārakta rabbanā
ya dha-l-jalāli wa-l-'ikrām

As-salāmu ʿalaykum wa raḥmatu-llāh wa bārakatuhu.

Praise be to Allāh and may the peace and blessings of Allāh be upon His Messenger and all the other prophets, and all of the guides, may Allāh be pleased with all of them. May peace and blessings be upon the spiritual guides, the gnostics and the loyal allies of Allāh—those who purified their hearts and cleaned themselves and purified their souls and intellects and offered all of the outer for direct knowledge of Allāh as an offering and sacrifice for Allāh.

Those are the ones who are carrying the message of unity, peace, beauty and excellent perfection. They carry the message of love and beauty and peace and justice for all, for everyone, without discrimination. They know only love and beauty for everyone. They have annihilated their lives and devoted them to Allāh and to the service of humanity. Allāh chose them and specialized them to carry the message of the prophets, to continue to carry that message and to die for it so that their lives become a sacrifice for all of those who are suffering on the earth. Their lives are devoted to serving sick people. They have devoted themselves to being healers of those who are in pain across the earth, whether this pain is coming from sickness in the bodies or from psychological disease or from a spiritual disease.

Peace be upon you my beloveds. Ladies and men and children and elders, I greet you with the tongue of godly love and of witnessing the divine things. It is a blessed day in which the angels are attending now and praying for the faithful. The angels are praying for those who rid themselves of their evil souls and animal souls and animal hearts. Those who came sincerely and faithfully, fully toward Allāh, I ask Allāh to grant you the way of the Truth, the way of unity, the way of all the prophets and messengers and saints. He is the One Who Responds to Prayer and Answers it.

Today I will continue searching more deeply into the diseases of the heart and the spirit and the intellect, so that I complete with you the full journey, the journey of healing, and explain to you how one can annihilate in his spiritual guide and in his brother and sister. Those who are walking on the Ṣūfī path, I will explain how to destroy the barriers between you and the others, and how to rid yourselves of the garments of hate and anger and jealousy, and how you can destroy the degrees and stations that you think you attained.

To Allāh there are no stations or levels or states. There is only one station with Allāh, which is the station of full unity. In that realm, there is no boss, and there is no teacher and student. We all become equally the children of Allāh. There is no young or old. We are equal. Allāh created us in one degree, from one soul, one heart. He says in the Qur'ān:

> He created you from a single soul. (Qur'ān 7:189)

He created you from one soul, not from multiple souls, not from a black soul or a yellow soul or a white soul. No, it is one and the same soul, a godly soul, a faithful, pure, beautiful and majestic soul. It is a soul that enjoys peace and love and mercy and justice for all. I ask Allāh to make me one of those in that station.

As the Prophet, ʿalayhi as-salātu as-salām, said:

> Deeds are judged by their intention,
> and everyone who intends something
> will have what he intended. (Ḥadīth)

The one who emigrates for the sake of having a woman or earning wealth, will get that. But the one whose pilgrimage is toward Allāh and who travels toward Allāh will get what he intends. So, look at your heart deeply and purify your intention and then actualize it. Follow his true laws, the s̲harīʿa, and follow the way of the Truth and Reality, and at that point you will come into the highest Garden, a garden that is full of meaning and beauty and love and mercy.

I would like to tell you a story about our Prophet, ʿalayhi as-salātu as-salām, because of the mention of this beautiful daughter (Ibrāhīm Jaffe's daughter had been on the stage with him and he asked Sidi for permission).

Story of the Prophet Staying in Prostration for His Grandsons' Comfort

The Prophet, ʿalayhi as-salātu as-salām, was leading the magẖrib prayer and there were thousands of people praying behind him. He is the leader of guidance, the imām al-ḥuda, the leader of mercy, the leader of justice, the leader of humanity, of the humane way. Many people do not know him; they lie about him and they accuse him with false accusations.

He started his prayer and when he prostrated, his two grandchildren, Ḥasan and Ḥusayn, who were very young at that time, one of them was two and a half, and the other was about four years old. So when the Prophet, ʿalayhi as-salātu as-salām, prostrated, they both climbed on his back, one on his shoulder and one on his back. The Prophet, ʿalayhi as-salātu as-salām, continued his prostration as they continued to play on his back because they were enjoying it, and he stayed like that for not less than half an hour.

He never got annoyed with them. He never bothered them or said, "Get off my back." He just let them satisfy their desire to play until they went away on their own, and then he continued the prayer. The people continued to prostrate along with him because he was the imām, the leader. When he said, "Allāhu akbar," people stood up and continued their prayer.

After the prayer, one of the them asked, "Did Allāh order you to prostrate longer this time or what happened?" He said, "No, He did not say it should be longer but my two grandchildren were riding on my back and I did not want to annoy them. I wanted them to have their joy, to be happy, and when they had their satisfaction, then I stood up from my prostration."

That is our teacher. That is the true teacher of how to become humble toward everyone, including children. It is not of the ethics of any prophet or spiritual guide to be annoyed with children or yell at them or be arrogant. They are usually humble with the young and respectful to the old. The mercy always comes, but you do not know to whom it is coming, so you must humble yourself to everyone and respect everyone. Because the Prophet, ʿalayhi as-salātu as-salām, once said:

> It is because of nursing babies
> and cattle grazing
> and elderly men prostrating themselves to Allāh,
> that Allāh sometimes withholds His wrath from people.
> (Ḥadīth̲)

Why? Because those people are in complete unity and purity. They do not know corruption, they do not know envy, they only know love and mercy. These cattle even, they have no intellect, but they do understand in their own language about Allāh and what Allāh teaches them.

It is because of the righteous and pious men and women who are carrying the message of love and mercy and justice and peace for everyone, and because of their prayers for everyone, it is because of that, that Allāh protects the people and withholds His wrath and punishment to come to the people who are unconscious and spreading corruption on the earth. So, to be merciful to the children is one of the ethics of the Prophet. It is from the godly, lofty ethics because those gnostics know only love in their hearts. Allāh and His Messenger want us to be like that—loving, sincere and truthful and respectful with everyone.

Now we will start talking to our children who gave the promise to make their hearts human hearts, to make their bodies human bodies and to purify them. Those who took that promise and wish to preserve and protect that promise, we continue to speak to them and by the permission of Allāh, after taking this promise the bodies that have diseases are healed and selves that have diseases are healed and spirits that have diseases are healed.

Today I speak with you about the animal soul that is sick and full of desires and pollution and dirt, like envy and hate and anger and jealousy. These souls are the houses of the s̲hayāṭīn, the devils, because these souls are dirty and are carrying all types of sicknesses and diseases and so they merge with the s̲hayāṭīn. How can a soul like that claim that it is capable of healing? We must teach everyone how his soul becomes a true humane soul, the soul of a human being, not the soul from the animal realm, a soul that is full of dirt and desires and in rebellion and disobedience to Allāh.

The characteristic of this type of soul, the animal soul, is to betray, to deceive, to spread corruption across the earth and to cheat on people. But Allāh says in the Qur'ān that Allāh will guide the one who comes to Him wholeheartedly with a pure soul and full heart. Because as Prophet Ibrāhīm said:

> I will emigrate for the sake of my Lord. (Qur'ān 29:26)
> It is He Who guides me (Qur'ān 26:78)

The human being has two types of intellect, a black animal intellect and a white, spiritual, godly intellect. Those two intellects are the most important thing, and the one who unifies with Allāh and wants to be a spiritual healer, must recognize those two intellects and be able to discern between them and have the white intellect.

Because how can his hand be godly and be healing if he is carrying an animal hand, an animal soul and intellect? How can his tongue speak the truth if he is an animal human? How can his eyes become godly if they are still full of desires and anger and envy? He must rid himself of and remove these animal qualities from himself so that his soul becomes a true human soul, a humane soul.

At that point, Allāh becomes his eyes by which he sees, his ears by which he hears, the tongue by which he speaks, the hands by which he deals and the feet by which he walks. He becomes totally a slave and servant of Allāh, a godly human being. When he rids himself of these animal qualities and gives everything back to Allāh, then Allāh fulfills his needs.

We must do as Maryam's mother did, may Allāh be pleased with her. She said, "Whatever is in my womb, I dedicate to You, Allāh. I devote it to You." And then she gave birth to Maryam. In the Qur'ān, Allāh says:

> Say: "The spirit is from the command of my Lord."
> (Qur'ān 17:85)

That means there are no games in it, there is no lying. No one can say, "I can see your spirit," or, "I know what is within you." That would be a lie, because the spirit is something divine. The spirit is a divine, godly secret that was given to you, and the spirit is the source of the life that Allāh has given you.

So the spirit can become a desiring soul or animal soul or materialistic soul but if your spirit preserves the qualities of Allāh and adorns itself with the lofty ethics of Allāh and devotes itself and everything to Allāh, then it is a godly spirit. So you must first actualize your annihilation in Allāh.

How do you do that? By surrendering and following every godly command and by avoiding every selfish and egoistic desire and animal quality. Your pilgrimage and traveling should be only toward Allāh, and you must absolutely submit yourself to Allāh and surrender to Him and to His messengers and to the teachings of the messengers of Allāh. Allāh says in the Qur'ān, on the tongue of His Prophet:

> If you truly love Allāh, then follow me. (Qur'ān 3:31)

Follow the Messenger of Allāh who is the leader of guidance, imām al-ḥuda.

So, the spiritual guide, the true leader, annihilates in the spirit of the Prophet, 'alayhi as-salātu as-salām, and any seeker's goal should be to annihilate in his spiritual guide so he can annihilate in the Prophet and then in Allāh. If he annihilates in his spiritual guide then he will have this fire that can burn the jinn and the devils and leave no space of evil. Because Allāh says in the Qur'ān to the s̱hayṭān:

> Certainly, you will have no authority over My slaves,
> except those who follow you of the astray ones. (Qur'ān 15:42)

So anyone who claims that he is so big and says, "I know; I do; I see; I heal," do not believe him unless his hand is fully in obedience to Allāh and you see that he is in complete surrender to the way of Allāh and fulfilling all the godly commands and all the worshiping rituals and all the spiritual practices. He cannot be envious or jealous. And if you see that when he serves he does not say, "Oh I served, I did that and I did this." If he has achieved that, then he is truly annihilated in Allāh and he becomes a true healer because his spirit becomes a godly light.

The prophet, 'alayhi as-salātu as-salām, said to one of his companions:

> Oh Jabbar, the first thing that Allāh created
> was the light of your Prophet. (Ḥadīth)

That light was put into Ādam. Who is Ādam? The human being. Allāh put that light within the human being in his purity and in his essence; He put it within him, within that spirit. All people are the children of Ādam. Some of them preserve the secret of Allāh—the essence that is given to him—and he keeps himself pure, so he will have sound intellect and white pure intellect and become the beloved to Allāh and Allāh's lover. So we must wash our souls from all the egoistic qualities, the selfish qualities, and be in Allāh's presence.

Throw yourself into the presence of Allāh. How can we throw ourselves into the presence of Allāh? It is by annihilating ourselves and getting consumed in Allāh. How? By getting consumed in the spiritual guide, the leader of guidance. If we do that, then we annihilate into the Prophet of unity, the Messenger of Allāh. Then you annihilate from everything, except Allāh. Are you not a divine reflection? Are you not an image of Allāh? So you must rid yourself of any other—the animal qualities, the qualities of the lower realm, the dirt and the pollution. Sweep it away and become free. When the spirit becomes totally light, pure light that has no darkness whatsoever, then it becomes a godly reflection.

I say the whole universe is light because I see only the Real manifesting through it. Did He manifest through it? Yes, of course He did through His name aḏẖ-Ḏẖāhir, the Manifest. Within all of these manifestations and pictures and forms there is His Light within, the essence is in it. So, the one who rids himself of all the outer pictures and surrenders to Allāh's commands and is polite with all of Allāh's creation, annihilates in that essence, in that light.

He must never boast about himself or belittle others or humiliate others. You cannot think of yourself as better than others. Allāh refuses that, that you become arrogant. He does not accept that. He wants you to become humble. He says in the Qur'ān that you should not walk across the earth thinking highly of yourself. All of this arrogance and conceit is abhorrent to Allāh.

The one who possesses the godly spirit, has godly walking, godly behavior, godly hearing, godly seeing becomes a messenger of Allāh, carrying Allāh's message to the black intellect, to the animal soul, because it illuminates that black intellect and dispels the darkness.

How can one attain the white intellect? By surrendering to Allāh, ridding himself of all pictures and illusions and lower desires and animal qualities. When that intellect controls the soul, then it becomes the godly spirit. But when the black intellect controls the dark soul, they start to spread corruption and destroy the lower realm, the physical realm, by inventing weapons of destruction because they use their intellect to destroy humanity; they use the black intellect. If they used the white intellect, they would not be destroying animals and trees and humans, they would not be doing that.

So, we must find that pure luminous light, that godly light within us, in our spirits, because that luminous light makes the spirit powerful and strong and s̱hayṭān cannot have any control over it. That is why it becomes a secret, because it is powerful and s̱hayṭān has no control over it. That is why Allāh says in the Qur'ān:

> Say: "The spirit is from the command of my Lord."
> (Qur'ān 17:85)

It has no limit and no boundaries, because there is nothing like unto Allāh. He is the All-Hearing, the All-Seeing, the Full of Knowledge. Allāh is the One Who has Power over everything. The heavens and the earth will be folded into His grasp on the Day of Judgment, the Day of Resurrection, and He has nothing unto Him. He is the One Who Has Full Knowledge. He is the All-Hearing.

He said:

> I have breathed into him from My spirit. (Qur'ān 15:29, 38:72)

That means you are only alive by Allāh, and when you pass away from this world to the other realm, it is by the command of Allāh. But understand you do not totally perish. Only the elements return to their origin and disappear from the human, but the human himself does not totally perish. This spirit returns to its original picture, which Allāh wants from him. So, He transforms him from the perishing realm to the eternal realm.

The faithful believer who has full goodness transforms to the other realm, to the Garden. This Garden has that which no ear has ever heard and no eye has ever seen and things that no one has ever even imagined.

It has rivers, and it has eternal provision and life without an end, eternal life, everlasting life. None knows it but he who has tasted it.

Allāh is not like those who have you do something for them and they say, "I will reward you later." No. Allāh gives you your reward right away. It is not one of His qualities to postpone His rewards and blessings to people. That is a quality of the greedy man, the animal soul who wants to say, "All right, I will pay you later."

But Allāh always gives what is good. He has always been giving. He does not give you a disease. He does not give you evil. He does not push you to do evil. It is by what your hand earned freely that you get what you get. So do not say, "Allāh brought that. Allāh pushed me into that. Allāh is the one who afflicted me with this." No, look at what your own hands did?

You say, "Oh my son is sick." Well, look at why your son is sick. Allāh wants to discipline you through that experience because it is what your own hands earned in life that brought that sickness to your son (Qur'ān 42:30). But the son is still pure and Allāh will reward that spirit. And if the man corrects himself then Allāh heals his son for him and gives him His pure help.

Do not ever think that Allāh is vengeful. No, Allāh is never vengeful; He just wants to discipline you, to train you, to teach you. He is the One Who Gave you your tongue after all. Did you say something to get it? Did you make some effort to get it or is it a blessing from Him? It is a trust He gave you and if He wants to take it back, it is His right, because it belongs to Him.

And if He takes the spirit of a child, He puts it in the loftiest garden so He never actually hurts the child. He never does what is evil. He always does what is good. Do not say, "It is not fair. Why is Allāh not sending me a beloved? Why did not he give me a child? Why this? Why that?" Allāh is Wise, so trust Him. Maybe He does not give to you because He knows you are not fully ready to receive that, and He knows.

He wants what is good for you. Maybe He does not want to give you a husband who will give you a hard time when you are not ready to actually accept the right one. So Allāh wants you to learn first until you are ready to have a good beloved who will treat you right. So do not listen to the foolish people and act like them.

Surrender yourself to Allāh. Trust Him and rely on Him. He is the One Who created us and He knows us better than we know ourselves. He is so kind toward us. Allāh never likes to imprison people. He is full of absolute beauty and love. He is full of pure goodness.

There is something else. How can we heal spiritual disease? Allāh said to us in all of the holy books and in the Qur'ān:

> If you love Allāh, then follow me
> and Allāh will bestow His love upon you (Qur'ān 3:31).

This means if you truly become the worshipful slave of Allāh and are eager to purify your soul, then follow the teachings of Allāh and His Messenger. Follow His law and purify yourself and your house. What if your house if full of dirt? Will you be able to live in it happily and comfortably? No, you cannot. You do not like to be living in a house full of dirt, so you will be sweeping it, and washing it. The same thing is true with your heart and spirit. What are the tools of cleaning them? It is not soap. It is not the physical tools, but it is something else.

The Prophet, ʿalayhi as-salātu as-salām, said:

> Cleansing is part of faith, of belief. (Ḥadīth)

That means that the human being always keeps himself pure because Allāh is the Beautiful and He loves beauty. He is the Perfect and He loves perfection and excellence. Allāh is the Loving and He loves the lovers. He is the Peace and He loves those who work for peace. He is the Just and He loves those who stand for justice. So, what is the tool by which we can clean our faults to be able to transform them from the animal level to the human level? How can we clean it from all the garbage and dirt that are seen and unseen?

I want to give you one secret; it is a deep secret. I was keeping it and I will only reveal it to my beloveds who are willing to carry the message and are ready. Are you ready to accept this trust? Allāh says in the Qur'ān:

> Truly, We did offer the trust
> to the heavens and the earth, and the mountains,
> but they declined to bear it and were afraid of it.
> But man bore it. (Qur'ān 33:72)

Who is that human? It is the human who is satisfied with the One Lord and with Muḥammad as the Messenger and slave of Allāh, and by the Ka'ba as the direction for prayer, and by the faithful believers as brothers and sisters; those who do not discriminate between the messengers like Mūsā (Moses), 'Īsā (Jesus), Muḥammad and Ibrāhīm (Abraham)—all of them. Those are the true lovers of Allāh, the beloveds of Allāh. If you are like that and ready to surrender to all Allāh's commands without any discrimination, then I will give you a secret, but know that the message is the same as the message that came to all the prophets.

There are many who have carried this message. There are truthful and sincere men who carried this message. All the prophets and messengers carried it. All the saints carried it. If you want to wipe off your souls and wash them and return them to be as spirits of the children in the presence of Allāh, who are sitting around the godly table of Allāh that Allāh sent down.

Do you want to sit at the same table that Allāh sent down to 'Īsā, 'alayhi as-salātu as-salām, where his disciple once asked him, "Can you ask Allāh to send down for us a table of provision from heaven?" We are not talking about the provision that is like food and fruit, materialistic things like that. We are talking about a table of divine knowledge and meaning that Allāh is providing for us. It gives us the tool of how to wash our spirits and souls and hearts.

We are talking about the children who are living in the presence of Allāh. How can we annihilate everything and be only with Allāh along with those children around that divine table? How can we make ourselves a divine life? By completely following...

I want you to write what I will say. Open your hearts and spirits and rid your intellect from every thought except the thought of Allāh, so that you can become the godly slave and servant of Allāh, as He wants you to be...

Practice to Purify the Body, Heart, Soul, Spirit and Intellect

I am giving you a spiritual prayer that you should do after ʿIshā.[29] Start on a Thursday night; begin it on any Thursday night that is convenient for you.

1. Pray two rakʿāh. During the prayer fully direct yourself toward Allāh with the intention, "Please Allāh, purify me, my body, my soul, my heart, my spirit, and my intellect."

2. Recite the following prayer 1,000 times, preferably in Arabic.

Yā Allāh,	Oh Allāh,
Allāhumm-j-ʿal fī badanī nūra(n)	please Allah put light in my body
wa fī nafsī nūra(n)	and light in my soul
wa fī qalbī nūra(n)	and light in my heart
wa fī rūḥī nūra(n)	and light in my spirit
wa fī ʿaqlī nūra(n)	and light in my intelect
wa-j-ʿal min amāmī nūra(n)	and put in front of me light
wa min k̲halfī nūra(n)	and behind me light
wa miñ fawqī nūra(n)	and above me light
wa miñ taḥta aqdāmī nūra(n)	and underneath my feet light
wa ʿan yamīnī nūra(n)	and light on my right side
wa ʿan yasāri nūra(n)	and light on my left side

   Note: recite the "n" at the end of the line if you are continuing on to the next line without pausing. If you are pausing, pronounce the last word of the line as "nurā."

3. Bring Sidi's spirit into your consciousness, and also the Prophet Muḥammad's spirit (which brings in the spirits of all the prophets). In this way enter into the Reality of Allāh.

4. Recite, "Yā Allāh" 1,000 times.

5. Then recite al-Fātiḥa once, asking Allāh to purify you from every blemish and to use you to serve in the way of the Truth.

6. Repeat this process (two rakāh, 1,000 recitations. al-Fātiḥa) on the next two consecutive nights.

7. Upon completing the process on the third night promise Allāh that you will fulfill your walking in the way of the truth.

8. Every month repeat this process, and by Allāh's permission you will annihilate; you will get consumed in Allāh and get purified.

---

[29] It is recommended that you take a special promise before doing this practice.

Through this process, you will purify your body, your heart, your soul, your spirit and your intellect. And if you continue to do this, you will actualize your annihilation in your spiritual guide, in the leader of your guidance. Nothing will separate you and Him. Nothing will serve as a barrier between you and Him. You must fully direct yourself toward Allāh and call upon the guide's spirit and it will rise to you. Then after that, the spirits of the prophets will also come to you when you call them and then the divine light will shower you and epiphanies will come directly toward you from Allāh. Allāh will come toward you from the realm of humanity to the divine realm.

So be straightforward and beware of sinning, beware of corrupting, beware of being arrogant, beware of envy, beware of boasting. Do not say "I." You have no "I." "I" belongs only to Allāh. He says in the Qur'ān, "I am Allāh" So if you want to ask, ask only Allāh. Do not ask any human. Ask directly, because Allāh says in the Qur'ān:

> And when My slaves ask you concerning Me,
> then [answer them], I am indeed near.
> I respond to prayers when they call upon Me. (Qur'ān 2:186)

And He says, "And let them respond to Me, as well." So what is the condition of responding to your prayer and supplication? You should respond to Allāh first, which means to obey Him, to obey His Messenger, for the one who is obeying the Messenger is obeying Allāh. Beware and do not think that Allāh can respond to your prayer before you are responding to the special guidance, the teachings, and following them, i.e., before you are following the teaching of the Messenger.

I came to you in this picture but I am talking to you by the tongue of the Truth, the tongue of Reality, the tongue of Allāh because I listen to Him and I obey. He says, "Obey Our commands. Obey Our commands because We will rend the veils from between Us..."

Did you listen? Did you hear what I said? Are you going to abide by this? Whoever is saying, "Yes," understand that this is the greatest covenant. Whoever wants to fulfill it, let him come. Whoever wants to turn back, he is free. This is a covenant and promise of Allāh to the young and old...

Nullify the Touch of the Shaytan or Jinn

Lā ʾilāha ʾilla-llāāāāāāh, Lā ʾilāha ʾilla-llāāāāāh, Lā ʾilāha ʾilla-llāāāāāh
Muḥammad rasūlu-llāh, Ibrāhīm rasūlu-llāh, Mūsā rasūlu-llāh,
ʿĪsā rasūlu-llāh ʿalayhim ṣalātu-llāh.

Allāhumma anta-s-salām wa minka-s-salām
wa ilayka ya'ūdu-s-salām
tabārakta rabbanā
ya dha-l-jalāli wa-l-'ikrām

As-salāmu ʿalaykum wa raḥmatu-llāh wa bārakatuhu.

Praise be to Allāh and may the peace and blessings of Allāh be upon our master guide and messenger Muḥammad and all the other prophets and messengers, our master guides. May the peace and blessings be upon the saints and gnostics and those who follow them and who carry the message of peace and love and beauty and perfection and majesty, those who carry the message of mercy and justice and pure goodness, those who are polite and humble, those who are carrying the subtle divinity who want to truly be and are satisfied to be the slave servants of Allāh, the worshippers of Allāh. Allāh says to Iblīs about them:

> Certainly, you will have no authority over My slaves,
> except those who follow you of the astray ones. (Qur'ān 15:42)

He says, "You do not have any control or power over My worshipful slaves. You only can affect those who are rebellious against Me and disobey Me and deviate from My way." He says that to the shayṭān, Iblīs. He is the one who disobeys Allāh and deviates from the Prophet of Allāh, and who keeps dwelling in the past that is passed away and keeps dwelling on the things that he did in the past and wants to bring all the difficulties that happened in his past into the present.

That is why I say, forget about your past, whatever you committed because you used to live in darkness. But Allāh bestowed upon you the gift and brought you to pure goodness and opened for you the door because He wants good for you and He wants you to be happy and well.

Why do you dwell in the past and say, "Oh such and such a brother did this to me and that happened in the past and I did this and that?" I know that many of the healers actually bring that to you and ask you, "Try to remember what happened in your past." But oh healer, the past is gone. Can you return and change it for the person? It is one of the mistakes that many of the ignorant healers fall into. Allāh says, do not dwell on the past; do not remember the past. He says:

> The one who comes with repentance and a full heart,
> I will transform their bad deeds into good deeds
> and rectify their deeds and his affairs. (Qur'ān 5:39)

So if someone did something wrong to you, your brother or sister abused you, it is gone. Why do you keep dwelling on it and remembering it? Why, as a healer, do you make people remember the suffering and pain and trivial things? Allāh did not command us to do this. Is this part of the healing or part of the disease? It is part of the sickness to live in the past. These are the goods of Sẖayṭān he is selling to you, to revive your anger and suffering and hate. Can you bring someone who has passed away back to life? You cannot change the past either.

It is a great mistake to keep dwelling in the past. If someone sick comes to you, tell him, "be the son or daughter of your moment." Do not dwell in the past.

Sidi speaking in English: The past, you cannot return to it again. It is gone. Why do you give lies? Do not lie. This is jinns. They like to play games. They would like to destroy everything inside of him.

This is not permissible. This is not healing. Healing is to tell him and explain to him, be the son of your moment, of the present. You cannot return an hour that is past. An hour ago, you cannot return it now; it is gone; it is over; it is finished. Give him new hope, a new creation, a new beginning. Give him new life. Give him hope. Give him hope, full of love, full of peace. Give him a chance or an opportunity to revive his life and to walk forward. Do not kill him. Do not submit him to Iblīs, the evil one.

Why do you open the door of Iblīs to him? Why do you open the door of evil? You are evil if you do so. You are the sick one, in fact, if you do that to someone. The true healing is to make him forget his disease, to help him forget the past, the abuse that is done to him by the evil one, to open the door to him for hope, and to achieve his fulfillment. Start healing him like that. Never tell someone there is a jinn inside him. Never! You are a madman if you tell someone that. Who told you there is a jinn or s̲hayṭān inside him or this or that. Allāh says, "For the faithful believer, s̲hayṭān has no control over him." I give you what is enough for you. I give you the way to destroy all the jinn and s̲hayāṭīn.

A month ago I brought to you a healing to destroy all the jinn and evil ones. And we did try this medicine and we destroyed a lot of evil jinn and s̲hayāṭīn and by Allāh's permission we will continue to do so. These days, by the favor of Allāh, we helped you already and we saved you from the evil soul and from the evil heart and from the evil spirit and from the evil intellect and it is over.

That is why I warn all of my children, do not go to the old, evil, mistaken techniques of healing others by making people dwell in the past. Tell everyone, "I see your beauty, how you are full of beauty and health." Give him mercy and hope and do not terrify him. Do not believe the liars and those who claim that they know but they do not know. Allāh knows that they do not know.

That is why we explained everything you may need to heal in the book. We explained herbal remedies that go back thousands of years and have been tried and we put a strategic divine plan against all the evil ones, the s̲hayāṭīn, that can possess and affect the poor people and the miserable ones. We also put remedies to discharge the effects of magic. We have the ability, by Allāh's favor, to provide you with the weapons to protect yourselves against those s̲hayāṭīn and to save the patients that come for your help from their evil ways. Through applying the remedies you can save your children and the whole of humanity from the effects of the evil one.

After the reading, we will explain how you can destroy the s̲hayāṭīn who can possess and effect the people who are miserable and are suffering. I want you to know that the evil ones can inflict diseases, like cancer, within humans, because they make them lose hope and they feel sick. With Allāh's permission, we will explain that. The evil ones can breathe into the human liver or kidney or brain and cause diseases and affect him through the evil ones and through the magicians, like black magic.

Once, Dr. Jaffe sent someone to me, he was a Palestinian man and that man called me while I was in Jerusalem and his wife talked to me. She said, "My husband is a young man, he is strong, he is healthy, he is good and he is a business man. But his mother and his sister, through going to a magician and evil one, gave him something to drink that made him lose his capacity for comprehension and his health deteriorated and he stopped... Ibrāhīm, can you describe his state when you met him?

Ibrāhīm: This was a very beautiful man, when you looked at him he was so beautiful, you could not believe it, but he had lost his mind. He had actually become, in western diagnosis, psychotic, and he came to us looking for healing from his psychosis. He was not thinking clearly; his thoughts ran all over the place; he was in illusion; he was making things up; there was nothing clear in his mind.

Sidi through Amany again: That person, I told him and I promised his wife, that if it was decreed for me that I would come to America that I would meet him and I would come to him and I would destroy that magic that affected him. I told him that s̲hayṭān possessed him. I am the enemy of the evil jinn and the s̲hayāṭīn. That will be, I promised her. When I arrived in this country, after two weeks, he came accompanied by two young men. Many of my beloved children like Ibrāhīm and Ṣāliḥ saw him and he was crying.

I looked at his eyes and I saw that something was given to him in a drink from two females who actually were helped by a cunning magician. It was a cunning, dirty, magic that affected the body and prevented the person from having sound comprehension, so that even walking had become difficult for him. If he sat down, he couldn't stand up, he actually needed help to stand and walk.

He was accompanied by two young men so I told one of them, "Write what I tell you." And I prescribed for him the healing which you will find in this book. But this medicine does not work until I give permission for it to work. It does not work until I give the permission to any of my beloved healers to use it. Why? Because I worry that someone will misuse it and use it in the wrong way, for an evil purpose. I care to give it to my beloveds, but in the right way. So, if someone tries to practice it without my permission, it will not work.

This is why I try to prescribe the medicine for these effects that can happen to a person. But I give you the chance to give me your promise, the promise of the body, the promise of the heart, the promise of the soul, the promise of the spirit and the promise of the intellect, and you did give me your pledge. You promised to be truthful and faithful and sincere, that is why I give you my permission to apply it, and by Allāh's permission, healing will happen through your hands. But watch Allāh, because He is watching you through your work of healing. Let your heart be merciful, loving, be full of sincerity and faith and truthfulness and then apply it in the way I explained to you.

I put in this book, about eighty-nine remedies for the body, for the soul. I also explained how to protect the body against diseases and how to heal diseases when they happen. I also put in how to get rid of insects. I even put that there, in a natural way. Even the rats, I did not forget about them and the cockroaches and all of that. Everything that can cause harm to people, the flies, the mosquitoes, I did not forget about it, because it is not their place to live in your house. They need to go live in the forest, in their natural habitat.

I write this because I care about you. You are a human being and I care about you, and I explained how you could make these remedies. I explained how you could do these remedies with the herbs with precise measurements. Every remedy is described and its measurement is mentioned in an accurate and precise way—the weight of every herb used and how to use it in which way. I explained it.

So, it is a must that you be honest, truthful, faithful and rid yourself of greed. Heal people for the love of Allāh, for the sake of Allāh. I do not tell you though, to waste your effort and time. No, take your reward, you can take a compensation for what you do for people, but be gentle, merciful, merciful to yourself and others, because Allāh does not like oppression and does not like anyone to violate the right of another.

Ṣāliḥ says: Tell them what you did to my greedy raccoon Sidi.

A raccoon occupied Ṣāliḥ's house. Every day he came to his kitchen and ate Ṣāliḥ's food. Eight times, he did that. It was not enough for the raccoon to do that. He even went to his bed and took a nap there.

Ṣāliḥ said, "What can we do with the raccoon, Sidi?"

I said, "It is very simple. It is a simple remedy. I do not want to kill an animal, but I will write a warning for him and a second warning and a third. If he returns to do the same thing after that, there is no choice then."

He left me no choice and Allāh will not question me, because Allāh does not want even animals to violate the rights of others. So we put the warning and the raccoon did not listen to the warning. He ate the sandwich that contained some medicine. He went away for two days and came back with two more raccoons with him because they love Ṣāliḥ.

So, I agreed with Ṣāliḥ now, they are really enemies now and we have to deal strongly with them, so we put a concentrated herbal medicine for them and after three days they were done. We found one dead and the others never came back. So I said, "Ṣāliḥ, we do not want to hurt anyone, unless they hurt us."

These insects and animals can cause diseases. That is why we deal with them strongly. If rats, for example, stay in the houses, they can cause serious disease for the people. Cockroaches can cause skin disease. That is why we rid our houses of them, and that is why I explained about a remedy for every insect,. He must go or lose his life. I give him a warning. Go and do not come again to harm us, otherwise, you will lose your life. Some of them listen to the warning and go away and do not come back. But if he is stubborn, then he loses his life by his own actions. This is how we were commanded to deal with these creatures.

I now ask Ṣāliḥ to read the introduction that came to our Messenger and Prophet. We took this from them. It explains that the human is created out of dust. Elements that are contained in the dust are also in the human body. As I explained before, the human body has the four elements: water, fire, air, and dust and also everything that exists in the earth around us. The air exists. The fire exists and the dust and the water too.

The Introduction from *Heal Yourself: There is Medicine for Every Illness* is read from the beginning to end.

I will start with you, so pay attention to what I will say. Many people who are spreading corruption across the earth, who are the students of Iblīs and his children and learned magic from him and from the rebellious jinn, who are in disobedience to Allāh and who disobeyed the messengers like Sulayman (Solomon) and Dāwūd (David) and Muḥammad and Mūsā

(Moses) and ʿĪsā (Jesus) and all the prophets, are the enemies of humanity. Some of them are males and some are females. Some of them are truly miserable and evil and they do associate and befriend some of the evil magicians and humans. But Allāh taught our prophets and messengers how to stop them within the limits and how to nullify the effect of their magic through words that come from Him, His glorious words. He taught us how to use them and how to repeat them. It is through the tongues of His prophets and messengers that we are taught to do so.

Recite Sūra Quraysh (106). This noble sūra in the Qurʾān can cure the one who is afflicted by the touch of the s̲hayṭān or jinn. Do you know this sūra? It is in the Qurʾān. How can we apply this ʾayāh to cure or nullify the effect of the touch of the jinn?

Nullification of the Touch of the S̲hayṭān or Jinn

1. Do ablution and pray two rakāh of prayer.

2. Put your hand on the afflicted one and recite Sūra Quraysh̲ seven times while putting your hand on his head from the right side.

Sūratu Quraysh̲ (106)
bismi-llāhi-r-raḥmāni-r-raḥīm

li-ʾīlāfi quraysh̲ (in)
ʾīlāfihim riḥlata-sh̲-sh̲itāāʾi wa-ṣ-ṣayf
fa-l-yaʿbudū rabba hādh̲a-l-bayt (i)
ʾal-l-ladh̲ī ʾaṭāʿamahum-miñ jūʿiñw-wa ʾāmanahum-min kh̲awf

3. After that, what should you do? Write it with saffron ink after you mix the saffron with rose water and make an ink out of it. Write the sūra with that ink. Write it on a white, clay pot so you can see the ink. After the ink dries, put pure water on it and mix it and the ink will melt into that water.

4. Then give that water to the patient, the afflicted one, and let him drink it.

5. Repeat this process for a whole week, once a day.

By the permission and help of Allāh, the person will be healed and cured of that effect. Do you understand what I said or do you want me to repeat it?

Where did such diseases come from—diseases of the heart, of the chest, or the stomach and the liver? From where do these diseases come? Let me explain. They come from meat that is not natural, that is the first cause, eating meat from animals that are fed with unnatural stuff full of chemicals. These chemicals cause diseases in the body because these animals did not grow the natural way in a natural climate and habitat as Allāh wanted it to be, so eating these animals causes these diseases.

The heart disease comes from where? The heart is a very important organ in the body, isn't it true? Obesity causes this. Eating more than you should can cause this heart disease, because it can cause the accumulation of cholesterol and also, adding to it, the eating of the unnatural meat and the food that is full of chemicals, because such a person does not listen to the Prophet's recommendation, that the worst vessel to fill to its fullness is the human stomach. But if he must eat, let him fill one third with food, one third with drink, and leave one third for air.

The arteries that come from the heart and feed the body and the organs, how many are there? There are seventeen thousand arteries, and some of them are known and some of them are very subtle, tiny, and the physician knows about them. After purifying the blood, and the blood could be mixed with cholesterol and chemicals as we explained, and then it goes to the heart to purify it and that can cause blockages in the heart, and so the human can actually have a heart attack and die.

There are so many arteries that two could stop working while others are still working and people can have open-heart surgeries and all of these things which are serious surgeries. The people go through that, but why? Because of what their own hands earned (Qur'ān 42:30), by listening to the whispers of s̲hayṭān, the cunning ways of s̲hayṭān and listening to the desires which s̲hayṭān strikes within people.

Allāh is Truthful. He said, say, "I seek refuge in Allāh, rabbi-n-nās." You know the meaning of this sūra. He taught you how to seek refuge and protection from the whispers of the s̲hayṭān and his temptations. I told you the story about my friend when once we went as guests to our master guide. I saw this with my own eyes. So, that guy started to eat and the host, as usual, said, "Please take more." So whenever the host said that, my friend took more and more and he kept eating. He filled his stomach with food, and there was no room for drink or air.

Our master guide kept laughing. I said, "Why are you laughing?"

He said, "You will see what will happen to him. He will learn a great lesson."

I ate only about three pieces of bread with something and that was enough. So, I went on my way back with my friend. We were riding our donkeys and my friend was unable to walk or even to ride on the donkey because he started to throw up and he fell on the ground.

He said, "What happened to me?"

I said, "What happened to you happened because you are a madman. I will show you how you are a madman."

We went to the well and I put the donkey's head in to get something to drink.

I said, "Oh please donkey, please take more for my sake."

But the donkey turned his head away and would not drink more than what would satisfy him even though I kept trying.

So I said to my friend, 'Now I know your donkey is more intelligent than you."

He said, "You speak the truth."

He said, "I will not teach him, that is why I did that."

Many here know this is the truth. They know the right way, but still, they eat more than the donkey would eat. So, have mercy upon yourself and be careful.

However, we must understand first, how to protect ourselves from diseases before they happen. The causes of most of the diseases are feeding on things that are unnatural. Even fish, they are raised in artificial farms or lakes and they give them chemicals and that is why a lot of diseases are spreading.

Cure for Diseases from Listening to the Sẖayṭān

If those diseases afflict a person because of the whisper of sẖayāṭīn or jinn, then you can apply a ruqya to heal him.

1. Write ʾayātu-l-kursi three times with the saffron and rosewater ink, in the same way, in the white clay pot.
2. Again, you add pure water until the ink dissolves into it,
3. Then give the water to the patient to drink. He must drink it first thing in the morning before he eats any breakfast.
4. Also, the healer can recite al-Fātiḥa seven times over pure water, then give it to the patient daily before breakfast.

By Allāh's permission, the person will be healed and benefit from this remedy.

I explained in detail in the book, but I want to mention to you the successful remedy of those who are afflicted by magic in their head or in their bodies, just as that man we mentioned earlier, was affected. I mentioned here, this remedy that can protect the human body and soul and the human heart and the human intellect. It can protect him from the touch of the sẖayṭān and jinn and magic.

You can actually take this remedy before you even get afflicted, as a protection. You can give it to your children, your loved ones, even before the effect appears on them, because the protection will affect the sẖayāṭīn's ability to affect them with their magic and whispers. This remedy will protect your body to be a true human body and protect your soul and protect your intellect to be truly human, not to be like the animal, but to be truly human.

All of you know how to recite al-Fātiḥa. You must first bring twenty liters of pure water, best if you can get it from a running source. Why should it be running? Why not from a pond, for example, that is stagnant and still? Because when there is a current and it is running, it gets rid of the viruses and insects. The viruses and germs and insects stay in stagnant water that is not running. Running water will always be clear and pure. So there is wisdom in collecting the water from a running source because it will be devoid of germs and viruses and microbes.

Purifying Water to Heal the Touch of the s̲hayṭān or jinn

1. Bring twenty liters of pure water from a pure source and put it in a clean container
2. Recite Sūrat al-Fātiḥa upon this water seventy times.
3. Recite ʾAyāt al-Kursī seventy times.
4. Recite Sūra al-Ik̲hlāṣ seventy times.
5. Recite Sūra al-Falāq seventy times.
6. Recite Sūra an-Nās seventy times.
7. Have your loved ones or ill ones drink from it on an empty stomach before breakfast.
8. See below for directions on bathing in this water.

So, now we have prepared these twenty liters of pure water and recited these sūras seventy times. You must recite all of these sūras over the water and drink from this water and let your children and loved ones drink from it and all the people whom you care for. Drink from it.

Or if there is someone sick and afflicted by the touch of s̲hayāṭīn or jinn, then have them drink from this water after you have recited from the Qurʾān in the way we have described.

But this drinking must be before the patient takes any breakfast. So, after the one who is afflicted by disease or touch of s̲hayṭān or magic, after he drinks it, take the rest of the water and in a pure place, let the patient take a bath in this water seven times.

When I say a bath, it does not mean you have to pour on him the twenty liters, but you can bring a piece of cloth and you soak it in the water and then you wipe his whole body and the place must be pure, not a dirty place. Not in the bathroom, no, in a pure place, like a room that is clean and purified and there is no dirt in it. Repeat this process twice.

The whole process should be repeated twice and this will not leave a trace of any jinn or s̲hayāṭīn, even if there are one thousand jinn which have affected the person, they will be destroyed and killed. Whatever their number is, they will be destroyed. And whenever you repeat it, you will kill more of them. Do not repeat it more than once on same day, but day after day or on two successive Fridays.

I mentioned to you before, oh healers, to shelter yourselves from the enemies of humanity, from the s̲hayāṭīn and the evil jinn. So shelter yourself from the s̲hayāṭīn of humanity, the evil humans and the evil jinn and preserve your bodies to be like human bodies, not like animal bodies.

Shelter yourself and do not listen to the animal soul, but make your soul stay human. Let your hearts be sheltered and be protected from being animal hearts. Be a human heart. Do not let your spirits be animal spirits, but preserve them and protect them to be true human spirits and protect your intellects from being black, animal intellects. Purify them, clean them, so they can become white, godly, intellects. That is why I made these remedies for you and I prescribed to you.

Before I came here, I wrote the protection papers for you. It is a new protection, not like the protection you took before; it is a new protection prayer, written on these papers. Whoever wants to protect his body, his heart, his soul, his intellect, let him come now because I open the door for you to come and take this protection. I advise you to make these remedies for yourself first, to protect you from the jinn and the s̲hayāṭīn, then to give it to your loved ones, so they can be protected too.

Come and take your share so your intellect and spirit and soul and body can be protected so that you can become strong and powerful and effective in healing others and you can destroy any evil jinn and defeat any human evil. I ask Allāh to protect you.

He gives the promise.

After the promise: The words of Allāh never end. If all the trees were pens and all the oceans were ink, they would vanish before the words of Allāh ended (Qur'ān 18:109). The oceans of the world can dry, but the words of Allāh can never end.

Is There Any Life but Rabia's?
"How Rābiʿa Loved Her Lord"
from *The Secret of the Love of God*

Lā ʾilāha ʾilla-llāāāāāāh, Lā ʾilāha ʾilla-llāāāāāh, Lā ʾilāha ʾilla-llāāāāāh
Muḥammad rasūlu-llāh, Ibrāhīm rasūlu-llāh, Mūsā rasūlu-llāh,
ʿĪsā rasūlu-llāh ʿalayhim ṣalātu-llāh.

Allāhumma anta-s-salām wa minka-s-salām
wa ilayka ya'ūdu-s-salām
tabārakta rabbanā
ya dha-l-jalāli wa-l-'ikrām

As-salāmu ʿalaykum wa raḥmatu-llāh wa bārakatuhu.

It is important to use your beads now. I invite all my children to come and to be prepared. Bring your quiet intellects, hearts and spirits so that they may be present here. Allāh will bestow a lot of goodness upon your hearts this morning. I will start by an opening and a completion to purify the bodies, hearts, souls, spirits and intellects. I will purify your right and your left sides, above you, and what is underneath your feet. This purification will be with light and I will bestow upon you how to use this remedy of medicine to heal yourselves and to heal others by the permission of Allāh, most High, glory be to Him.

Whoever wants to receive this purification, let him stay. Whoever does not want this purification is free to leave. If you want to be present with Allāh, present with the spirits of the angels, the prophets, the messengers and the saints as well as be surrounded by the close angels, then stay.

Every person must have the intention to be fully present and fully prepared to carry this true message. It is pure goodness cannot be counted or measured. It is invaluable and it will purify. The invocation and supplication, which we will say, will purify us by the water of the unseen, the godly or divine water. When I start I want you to repeat what I am saying with full consciousness. The supplication may last for an hour or whatever Allāh wills. Let each human be present in full consciousness.

Leave everything from the lower realm behind. Empty your heart of everything and make your body and your heart a vessel, a locus for Allāh. Be conscious of everything around you, in your heart, on your right side, left side, above and below you. This invocation will not only benefit you but it will benefit all of your loved ones, your family, friends, your house, your neighbors and everyone you care for. This pure goodness will reach this life, your house, neighbors, and everyone you come across. Allāh will heal everyone and will heal their afflictions. It will protect whichever city you live in and it can expand to benefit all of humanity by Allāh's will and permission. It is not from me. I am only a poor slave and servant. My supplication is as Mūsā invoked his Lord before me.

Mūsā said, "Oh Allāh You have given me great bounty and riches but I am still your poor slave in need." The Prophet, ʿalayhi as-salātu as-salām, said that we are always in need of Allāh and Allāh is the Self-Sufficient and worthy of praise. Are you ready to offer everything to Allāh?

Oh generous One,
Oh tremendous, glorious and powerful One.
You have the generous names and qualities.
You are the Creator of the heavens and the earth.
You are the One Who Knows the secrets
of what is hidden and what is concealed.
You know that we are fully directing ourselves to You,
standing at Your door.
Please do not turn us away from Your door disappointed.

Oh Beloved, do not forsake us.
Our final abode is You and we are in need of You, most glorious.
Please purify our bodies, hearts and souls.

Please bestow upon us Your light
and purify and protect our hearts, souls, and intellect
by Your Light, oh Protector.
Please put light into our bodies, hearts, souls, spirits and intellect.
Put light in front of us, behind us,
on our right and left sides,
above us and underneath our feet.

Make us light.

We promise to be Your true worshippers
and to keep and fulfill our promise with You.

We are the poor and in need of You.
We promise to be sincere and truthful,
following what You give us and standing at Your door.

Please send peace across the earth.
Send mercy across the earth.
Protect Your children and Your creation.
Lift the suffering and the pain from them.
Heal them and send them love, mercy and beauty.
Let pure goodness spread into this lower realm.

Please protect this country
and all other countries across the world
by Your mercy and justice.

Bestow Your Light upon us and upon all Your people.

We promise to be truthful, faithful believers,
humble and surrendering to You.

We are accepting You as our Lord without partners.
You are our life.

Please make us steadfast and firm
and among the faithful believers.

Protect us from the suffering of the Hellfire.
Make us of the pious ones.

We praise You for what You give us.
You let us see Your light and we praise You for it.

Send Your peace and blessings for
Your prophets Muḥammad, Nūh, Yaqūb, Ibrāhīm and Mūsā
who spoke directly to You.

Recitation of al-Fātiḥa

This is a blessed morning. It is a morning of an opening for purifying the bodies, hearts, souls, spirits and intellects. It purifies what is above us, below us, in front of us, behind us, to our right and to our left and underneath us. At this time I would like to invite everyone to offer a sacrifice on behalf of his body, heart, soul, spirit and intellect. Also to offer a sacrifice for his children, parents, wealth, house, property and all of his loved ones. Give a sacrifice for people of the past so that they may live and walk in the light.

I ask Allāh to accept all of you and I bless all of you. Watch yourself, your children and care for everyone. I want you to be true healers and keep the trust. Through my weeping to Him, I ask Allāh to accept this invocation in order to accept you and make you true healers.

Oh Allāh I have conveyed the message
I have conveyed the message
I have conveyed the message
You are the best witness.
I bear witness that there is no god but Allāh
and Muḥammad is his prophet and messenger.
I bless you all.
As-salāmu ʿalaykum.

Ṣāliḥ is collecting the sacrifices for those who wanted to clean their bodies, hearts, souls and intellects. Give your sacrifice for your bodies, hearts, spirits, and souls. Give it with sincerity and from your heart and know that it will go to help the poor, the miserable and the suffering ones from the earth. Allāh is witnessing what you are doing. Āmīn.

This command to do this spiritual practice descended upon my heart this blessed morning. Stand and be polite with Allāh when you offer your sacrifice. The angels are here and they rejoice when they see you come and give your sacrifice in a polite and humble way.

Whenever you offer a sacrifice, angels are around you at once. It is a glorious, blessed day to Allāh and I want you to always remember it and praise Allāh for it. It is a feast, an ʿEid day. It celebrates your body, heart and soul. It is a feast of light. Many other people celebrate their own feast but we celebrate our Lord and his angels. This is a divine wedding.

The healer is Allāh and I am certain that whoever is sick will be healed because they cried out to Allāh a thousand times from the bottom of their hearts. I am sure whoever is suffering will be healed and the sinner will be forgiven no matter how big his sin is. Allāh will forgive him because he cried out for him. I ask Allāh to accept you.

After this holy blessing, I would like Ṣāliḥ to read the story of the flag of the love. This is the story of Rābiʿa. I want everyone to smell the fragrance of Rābiʿa, through feeling her truthful love.

I ask Allāh to provide you with love like hers. She did not love except for Allāh. She said to Allāh:

> I love You with two types of love.
> The first is a love of passion
> and the second is a love because You ought to be loved
> in Your excellence and perfection.

Would you like this love to be actualized in you? It was actualized for her and she realized it. Listen to her love story and do not listen to any other because she is a sultan of love. She carried the flag of the most noble, lofty, pure and clean love to her Protector. He protected her and she loved him sensually. She annihilated in Allāh while she was still living on earth. She lived her life devoted in giving. Look at her wedding. She is one who fell in love and went into a divine wedding. I am the one annihilated in her and she also annihilated in me in pre-eternity. She overshadowed me by her shadow and love. I look at her and I prostrate. She walks in her realm forever, for eternity and ancient times.

The life of love never ends. This is the way of the ones penetrated with love and with love of Allāh. They sing the song of love. Their words are the words of unity and their walking on earth is one of glorifying Allāh. They weep from melting in the love. They are the mercy of Allāh, a gift given to people. They live for Allāh and for serving his people. Live day and night in the shadow of the one who loves Allāh and you will see the light. This is just a continuous poetry and I hope that I translated it to the best of my ability.

"How Rābiʿa Loved Her Lord" from page 243 of *The Secret of the Love of God* is read from the beginning.

There is no he or she.

The reading begins, "Who is Rābiʿa? She appeared in the second century...."

She said to Allāh:

> You are very sweet while life is bitter.
>
> May You always be pleased and content with me
> as well as with others.
>
> May whatever is between You and me remain
> while what is between me and the whole world becomes ruined.
>
> There is no life but Yours.
>
> My Lord, You are the one who perfected and originated me in excellence.
>
> Everything is from You, to You
> and I am very pleased and content with that.
>
> You did not call me the first, second, or third
> but You named me the fourth, Rābiʿa.
> I am content with that.
>
> I annihilated all the stations in You
> and I became one and single in the name of love, alone for You.
>
> I am always drunk in the eternal wine
> and I am always absent in the presence and pleased by that.

The reading continues to page 244, "She was known as Umm-l-Kh̲ayr, the Mother of Goodness..."

It is a necessity that every mother becomes the mother of goodness. Also the father must be the father of all goodness. This is what is required and this is our walking.

The reading continues, "Her mother wept when she gave birth to her."

Her mother wept because she became the fourth girl, not knowing that she had birthed the sultan of all ladies. What can I say about all of you ladies? I love all of you because each one of you is Rābiʿa. If you return to your original essence and believe in your reality, then you will know who you truly are. Are you not the mother of the creation, the mother, the sister and the daughter of every man? Only a woman can contain a man. Love must be clean, truthful and pure. It must have sincerity, truthfulness and faith. It must be within the divine boundaries and limits according to the law of Allāh.

The woman is a gem that must be maintained and be taken care of. However it is not permissible for the lady to break the heart of her beloved. This is the life that Allāh created and wants us to have. He did not create life so that we could break hearts. Allāh created life for true love without discrimination between people. Allāh wants life to be beautiful, pure and polite, not to destroy love.

The reading continues, "Then he gave him everything his family needed, and took a pledge to care for the newly born daughter and her family."

What does a woman need more than this station? Allāh cares for his beloved. Whoever trusts and relies completely on Allāh, will never be forsaken by Him. Never ask another, only ask Allāh. Allāh says:

> And when My slaves ask you concerning Me,
> then [answer them], I am indeed near.
> I respond to prayers when they call upon Me. (Qurʾān 2:186)

Talk to Allāh and invoke him. His door is open. Do not hesitate or turn left or right. Allāh will meet you and embrace you.

A man bought her to be a slave and a servant for him. This still happens. Humans can sometimes be cruel. Actually slavery has not come to an end; it still exists. They used to say that people had been bought and sold in the past. Today every president of every country considers the people underneath him to be slaves and servants to him. He buys and sells them. Slavery never ended. Slavery of the whole nation still exists. This slavery is much worse than the slavery of the past.

Allāh created everyone free. Your mother gave birth to you free and you have been free since day one. Why do you enslave yourself or others? Why rob houses, take their money or hurt people? This is not the law of Allāh. It is not the s̲harīʿa. The law of Allāh demands that each human have a house of his own. What happens today is that people live in a house which is owned by the bank. If you miss a payment, the bank comes, kicks you out and takes the house. You are left homeless.

If a person is sick, he cannot heal himself because he cannot buy medicine. He has no insurance. Is this not true? Is this what Allāh wants? Is this not slavery? We want everyone to have a noble life that will protect every human body, heart, soul, children, family and house. Allāh did not create us to be hungry and homeless. He created us to be free and live a noble life. The human today is tied up and led like a donkey. This is the life of people today. This is the oppressing law that the human invented.

Allāh's treasure is all across the earth. Yet is it justice that those who were naked and barefoot living in the Gulf area and are now making millions and billions of dollars leave others to be hungry and homeless? We see people who exert their effort to study and graduate and then they cannot find a job. Is this justice?

Allāh says in his Holy Book that you will never feel hungry in His Garden. You will never be naked, thirsty or homeless. This means that it is the duty of the president and the leaders to achieve justice and happiness for all so that everyone will be safe and have a home and the care that he deserve as a human being. This is the philosophy of the religion of Allāh. This is the religion of justice, goodness, equality, love, beauty, and peace.

However when you walk in the street today, you smell the odor of death because of what people do which spreads corruption. May Allāh protect you from this. It is this that keeps me awake day and night. My prayers are for those who are suffering in pain across the earth without discrimination. I love all my beloveds whether they are Jewish, Christian, Buddhist, or Muslim, white or black. They are all my beloveds and I care and pray for every one of them. Allāh says:

> Truly! This, your religion (or nation) is one religion (or nation), and I am your Lord, therefore worship Me. (Qur'ān 21:92)

There are no different or multiple gods. We are all equal. All of us are beloveds and children of Ādam and Ādam came from dust.

The reading continues until, "She used to intimately call upon..."

He heard about the story of Jalāl ad-Dīn. Do you know who Jalāl ad-Dīn Rūmī is? I am Jalāl ad-Dīn Rūmī. I see him many times through his spirit. He is my beloved, my father from his spirit. Always I speak about Jalāl ad-Dīn Rūmī and his song. He gives me his spirit and I speak his poems.

The reading continues to the bottom of page 245.

My beloveds who are listening to my singing, I love you.
No matter what state you are in, wherever you are,
direct yourselves toward unity.
Come with me and sing with me
for I am singing for the One and Only.
I love you because Allāh is your creation.
I do not know envy, hate, or jealousy and I love everyone.
This is the song of Jalāl ad-Dīn Rūmī.

The reading continues, "...if you want to leave, you can leave."

She is in the real wedding with Allāh. He saw a simple glimpse of her realm and he said that he would be her servant. She said "No, I am a servant of Allāh." This is the real prison. She destroyed all the prisons. No prison can contain her. She is not chained and she crossed all limits without a passport to freedom.

The reading continues to, "I seek refuge in you from every barrier."

Who wants to carry anyone on his shoulders and who wants to be carried by the One? Everyone is crying out, "Who can carry me?" No, you cannot. The price is not easy. Give everything to Allāh and Allāh will give you everything.

The reading continues until, "...so that You may give her one glance by which You prevent her from sleep so that she may serve You night and day until she meets You."

What do you give Allāh? Nothing.

I want nothing but you. This is the right way. Everything will perish except for the face of Allāh. I ask all of the ladies, do you want what is perishable or what is eternal? This is why Rābiʿa chose Allāh, because she did not want something that was perishable. She wanted what was eternal, Allāh, the true Beloved. This is our way. I would like to put everyone with Allāh directly. Be with me one moment, with everything and you will see your Beloved. Allāh, bismillah.

The reading continues to, "My Cup, my Wine and the drinking Friend are three,"

Is there any life like hers? It is not a life that can be imported. The door of love is open for her and for everyone else. The ocean of Allāh's love is vast and it is calling people to come and rejoice. He is never absent from me. I see Him always. Do you see anything else in existence other than Him? When I look, I look only to Him. I see nothing but Him. I am Him from pre-existence, (the pre-eternity), in the realm of witnessing.

The reading continues to the end of the poem on page 246.

How sweet are the tears of love. How sweet are the tears of a lover who weeps, yearning for his beloved. I become absent in my beloved and my beloved becomes absent in me. This is the meeting in which we drink the wine of love.

The reading continues until, "Rābiʿa gave us one of the greatest examples of renunciation (zuhd), worship and love for Allāh...".

Rābiʿa never said that she was a kẖalīfa, a vicegerent, a sẖaykẖ or a boss. She always said that she was a very poor slave of Allāh. This is the highest of the loftiest station. I say as she did, that I am a very, very poor slave.

The reading continues to, "The goal of my seclusion today..."

The lady said, "My God, my Beloved, my Lord, I did not worship You because of fear of the Hellfire or because of greed to attain the eternal garden. I worshipped You and loved You because You ought to be worshipped and loved. I worshipped You because I loved You and not because of the Garden or the Hellfire." This is the true love that emerges from gnosis, the true direct knowledge of Allāh.

The reading continues to page 247, "...so tell me now if You have accepted my night of prayer so that I may rejoice..."

Did you see how glorious it is? The arrival to Allāh is glorious as is described by Rābiʿa. She was very keen to pray all night because Allāh is her beloved and she is obedient to her beloved. She wants to please Him and cares about the trust between them. She is faithful and sincere.

Sidi prays the Fātiḥa.

I think this is enough now. There is no end. I am sure.

University of Spiritual Healing and Sufism Year 1

My beloveds, are you ready for this?

If you are truly ready for this and prepared to carry
this message of the Real, of the Truth
the message of Allā,
the message of unity
the message of love, peace and beauty
the message of true knowledge and gnosis
and the message of pure goodness
then you must rid yourself of all of these qualities.

If you are ready I will give you fully
my whole heart,
my soul,
my spirit
and my intellect.

If you are ready, then let me hear, "Yes."
If you are ready say, "I am ready."

The True Beginning of Healing
Sidi's Teachings of the Ṣūfi Path, 101

Lā ʾilāha ʾilla-llāāāāāāh, Lā ʾilāha ʾilla-llāāāāāh, Lā ʾilāha ʾilla-llāāāāāh
Muḥammad rasūlu-llāh, Ibrāhīm rasūlu-llāh, Mūsā rasūlu-llāh,
ʿĪsā rasūlu-llāh ʿalayhim ṣalātu-llāh.

Allāhumma anta-s-salām wa minka-s-salām
wa ilayka yaʿūdu-s-salām
tabārakta rabbanā
ya ḏha-l-jalāli wa-l-ʾikrām

As-salāmu ʿalaykum wa raḥmatu-llāh wa bārakatuhu.

Peace be upon you beloveds of Allāh. You are the ones carrying the flag of peace, mercy, love and justice, and the flag of goodness and beauty. You are carrying all the beautiful qualities of Allāh, the godly qualities that have unified the world since pre-eternity and since Allāh created the world. He made mankind into one nation. He said in the Qurʾān:

> Truly! This, your religion (or nation) is one religion (or nation),
> and I am your Lord, therefore worship Me. (Qurʾān 21:92)

Praise be to You, Allāh, that You have created us from a single soul (Qurʾān 7:189).

He created you from a single soul (Qurʾān 7\:189) and out of that soul He created its mate and then generations and generations, without discriminating between their ethnicity or color, white, black or red. He is a just God and He wanted people to be like one nation, carrying one message, which is the message of unity that brings people together. He created us from one soul and we must be one soul, having one hand, one heart and one body. Because no matter what our race or ethnicity is, we have the same soul. Allāh wants us to be like that, to live in unity, because He created us from a single mother and a single father.

But people wanted to discriminate and to make separation between one another, so they say, "These are men, these are women, these are white, these are black." They separate or isolate themselves into groups. But Allāh created them pure and full of love and peace. They are originally full of mercy and beauty. The reality of the human being is divine beauty, godly beauty. Allāh created the human as a divine being, not as an animal being. But the human being has dressed himself in the garment of an animal. The divine soul is pure and clear and full of justice and mercy for all people and all of creation.

Allāh, glory be to Him, Most High, ordered the angels to prostrate to the human being as it is mentioned in the Qur'ān:

> When your Lord said to the angels,
> "prostrate yourselves to Ādam," they prostrated.
> (Qur'ān 2:34, 7:11, 17:61, 18:50, 20:116 *and see* 15:29-30, 38:71-72)

But they prostrated to the divine human being; they did not prostrate to the animal human being, not to you while you are carrying animal qualities. No, He ordered them to prostrate to the pure essence of the human being, which is divine.

In your reality, in your original essence, you are carrying the image of the Truth, the Real. You are the manifestation of His manifestation. You are His reflection. So in your deepest essence you are a godly being, a divine being and you are loftier in rank than the angels. That is why Allāh said in the Qur'ān that He ordered the angels to prostrate to Ādam. Allāh never changes His word. This is affirmed not only in the Qur'ān but also in the Gospel and the Torah. It is affirmed in the scrolls of Ibrāhīm and the scrolls of the ancient prophets. But the rebellious human being that pollutes himself, pollutes his heart, his soul, his intellect, reaches the states he is in now. How can this human being be pure and clean as Allāh wants him to be when he allows things to accumulate in himself that should not be allowed to accumulate? He pollutes himself.

All the prophets and messengers were sent by Allāh to purify the human being, to return him to his original essence as a godly being, a divine being. They were to return him to his divine reflection, his divine image. They do not want the human being to wear an animal garment and have animal qualities. I love you from the bottom of my heart and soul, that is why I tell you this, that is why I come here to you. It is a great honor to me to start to wash your feet and purify you. It is a great honor for me to become your servant, and I am not better than you are, I am one of you. I am also a human being, but I am carrying the qualities Allāh gave me that allow me to serve you. I came here to return you to your original essence, your divine essence.

What the human being is carrying now is like an animal body. The human being today is carrying an animal soul, an animal heart, an animal spirit and an animal intellect. These are like diseases that afflict the human being, so we must heal these diseases so we can return to our original essence, a divine being, a mirror for the godly qualities. I want the human being, when he looks within, to see not his animal body, animal heart, animal soul and animal mind; I want him to see his true essence, his divine essence.

You came here to learn how to become true healers, but before you become true healers you must purify yourselves, clean your selves to return to the original reality, as it was created. What is this reality? It is a reality full of peace, mercy, love, justice, and goodness. It does not know any discrimination. It does not discriminate between people. It considers people as one family, one nation. If you are ready and prepared to purify yourselves—your bodies, your selfs, your hearts, your spirits and your intellects—then you must listen to what I say and follow it. These instructions or teachings that I will give you I have given before to all the teachers and spiritual guides. These are the same as those I will give you because the meaning of Ṣūfism is purity. The word taṣawwuf, originally from Arabic, means "to purify."

The whole way can be described with two words: renunciation and beautification.[30] Renunciation means to renounce every quality that is not original in you, all of the animals qualities. Allāh wants to wash you with pure divine water so that you transform from this realm of physical manifestation, to the realm of the angels, to the realm of divinity. If you really follow the teachings and instructions that I wrote and described for you, it will help you to reach that step.

---

[30] "Takhlīyya (to divest and strip bare): In this process he divests himself and empties himself of all that draws his nafs down to the lower world, such as pleasure, pain, evil, and disobedience to the commands of Allah.
Tahlīya (to clothe and ornament): In this process he ornaments himself with beautiful character traits and spiritual virtues, which draws human nature up to the highest levels of the soul, and this includes confirmation and obedience to the commands of Allah" page 21 of *How the Arrival is Realized, O People of Hearts and Souls and Intellects,* which can be purchased from Sidi Muḥammad Press.

I mentioned this especially in the deep book entitled *He Who knows Himself, Knows His Lord*. I put everything you may need in it. I did not leave anything out that needs to be healed. If there is something that needs to be healed I prescribed a remedy for it, regardless of whether the disease is physical, spiritual or psychological. This is why I recommend that you read, write and understand it in a deep way, and that you follow its teachings. This will enable you to become a true healer of others, and you will not stop with illusions, imaginings and pictures. You will not see things that are not real.

If you follow what I say then you will become a godly human being, a divine being. Your own eyes will become divine eyes, your ears will become divine ears; your hands, your feet, everything in you becomes luminous, and the light of God will be always with you. Your hearing will become light; Allāh will make your hearing luminous. Your vision will be luminous and clear. Your own intellect will be full of light, and you will see the Reality as a favor from Him. You will not imagine or see illusions and pictures that are not real, but you will see the Reality as it is in the people.

If you are honest and sincere and you surrender to the spiritual guidance of the leader of guidance, who is your beloved and who loves you, then you will reach that state. This is because the spiritual guide receives this light and receives this knowledge of Reality. He will pass it to you if you follow all of his teachings and if you follow the commands of Allāh and avoid His prohibitions. Then you will arrive at your original essence. So, the one who would like to be a true healer must fully surrender just as the corpse surrenders to the washer before burial. Do you see the corpse moving? No. What I mean is that you have to let all the human and animal qualities that do not belong to your very essence, to die so your original essence can be revived and you can be a true healer who can heal others.

My beloveds, are you ready for this?

If you are truly ready for this and prepared to carry
this message of the Real, of the Truth
the message of Allāh
the message of unity
the message of love and peace and beauty
the message of true knowledge and gnosis

and the message of pure goodness
then you must rid yourself of all of these qualities.

If you are ready I will give you fully
my whole heart
my soul
my spirit
and my intellect.

If you are ready, then let me hear, "Yes."
If you are ready say, "I am ready."

Allāh ordered us to be His worshippers. He says in the Qur'ān:

> And when your Lord brought forth from the children of Ādam,
> from their loins, their seed
> and made them testify as to themselves (saying):
> "Am I not your Lord?"
> They said: "Yes! We testify,"
> lest you should say on the Day of Resurrection:
> "Truly, we have been unaware of this." (Qur'ān 7:172)

The Messenger of Allāh says:

> The one who believes in me today is in the Garden. (Ḥadīth)

He did not say, "Tomorrow he will enter the Garden." He said, "Today he is in the Garden." Allāh, Most High says:

> To whom is the true dominion?

and He answered Himself,

> The Lord of the universes, the Lord of the worlds,
> the Irresistible, the Powerful. (See Qur'ān 5:40)

I will start now to explain how to heal physical diseases, because there are many different kinds of diseases. There are physical diseases, psychological diseases, spiritual diseases, and intellectual diseases. First I will explain to you how to heal the physical diseases, and move from the dense realm of the physical positions to the subtle realm of the angelic realm.

Wash with the Water of the Unseen and Do what the Prophets and Saints Did

This is the beginning of receiving spiritual healing. We have to look at every aspect of the human being so that we can wash and purify them with divine, godly water. That is why I say: perform your ablutions with the unseen godly water. How? You do this by opening your heart, by opening your soul and surrendering to Allāh alone, not to anything else, and by following His commands and avoiding His prohibitions. Say what the saints and the prophets said "We listen and we obey." They surrendered themselves fully to Allāh and they said, "We listen and we obey, so please forgive us for our trespasses and our mistakes." That is why as your first step you must declare your repentance. You must repent, There are different levels of repentance, including the repentance of the physical body, the repentance of the heart, the repentance of the soul. Are you ready to repent the special repentance of the physical body, the heart and the soul?

What it Means to Repent

What does it mean to repent? It is to return to Allāh and to step out of all of your past sins and what you did before. Step out of everything you did in the past, regardless of whether it was stealing, cheating, betraying another, or envying or being jealous of someone. You step out of all of these bad actions from your past. You promise Allāh to offer your physical being as well as your heart, your soul, your spirit and intellect as a sacrifice for Allāh. This is what Ibrāhīm, ʿalayhi as-salām, did with his son.

What it means to Take the Promise

What does it mean to give a promise to Allāh, to make a covenant with Allāh? Allāh says in the Qur'ān:

> *ʾinna-l-ladhīna yubāyiʿūnaka ʾinnamā yubāyiʿuna-llāh;*
> Truly, those who swear allegiance to you [a guide or the Prophet] swear allegiance to Allāh;
>
> *yadu-llāhi fowqa ʾaydīhim:*
> the hand of Allāh is over their hands
>
> *fa-man-nakatha fa-ʾinnamā yañkuthu ʿalā nafsih:*
> The one who breaks [the promise] breaks it to the loss of his

own self.

> *wa man owfā bi-mā ʿāhada ʿalayhu-llāha fasayuʾtīhi ʾajran ʿadhīmā*
> And whoever keeps his oath with Allāh, upon him will be an immense reward. (Qurʾān 48:10)

Why We Offer a Sacrifice

Who is Ibrāhīm? Ibrāhīm is the father of all the prophets. He is the father of all the prophets and Allāh once inspired him in his sleep. Ibrāhīm explained to his son that he saw a vision in which he was slaughtering him. He saw him not in a dream or vision, but it was a true state of seeing. He said, "I see that I am slaughtering you." But it did not mean slaughtering in the way that people think. It has a deep meaning. It has a very deep meaning, which means, "I am slaughtering all of the animal qualities within myself. I am slaughtering the physical diseases; I am slaughtering the psychological diseases, and all the selfish and non-godly qualities."

> And, when he (his son) was old enough to walk with him,
> he [Ibrāhīm] said: "Oh my son! I have seen in a dream
> that I am slaughtering you (offer you in sacrifice to Allāh),
> so look what you think!"
>
> He said: "Oh my father! Do that which you are commanded,
> inshāʾa-llāh (if Allāh will),
> you will find me to be one of the patient ones." (Qurʾān 37:102)

The child of Ibrāhīm was also a prophet. He was around nine years old and he said to his father Ibrāhīm, "Oh my father, do as you were commanded." Because he understood that what Ibrāhīm was telling him was, "I want to purify you." So he said, "Purify me; do as you were commanded," because he believed that the one who commanded his father was Allāh. Because the prophet's vision is a godly vision, it is direct knowledge from Allāh. He knows that Ibrāhīm was his father, biologically speaking, but he was Ibrāhīm's very soul, when we talk from the spiritual perspective.

When Ibrāhīm took his son to the mountain of Arafat...this mountain is where Muslims go for pilgrimage and there is a belief that all of the prophets went to this mountain. Mūsā went to this mountain and all other prophets went there, as well. It is not as some ignorant Muslims and other ignorant people understand it. I also visited that mountain for seven years and I saw divine visions in it, scenes in it, in a true way of seeing.

Going back to our story, Ibrāhīm took his son and put him on the altar and took the knife in his hand. People thought that he was truly going to kill his son, but who could ever kill his son? What happened to the sharp knife at this point? It became water. It was moving as water moves. It was a purification operation, it was not a true killing. He kept trying to use the knife, but it turned to water. When the knife turned to water, it could not really slaughter his son.

Ibrāhīm's name has two syllables. Ib-rahīm. It means to become the merciful father, which means to become absent from everything except Allāh. It means to be absent from your animal self and to get in touch with your divine essence. The divine essence is far from the animal essence; it is the godly essence. In this instance Ibrāhīm's hand was a divine hand, his hearing, his seeing, all of his senses were luminous. He was full of light. All of his senses were full of light and he was a luminous being. Ismā'īl (Ishmael), his son, was also full of luminous light. Can a knife really slaughter light? It cannot go through light and hurt it. So, they became light, and that is why the knife couldn't slaughter him.

Do you truly want to be like that, to be an Ibrāhīmic being or an Isḥāq (Issac) being or an Ismā'īl (Ishmael) being? Do you want to be like those beings, to be one with them? So, do what Ismā'īl did. He said, "My father I surrender fully to you. Do as you were commanded by Allāh." He surrendered to all the commands of Allāh. But he did not surrender to Ibrāhīm as a human being, no. He surrendered to the divine essence, to Allāh as reflected in Ibrāhīm. He surrendered to the divine image, to the divine reflection that was coming through Ibrāhīm.

Ismā'īl said, "Father, do as you were commanded." Ibrāhīm tried seven times, but the knife would not slaughter Ismā'īl. Then Allāh sent something to ransom him and to purify him. He sent blood that would purify him. Allāh sent down archangel Jibrīl and Jibrīl said: "Oh Ibrāhīm, you were truthful and you believed in the vision. You were doing what we asked, and We will ransom your son with a great sacrifice." And Allāh made this sacrifice as a way of purifying him.

> Then, when they had both submitted themselves,
> and he had laid him prostrate on his forehead,
> And We called out to him: "Oh Ibrāhīm!
> You have fulfilled the dream (vision)!"
> Truly! In this way We reward the good-doers.
> Truly, that was a manifest trial

> And We ransomed him with a great sacrifice;
> And We left for him [a good teaching]
> among generations in later times. (Qur'ān 37:103 – 37:108)

So this great lamb came from the heavenly Garden as a sacrifice to purify the human being. This great sacrifice is equivalent to all of the animals, all of the birds, and all of the human beings. This way of purifying oneself became the accepted way, from that time until today, until eternity. It became the way of purification that we must follow. But it is not as people understand; it is not to just slaughter an animal and eat it. It was a way of granting sacrifice and purification. So, the angel said to Ibrāhīm, "You believed in the divine vision and so We will ransom you. We will save you and your son; we will purify you." That is why anyone who wants to walk this path must also offer a sacrifice on behalf of his physical being, his heart, his soul, and his spirit. This is the first step to walking the path of purification, the path toward Allāh, in the way of the people of Allāh, the people who walk in the way of purity. We have to offer a sacrifice to purify ourselves.

Repentance through Taking the Promise

What are the conditions for walking in this way? Step one is to repent, to step out of your past sins, to promise Allāh fully and completely and sincerely not to return to these things again. You do this by taking the hand of the spiritual guide who is walking this way, and who has arrived [at the Reality] in this way. You must have this intention to repent, to offer a sacrifice so that you can walk in this way toward Allāh upon the path of purification. Do not hesitate to promise Allāh. Do not hesitate for the twinkle of an eye. Do not listen to s̲hayṭān and listen to his whispers, which make you hesitate. Do not listen to him when he says, "No, do not do that, it is not necessary," whispers that make you doubt. Be like Ibrāhīm; be strong. He said, "I will listen to Allāh's command." That is why when Muslims go on the pilgrimage they throw pebbles at the s̲hayṭānic symbol, to rid themselves of all doubts and s̲hayṭānic whispers; they do this to rid themselves of these qualities and to purify themselves.

When I give my teaching in al-Masjid al-Aqṣā (the al-Aqṣā Mosque) in Jerusalem I say to the Muslims there, "You are not really throwing pebbles at someone else, you are throwing them at yourself in order to rid yourself of doubts, bad thoughts, and bad qualities, and to purify your physical being, your heart, your soul and your spirit." Do not be like a donkey who carries books and does not understand anything, because if you go on the pilgrimage like a donkey with these books on your back, you will return with more burden. You will not be relieved of this burden. Allāh will not accept your pilgrimage if you go just carrying an outer teaching, without really understanding it and applying it in a deep way. What does this mean? It means to empty your heart of envy, to empty your heart of arrogance. Do not leave room in your heart for any of the polluted qualities, the negative or the bad qualities, the animal qualities. You must purify your body and your heart from all disease, whether these diseases are physical, psychological or spiritual. You must not continue to be a murderer, one who hates peace, hates beauty, hates and envies others, steals from others, and cheats others. No, you must stop this and be a true human being with humane qualities, godly qualities. Do not carry qualities that make you destroy the earth, pollute it, create corruption, kill people and destroy their property and then claim, "I am a religious person." No, you must bring yourself to accountability before you are brought to accountability for what you do.

Achieve True Healing by Following Allāh's Commands and Prohibitions

This is true healing. This is true walking toward Allāh—following His true commands and avoiding His prohibitions. It is not achieved by talking and claiming to be religious. It is achieved by making your hand godly, by returning your hand to its divine essence. Stealing and cheating with your hand makes your hand polluted, dirty, and if your tongue lied, cheated, backbit and hurt people, then it will become polluted; it will not become divine and godly. If your heart is full of beauty, mercy and love, then this is your true essence. But if your heart is devoid of these good qualities, it is worse than Iblīs, the leader of the s̱hayṭān.

You will become worse. Your pollution will become worse than Iblīs'. How can you heal at that point? How can you heal by your tongue if your tongue is doing dirty things—lying, backbiting or cheating? You must wash yourself. How do you wash yourself? You purify yourself by following the commands of Allāh and by avoiding His prohibitions. You must also do the spiritual practices that will purify you—prayer (aṣ-ṣalāh) and fasting. Then your hand will become full of goodness, your tongue full of goodness, your heart will never know envy, hate, anger and jealousy, all of the bad qualities. This is true healing for your body, heart and soul.

Allāh created the physical body in the best mold, pure and beautiful. But look at what you did to it! Look at what the human being does to it. Allāh created the earth pure and clean for the human being. He put all of the resources the human body might need in the earth. These resources contain healing for the physical body, as well, because there is no disease that Allāh did not create a cure for. Allāh taught Ādam this truth at the beginning of time. First He asked the angels, at the beginning of creation:

> And He taught Ādam the names of everything,
> then He showed them to the angels and said,
> "Tell Me the names of these if you are truthful."
>
> They said: "Glory be to You, we have no knowledge except what you have taught us.
> Truly, it is You are the All-Knower, the All-Wise."
> (Qur'ān 2:31-3:32)

Then He talked to the godly human being whom He created as His reflection, pure and clean. He said to that godly essence:

> He said: "Oh Ādam! Inform them of their names." (Qur'ān 2:33)

We are talking about Ādam as the true, godly human being, not the animal human being. And Ādam started to teach the angels and tell them all of the animals' names and what will happen on earth from beginning to end.

So you, human being, you are the child of Ādam. You are the viceregent of Ādam and you also carry this knowledge, like him. Allāh says in the Qur'ān:

> Truly, We did offer the trust
> to the heavens and the earth, and the mountains,
> but they declined to bear it and were afraid of it.
> But man bore it. (Qur'ān 33:72)

Who carries that trust? The human being does. You as a human being are carrying the trust. They said, "We will carry the trust."

If you carry the trust, you must preserve it. Are you qualified to carry the trust? Yes, you are. You are qualified to carry the trust, but you must preserve it. How? By keeping your promise and fulfilling it, by obeying Allāh's commands and avoiding His prohibitions. You must keep your physical body pure and clean. You must keep your soul and your heart pure and clean. And then, when you are totally and completely purified in this way, Allāh will reveal knowledge to you directly.

When a child comes to life, when he comes from the womb, he comes crying and weeping, sad. But everyone around him is laughing and happy. But the child is weeping and crying, Why? Because he stepped out of the pure realm, and he was enjoying that pure realm. They put him in the uterus of the mother and were taking care of him, feeding him from her through her blood. Who can do something like that except Allāh, the Creator? How beautiful the child is when he comes out of his mother's womb.

During birth, the mother feels tremendous pain, is that not true? She feels tremendous pain, but when she takes the child in her hands, all the pain disappears. She forgets the pain and the child automatically begins to breastfeed from her. Why does he do that? Why does he not just go and suck something else? Because he is pure in heart and soul. He is inspired and guided by Allāh through His angels to do what he should to preserve himself. So he takes nutrition which is pure and nutritious for him. It makes him grow and it makes his bones strong. Also the qualities of the woman and the man, the parents, can pass through the child. Milk that is nutritious for the child does not belong to the mother alone—it carries the qualities of the father, as well. If there were nothing coming from the father, the child would not have been.

Can someone bring a child into this world without a father? No, except for one exception, which happened by Allāh's will. We are speaking about Maryam, may Allāh be pleased with her, when she gave birth to ʿĪsā (Jesus), ʿĪsā, ʿalayhi as-salām. That happened without a father. People asked her, "How can that happen?"

> Then she [Maryam] pointed to him [ʿĪsā].
>
> They said, "How can we talk to a child in the cradle?"
>
> He [ʿĪsā] said, "Truly! I am a slave of Allāh,
> He has given me the Scripture and made me a Prophet.
> And He has made me blessed wheresoever I be,
> and has enjoined on me prayer, and zakāh, as long as I live.
> And dutiful to my mother, and made me not arrogant, unblest." (Qurʾān 19:29 – 19:32)

ʿĪsā said, "I am a slave and servant of Allāh. He made me a prophet, a messenger who is carrying the message of unity. My Lord is Allāh; He is one God, and my mother is a holy woman. She is a holy being and has not done anything wrong."

This is something we must firmly believe in. ʿĪsā, ʿalayhi as-salām, will return to earth again. He was lifted to heaven when he was thirty-three years old, and he will return to the earth to spread peace on earth, to make earth full of love, justice and mercy. Whether people like it or not, he will wash the earth of all its corrupters and liars. He is our beloved prophet, our messenger. He is the Sultan of Love and we are carrying his message. This is the message of ʿĪsā, ʿalayhi as-salām, Jesus Christ.

It is also the message of Muḥammad, Mūsā and Ibrāhīm, ṣalla-llāhu ʿalayhim wa sallam. We do not discriminate between the messengers. We consider them one spirit. We look at them with the eye of love, the eye of peace, the eye of unity. This is the way of Allāh's gnostics, those who truly know Allāh. Do you want to be like that? If you would like to, then know that the doors of Allāh are open.

This is the reality of existence.

Heal the Physical Body through Restoring the Family Unit and Living in the Natural Way of our Ancestors

We talked about the spiritual perspective, but we will also talk about how to heal your physical bodies. Allāh put everything on earth that the human being might need. He created everything pure, clean and available to all people. If you look at your ancestors one hundred years ago or so, you will see how your great-grandfathers, two or three hundred years ago, lived in a natural way—with a wife, children and parents. It was a life full of love and unity. The father was full of tenderness and kindness, and the wife, also, was full of love and worked to serve and unite the family. The children were also full of love and respect for their parents. But look at the family now, in this lower realm. It is not the way it should be, because the father should care about his daughter, whether she is more than twenty years old. He should still care and be there so that no one who harms her. He protects her; he helps her; he supports her, and he cares that she may always be pure.

Look at what people have done today. The first step [the evil ones took] was to destroy the family. The family is destroyed now, and the physical being is destroyed as well, because they do not use their natural resources well. Now we see that when the son or daughter turns eighteen he turns his back on his parents, and his parents turn their backs on him. They claim he is free, but it is not true freedom. It is a false freedom full of diseases, full of pollution. This false freedom will not serve people well. It destroys people.

Who creates this? All of the governors and rulers across the world in all countries create this situation, because they do not serve the people as they should. Allāh ordered leaders to care for people and to serve them. He ordered them to carry the message of unity, justice, peace, love, beauty, and pure goodness for all. But these false rulers or tyrant rulers say to people, "Oh we want to advance you; we want to help you," but they invent things that are not good for humanity.

Look at your ancestors. They used to eat natural things they grew from the earth, and their animals used to feed naturally from God's plants. That is why they did not have as many diseases as we have now, because they used to feed from the source from which your own body came. It was all a natural cycle. But now you see that they feed every plant with chemicals and hormones, and they change its nature. They think it is good, but the human body is full of poison, because it changes the natural way, the divine way. That is how they changed the human body and the human body started to have new diseases.

In ancient times there was no cancer, AIDS, or many of the new diseases. More than one hundred diseases are new. They did not exist in ancient times. You know that people in the past lived longer than we do today. Nuh lived nine hundred and ninety-nine years; Ibrāhīm lived more than four hundred years. Why? Because they were true, faithful believers. They believed in unity and they always ate natural things that they planted with their own hands. Look at the meat you eat today. A chicken that is two months old you will find weighs about five pounds. How does this happen? How does it grow so fast and so big? Because they feed the chicken things that are not natural. The chicken that you grow at your own farm or backyard, at that age, will be one and a half pounds, but pure, clean and free of poisons. Even the cows, sheep and fish are fed with artificial hormones, chemicals and poisonous stuff.

They do not care about the human body. They do not care if they destroy it. And now they have invented factories and machines. Allāh gave us the ability to invent these things to use for good, to use in service to the human being, not to destroy the human being. The factories that we have today—are they really working for the happiness of humanity, to serve humanity? They say we have become more civilized—we do this, and we invent that. But does this achieve happiness for humans? We do not mean that we should not invent things – no. We say: invent things that will serve the human being, and make him happy and healthy. We just ask: why do you invent things that destroy humans and kill them? Why do you invent weapons, rockets and weapons of destruction? Did Allāh order us to do this? No. Did Allāh say to invent poisons and chemical weapons to destroy ourselves? Did he say to feed animals chemicals? No, He never did.

Now the earth is full of pollution and harm to the human. We want to invent things that will serve the human being, that will help him and keep his health. Yes, you can invent an airplane to help people travel long distances, but do not use airplanes to hurt others, to destroy houses, to burn plants, animals and people. We say, "Yes," to peace. We say, "No," to war, "No," to destruction, "No," to killing. We want a happy life for all people. In our way we never approve of this behavior. Anyone who kills others is our enemy. Because Allāh says in the Qur'ān:

> If anyone kills a person, or spreads mischief in the land
> it would be as if he killed all humankind,
> and if anyone saves a life, it would be as if
> he saved the life of all humankind. (Qur'ān 5:32)

The Qur'ān asks us to care of human beings, to produce and eat food that is good for human beings. It asks us to invent things that will serve the happiness of the human being.

There is a lot of land that has no one to farm it, and the land is crying and calling to people to care for it and to produce. Why do you not help the earth produce healthy things to feed humans across the earth? Why do you use chemicals, which make the earth cry? Even the medicines that people use today are full of chemicals and pollution. We are the enemies of whoever becomes an enemy of humanity and whoever breaks the hearts of the human beings. We want to heal all humans with a divine healing. Divine healing preserves our bodies, the bodies of all others, and preserves souls and the essence of the human being. The spiritual, godly, divine healing is that which cares about healing all diseases that are in the body, heart, soul, and intellect. It heals all diseases like envy, backbiting, cheating, betraying. It heals all of these because we want only justice, love, mercy and freedom for all human beings.

We want the earth to be full of happiness and beauty. How can we achieve this? By following the divine commands and avoiding Allāh's prohibitions. By following His messengers and prophets. If we do so, then your heart becomes a godly heart, a divine heart. Even the physical body becomes a godly body, a divine body, and the soul becomes a divine soul. This is what we care about and what you must care about, my children, my beloveds. This is the true beginning of healing. I came here to give you the true message, the message of the Reality as I gave it to my children before you; they who now carry the message between their hands and who promised Allāh to be as He wants them to be. So we must get our luggage ready to travel from the realm of creation to the realm of the Creator.

Allāh is with you wherever you are. He is with you. He is not veiled. But you are veiled. Why are you veiled? Because you have accumulated these qualities; your body became like an animal's body and your heart became like an animal's heart. You must purify it to return to your original essence, to remove your veil and see that the divine presence is closer to you than your jugular vein (Qur'ān 50:16). If you do that, then Allāh will say, "I am at your service, oh pious one." That means He will not leave you in need; He will fulfill you. He says in the Qur'ān:

> And when My slaves ask you concerning Me,
> then [answer them], I am indeed near.
> I respond to prayers when they call upon Me. (Qur'ān 2:186)

And He says, "and you must also respond to My call." How would Allāh ever respond to your prayer if you are asking for something evil, if you are an evil, rebellious one who breaks people's hearts, destroys love on earth, and steals, cheat, and lies to people? No, you must first purify yourself and answer the divine call so that Allāh may fulfill your needs.

Do not say, "I am going to heal people." Purify and heal yourself first to become a true healer, as I have told you. If you are ready to follow what I have said, I am ready to look at you and extend my heart and my hand to help and support you in your walking on the path of purity. I say that I am ready, and also my children here are ready. They have learned how to heal, and you must surrender to them and listen to them. You must realize that this university is unique in your country, the only one of its kind. The knowledge offered in it is spiritual knowledge that is not given to just anyone, but only to those who are ready. Do you know the great mystic Jalāl ad-Dīn Rūmī? I am carrying his spirit. I am carrying his message as well.

This is the very same message of ʿĪsā and all of the other prophets and messengers. If you come to me with the intention of pleasing Allāh and following this message, of being healed and using the healing of this way, then Allāh will be pleased with you and He will lift diseases of humanity through your hands by His permission. Whoever is ready, let him come, I will bless him and make my supplication to Him.

Oh Allāh, I have conveyed the message.
I have conveyed the message.
I have conveyed the message,
so be my witness.

Oh Allāh, I did not leave out anything You have given me
and I will not leave out anything You have given me,
but I will share it with my truthful and sincere children.

Whoever would like to come and give their covenant to follow this way of purity, let him come and take the Ibrāhīmic promise. This is the same promise Ibrāhīm and his children gave, so giving it you become the Ibrāhīm of your time. You become the Isḥāq (Issac) of your time, and Allāh will stretch His hands to you and support you and heal many people through your hands. You have to confirm inside yourself andd be firm and steadfast that you are ready to give this promise. That you are ready to give it, follow it and fulfill it. You are free to come and give this promise with sincerity. Take your chance, because this chance might not come to you again. This is a great opportunity to start the way of healing and purity.

Sidi gives the promise.

The Basics of Divine Love and Healing

"The Love" from *The Path to Allāh, Most High*

Lā ʾilāha ʾilla-llāāāāāāh, Lā ʾilāha ʾilla-llāāāāāh, Lā ʾilāha ʾilla-llāāāāāh
Muḥammad rasūlu-llāh, Ibrāhīm rasūlu-llāh, Mūsā rasūlu-llāh,
ʿĪsā rasūlu-llāh ʿalayhim ṣalātu-llāh.

Allāhumma anta-s-salām wa minka-s-salām
wa ilayka ya'ūdu-s-salām
tabārakta rabbanā
ya d̲ha-l-jalāli wa-l-'ikrām

As-salāmu ʿalaykum wa raḥmatu-llāh wa bārakatuhu.

Oh Allāh, You are the Source of Peace. Peace comes from You. Peace relies on You, Oh Most High, glory be to You, Lord of Bounties and Majesty. Please let us live in peace. Let the suffering world return to live in peace. Let those who are suffering across the world live in peace and mercy and justice and love. Grant this for all people across the world.

Praise be to Allāh, and may the peace and blessings of Allāh be upon His Messenger Muḥammad, and all the prophets and messengers of Allāh, and the beloveds of Allāh. May the peace and blessings of Allāh be upon the saints and upon all those who devoted their lives to the message of peace, beauty, love, justice, mercy and freedom.

I also greet you, my beloveds, with the greeting of peace and love, with all the signs of mercy that Allāh made us carry to all people across the world, without discrimination. I ask Allāh to allow you to understand me, to understand Him, to understand His words, and to understand the truth and reality of the way of Ṣūfism, the way of purity, and to apply it and follow it.

I mentioned to you earlier this morning how the human can heal the animal body, animal soul and animal heart. Now I would like to explain to you the successful way to heal and purify this heart, and soul and intellect. I am telling you the truth. The whole matter is based upon love. It is based upon peace, security, safety and mercy.

First we will start with love, because no one across the earth can live without love. There is no one in existence, no creature even birds or other animals who can live without love. There is not even a plant on the earth that can live without love. Even the worlds of solid matter need love. It is love that keeps the mountains in place. Allāh says in His Qur'ān:

> Had We sent down this Qur'ān on a mountain,
> you would surely have seen it humbling itself
> and rending asunder by the fear of Allāh.
> Such are the parables
> which We put forward to humankind that they may reflect.
> (Qur'ān 59:21)

Do you not see the water gush forth out of the rocks? It is the mountain that you live by and drink. It sometimes comes out of the mountains. This water has everything the human needs. All mountains contain minerals, and underneath them are metals that the human body needs. These resources can be used for the happiness of the human being, or to destroy the human being.

Do you not see that underneath the surface of the earth there are all of the metals and materials the human being may need? There is: oil, fire, all metals, gold and silver, charcoal. And even this matter cannot live without love.

What is love? Love is water. Do you not see that tremendous fires cannot be calmed down except by water? Why? Because water is full of love. When water is sent down to fire, what happens? It turns the fire off. So water prevents suffering. If fire spreads, what happens? For example we see the volcanoes gushing forth burning lava. What prevents this from happening is the water across the earth? If it happens, it is water that turns it off. This means that water is an indication of love. It is a sign of love. If water is used in the right way, it is a sign of love and it will revive life. Even in the mountains everything becomes calm and safe from water.

From where does water come? It is sent down from the sky. It comes down by the Lord of Love, the Lord who created love within our hearts. The name of that lover is Allāh, which in your language is, "God." Is that not true? In all languages there is a name that refers to that Being Who is the Creator, the One and Only.

Let us now search in love. We explained the different signs of love across the earth. If people used water in a holy way then the whole earth and its people would be happy, but if people use water to destroy and harm, then it will make the human sick and miserable. We must use the water of love that Allāh sent down to earth in a good way.

Allāh fills the oceans and seas with this water of love. Look at the oceans and seas. What do they contain? The vapor from these oceans rises into the skies. By the command of the Almighty, the Wise, the water accumulates and forms clouds. The clouds are lead by winds to the parts of the earth that are barren and without plants. When water is sent down as rain to these lands it brings forth things that carry the fragrance of absolute beauty that the human being needs. It is a sign that shows the love of Allāh for the human being. It talks to the human being and says, "Look at me. Do not pollute me. Keep me beautiful so that you can become beautiful, too."

When you walk by fruits and flowers they call you to witness their beauty. They say, "Come to me. I will teach you about love. I will teach you to be beautiful." Everything in creation talks to you. Allāh also says in the Qur'ān:

> Everything in creation knows its prayer and glorification of Allāh. (see Qur'ān 24:41)

Do you not hear the trees talking as they sway back and forth? They chant with the divine tongue. Do you not also hear the birds singing and chanting the praise of Allāh? Everything glorifies Allāh in prayer (Qur'ān 24:41).

Allāh wants you to be a beloved, not a destroyer or a corruptor. He wants you to be beautiful, full of mercy for everything. He wants you to be merciful to the birds, to the trees, to everything. Do you not hear the currents of water running in the river praising Allāh and thanking Him? He waters all the fruits and vegetables and trees for you. Isn't that the essence of love? Allāh serves you. Allāh made everything for you. He offered you the water of love. People need love. They need the pure and clean water of love.

My son and my daughter, how can you heal people unless your heart is full of love? This heart must be full of love and peace and security. The house of your heart must become the mercy. Those are three things: love, peace, and mercy. If your heart is full of these qualities and you put your hand on the patient and you say, "Oh Allāh, in your name 'the healer' (as̲h̲-s̲h̲āfī)," then you are using the water of love that Allāh put inside you and you can heal that person. However, you must ask Allāh, "Please let the healing come through my hands."

So when the patient comes to you, you must first make him feel safe and at peace. You must first smile at his face with a heart full of love and beauty. You must take all the sadness out of his heart. You must be gentle and kind with him. You should never utter a word that may change him in a bad way or frighten him.

First ask him, "What do you feel?" or "What is your complaint?" Make him speak. You must be gentle and kind and not speak rough words to him. You must make him feel at ease and at peace. You must try to make him happy and joyful. Illuminate the love within his body and heart. Water him with the water of love. He will be healed when he feels the love, the peace and the mercy. He will trust and respect you because you give him this love and mercy.

He will know that you are truly his brother. The only difference is that you are carrying a godly heart. This spiritual heart must be rejoicing in peace and mercy and love. You do not ask the patient, "Tell me about your history" in a way that he has to remember the things in the past that have hurt him. Do not try to know his secrets. Everyone has his or her privacy. Sometimes the secrets are painful secrets, horrible secrets. You should not open this.

On the contrary, you can encourage him to say whatever is on his heart but you must be gentle and subtle. Then that person might actually confess, "My father abused me," or "My father raped me," or "My mother treated me badly," and "It is painful for me. I cannot forget about it." These people might then continue on and on to say, "And my brother did this to me, and my friend did that to me, and my wife did this to me."

He is allowed to tell you all of this, but as a healer you must explain to him that, "These events took place in the past. These things took place because you were ignorant or helpless or young. Whatever happened it is over now. You must never return to the past. Forget it. Let it go." Tell the patient, "This is the hour that you will dress in a new garment. It is a new beginning, a new creation. You will be created anew. You will not remember the past. You cannot return to the past to change it. It is already past."

Can any one here return to the past to change it? No! Can you even bring yesterday to be today? Whatever you did for forty years, it is over and gone. You cannot change it. That is why as a healer you should not keep talking about the past and keep the patient thinking about it. You just tell him that, "The door of repentance, the door of returning to Allāh is open. You are now a new child with a new creation. You must now start to wash your heart with the water of love and the water of mercy."

"No matter what your father or brother or friend or abuser did to you, leave him to Allāh. Allāh knows him. Allāh will judge him and bring him to accountability."

So whoever abused his daughter or his sister or any human Allāh will judge him. Leave him to Allāh. You, however, must always repent to Allāh, return to Allāh, and renew your promise with Allāh and become the son or daughter of the moment. Allāh says:

> The one who comes with repentance and a full heart,
> I will transform their bad deeds into good deeds
> and rectify their deeds and his affairs. (Qur'ān 5:39)

You were deprived of love; Allāh is giving you a chance to know His love. He brought you here. He washed you with the water of love. He bestowed His mercy and forgiveness upon you. He always took care of you.

As a healer you must always wash the patient's heart with the water of love by showing him love and by asking him to be forgiving, to leave the past and to know that the abuser will be judged by Allāh. Allāh says in the Qur'ān:

> Whoever does an atom's weight of good will receive its reward
> and whoever makes an atom's weight of evil will suffer the consequences. (Qur'ān 99:7-99:8)

So you must first make the patient feel loved, and not feel that he is hated, or that he is a bad person. Let him feel he is equal to you. He is not worse than you. Make him feel that you are equal and that he is a good human.

Allāh says:

> Let them pardon and forgive.
> Do you not love that Allāh should forgive you? (Qur'ān 24:22)

Allāh says in the Ḥadīth Qudsī:

> If you had not made mistakes
> I would have brought forth another creature
> who would make mistakes
> so that I may bestow My forgiveness upon him.

As you continue to speak with your patient say, "Understand that to Allāh is our final return. Everyone, young or old, kind or not, will return to Allāh. We must realize that we will return to Allāh. So whoever abused you will be brought to Allāh in front of your very eyes. You will see him suffering if you do not forgive him. Allāh will bring him to accountability and will judge him. He will suffer the consequences of his abusive actions. He will suffer in the Hellfire that is prepared for the evil ones."

But Allāh is merciful. Whoever repents from his sins can turn back to Allāh and say, "I confess my sins. Please forgive me." If he then sincerely promises Allāh not to do that again, then Allāh will forgive him. On the Day of Judgment Allāh will bring the person who was violated and say, "Look at this sinner who abused you and offended you. He repented and realized his mistake. Do you still want him to be punished?" If the person says, "I will forgive him," then Allāh will say, "I am More Forgiving and More Merciful." Then He will reward the abused with more blessings. He will compensate him for his injury and for all of the violations he suffered. He will give him a great reward and blessing, as well as compensation for what he suffered.

Understand that all human beings have committed sins in one way or another. Even Ādam. Allāh says about him in the Qur'ān:

> Thus did Ādam disobey his Lord. (Qur'ān 20:121)

Allāh said to him, "Do not eat from this tree" but the accursed shayṭān, Iblīs, whispered in his ear and lead him to eat from the forbidden tree. Why? Because there was wisdom in it. If Ādam had not eaten from the tree then we would not have seen you or you. (Sidi points to two of his students in the audience.) It was decreed. Allāh says that He accepted the repentance of Ādam and forgave him. Ādam came from the Garden to the lower realm of this world to build on it, to construct it, and to produce all of his offspring.

What did he do in the beginning? He ate the tree of love that is pure. You came from that tree. Allāh wants you to live by this tree. He wants you to know true love, to know that Allāh is your true Lord, and to know the true way of His love and mercy. These are the qualities that must be in the true healer. These are the foundations and the basics of healing.

For you to be a true healer you must have a heart full of love and mercy and peace. This will be the secret of your ability to heal. Carrying these qualities is the secret of healing.

Know that Ṣūfism, the way of purity, and the way of healing are one and the same. The message of Ṣūfism, the message of purity, depends upon the qualities of love, peace, mercy, pure goodness, beauty, justice and freedom. These are the foundations of Ṣūfism, of purity. These foundations teach you, oh human, where you come from, why you were created, and what your purpose is. You must carry these qualities and purify your heart and not allow s̲hayṭān to whisper in your heart or to leave any of his traces in you. Listen only to the words of Allāh and always remember the name of Allāh.

Follow the s̲harī'a, the law of Muḥammad, Ibrāhīm (Abraham), Mūsā (Moses) and 'Īsā (Jesus), ṣalla-llāhu 'alayhi wa sallam. You must follow its teachings and instructions. There is no Ṣūfism without following the law. If anyone claims to be a Ṣūfī without following the divine law, the s̲harī'a, he is a liar. Such a person will be afflicted with diseases and problems. Allāh will never heal people through his hands because Allāh only heals through love, mercy and peace. These are the teachings that came through the tongues of all the messengers of Allāh: Ibrāhīm, Mūsā, 'Īsā and Muḥammad. We must follow them and carry the message of true unity. There is no difference between these prophets. If you look with your heart and listen carefully to their words, it is the same message.

Look at this child (Sidi is pointing to a young child who had just come up front to sit with her dad). Is she not a reflection of divine mercy and beauty? Can you see that she is in complete surrender to Allāh? She does not care about anything other than the search for love. When she finds love, she clings to it. She finds it now through her father. That is why she goes to him.

(Turning back to address all his students): you must also be like that: a child in the presence of Allāh, clinging to Him to be fulfilled in love. Those are the children that are beloved to Allāh. So sit with them around the table of Allāh. Who are the children? The children of Allāh are the prophets and messengers of Allāh, the pure ones who were completely purified. Return to your true essence. All of us must return to our real essence as a divine reflection.

My beloved sisters and brothers, daughters and sons, please do not return to the past again and open these painful memories to the patient and make him sicker than he was. Do not open this for them! You must make their world full of love, mercy and peace. Tell the patient to forget about the past and to be the son or daughter of their moment. This is the way of Allāh, the way of all the prophets and messengers. I hope you have comprehended these words and will keep them in your hearts. I hope you will purify your hearts by these words.

For the one who does not have love, it is better if he throws himself into the Hellfire because he actually wants the Hellfire. He must pursue love so that he can find the Garden. If he does not pursue love he will continue to be in the Hellfire. He has free choice. Does he want to be in the Garden or in the Hellfire? Only through love can you live in the Garden. You cannot find sufficiency without love.

Breaking hearts is the most offensive sin. To break the heart of another person is the most tremendous crime that humanity can experience. Even animals—you should never break the heart of an animal. For example, if you have a dog it is important to understand that this dog has seven divine qualities. What are these qualities?

Seven Qualities of the Dog

1. The first one is love. The dog carries love because he loves his friend with the pure love of eternity. He teaches you about love.
2. Surrender
3. Sincerity
4. Truthfulness
5. Faithfulness

6. Friendship.
7. Discipline and patience to say "no" to the nafs and s̲hayṭān

Do you see these seven qualities in one human? Show me that human! If I see him I will kiss his feet, because that would mean he is one of the saints, one of the loyal friends and allies of Allāh.

The Prophet Muḥammad, ṣalla-llāhu ʿalayhi wa sallam, said that one man went directly into the Garden when he found a dog that was panting from thirst. There was no water. The man used to be a thief, a robber who traveled and violated other people and stole things from them. He was walking on the hot desert. He was thirsty and drank water from a well along the way. He found the dog and felt for the dog. "Oh, this dog is so thirsty. He cannot reach the water in the well." He took off his shoes, filled them with water and brought the water to the dog. He offered the water to the dog, who drank it until his thirst was satisfied. So Allāh, Most High, glory be to Him, sent down the archangel Jibrīl who revealed to the Prophet:

> There is a man who watered a thirsty dog in the desert.
> When he comes to you, oh Prophet,
> give him the good news that he will dwell in the Garden. (Ḥadīt̲h̲)

What if any of you have the desire in your heart to water the thirsty heart of a child, or to offer food to a homeless family in Africa, or in any other country including this country? What if we offered this food and clean water to these people, to the homeless people and the poor ones? In this country are there not people in need of help? Yes! Here and everywhere else.

The one who is devoid of love is devoid of mercy as well. Love and mercy go together. Allāh and His Prophet say to us:

> Have mercy on those on earth
> so that the One in heaven will bestow His mercy upon you.
> (Ḥadīt̲h̲)

The one who does not show any mercy will not receive any mercy. Our message is the message of love, mercy and peace. Those are the three qualities that all people on earth need, including the sick ones and the homeless ones. The one who carries these qualities and rejoices in them is a true healer and Allāh will grant healing through his hands.

Love has different degrees and levels that Ṣāliḥ will read about for us. So Ṣāliḥ, if you have love in your heart, read for us. I am sure that he is full of love. Everyone has the love. Show me anyone who does not have any love in his heart. Anyone who is devoid of love will be deprived of life. Love is life. Love is the essence of life and life is the essence of love.

"The Love" on page 77 of *The Path to Allāh, Most High* (second, revised edition) is read from page 83, "Love has four names or categories. The first is passion (al-hawā). Passion is love's descent into the heart, which is its appearance, its manifestation from the unseen to the seen. This descent is caused by a gaze or by hearing... Passion may cause a person to love something that his Lord orders him to not love."

The one who has the lower passions does not know about true love. Let him go learn about love. Let him keep knocking on the door until he can find someone whom he can love with sincerity, in a pure way. Let him give love in a pure, clean way and then he will receive love. Do not let him break any hearts. Let him come in humility and humbleness and ask for love in a true and pure way. Then Allāh will provide for him a true lover.

If love actualizes in you and you become consumed in another person whom you love then know you did not lose yourself to a human because that human is a divine reflection, a divine image. If you truly love in a pure way, you are loving the divine essence through this divine mirror. If you look at the one whom you love and you see only your own face, then you are not yet in love. If you are in true love then you will look at the one you love and you see your own (essential, divine) face.

It does not mean you got annihilated or consumed or got lost to someone. It means that Allāh revealed to you the secrets of His love through His creation. So be polite with the divine manifestations and give them the love and mercy. Help them and support them. Then you will be fulfilled in love and receive the divine love. Allāh says to His Prophet:

> If you love Allā then follow me, and Allāh will love you.
> (Qur'ān 3:31)

That means you must follow the Messenger of Allāh in all of his actions. Then your heart will be open to love all of the divine manifestations and to love all people. In fact, one does not hate the human being; one hates the actions that are in deviation of divine law. So instead of hating someone else, just try gently and with love to correct his way.

The reading continues, "the Deep Love is the love that takes over the person, making the person blind to other than the Beloved. This love takes over the spirit and all of the limbs..."

We do not mean by "blind" someone who cannot see with his physical eyes. No. We mean the one whose heart is blind; the inner eyes within his heart cannot see. He has no insight. He cannot see the Reality. He does not have any knowledge. Allāh said:

> The heavens and the earth cannot contain Me,
> but the heart of My faithful believer and lover contains Me.
> (Ḥadīth Qudsī)

Your heart can contain Allāh. He said, "My heavens and earth cannot contain Me, but the heart of My slave worshipper, My lover, contains Me."

Do you not want to be Allāh's lover and beloved so Allāh fulfills you and gives you what you need, and become the eyes through which He sees and the ears through which He hears? If you want that then come to the way of Allāh, the way of love. This is the way of Allāh. There is no other way. This is the way of the lovers, the way of the prophets and messengers, the way of those who lost themselves in Allāh and do not take anything except from Allāh. They do not understand any language except the language of Allāh. They are not holding any qualities except the divine attributes and the lofty ethics of Allāh.

The reading continues, "This love takes over his spirit and all of his limbs... (to) his speech and his hearing are from Him and to Him..."

It is true. He will talk by the tongue of Allāh. Know that you do not have anything except that which Allāh gives you. Do not talk by the language of the selfish ego or the animal self. Do not talk in an impolite way or any way that is a violation of the lofty ethics of Allāh. Do not backbite people. Do not speak badly about people, describing them by negative attributes.

If you do that your prayers are not beneficial for you. How many people are praying and they have no benefit from their prayers because their prayers will turn against them. The prayer will tell the person that he is dirty, polluted. Why? Because he does not respect the prayer and nor does he give the prayer its true rights. Prayer is connection and communication with Allāh. When you say, "Allāhu akbar" it means that He is the Greatest, greater than anything else. So why bother with anything else? Allāh says:

> Remember Me and I will remember you. (Qur'ān 2:152)
> [Sidi: by fulfilling you and by giving you My garden, My love, My peace, My healing, My happiness, My pure goodness and beauty.]

Who does not love beauty, except for a diseased person? I am a slave of beauty wherever I go. I am a worshipper of beauty. I prostrate and bow down to beauty. These are the poetic verses of Jalāl ad-Dīn Rūmī. I love everything across the earth because I see only Him in the whole world. So silent one who is still in your state, listen and understand. Live by love and lose yourself in love and you will learn the true divine essence. The one who tastes, knows. How can the one who has no tasting, distinguish between the honey and the onion? He will not be able to. The one who lost his sense of tasting will not be able to distinguish between the honey and the onion.

Did you taste the true taste of love? We do not mean when you are making physical love. We mean the pure, strong, powerful love that loves everything and everyone without limits or boundaries. There is no end to the divine life. It is eternal. So die before you die. Let everything in your life die except the truth and reality of Allāh. Let go of the illusions and pictures. Transform from this realm of illusions to the divine reality that is full of love and peace and mercy. The Gnostic told us this.

Story about the Man Who Learned Love Through a Donkey

I will tell you a story that happened in the past. Once a person came to my master guide in Damascus, Syria. He asked my guide to give him the promise. My guide said, "How can I give you the covenant while you have this offensive physical odor about you? I do not think you know love. Have you ever fallen in love?"

The man said, "No."

So my master guide said to him, "Go and find love. Love even a donkey. Taste the true taste of love and then come back to me to give me the promise."

I was beside my master guide and I laughed and asked my guide, "What is there in the donkey that he should love?"

He said, "The donkey carries a love that is greater than the love of the human being." I had my own donkey at that time but I had not yet smelled the love that the donkey carries.

So my guide told me to pull on the donkey's head with his leash. "Look. Will not he come you and respond to your call? Does not he stop when you say stop? Do you not ride on his back and he accepts you? And when you feed him he eats? And when you do not feed him he still remains silent and does not complain or rebel? He is obedient to you."

I said, "Yes, my master guide, that is true."

He said, "Isn't that an indication of love, of pure love?"

Everything Allāh created carries this love. So carry it to. Give it to the child and to the elderly. Give it to all people. Give it to the animals. Allāh will bestow mercy on those who bestow their mercy on people.

So, the man (left my master guide) and went out to find love. All of the ladies refused him. No woman ever said to him, "Come to me my beloved." No one told him that. He came back to my master guide weeping bitterly. He kept weeping and weeping in his search for love until he lost his own eyesight.

At this point my master guide said to him, "Now your love is sincere and true. Come here." My guide was one hundred and thirteen years old at that time. He took some of his own saliva on his fingertips and touched the eyes of the man asking him, "What is your name?"

The man replied, "My name is Aḥmad."

My guide asked, "Do you see me now?"

The man said, "Yes, I do see you now. All of a sudden my eyesight has returned."

My guide pointed out, "This is when you surrendered fully. Allāh made your heart full of love."

The man said to the s̲hayk̲h, "I know your saliva was not just saliva. It was the water of love that wanted to reach me and touch me. That is why it made me gain my sight back. Now I experience love from you. I now know the divine love through you."

Love causes everything to die except life – the pure, beautiful, true life needed by every creature that Allāh created. There are other types of people who love lots of other people. They love a woman and then marry her. Then they divorce her and marry another person. No! In our way, in the way of Allāh and the s̲harī'a, there is no divorce or separation. We do not let people marry with the intention of separating later.

We consider love as something very holy. We respect the human being as the divine mirror. We want to purify it and to preserve it as pure and clear. Everyone came through love. I ask men, "Who of you came (i.e., were born) outside of the way of love? So how can you go and break hearts? How can you ladies also break hearts? Did you not receive love through your father when he gave his own water for you to be conceived?"

Allāh is love. Allāh is beauty. Allāh is mercy. Allāh is purity. That is why he starts the Qur'ān:

> In the name of Allāh, the Compassionate, the Merciful. (Qur'ān 1:1)

One of his names is "the Giving." One of his names is "the Merciful." One is "the Compassionate." I am trying to explain to you just a glimpse of the meaning of love. I hope you will understand it. If you comprehend this love in the true way, the way of Allāh, then you will be able to heal. This is the way of healing. The way of healing is the way of love, mercy and peace. The one who does not have these qualities will not be able to heal. The principle foundations of healing and the healer are these qualities. This is our law.

The reading continues, "he sees Him in every image that he sees. 'There is no limb or joint, except that it has the remembrance of You.' These lovers are consumed...(through)...and not changed in this state of love by anything, whether it is pleasant or unpleasant,"

Drink my son, my daughter! Drink from the wine of love so that you can rejoice and live in happiness. Do not wait and deprive yourself of this pure drink. If you have not gained even a sip of this wine then you will lose all of your life. Swim in the ocean of the Beloved so that you may see His marvelous actions that you've never seen before in your life. This poetry came through the spirit of Jalāl ad-Dīn Rūmī, the great Ṣūfī guide. I think this is enough now, enough drinking.

Appendices & Indices

Appendix I: Prophets, Angels, Awliya

Prophets

May the blessings and peace of Allāh be upon them.

English	Arabic	Function/Relationship
Abraham	Ibrāhīm	Father of the prophets Friend of Allāh Father of Ismā'īl and Isḥāq Builder of the Ka'ba
Adam	Ādam	Father of humanity The first prophet in the body
David	Dāwūd	Bringer of the Zabūr (Psalms) Slayer of Jalūt (Goliath)
Enoch	Idrīs	Predecessor to Nūḥ Raised to Heaven by Allāh
Issac	Isḥāq	Father of the Jewish line Second-born son to Ibrāhīm via Sara
Ishmael	Ismā'īl	Father of the Islāmic line (Arabs) First-born son to Ibrāhīm via Hajjar
Jacob	Ya'qūb	Father of Yūsuf and the 12 tribes of Israel Son of Isḥāq
Jesus	'Īsā	Son of Maryam (Mary) The Spirit of Allāh The Messiah (al-masīḥ) Bringer of the Injīl (Gospel)
John the Baptist	Yaḥyā	Son of Zakariyyā Forerunner of 'Īsā
Jonah	Yūnus	Swallowed by a large fish (whale) Prophet in Ninevah
Joseph	Yūsuf	Son of Ya'qūb Prophetic dreamer
Lot	Lūṭ	Prophet of Sodom and Gomorrah Wife turned into a pillar of salt

Prophets

May the blessings and peace of Allāh be upon them.

Moses	Mūsā	Converser with Allāh Freed Jewish slaves from Egypt Bringer of the 10 commandments Bringer of the Torah
Muḥammad	Muḥammad	The Seal of the Prophets The Beloved of Allāh The Light of Allāh's Face First prophet in spirit Bringer of the Qur'ān
Noah	Nūḥ	Built the ark and the ship of safety
Solomon	Sulayman	Son the Dāwūd Has command over all creatures, including the jinn (spirits)

Angels

May the blessings and peace of Allāh be upon them.

Raphael	Isrāfīl	He will blow the horn at the end of time, announcing the Day of Resurrection
Azrael	Izrā'īl	The angel of death
Gabriel	Jibrīl	The angel of Revelation to the Prophet Muḥammad (*ṣalla-llāhu 'alayhi wa sallam*) The Holy Spirit
Michael	Mikā'il	The angel of health

ʾĀwliya

May the blessings and peace of Allāh be upon them.

ʿAbd as-Salām ibn Mas<u>h</u>ī<u>sh</u>	The guide for Abu-l-Ḥasan as<u>h</u>-S<u>h</u>ād<u>h</u>ulī
Abu Bakr aṣ-Ṣādiq	Was one of the Prophet's closest companions. He gave all of his wealth to help Islām survive. The Prophet married his daughter, ʿĀʾis<u>h</u>a. He was the first caliph after the Prophet passed away.
Abu-l-Ḥasan as<u>h</u>-S<u>h</u>ād<u>h</u>ulī,	The guide for our ṭarīqa.
ʿĀli ibn Abī Ṭālib	Was the cousin of the Prophet and one is his closest companions. He was married to the Prophet's daughter Fāṭima, and together they embodied the highest spiritual teachings of Islām. ʿAlī was the fourth caliph (ruler) after the Prophet passed away.
Al-Mahdī	The guided one who will appear to restore righteousness and announce the second coming of ʿĪsā.
Bilqīs	Wife of the Prophet Sulayman
Hajjar	Wife of the Prophet Ibrāhīm, mother of the Prophet Ismāʾīl
Maryam (Mary)	Mother of ʿĪsā [Jesus] ʿalayhi as-salām)
Muḥyi-ḍ-ḍīn ibn al-ʿArabī	One of the most famous and influential Ṣūfī saints, scholars, writers in the history of Islām. He lived in the 12th century A.D., and is known as the "S<u>h</u>ayk<u>h</u> al-Akbar."
Rābiʿa al-Adawiyya	Was a passionate lover of God and the first Ṣūfī saint. She extolled the way of Divine love and intimacy with Allāh.
ʿUmar ibn al-K<u>h</u>aṭṭāb	Was one of the Prophet's closest companions. Known for his strength of character the Prophet said, "Even the s<u>h</u>ayṭān would be frightened of you."

Appendix II: Glossary of Arabic Terms

Adab: politeness, manners.

Al-ḥamdu li-llāh: literally translated as "all praises to God." It is polite and customary to say this in response to a query about your state or your health (i.e. how are you?). In doing so you recognize that no matter what is happening in your life, Allāh is to be praised because everything in your life is from His Raḥmān (never-ending mercy).

'Alaq: literally means a clot of blood. In the Qur'ān its outward meaning is the second stage of embryonic development, where the fetus appears as a clot of blood.

'Alayhi as-salām: literally translated as "peace be upon him." It is polite and customary to say this after mentioning any of the prophets, 'alayhim as-salām.

'Alayhim as-salām: the plural of 'alayhi-s-salām.

Āmīn: Amen. Assent. "So be it."

As-salāmu 'alaykum: This is the greeting Allāh told the Prophet Muḥammad, may the blessings and peace of Allāh be upon him, to use when greeting believers. It means "peace be upon you."

As-salāmu 'alaykum wa raḥmatu-llāh wa bārakatuhu: An extended version of "as-salāmu 'alaykum," this translates as "May the peace of God be upon you, and His mercy and blessings."

Astaghfiru-llāh al-'aḏhīm: This phrase is used during tawba to ask for Allāh's forgiveness. When using it you are asking Allāh to veil your faults and forgive you while acknowledging His Enormity, Greatness and Power to do so.

Ākhira: the hereafter, the next life.

Awrād: plural for *wird*. See *wird*.

'Āyah: a verse in the holy Qur'ān.

Azal, al-: pre-eternity, eternity without beginning.

Baṣīr, al-: The name of God that means, "The All-Seeing." Allāh lends us His quality of seeing, and that is why we can see.

Baqā': subsistence; the state of subsistence which occurs after the fanā' where you are established in and by the qualities of Allāh.

Bay'a: the promise made by a novice with God through the spiritual master; originally the covenant between Allāh and the believers in the soul world when He asked them, "Am I not your Lord?" They answered, "Yes (bala), You are our Lord in truth."

Bismi-llāh: literally means, "In the name of Allāh." It is traditional to say, "Bismi-llāh" before undertaking any action in order to sanctify it.

Bismi-llāhi-r-Raḥmāni-r-Raḥīm: "In the name of Allāh, universally Merciful, specifically Compassionate."

Dhikr: the remembrance of God through the remembrance of the tongue, the remembrance of the heart or the remembrance of the spirit.

Dunyā: the material world.

Fanā': the death of the nafs/self/ego; to die before one dies; to die to the world; to annihilate into God's reality.

Fātiḥa, al-: Al-Fātiḥa is the opening chapter, or sūra, of the holy Qur'ān. It is said to contain the essence of the entire Qur'ān within it. Al-Fātiḥa is recited at least seventeen times daily by Ṣūfis and Muslims during the obligatory, five times a day prayer (ṣalāh). This sūra is fundamental to the Ṣūfi's understanding of his religion.

Ḥadīth: traditions relating to the actions and sayings of the Prophet, may the blessings and peace of Allāh be upon him, recounted by his companions. Sayings from the Ḥadīth Qudsī are sayings where Allāh speaks with the tongue of the Prophet (where the "I" refers to Allāh speaking in the first person).

Ḥajj: the pilgrimage to Mecca to circumambulate the Ka'ba, the holy house the Prophet Ibrāhīm [Ibrāhīm] built with his son Ismā'īl [Ishmael], and perform the other sacred rites as a testament to one's belief in monotheism. Going on Ḥajj is one of the five pillars of Islām. The five pillars are the five core, obligatory practices for Ṣūfis and Muslims practicing "the real Islām."

Ḥaqīqa: the truth, reality or essential reality of Allāh.

Iblīs: Satan. Iblīs is the personal name for the devil (ash-shayṭān); originally the jinn who refused to bow to Ādam.

Iḥsān: excellence in action. Worshipping God as if you see Him. The highest of three levels of worship.

Imān: faith, trust, belief; The second of three levels of worship.

Injīl: the Gospel, the holy Book brought by the Prophet 'Īsā ['Īsā] (*'alayhi-s-salām*).

Inshā'a-llāh: literally means "if God wills." It is used to express the dependence of man's will on God's will. We are told not to say regarding

anything, "I'm going to do that tomorrow," without also saying, "if God wills." (Ḥadīth).
Islām: surrender; the word Islām is derived from the word as-Salām (peace); The first of the three levels of worship (Islām, Imān, Iḥsān). Islām is the religion brought by the Prophet Muḥammad *(ṣalla-llāhu 'alayhi wa sallam).*
Jabarūt: formless world; world of infinite eternal power and possibility.
Jihād: holy war; inner struggle. This term refers both to the outer struggle which can manifest as a holy war between people or cultures, and the inner struggle that occurs when the nafs are not in surrender and obedience to Allāh.
Jinn: inhabitants of the world of the Malakūt, the subtle world created of "smokeless fire." There are believing jinn and unbelieving jinn.
Jumu'a: the Friday congregational prayer.
Ka'ba: the holy house in Mecca first built by Ādam and re-built by Ibrāhīm [Ibrāhīm], Ismā'īl [Ishmael], and Isḥāq ['Īsāac] *('alayhimi-s-salām).* The place of pilgrimage. The house contains the black stone which came from heaven. It was white but now is black from the sins of those who have touched it.
Khalwa: spiritual retreat where chants are recited all night until dawn.
Khuṭba: the sermons given during Jumu'a, the Friday congregational prayer.
Lā 'ilāha 'illa-llāh: translated as: "there is nothing worthy of worship except God." Attesting to the truth of this statement is one half of ṭawhīd, the declaration of God's oneness and unity.
Lāhūt: the world of the Divine essence.
Laylā: the essence of the deep, secret love of Allāh. Also, the beloved of Qays.
Lawamma: the station of still questioning.
Malakūt: the world of the heart and soul which contains the spiritual presence of the Prophet, may the blessings and peace of Allāh be upon him. It's the world of the unseen, the angels, the jinn, heaven, and hell. It's where we go after we die, also known as the second world, until we travel through all of the worlds to reach Allāh.
Maqām: spiritual station.
Masjid: a mosque; where Muslims gather to pray.
Masjid al-Aqṣā: the mosque in Jerusalem at the Dome of the Rock. This is where Sidi works.
Misbaḥa: prayer beads hung on a string for easy counting.
Monotheism: the belief that there is only one God.
Muḥammadan light: The light that Allāh originally took from His face (His essence) when He gave the first command, "Be." This is the essential light upon which everything else rests, and it is the highest light in existence. It is

most strongly embodied in the Prophet Muḥammad *(ṣalla-llāhu ʿalayhi wa sallam).*

Muḥyī, al-: the name of Allāh that means, "The Giver of Life."

Mulk: the physical state or material world. All that you can see and everything you can experience with the five outer senses.

Muqaddam: the word is derived from the quality of Allāh, "the Initiator." A muqaddam is typically the representative of a s̲haykẖ or spiritual master. One who is authorized to give instruction and initiate disciples in certain Ṣūfī orders. In Sidi Muḥammad's order, the muqaddam is given the responsibility of opening the doors of the local community, to invite new people to the path, and to give the message of God's peace, love, mercy, justice, and freedom without discrimination.

Murabbi: a rank in Sidi Muḥammad's ṭarīqa given to those who deeply support the spiritual walking of all people in the ṭarīqa. These beloveds provide organizational development and administrative support for the University of Spiritual Healing and Ṣūfism, and the ṭarīqa as a whole.

Murīd: the seeker on the path to Allāh.

Nafs: the self, the soul which resides alongside the spirit. Sidi Muḥammad defines the nafs as: "your perceptions, hearing, feeling, the voices in your mind, and the desires of your heart that say this and that or ask why or what." (page 47 of Music of the Soul, Sidi Muḥammad Press)

Naqīb: literally means, "One who cares for the people." It's a rank and a responsibility Sidi gives some of his students in different communities around the country.

Pharaoh: used specifically to reference the Pharaoh who oppressed the Jews, Tutankhamun. Used generally to refer to an oppressor.

Qibla: the direction the seeker faces when praying ṣalāh. Initially, the qibla was Jerusalem, but during the Prophet's lifetime Allāh revealed that it should be changed to the Kaʿba in Mecca.

Rakāh: one cycle of standing, bowing, kneeling and prostrating in the ṣalāh.

Ramaḍān: the 9th month of the Islāmic calendar, Ramaḍān is considered the holiest month of the year. Muslims spend the month fasting from dawn until dusk, offering extra worship, giving charity to the poor, and deeply drinking from the overflowing blessings of Allāh.

Ṣabūr, aṣ-: The name of Allāh that means, "The Patient."

Sacrifice: an important and deeply holy act of self-purification. A "sacrifice" is given when you need to repent for something you've done and cannot complete it (because you cannot right the wrong). A sacrifice is a donation of $500 which is used to buy and painlessly kill a sheep in a sacred way. The meat is given to the poor and hungry as food.

Ṣafā: purity. A word from which "Ṣūfīsm" is etymologically derived.
Ṣalāh: Ṣalāh is a physical act of worship, done in groups or by oneself, that engages the body, mind, heart, soul, and spirit. The form, which includes standing, reciting, bowing, kneeling, and prostrating, is specific and is done in the same way all around the world. It is one of the five pillars of Islām.
Ṣalla-llāhu 'alayhi wa sallam: literally: may the blessings and peace of Allāh be upon him. It is polite and customary to always say this after mentioning the name of the Prophet Muḥammad, may the blessings and peace of Allāh be upon him.
Sayyid/Sayyida: master.
Sh̲arīʿa: the law of Islām as revealed in al-Qurʾān and the sunna—the traditions of the Prophet, may the blessings and peace of Allāh be upon him.
Sh̲ayṭān: satan, the devil, Iblīs.
Sh̲aykh̲: literally: old man or elder. The master who can give effective instruction for students on the spiritual path. He possesses a degree of spiritual realization and can bring others to his degree.
Sh̲irk: considered the greatest transgression in Islām. It is the worship of something other than Allāh. This can range from the obvious, such as worshipping a statue of a cow, to the subtle, such as worshipping power, money, beauty, etc.
Soul: the soul was formed when Allāh breathed His spirit into the dust which became Ādam [humankind]. It rose as a vapor.
Subḥāna-llāh: literally: all exaltation to Allāh.
Ṣūfī: see faqīr. The name is thought to have come from the rough woolen garments worn by the early Ṣūfīs.
Ṣūfīsm: the science of direct knowing of Allāh.
Sunna: the spoken words and actions of the Prophet, may the blessings and peace of Allāh be upon him, that have become the example to follow.
Sūra: a chapter from the holy Qurʾān.
Tajallī: revelation; coming forth into the light; the unveiling of Divine secrets; illumination.
Taqwā: reverence, piety, awe of God.
Tarāwīḥ prayers: additional prayers (cycles of ṣalāh) offered each night during the month of Ramaḍān. The blessings given during tarāwīḥ prayers are extraordinary. The tradition of the Prophet *(ṣalla-llāhu ʿalayhi wa sallam)* was to do at least eight rakʿah per night during Ramaḍān.
Ṭarīqa: the path, the way, school or brotherhood of mystics. It is the bridge between the sh̲arīʿa and the ḥaqīqa.

Tawba: literally: to return. It indicates the process of repentance that the Prophet, may the blessings and peace of Allāh be upon him, did seventy times each day (Ḥadīṯh).
Tawḥīd: unity of Allāh.
Torah: the holy Book brought to the Jewish people by the Prophet Mūsā [Mūsā] *('alayhi-s-salām).*
Wird: A "wird" is a specific set of recitations given to the seeker by his guide. The standard wird in Sidi Muḥammad's ṭarīqa is to recite the following twice a day: "astagḫfiru-llāh al-'aḍḫīm" 100 times, "Allāhumma salli 'alā sayyidinā Muḥammad wa ālihi wa sallam," 100 times, "Lā 'ilāha 'illa-llāh," 100 times and, "Allāh" 100 times.
Wuḍu': ablution, ritual purification. For information on how to do wuḍu' see The Reliance of the Traveler by Ahmad ibn Naqib al-Misri.
Zabūr: the Psalms brought by the Prophet Dāwūd [David] *('alayhi-s-salām).*
Zakāh: obligatory charity. One of the five pillars of Islām.

Index

A

F

G

H

I

J

N

O

S

U

V

W

Y

Z

Index of Qur'an Quotes

A

[Allāh said] "Tell Me the names of these if you are truthful." (Qur'ān 2:31-2:33), 70
Alif Lām Mīm (Qur'ān 2:1, 29:1, 30:1, 31:1, 32:1), 69
Allāh says in the Qur'ān that there is the one who witnesses and (Qur'ān 85:3), 240
Am I not your Lord? (Qur'ān 7:172), 370
An olive tree that is not from the east or the west (Qur'ān 24:35), 90
And (remember) when your Lord said to the angels: "Truly, I am going to place on earth generation after generation (of humans)." (Qur'ān 2:30), 151
And [remember] when Allāh took the covenant from the prophets (Qur'ān 3:81), 17
And Allāh's punishment is severe. (many places in the Qur'ān), 303
And do not spy on or backbite one another (Qur'ān 49:12), 111, 138
And had you been severe and harsh hearted (Qur'ān 3:159), 110, 139, 263, 317, 321
And He made you vicegerents upon the earth (Qur'ān 57:7, 6:165), 18
And He taught Ādam the names of everything (Qur'ān 2:31 - 2:33), 212, 429
And hold fast, all of you together, to the rope of Allāh (Qur'ān 3:103), 261
And I blame myself (Qur'ān 12:53), 187, 198
And indeed, there are stones out of which rivers gush forth (Qur'ān 2:274), 173
And my breast tightens, and my tongue expresses not well, 260
And some people argue about this matter of Allāh (Qur'ān 6:25), 303
And they ask you about the Spirit (17:85), 11
And those who hoard up gold and silver (Qur'ān 9:34), 184, 284
And undoubtedly We have honored the children of Ādam (Qur'ān 17:70), 138, 247
And We are nearer to him than his jugular vein. (Qur'ān 50:16), 86, 88, 122, 189, 250
And whatever of misfortune befalls you, it is because of what your hands have earned. (Qur'ān 42:30), 97
And when I am ill, it is He Who cures me. (Qur'ān 26:79-80), 121, 131, 358
And when Mūsā came at the time and place appointed by Us, (Qur'ān 7:143), 88
And when My slaves ask you concerning Me, (Qur'ān 2
And when My slaves ask you concerning Me, (Qur'ān 2:186), 86, 121, 169, 232, 236, 266, 361, 374, 392, 411, 434
And when your Lord brought forth from the children of Ādam (Qur'ān 7:172), 423
And, when he (his son) was old enough to walk with him, he [Ibrāhīm] said: "Oh my son! (Qur'ān 37:102), 425
Anything the human utters is recorded by two mighty angels (Qur'ān 50:17), 228

B

But Allāh is rich, and you are poor. (Qur'ān 47:38), 140

C

Certainly, you will have no authority over My slaves (Qur'ān 15:42), 126, 128, 255, 385, 393

D

Do you think [that We created you as a game] (Qur'ān 28:39), 298

E

F

G

H

I

O

P

R

S

T

U

V

W

Y

Index of Hadith Quotes

A

C

D

E

F

H

I

M

O

R

S

T

W

Y

Index of Hadíth Qudsí Quotes

Jewel Prayer from Portland

Jewel Prayer from Portland

al-ḥamdu li-llāhi rabbi-l-ʻamīn
wa-ṣ-ṣalātu was-s-salāmu ʻala- l-ḥabībi-l-aʻḍẖam
Muḥammadir-rasūli-llāhi ṣallā-llāhu ʻ alayhi wa sallama
wa ālihī wa saḥbihī wa sā'iri-l-anbiyā'i wa-l-mursalīn

Praise to Allāh, Lord of the Worlds
and may the peace and blessings of Allāh be upon the most beloved:
Muḥammad, the Messenger of Allāh
and upon his family, companions and followers and upon all the prophets and messengers.

As'aluka yā Allāh añ taghfira lī dhunūbī bi-nūri ḥubbika-l-ilāhī
As'aluka yā Allāh añ tuṭāhira badanī bi-nūri ḥubbika
As'aluka yā Allāh añ tuṭāhira nafsī bi-nūri ḥubbika
As'aluka yā Allāh añ tuṭāhira qalbī bi-nūri ḥubbika
As'aluka yā Allāh añ tuṭāhira ruḥī bi-nūri ḥubbika
As'aluka yā Allāh añ tuṭāhira ʻaqlī bi-nūri ḥubbika

I ask You, oh Allāh, to forgive my sins by the light of Your divine love.
I ask You, oh Allāh, to purify my body by the light of Your love.
I ask You, oh Allāh, to purify my soul by the light of Your love
I ask You, oh Allāh, to purify my heart by the light of Your love
I ask You, oh Allāh, to purify my spirit by the light of Your love
I ask You, oh Allāh, to purify my intellect by the light of Your love

الحَمدُ لِلَّهِ رَبِّ العَالَمِينَ
وَالصَّلاَةُ وَالسَّلاَمُ عَلىَ الحَبِيبِ الأَعظَم
مُحَمَّدٍ رَسُولِ الله صَلَّى اللهُ عَلَيهِ وَسَلَّمَ
وَآلِهِ وَصَحْبِهِ وَسَائِرِ الأَنبِيَاءِ وَالْمُرْسَلِينَ

أَسْأَلُكَ يَا اللهُ أَن تَغْفِرَ لِي ذُنُوبِي بِنُورِ حُبِّكَ الإِلاَهِي
أَسْأَلُكَ يَا اللهُ أَن تُطَاهِرَ بَدَنِي بِنُورِ حُبِّكَ
أَسْأَلُكَ يَا اللهُ أَن تُطَاهِرَ نَفْسِي بِنُورِ حُبِّكَ
أَسْأَلُكَ يَا اللهُ أَن تُطَاهِرَ قَلْبِي بِنُورِ حُبِّكَ
أَسْأَلُكَ يَا اللهُ أَن تُطَاهِرَ رُوحِي بِنُورِ حُبِّكَ
أَسْأَلُكَ يَا اللهُ أَن تُطَاهِرَ عَقْلِي بِنُورِ حُبِّكَ

As'aluka yā Allāh añ taḥmī badanī bi-nūri ḥubbika
As'aluka yā Allāh añ taḥmī nafsī bi-nūri ḥubbika
As'aluka yā Allāh añ taḥmī qalbī bi-nūri ḥubbika
As'aluka yā Allāh añ taḥmī ruḥī bi-nūri ḥubbika
As'aluka yā Allāh añ taḥmī 'aqlī bi-nūri ḥubbika

I ask You, oh Allāh, to protect my body by the light of Your love.
I ask You, oh Allāh, to protect my soul by the light of Your love
I ask You, oh Allāh, to protect my heart by the light of Your love
I ask You, oh Allāh, to protect my spirit by the light of Your love
I ask You, oh Allāh, to protect my intellect by the light of Your love

As'aluka yā Allāh añ tashfī badanī bi-nūri ḥubbika
As'aluka yā Allāh añ tashfī nafsī bi-nūri ḥubbika
As'aluka yā Allāh añ tashfī qalbī bi-nūri ḥubbika
As'aluka yā Allāh añ tashfī ruḥī bi-nūri ḥubbika
As'aluka yā Allāh añ tashfī 'aqlī bi-nūri ḥubbika

I ask You, oh Allāh, to heal my body by the light of Your love.
I ask You, oh Allāh, to heal my soul by the light of Your love
I ask You, oh Allāh, to heal my heart by the light of Your love
I ask You, oh Allāh, to heal my spirit by the light of Your love
I ask You, oh Allāh, to heal my intellect by the light of Your love

أَسْأَلُكَ يَا اللهُ أَن تَحْمِي بَدَنِي بِنُورِ حُبِّكَ
أَسْأَلُكَ يَا اللهُ أَن تَحْمِي نَفْسِي بِنُورِ حُبِّكَ
أَسْأَلُكَ يَا اللهُ أَن تَحْمِي قَلْبِي بِنُورِ حُبِّكَ
أَسْأَلُكَ يَا اللهُ أَن تَحْمِي رُوحِي بِنُورِ حُبِّكَ
أَسْأَلُكَ يَا اللهُ أَن تَحْمِي عَقْلِي بِنُورِ حُبِّكَ

أَسْأَلُكَ يَا اللهُ أَن تَشْفِي بَدَنِي بِنُورِ حُبِّكَ
أَسْأَلُكَ يَا اللهُ أَن تَشْفِي نَفْسِي بِنُورِ حُبِّكَ
أَسْأَلُكَ يَا اللهُ أَن تَشْفِي قَلْبِي بِنُورِ حُبِّكَ
أَسْأَلُكَ يَا اللهُ أَن تَشْفِي رُوحِي بِنُورِ حُبِّكَ
أَسْأَلُكَ يَا اللهُ أَن تَشْفِي عَقْلِي بِنُورِ حُبِّكَ

As'aluka yā Allāh añ tuthābitanī 'alā dīnika bi-nūri ḥubbika
As'aluka yā Allāh añ tuthābita badanī 'alā dīnika bi-nūri ḥubbika yā karīm
As'aluka yā Allāh añ tuthābita nafsī 'alā dīnika bi-nūri ḥubbika yā karīm
As'aluka yā Allāh añ tuthābita qalbī 'alā dīnika bi-nūri ḥubbika yā karīm
As'aluka yā Allāh añ tuthābita ruḥī 'alā dīnika bi-nūri ḥubbika yā karīm
As'aluka yā Allāh añ tuthābita 'aqlī 'alā dīnika bi-nūri ḥubbika yā karīm

I ask You, oh Allāh, to make me firm and steadfast in following Your religion by the light of Your love.

I ask You, oh Allāh, to make my body steadfast in following Your religion by the light of Your love, oh Most Generous

I ask You, oh Allāh, to make my soul steadfast in following Your religion by the light of Your love, oh Most Generous

I ask You, oh Allāh, to make my heart steadfast in following Your religion by the light of Your love, oh Most Generous

I ask You, oh Allāh, to make my spirit steadfast in followingYour religion by the light of Your love, oh Most Generous

I ask You, oh Allāh, to make my intellect steadfast in following Your religion by the light of Your love, oh Most Generous

أَسْأَلُكَ يَا اللهُ أَن تُثَابِتَنِي عَلَى دِينِكَ بَدَنِي بِنُورِ حُبِّكَ يَا كَرِيمُ

أَسْأَلُكَ يَا اللهُ أَن تُثَابِتَنِي عَلَى دِينِكَ نَفْسِي بِنُورِ حُبِّكَ يَا كَرِيمُ

أَسْأَلُكَ يَا اللهُ أَن تُثَابِتَنِي عَلَى دِينِكَ قَلْبِي بِنُورِ حُبِّكَ يَا كَرِيمُ

أَسْأَلُكَ يَا اللهُ أَن تُثَابِتَنِي عَلَى دِينِكَ رُوحِي بِنُورِ حُبِّكَ يَا كَرِيمُ

أَسْأَلُكَ يَا اللهُ أَن تُثَابِتَنِي عَلَى دِينِكَ عَقْلِي بِنُورِ حُبِّكَ يَا كَرِيمُ

As'aluka bismika-l-a'ḏẖam yā Allāh
wa bi-asrārika al-'uḏẖmā añ tastajiba du'ā'ī

Wa taḥfiḏẖ aḥibbā'ī miñ kulli dhi-sharr
wa miñ sharri kulli dābbah añta ākhidhum-bi-nāṣiyatihā

Yā Allāh atawājahu ilayka bi-rūḥi nabiyyika
wa bi-arwāḥi jamī'i-l-ambiyā'i
wa bi-asmā'ika-l-ḥusnā al-lā tarūdu du'ā'ī

Bi-ḥaqqi asrāri-l-fātiḥah.

[Recite al-Fātiḥa.]

Allāhumma, āmīn. Allāhumma, āmīn. Allāhumma, āmīn

I ask You, oh Allāh, by Your glorious name
and by Your greatest secrets that You accept my calling

And protect all my beloveds from every evil-doer
and from the evil of every creature whose forelock You hold.

Oh Allāh, I beseech You by the spirit of Your Prophet,
by the spirits of all the prophets
and by Your beautiful names that You reject not my call!

I ask you to grant this by right of the secrets of al-Fātiḥa

[Recite al-Fātiḥa.]

Please grant this, please grant this, please grant this.

أَسْأَلُكَ بِسْمِكَ الأَعْظَمِ يَا اللهُ
وَبِأَسْرَارِكَ الْعُظْمِى أَن تَسْتَجِبَ دُعَاءِي
وَتَحْفِظْ أَحِبَّاءِي مِن كُلِّ ذِي شَرٍ
وَمِن شَرِّ كُلِّ دَابَّةٍ أَنتَ آخِذٌ بِنَاصِيَتِهَا
يَا اللهُ أَتَوَاجَهُ إِلَيْكَ بِرُوحِ نَبِيِّكَ
وبِأَرْوَاحِ جَمِيعِ الأَنبِيَاءِ
وَبِأَسْمَاءِكَ الحُسْنَى ألاَّ تَرُودُ دُعَاءِي

بِحَقِّ أَسْرَارِ الْفَاتِحَةِ [إقرأ الفاتحة]
اللَّهُمَّ آمِينَ اللَّهُمَّ آمِينَ اللَّهُمَّ آمِينَ

Made in the USA
San Bernardino, CA
16 April 2019